Material Management
Indian Railways

MATERIAL MANAGEMENT INDIAN RAILWAYS

By

Dr. C.L. BANSOTRA

B.Sc. Engg. (Mech.) Hon. DIM, DBM, Ph.D.

Formerly, Controller of Stores, Indian Railway

UNIVERSITY SCIENCE PRESS

(An Imprint of Laxmi Publications Pvt. Ltd.)

An ISO 9001:2008 Company

BENGALURU • CHENNAI • COCHIN • GUWAHATI • HYDERABAD
JALANDHAR • KOLKATA • LUCKNOW • MUMBAI • RANCHI • NEW DELHI
BOSTON (USA) • NAIROBI (KENYA)

Printed and bound in India
First Edition : 2010, 2017; *Edition* : 2025
***ISBN* :** 978-93-80356-57-7

Branches

✆	Bengaluru	080-26 75 69 30
✆	Chennai	044-24 34 47 26
✆	Guwahati	0361-254 36 69
✆	Hyderabad	040-27 55 53 83
✆	Kochi	0484-405 13 03
✆	Kolkata	033-40 04 77 79
✆	Lucknow	0522-430 36 13
✆	Ranchi	0651-224 24 64

PUBLISHED IN INDIA BY

UNIVERSITY SCIENCE PRESS
(An Imprint of Laxmi Publications Pvt. Ltd.)

An ISO 9001:2015 Company
113, GOLDEN HOUSE, GURUDWARA ROAD, DARYAGANJ,
NEW DELHI - 110002, INDIA

Corporate Office : B-33, Sector-5, Noida,
Gautambuddha Nagar (U.P.) - 201 301, INDIA
Telephone : +91-120-44 46 900
www.laxmipublications.com
info@laxmipublications.com

Dedicated
To
The Memory of
my beloved
Grandfather and Father

Contents

ACKNOWLEDGEMENT

I am grateful to Railway Board / Ministry of Railways for appointing me to the Indian Railway Stores Service (IRSS), vide their letter No. E (GR) I- 66 RC] 5-2, New Delhi, dated 28th October 1966.

I am grateful to GM (P), Northern Railway, Baroda House, for in using my first year training programme vide letter No. 884-E/26/E1a, dated November 1996, and second year training at programme vide 844-E/26/E1a dated 9/11/1967.

I am grateful to COS/NR, Shri P.C Vaish, Shri Gulshan Rai, Dy COS, N.M Shah and Dy COS, Shri R.K Mittal for giving me training for the year. Who were incharge of training for those two year when I was working as probationary officer for the first two year of my training.

I am grateful to Shri S.N. Biswas, COS's/NER/Gorakhpur and Shri. M.K Sarkar, Dy COS's, S.K Gurnani, P.C Ojha and R.N. Ghate.

I am grateful to Dy COS, A.B Bannerjce, and COS, M.K Sarkar/ D.L.W.

I am also grateful to COS, N.R, Shri S.K Sabbarwal, Supertendent stores, Shri J.P Moorjani and Dy COS's, Shri V.R. Mehta and Shri Kanti Swaroop, SSO, Shri Om Parkash Northern Railway, Baroda House DCO S's Shri Naubat Lal, Shri D.N Chatterji, Shri P.C Gupta, Northern Railway Jodhpur.

I am grateful to COS Northern Railway, Gorakhpur, Shri S.B.J. Rajash, D COS/ SPJ, Shri B.K Singh, D.S, Shri Sharma / SPJ Division DRM, Shri R.N Tewari, CO S's Gorakhapur, B.C. Chaudaiah, Shri P.K. Datta, Shri Shyamji Shinghal, Dy FA & CAO R.N. Tiwary, D.C. Bhattacharya.

I am grateful to Shi Verandar Kumar, CE (Con) Northern Railway Gorakhpur, Shri Gauri Shankar CE (Con) Northern Railway Gorakhpur, Shri J.P Char, Shri S.K. Gurnane, Shri B.K. Singh COS/NE Railway Gorakhpur. Shri. P.C. Oack, COS/ Northern Railway Gorakhpur, Shri. S.N. Andley, Shri. Daulal Datt, Shri. V.R Krishna Murthy and Shri K. Veera Rghvan, COS's NE Railway Gorakhpur, C.E (Con) Gorakhpur. Shri Pendse.

I am grateful to Shri C.P Subriamanian COS/NF Railway/MLG/ Guwahati, Shri N.K Prashad, CO S/MLG/NF Railway, Shri S.S.D Aggarwal, CO S/ Northern Railway, Shri N.R Nair CO S/ Northern Railway Shri S. Paul. COS/ Northern Railway/MLG, Shri R.N Malik, GM (Con) Northern Railway MLG.

I am grateful to Shri SA Singh CAO/COF MOW for giving me advice in all these matter.

I also grateful to GM of all the Railway where I worked.

I am grateful to Director Stores/ Adviser Store/ AM (RS) under whom I worked, I am grateful to Secretary Railway Board.

I am grateful to Member Mechanical without their advice and guidance this venture would not have been a success.

—Author

PREFACE

This book deals with organization of Store department, Stores nomenclature and Price list, Purchase of stores, Purchase policy and Rules contracts, Scrutiny of contract, Indent for supply of stores and certification of funds by the Accounts department, Contract estimates, Purchase procedure, Direct purchase by the administration, Purchase through DGS&D, Purchase of sleepers, Purchase of stationery and printing stores and printing forms. Stores depots, Receipt and custody of stores depot ledger, Procedure in ledger section, Issue to and receipt from Railway workshop, Issue to workshop, Returned stores, Empties, Imprest stores, Engineering plant, Reserves, Custody, Receipt issue, Carriage of railway materials, Packing and loading of materials, Surplus stocks, Scrap and Auction sales priced ledgers, Cheque and payment of bills transfer traction, Annual statement of stores transaction, the store budget, Stock verification of stores depot by Accounts department.

I am grateful to those who have helped me to write this book.

Suggestions are welcomed to further improvement of this book.

—Author

1

IMPORTANCE OF PURCHASING FUNCTION

1.1 PURCHASING FUNCTION—AN INTRODUCTION

Purchasing plays an important part in business success. It is quite usual to find that raw materials and bought-out components account for approximately 50 per cent of manufacturing costs and that labour for only about 10 per cent.

The purchasing function is therefore in a very favourable position to contribute towards both control of existing cost and the reduction of costs. Although maintenance of profit lose and increase in profit, result from the efforts of the organisation as a whole, the purchasing section is generally in a position to make the greatest contribution to profit. This is influenced by the nature of an organisation and the extent to which materials and bought-out items contribute to product costs.

Duty of Purchasing Function

The duty of the purchasing function is to know where to obtain materials of the required quality at reasonable prices. It must be well informed about fluctuations in the cost of materials used in the industry in order to decide when to purchase supplies the best advantage, thereby saving the company, what may well amount to large sums of money.

Requirements for Successful Purchase

Successful purchasing involves three main requirements, these are:

1. Discovering reliable firms who can supply specific materials.
2. Reaching agreement with such suppliers on prices, qualities, and delivery sales.
3. Ensuring that the terms of all such agreements are fulfilled.

Before we discuss the techniques of purchasing to accomplish these things, it is appropriate to outline the changes which have occurred, and are occurring in the purchasing role.

With the setting up of organisations such as EFTA and OEEC, tariff barrier throughout the world are tending to get progressively lower and ultimately may be removed entirely. This has the effect of enlaying the buying opportunities for the purchasing function and coupled with the growth of multinational organisations, whose activities are not confined to one location or area. The role of the purchasing is undergoing an expansion which will give rise to increased demands on those engages in this function. This leads to a need for a change in the breadth of training requirements and to a demand for higher qualification by those, who are in the broad area of supplies procurement and inventory control.

A sign of this is the increasing interest shown by management in the professionally bodies and consulting services connected with purchasing. Far more training courses in inventory control and other aspects of the materials management and in the selection and value analysis of materials are being offered than was the case a few year ago.

Now managements are becoming more interested in establishing methods of assessing productivity in the purchasing function, using standards ranging from output per hour worked for task that are largely routine to other standards which are much more difficult to establish and use as applied, for example to effectiveness of supplier selection or improvement in quality of bought-out items arising from efforts of the purchasing function.

1.2 SYSTEMATIC PURCHASE ANALYSIS

The introduction of a systematic analysis of what has been achieved by buying transactions coupled with the use of the technique of value analysis, is tending to broaden the scope of the purchasing function from being solely concerned with the effectiveness of buying to the concept of being involved with other function, such as design or production planning in obtaining the best value for money—as opposed to minimising the cost of determined and fixed requirements.

A rising from the considerations in purchase analysis, the organisational position and status has changed from the old concept of isolated specialist function with what is now an outmoded status arising from this isolated to a function with others in the total concept of an organisation.

To run a business you need what is often referred to as the five M's—Men, Machines, Money, Management, and Materials.

To considered systematic analysis, following points should be follows:

You cannot do without Materials. You cannot do without materials, and the function which, procure and control them. The purchasing function is therefore a vital one.

Superior Performance in Purchasing. Superior performance in purchasing can well make the difference between profit and loss or between moderate and very satisfactory results in business enterprise.

CHAPTER

2

STORE ORGANISATION AND FUNCTION

2.1 MINISTRY OF RAILWAYS (RAILWAY BOARD)

Rules have been framed by President for the convenient transaction to business of Government of India. The jobs allocated to the Ministry of Railway (Railway Board) are in the charge of the Minister of Railway, who is a Minister cabinet rank. He is assisted by one or more ministers who are of the status of Minister of state or Deputy Minister. These ministers perform such functions as may be assigned to them in relation to the business allocated to Ministry of Railways.

The Railway Board is the chief administrative and executive body assisting the Minister of Railway in the discharge of his functions. It was constituted by a resolution of Government of India on 18th February, 1905.

The Railway Board at present consists of:

1. Chairman
2. Financial commissioner and
3. Member traffic, Staff, Mechanical Engineer. Civil engineer and Electrical Engineer., SLT.

Chairman in Railway Board is excutive office Principal, secondary to Government of India in the Ministry of Railways.

He is soley responsible under the Minister of Railway for arriving at decision on technical matter and advising the Government of India on the matters of Railways policy. The chairman also functions as member in respect of one another subjects as decided by the minister and is also responsible for co-ordination.

The Financial Commissioner for railways represents the Ministry of Finance on the Board and also function as executive officer secretary to Government of India in the Ministry of Railways in financial matters. He has direct contact with the Finance Minister whom he keep informed to development in the Ministry of Railways.

2.2 MEMBERS OF THE RAILWAY BOARD

The **members of Railway Board** are separately incharge of matter relating to Staff, Civil Engg, Traffic, Electrical Engg, Mechanical Engg., Signals Telecom, they function as executive-office secretary to the Government of India in the respective sphere. Every member is responsible for obtains with the all aspects of the technical subjects of which he is incharge. Where a question impinges of the function of another member, his concur is to be obtained and in of any persistent difference, the issue is to be referred Chairman Railway Board for a decision.

2.3 RAILWAY BOARD AND THEIR SUBORDINATE OFFICES

Railway Board is assisted by Additional Members Executive, direction incharge to performed various functions for smooth and efficient looking of Railways.

The Railway Board has the following attached subordinate offices.

1. The Research Design and Standards Organisation
2. Office of Railway Lesson Officer with DGSID
3. Railway Recruitment Boards (about 20 in India)
4. Railway Staff College, Vadodara
5. Indian Railway Engineering Institute, Pune
6. Indian Railway Institute of Signal Engineering and Telecommunication, Secundrabad
7. Indian Railway Institute of Electrical Engineering, Nasik
8. Indian Railway Institute of Mechanical & Electrical Engineering, Jamalpur
9. Railway Rates Tribunal Madras
10. Railway inspection Branch, London
11. The Railway Advisers to the High Commissioner for India in United Kingdom
12. Commissioner Railway Saftey on each Railway "Railway Claimstribunal" Ircham Tech., Gwalior.

2.4 ZONAL RAILWAY MANAGEMENT

On the basis of operational and management consideration, the Indian Railways have been divided into fifteen zones in order to have smooth and efficient working. These zones are placed in the charge of General Manager or Officer on Special Duty (OSD), who will be Chief Administrator officer, answerable to Railway Board for all matters affecting the working of the Railways.

In order to discharge the administrative functions, each General Manager is assisted by Additional General Manager, Senior Deputy General Manager, Deputy General Manager, Chief Public Relation Officer, Chief Planning Officer, and various Heads of Department for the following function:

1. Operating—Chief Operating Manager
2. Engineering—Chief Engineer

3. Mechanical—Chief Mechanical Engineer
4. Electrical—Chief Electrical Engineer
5. Signal and Tele Communication—Chief Signal and Tele Communication Engineer
6. Accounts—Financial Adviser and Chief Accounts Officer
7. Commercial—Chief Commercial Manager
8. Personal—Chief Personal Officer
9. Store—Controller of Stores
10. Medical—Chief Medical Director
11. Security—Chief Security Commissioner

The above mentioned Heads of the department are the Principal Officers of their respective department and they are responsible for functions of their department efficiently and directly answerable to the General Manager for all matter concerning their department. All Policy and important matter shall be discussed by these Principal HODs with General Manager if so desired.

Zonal Railway are further divided into Divisional and Extra Divisional Organisations. Divisional Organisations are placed under the charge of Divisional Railway Manager, who will the Administrative officer for the Diversion, and all Senior Branch officers are answerable to Divisional Railway Manager for all matters concerning to Division. The Divisional Railway Manager is treated as General Manager of the division. Each Divisional Railway Manger is assisted by junior administrative officers being head of various functions such as operating, Civil Engg., Mechanical Engineering, Electrical, SLT, Commercial, Personal Mechanical, Account, Store, Security. Each head is provided with senior scale officer, junior scale officer, and non gazetted staff for discharging the duties allotted to them efficiently in accordance to the rules and regulations, provided in codes and instructions received from Head of Department and Railway Board.

Objective of Railway Management

The corporate management objectives of the Railway undertakings are as under:

1. To provide rail transport for both passengers and goods adequate to meet the demand in areas where Railway operations confers optimum benefit to the economy having due regard to the Government's policy of development backward areas.
2. To provide such rail transport at the lower cost consistent with:
   (*i*) Requirements of the railway users and safety of operation.
   (*ii*) Adequate provision for replacement of assets and some provision for development of business.
   (*iii*) The least amount of pollution of the environment.
3. To work in association with or utilize other modes of transportation such as pipeline and road transport, and to encourage in ancillary activities necessary to subsequence the above two objectives.
4. To establish a corporate image of the Railway as being an up-to-date business organisation with the interest of the public and of the nation as its prime objectives.
5. To develop organisational effective personnel with pride in their job and forth in Managements

Functions of Railway Material Management

1. Evolution and regulation of Policy in respect of various functions of Material Management procurement, inspection, standing disposal inventory control indigenisation, Material Budget.
2. Monitoring and issue directives after study on the Material Management reports of the Railway received from time to time.
3. Review of performing on integrated Material Budget and inventory control in Railways monitoring and assure of directive
4. Framing and execution of Rolling-stock Budget.
5. Evolving a co-ordinate development of system of computerisation of Material Management functions on the Railway monitoring and implementation.
6. Liasion with various Ministries including the department of Supply. ISM Washington /London, Joint plant committee, SAIL in connection with problems of Material Management.
7. Policy on import substitution.

2.5 CONTROLLER OF STORE

The administration and control of stores of Railway is conducted by the stores department under supervision of a controller of stores who is the principle officer of the store department. This department is centrally controlled from head quarters. He is assisted by chief material manager, junior administrative officer, senior scale and junior scale officer and non-gazette staff for handling and competently efficiently. The inventory Management in Indian Railway is very important which function as to deal from common consumable stores to most complicated items such as parts of sophisticated rolling stock, signaling, telecommunication equipment etc.

The fundamental principle of inventory management is to see that the right quality of material in right quantity is bought at right price and at the right time from the right source. The organisation for inventory management thus involves planning and programming for purchase, procurement, inspection storage, handling of material inside depot.

Due to fact that capital expenditure is incurred for purchase of stores the material kept in the stores. Depots can be termed as unproductive cash till it is consumed. More so prolong stores keeping may also effect more payment of dividend to the general revenues. Therefore, it becomes essential on the part of stores department to have proper upkeep to safeguards from thefts, damage, leakage careless handling and have periodical inspection and ahead is departmentally and by account department.

Store keeping embraces the following main factors.

1. Receipt, inspection, custody,
2. Issue and dispatch
3. Frequent verification of ground balances with that of book balance.

In order to achieve the above objectives and efficient working of department, there are various depots located near the workshops and convenient places for catering the needs of users. Each depot of any importance is under the supervision of a Gazetted officer of store department directly subordinate to the controller of stores. He is referred to as the "Depot Officer" and is responsible to the controller of stores for :

1. Receipt and inspection of stores
2. Efficient maintenance of stock of stores
3. Prompt service of the territory served by his depot
4. The safe custody of stores in stock
5. The correct tally of such stock at any time with balance shown in the ledgers
6. The correct preparation and posting of all initial documents, ledgers and subsidiary registers.
7. Submission of relevant vouchers and documents to accounts officer on prescribed date, and
8. Disposal of surplus and scrap stores.

Objectives of Inventory Management

The main objectives are :

1. Ascertaining the needs of various departments for stores.
2. Preparing a correct estimate of quantities of stores to be purchased or manufactured in Railway workshops each year.
3. Obtaining stores of desired quality at competitive price.
4. Ensuring supply of stores in the quantity in the most efficient, economical and expeditious manner.
5. Maintaining an economic level of investment in the inventory.
6. Receipt, inspection, stocking, distribution of stores to various consuming centres as and when required.
7. Identifying and arranging disposal of shop and other object materials with in the shortest possible time to the best advantages of the Railway.
8. Developing ancilliary industries and indigenuous sources of supply to replace the import.
9. Finally, maintaining its constant touch with the market to ensure steady flow of materials.

All stock of stores in hand whether with stores department or other departments of the Railway, represents funds that are unproductive and blocking of capital.

It is therefore essential that stocks should be such stores required by Railway are readly available, they should be as small as possible and losses due to obsolescence deterioration should be the minimum practicable, the centralized control that is required for the purpose will vest in the controller of stores and will be responsible for the :

(*a*) Purchase and inspection.

(*b*) Custody and issue of Railway stores.

All material and stores for which the consumer departments have no immediate use should be returned to stores depots. Controller of stores is responsible for the survey valuation and for disposal for sale or otherwise. He has also to deal with all the surplus and unserviceable materials of Railway.

The controller of stores should arrange for submission to him of such statement and returns as may be necessary to keep him informed of the stock available on the depots, the manner in which the requisitions of the departments are being complied with the inflow of materials not required by the departments and the steps taken for disposal of surplus and unserviceable stores. Therefore, his functions in regard to inventory management shall be:

1. To ensure availability of raw materials, semi-finished and finished components, consumable and for general stores, machinery and plants, and spares for the production maintenance, operational requirements.
2. To maintain uninterrupted supplies and quality materials in time to user departments at minimum cost.
3. To minimize investment in inventories, purchasing cost, inventory carrying cost number of stockouts, and percentage of obsessing materials.
4. To reduce materials costs through standardisation, variety reduction value analysis, import substitution and by application of other techniques contributing towards reduction of the overall cost.
5. To satisfy the public accountability at all stages of the transportation relating to purchase, storage issue, and sale of materials in the best interest of the organisation.
6. To release the working capital for more useful, purposes by an efficient control of inventories.
7. To avoid losses to the Government due theft, breakage, leakage and deterioration while dealing with specific aspect of inventory management department in railway. Several measures recommended by various committees, in regard to proper delegation of power at various levels for purchase disposal, streamlining/simplification of system, procedure, organising an integrated approach to inventory management, proper use of computerisation having a centralised total management, information system, shall be adopted. Those measures will have the effect of toning up the organisation, so that decision should be taken expeditiously and machinery can be geared up for meeting the objective.

Standards/Canons of Financial Property

In regards to powers delegated to the controller of stores, he should pay strict regard to the standard cannons of financial property among which are the following:

1. The expenditure should not prime face be more the occasion demands and that every government servant should exercise the some vigilance in respect of expenditure incurred from public money as a person of ordinary product would exercise in respect of the expenditure of his money.
2. No authority should exercise its powers of sanctioning expenditure to pass and order which will be directly or indirectly to its own advantage.
3. Public money should not be utilised for the benefit of particular person or section of communication less:
   (*i*) The amount of expenditure involved is insignificant.
   (*ii*) A claim for the amount could be enforced in account of law.
   (*iii*) The expenditure is in pursuance of a recognised policy or custom.
4. The amount of allowance, such as traveling allowances, granted to meet expenditure of particle type, should be so regulated that the allowances are not on the whole sources of profit to the recipients.

Note: All proposals involving financial implication except those which have been specifically exampled for this purpose should be referred to finance branch for advice before these are sanctioned.

Applications of Canons of Financial Property in Stores Matters

In store department heavy capital investments are made in purchases and procurement of stores, while incising such expenditure, every Purchase officer should bear in mind the principles of cannons of Financial property that expenditure to be incurred from public money, he should exercise the some vigilance as he would excise in respect of his own money.

Every Purchase Officer should ensure that:

1. He should not incur such expenditure from public money which is beyond his power.
2. He should not incur expenditure which not yet authorised or sanctioned under the rules.
3. He should not sanction an expenditure which against the policy of the Government.
4. In spending, he gets the offer which is cheapest, economical and competitive.

However, all functions of store department such as purchase, sale, inspection quality control, preservation stock, payment disposal of scrap, damage, deterioration etc. are governed by the principle of cannons of financial property.

2.6 DELEGATION OF POWERS

Purchase is one of the vital functions of the controller of stores as it effect the capital and cash flow of Railways. It should be ensured that there should be no blockage of capital for which a definite rate of dividend is payable to General revenues. In order to reduce the capital-at-charge thus saving, ultimately the payment of dividend and also to ensure efficient guide and smooth working of Railway, the Railway Board have delegated certain powers to the General Manager in the matter of purchase, sale etc. of stores. Subject to safeguard Railways interest, the General Manager may re-delegate these powers (within the limits specified to COS/CMM and other officers subordinate to them, in consolation with the financial adviser and chief accounts officer excepting those where level of delegation have been fixed by Railway Board.

While exercising these powers, the finance branch of the FA/CAD office shall be consulted and the vetting shall be obtained before commitments or incurirng any expenditure. The role of finance branch is involved mainly in the following types of cases:

1. For all proposals of purchases and sales
2. In the proceeding of tender committee at appropriate level.
3. Spot purchase committee
4. Foreign exchange matters
5. Variation in quantities beyond permissable limit
6. Vetting of requisition and purchase order valued Rs 40,000 and above
7. While delegating power to lower authorities
8. Financial concurrence where financial implications are involved
9. Variations of rate of items
10. Extension of delivery date subject 445 5©
11. Relaxations in specifications and drawings
12. Variation in IRS conditions.

CHAPTER

3

STORES NOMENCLATURE AND PRICE LISTS

3.1 STANDARD CLASSIFICATION OF STORES

For exercising control is the classification of stores, essential. It is a pre-requisite for codification. Stores are grouped or classified according to certain principles, which may be either according to trade or according to end use. The DGS & D classifies stores according purpose. Import Trade Controller has his own classification. Customs Tariff is based on Brussels nomenclature for classification BIS has a system of classification. Railways classify stores according to purpose. Defence adopts "Cat. part no." system. Private sector classify stores according to purpose in use. Classification by end-use creates some hurdles when one item has more than one end-use. A wire rope is used as guy in telephone post, it is used as whistle cord for locomotive drivers; it is used as a hauling rope for cranes. In such cases, cross-reference will be shown in the catalogue without altering the numerical reference. Classification by design features was introduced by **Brisch** in which system all integers in a part number has prices and unique significance, allowing minute description to be incorporated in a code number. Kodak system consists of 10 digits of numerical value. V.E.D. Classification indicates criticality of material.

Grouping of Railway

Grouping of Railway stores is extracted below. In this Group a "part" is something without which the whole will not function. A "fitting" is something, which is an attachment, the absence of which will not prevent the main article from functioning though its presence might improve it.

The entire range of Railway stores is divided into 98 groups and codified in an 8 metric coding structure (XX XX XXX X) as under:

First 2 digits - Group/class

Next 2 digits - Subgroup under each group

Next 3 digits - Serial number of item under sub group

Eighth digit - Check digit

Check digit is calculated on "MODULUS 11", method, required for computerization purpose.

Groups and their details are tabulated as follows:

Table 3.1

Group	*Group Details*
00–09	Steam locomotives parts and fitting
00	WP/WG/WL/WT/ BG locomotive
01	Other IRS Steam loco BG
02	Non IRS loco bg
03	YP/YL/YG/YT metre Gauge loco
04	Other IRS Steam locos MG
05	Non IRS loco MG
06	All steam locos narrow gauge
07	Rail mounted steam cranes BG/MG/NG
08	Rail mounted diesel cranes BG/MG/NG
10–19	Diesel electric locomotive BG/MG/NG
10	Diesel electric locomotives BG/MG/NG
11	Diesel electric locomotives (Vehicle)
12	Diesel electric locomotives (Transmission)
13	Diesel hydraulic locomotive BG/MG/NG
14	Diesel hydraulic locomotive (Vehicle)
15	General motors diesel electric locomotive BG/MG
17	Henschel diesel hydraulic locomotives
19	Non-standard diesel locomotives
20–29	Electrical locomotives part and fitting
21	DC ele loco BG (per-war)
22	DC ele loco BG (post-war)
23	AC ele loco
24	AC ele loco (Japanies Design)
25	AC ele loco (C.L.W)
27	AC/DC ele loco BG
28	AC ele loco MG
30–39	Cariage, Wagon, EMU, Railcar parts fittings
30	ICF coaches BG MG
31	ICF EMU Coaches BG & MG
32	Diesel railcar BG/MG/NG
33	BEML coachas BG & MG
34	Jessop coaches BG & MG
35	EMU coaches BG & MG (Jessop , Breda)
36	Other coaching stock BG & MG
37	OlD IRS designed wagons
38	New IRS design wagon
39	Other goods stock (IRCA & non IRCA)
40–49	Electrical stores
40	Cables

41	Insulators
42	Elec. fitting
43	All instruments
44–45	Train lighting equipment
46	substation equipment
47	Electrical machinery and parts
50–59	
50	Telegraph and telephone equipment
52	Wireless equipment
54	Mechanical signalling equipment (single-)
55	Mechanical signalling equipment (double **)
56	Electrical signaling Equipments
60–60	Engineering Plant Machinery parts
60	Permanent way track tools and bridge work
61	Building materials
62	Pipes
65	Plant and machinery
66	spares for plant (Machinery)
67	Road motor
70–98	General stores
70	Abrasives
71	Brushes, Baskets, Bamboo products
72	Tools accessories components
73	Hardware's (fasteners)
74	Hardware (other than fastener)
75	India rubber
76	Electrodes
77	Paints enamels varnishes
78	Crockery and cutlery
79	Cloth and clothing
80	POL
81	Acids chemicals
82	Drugs or pharmaceuticals
83	Stationery forms
84	Refractory
85	Bearings
90	Metals (ferrous)
91	Metals (non ferrous)
92	Fuel
93	Timber
97	Rolling stock complete units
98	Scrap
99	Miscellaneous

3.2 STANDARD SPECIFICATION AND DRAWINGS

Standard specification and drawings of raw materials manufactured items are prescribed by the Railway Board RDSO and General Manager and price list should give a reference to the code of such specifications. First of such standard specification which have been adopted for use on Indian Railway are issued by Railway Board RDS from time to time for certain items. List of items for which IRS drawing exists are casulated through the quarterly notification issued by RDSO. All materials indented be the consumer and procured by COS should, where IR standard exist conform to such standard.

Table 3.2 Codes for Units of Account

Code No	*Units of Account*
01	Number
02	Pair
03	Set
04	In hundred number
05	In thousand number
06	Gross
07	Quite
08	Ream
09	Dozon
11	Milligramm
12	Gram
13	Kilogram
14	Quintal
15	Metric Ton
16	H
17	Coot
18	Long Ton
19	Short Ton
21	Millimetre
22	Metre
23	Kilometre
24	100 Metre
25	Centimetre
26	Inch
27	Foot
28	Yard
31	Square metre
32	Square centimetre
36	Sqr foot
41	Cubic central
42	Cubic diametre
43	Cubicmetre
51	Litre
52	Kilolitre

CHAPTER

4

PURCHASE OF STORES POLICY AND RULES PURCHASE POLICY

4.1 SOURCES OF SUPPLY

There are four sources of supply for receipt of materials required by Railway. These are:

1. Purchase
2. Manufactured by Railway works ahead
3. Returned stores
4. Transfer of stores from other Railway departments.

The purchase of stores is the most important and this chapter deals with the rules prescribed for the purchase of store. The rules are in accordance with the policy of the Government of India to make these purchases of stores for the public series no, in such a way as to encourage the development of the industries of the country to the utmost possible extent consistent with.

4.2 ORDER OF PREFERENCE

In making purchases, preference will be given in the following order:

Firstly, to articles which are produced in India in the form of raw materials or are manufactures in India from raw material produced in India preorder that the quantity is sufficiently good for the purpose.

Secondly, to articles wholly or partly manufacturing in India from imported material, provided that the quality is sufficiently good for the purpose.

Thirdly, to articles of foreign many achieve held in stock in India provides that they are of suitable type and requested quality.

Fourthly, to articles manufactured abroad which need to be specially imported.

4.3 PRICE PREFERENCE

Price preference may be granted to the purchase of articles produces in India either wholly or in part, or to imported articles available in India ex-stock, without releasing of foreign exchange latest policy should be followed.

Price Preference to Products of Small Scale Industries

The Railways purchases may be made/divided into the following groups.

GROUP-I Items which can be purchased only from large scale units

GROUP-II Items which can be purchased only from large scale units, but where it is possible for the large units to sub contract ancilliary and components to small scale unit

GROUP-III Items which can be procured from large scale as well as small scale units

GROUP-IV Items which may be entirely reserved for procurement from small scale units.

List of items under Group I and II shall be main termed by Railways and revised from time to time in consolation with the Regional Lesson Officer of the NSIC.

1. No price preference need to be given for items falling in these groups.
2. In case of items falling under GROUP III; reasonable price preference may be given maximum up to 15%.
3. Items under Group IV shall be procured exclusively from small scale industry units:, which are recognised by NSIC.
4. **Currency of Payment:** All terms which are procured from Indian industries, payment shall be made in rupees in India. The items, which are to be imported, payment shall be made in the currency of country of origin. Agency commission shall also be made in rupee.
5. **Payment:** Full payment should be made after receipt inspection and acceptance for others advance 90% – 10%, 95% – 5% –98% , –2% should be made against clear dispatch. Document inspection certificate is used by the inspection authority as mentioned in the contract.
6. **To Invite Tenders Abroad:** The discreation shall rest with the General Manager.
7. **Evolution of Officers:** Involving payment in foreign currency; the officer should evaluated in Indian rupee prevailing on the date of opening of tenders.
8. **Place of Delivery:** Place of delivery should be so decided as to give equal opportunity to all the genders.
9. **Price Preferences for Earlier Delivery:** A suitable clause should be added in tenders to Safeguard the Railway interest.
10. **Indian Agents for Tenders Abroad:** The tenders abroad should mention their Indian agent and his authority and confirmed agents commission shall be acceptable in Indians rupee.
11. **Classes of Tender:** The following are the classes of tenders:
    (*i*) Advertised tender (open tender)
    (*ii*) By direct invitation to a limited number of firm (limited tender)
    (*iii*) By invitation to one firms only single tender
12. **The 'OPEN' Tender System:** When tenders are invited by Public advertisement; they submitting their offer on the prescribed form also submit the following:
    (*i*) Income Tax Clearance certificate
    (*ii*) The name and full address of their bankers.

(*iii*) Particulars of theirs previous performance regarding supply of stores similar to those under purchase.

(*iv*) Details of inner equipment they possess for manufactured of the stores including quality and control.

(*v*) The detail of technical staff employed by them.

13. **The Limited Tender System:** Limited tenders are issued to few firms who are approved suppliers for the item underpurchase.

14. **The Single Tender System:** Single tender is issued to one firm as delegation of power to issue single tender.

15. **Tender Notices Shall State:**

(*i*) The short particular of stores to be supplied or work to be done, in specified quantity.

(*ii*) Where and when the tender documents can be seen and obtained also the amount, if any to be paid for such documents.

(*iii*) The place where the date and time up to, which the completed tender form will be received and time, fixed for opening of the tender.

16. **Tender Documents:** Tender documents comprise of :

(*i*) Instruction to tenders

(*ii*) IRS and special conditions of contract

(*iii*) Specifications standard or and special plans drawings as necessary

(*iv*) Schedules to the tender giving full particulars of stores to be supplied or work to be done

(*v*) Agreement form to be signed by tenderer

(*vi*) A statement of deviation from the specification.

(*vii*) A statement of deviation from the condition of contract.

17. Tender form shall state interail

(*a*) The amount of earnest money to accompany the tender and nature of security deposit if any, required in case of accepted tender.

(*b*) With whom or what authority the acceptance of tender shall rest

(*c*) Whether or not tender containing erassures and alteration of the tender document will be considered.

The forms for tender enqueries must provide for the acceptance by the tendering contractor of IRS conditions of contract and special condition contract.

18. **Opening of Tenders:** Tender should be opened as per guideline issued by the Railway Board from time to time.

19. **Constitution of Tender Committee Subject to Directives Issued by Railway Board:** A Tender Committee, consisting of a minimum of three members; one each from Stores, Accounts and Indenting Department, shall be constituted by the authority competent to accept tenders. When General Manager is the accepting authority, the Head of Department shall arrange to constitute the Tender committee.

20. **A Statement of Comparatives Rates and other Tender Conditions** should be prepared by branch concerned and verified by the Accounts department. It must be ensured that all tenders received including the late tenders and delayed tenders, are tabulated in the comparation statement and put up to the Tender committee.

21. **Tenders Should be Finalised Within the Validity:** The lowest tender should ordinary be accepted. Acceptance or rejection of tender is left entirely to the discretion of the authority entrusted with the duty and no explanation can be demanded of cause of rejection of his offer by any person making a tender. Reasons of rejection should be recorded.

22. **Intimation of Acceptance of Tenders:** A contract is concluded upon communication of the acceptance which must be within the time prescribed where post is the medium of communication between the parties. The acceptances is complete as soon as it is posted by the registered part or under certification of posting.

    Freight factor should also be considered while calculating the monetary value of tender.

23. **Inspection:** All articles whether manufactured in India or abroad should be subjected to inspection before acceptance and articles for which specification and tests, have been prescribed by component authority, should be required to confirm to specification and/or to satisfy the prescribed test or tests which may be carried out during manufacture and before or after dispatch from suppliers premises.

24. **Nomenclature:** As far as practicable standard form of nomenclature or description should be employed in the invitation to the tender to encourage free competition and the terminology in all areas should be such as to show beyond all reasonable double what exactly is required the place of delivery or installation the warranty and maintenance an other pertinent terms.

25. **Composition of Tender Committee:** For dealing with tenders for purchase of stores and power of stores officers for acceptance of tenders as determined by Railway Board.

CHAPTER

5

CONTRACTS

5.1 RULES FOR CONTRACT AND AGREEMENT

1. Rules apply only to contracts, agreements enforceable by law. The rules do not apply to petty purchases of Rs 10,000 and under.
2. The following fundamentals principles are enumerated for the guidance of the authorities who have to enter into contracts or agreement.
   (*i*) The terms of a contract must be precise and definite and there must be room for ambiguity or mis-construction there in.
   (*ii*) As far as possible legal and financial adviser should be taken in the drafting of contracts before they are finally entered into.
   (*iii*) Standard forms of contracts should be adopted.
   (*iv*) The terms of contract once entered into should not be materialy varied except in consultation with the competent financial authority.
   (*v*) If there is any uncertain or indefinite liability, unusual issue, previous consent of the competent financial authority should be taken.
   (*vi*) Contracts should be placed only after tenders have been openly invited and in cases where the lowest tender is not acceptable reasons should be recorded.
   (*vii*) The financial status of the tenders or firms should be taken into consideration.
   (*viii*) No contract should be placed without at least a written agreement as to price.
   (*ix*) Provision must be made in the contract for safeguarding government property entrusted to a contractor.
   (*x*) In case of long-term agreements or contracts; unconditional power should be given to the railway to cancel the contract at any time after the expiry of six months notice to that effect.
   (*xi*) The Auditor-General and under his direction, other audit authorities have power to examine contracts and to bring before the Public Accounts committee in any cases where competitive tender have not been sought, or where high tender have been accepted, or where other irregularities in procedure have come to light.

3. **'lump sum' Contract:** The contract is given a contract for a piece of work for lump sum amount.
4. **piece-work Contract:** The contract is entered with for price per unit of material without mentioning total quantity.

   Rate Contract: This contract is for supplying at a price fined per unit to supply any quantity during the validity of rate contract.
5. **Running Contract:** This contract is for supplying a fixed quantity within the validity of contract.
6. **Conditions of Contract:** The conditions of contract may either be standard or special. The standard conditions of contract and * coil condition of contract are prescribed by Railway Board.

   Specifications: The stores should be purchased to specification.

   There are Indian Railways standard Specification/DGSD specifications DIN, ASTM Specification.
7. **Warranty:** Contractor will gives commentry for the material supplied by him for a period of 18 months from the date of dispatch and 12 months from the date of received of consignment.

Competency of Authorities

Competency of authorities to vary the contract of variation, of Indian Railways standard conditions of contract are as follows:

(*i*) All other variations including minor relaxation in specifications and drawings

(*ii*) Variation of the rates of items

(*iii*) Variation of quantities of any item

(*iv*) Repeat order

(*v*) Variation of items

(*vi*) Extension of delivery dates

(*vii*) Modification

(*viii*) Security

1. **General:** Where the rules in this chapter call for a consultation between the General manager and his Financial adviser and their views are at variance, a reference should be made to the Railway Board.
2. **Stamp Duty:** Contracts are exempt from stamp duty.

Execution of contract prior to commencement of work or supplies. No contract should be permitted to commence work or supply materials until the relevant contract has been signed by the parties competent to do so.

CHAPTER

6

SCRUTINY OF CONTRACT/INDENTS

1. Copies of all indent, a central purchase agencies and contracts for stores and works valued over Rs 40,000/ should be finished to the chief accounts officer for prior scrutiny and vetting.

   The scruting of contracts/acceptance of tender should be conducted with reference to the purchase policy and rules. Indian railways standard conditions of contract and general instructions issued by Railway Board or any other competent authority from time to time. Any departure there from should be reported to the authority concerned for rectification.

2. The existing price list rate, the last purchase rate and the date of such last purchase rate should be considered in checking the rate of contract, if any large difference exists, it should be specially examined to make sure that the difference is not due to any faileure to follow faithfully the procedure prescribed for the purpose of securing the lowest role. It should also be seen that no unusual causes exists in the agreement, which are likely to lead to loss, in case of acceptance of tenders other than the lowest the justification setforth in support should be examined to see if it is in order.

   It should further be seen if the contract provides for the leave of liquidate damages from the supplier in case of delay in the delivery of stores and for such other safeguards in the interest of the administration.

3. **Register of Agreements.** After audit the main particulars of the agreement should be entered into a spectral register maintenance for the purpose and the agreement filed for safe custody, the register should show the following particulars.

   (*a*) Name of the contractor and period of contract

   (*b*) Particulars of contracts

   (*c*) Quantity

   (*d*) Rate and important terms of delivery

   (*e*) Amount of security, and

   (*f*) Penalty if any.

4. Whether the funds exist to meet the liabilities, as the indent/contracts should be examined by reference to the fund register of indents/contracts. Acceptance of tenders certified accordingly.
5. **Budget Allotment.** The funds sanctioned each year for purchases are in respect of
   (*i*) Stores for capital works
   (*ii*) Stores for works chargeable to depreciation reserve funds; developments in foundation line works (Revenue)
   (*iii*) Stores required for general purpose.
6. **Fund Register.** A Manuscript Register should be maintained for the purpose of watching the incurrence of liabilities against the budget grant distributed as shown below.

Year ... Allotment Date of...

S.No.	*Class of Stores Budget*
1.	Steam locos parts and fitting
2.	Diesel locos parts and fitting
3.	Electric locos parts and fitting
4.	Carriage wagon EM,E, paints and fittings
5.	Electrical stores
6.	Signals and telecommunication store
7.	P way materials, track tools and bridge working
8.	Engineering Stores covering building materials, plants and machinery
9.	Abrasives, tools and hardwares
10.	Brushes and brush wares
11.	Indian rubber and leather canvas
12.	Electrodes and welding accessories
13.	Paints engages and varnish
14.	Crockery cutleries and vapery
15.	Cloth, clothing and personal equipment
16.	Petroleum products the fuel oil
17.	Refractions packing materials
18.	Ball and roller bearings
19.	General stores covering acids, chemicals drugs, pharmaceuticals and other mix store such as fire fighting equipment
20.	stationery forms
21.	Metals Ferrous
22.	Metals Non-ferrous
23.	Fuel-coal/coke
24.	Fuel oil
25.	Timber
26.	Scrap
27.	Rolling stock complete units

7. **Certification of Functions:** Before placing any order or indents, a certificate regarding availability of funds, should be invariably obtained from the accounts officer store.

CHAPTER

7

CONTRACT ESTIMATES

7.1 ESTIMATE FOR PROCUREMENT

1. The controller of stores has to estimate in advance the requirement of each item he holds in stock with a view to make timely procurement. The actual procurement may be through a central agency (DGS&DS) Railway Board) or directly by the controller of stores.

   For items procured through a central agency, the estimate should be prepared on annual requirement basis to be submitted to the central agency as perfectly fixed by them.

   The 12 months period for which the requirement is estimated is called 'contract period" and the period between the date of preparation of estimate sheet and beginning of the contract period is called the "Interim period".

   For the items procured by the controller of stores directly, the estimate may be on annual basis or on maximum/minimum basis, as decided by controller of stores.
2. Depending upon the time table fixed by the controller of store, the depot in time should decide upon their own time table to ensure timely submission of their contract estimates to the controller of stores.

7.2 GUIDELINES ON FILLING UP CONTRACTS-ESTIMATE SHEETS

1. Theoretically speaking, the requirement for the interim period should be nil, and for the contract period it should 12 months average consumption. However, in actual practice there may be various cases may occur where the quantities ordered for the contract period prove to be either successive or insufficient.
2. The depots prepare their contract-estimate sheets, a few months in advance of the contract period. This gives an opportunity for an automatic review of the current contract period (which is interim period for the next contract period), depending upon the actual position requirements for the interim period and contract period should be calculated by the depot.
3. There may be cases that the estimated requirement shown by the depot would be negative indicating that the depot has the excess stocks.

4. **True Issues.** In making up their forecast, the depot should take into consideration "True Issues" only. 'True issues' or as they are generally termed consumption comprise that portion of the ordinary store, issues for which ordinary stores stock is maintained, "True Issue," therefore, exclude depot transfer, issues to non-recurring capital works, sales adjustment and other non-recurring issues and include only issues to home line indentors against regular routine demands and to recoup imprest stock.
5. **Action for Procurement.** The contract groupings form will be sent to central indent section of COS office, for submitting indent to the central agency as per their time table, for items which are centrally procure. For other items procured directly by COS's office, the grouping form should be sent to the purchase section concerned for taking purchase action.

   The grouping form or an extract of for part quantity. For indent items will also be forwarded to the purchase section where an emergency purchase is required in view of the low stock position. The purchase section will initiate purchase action and open the case with the contract grouping form with its extract.

CHAPTER

8

PURCHASE PROCEDURE: DIRECT PURCHASES BY THE ADMINISTRATION

8.1 AGENCY FOR SUPPLY

The Agency of stores department will be used in ordering the supply of all stores required for the use of railways, whether for stock purpose or for immediate consumption on works. The controller of stores is the only officer, through whom purchase should be made and will have complete authority to insist upon executive officers drawing stores from stocks until they are used up before indenting for new stores. He will scrutinize every indent and decline to purchase, where he considers that the existing stocks is insufficient and suitable and his orders shall be final unless he is overruled by the General manager.

The General manager may, however, delegate the powers of the local purchase to the Divisional railway manager subject to the provision.

Exceptions

As an exception to the above rule the following articles which supplied in large quantities may subject to approval by competent authorities be ordered by the Departmental officer concerned.

8.2 CLASS OF STORES

I. Under the Railway board contract purchase made by chief engineer are as follows:
   (*i*) Rails and fish plates
   (*ii*) Sleepers of all kinds such as:
   Cost iron, pressed sleepper, prestressed cement concrete, and wooden and steel turn out sleepers
   (*iii*) Point and gassings (including cost manganese steel crossings)
   (*iv*) Specified track laying/renewal machines and track maintenance machines.

II. Through chief mining Adviser Railway Board purchase made by
1. Coal steam small and soft coke chief operation manager.
2. Hard coke chief mechanical engineer.

The General manager of a Railway may sanction additions to the above list to suit local requirement of his administration.

8.3 AGENCY FOR PURCHASE

Purchase of materials of railways are arranged either:

1. By Railway board or directly by the Railway administration.
2. Through the Agency of other Government department:
   (i) The Directorate general of supply and disposal.
   (ii) The Controller of stationery and printing for printing and stationery store.
   (iii) Government medical stores depots for medical stores.

Purchase by the Railway Board

The Railway board have reserved to themselves the might to call tenders and let contracts for the supply of the following articles.

1. Locomotive, carriage, under frames, wagons and certain nominated spans/components
2. Wheel tyres axles.
3. Coal, including steam coal, small and soft coke.

The Railway Board also enters into long-term contract, from time to time for the supply of the following articles to Railways:

1. Rail, fish-plates and points and crossings
2. Sleepers of all kinds cost iron, pressed steel, prestressed cement conclude and wooden including pigskin for conversion into sleepers and sleep out sleepers.
3. Specified hack laying track maintenance machines.
4. Specified items of stores/equipment for Railways electrifications and signaling.

Purchase Arranged by the Administration

The administration may purchase all articles other than those purchase which is arranged by the Railway Board or as obligation through the Directorate general of supplies disposals and or other Government departments as prescribed by rules issued by the Railway board from time to times.

8.4 DIRECT PURCHASE OF DIRECTORATE GENERAL OF SUPPLIER AND DISPOSAL ITEMS

Except for items of stores for which the DGS&DS has entered into Rate of Running contract, the controller of stores may not use the Agency of DGS&P for any purchase upto Rs 1,00,000/ and under in each case. In emergency where non-acquisition of articles concerned is likely to whole up power purchases limited to the quantity sequenced to tide over the emergencies may mgs. The Controllers of stores, exercising these prowers up to limit of Rs 25 lakhs for each item, beyond this sanction of the General manager should be obtained. The controller of stores will decide when, for what quantity and in what manner, such emergency purchase shall be made.

Mode of Direct Purchase

- The Controller of stores will arrange purchases on behalf of the administration either through
  (*a*) Advertised (open) Tender (special or annual)
  (*b*) Limited Tender
  (*c*) Single Tender
- **Bulletins and Daily Tender:** For items, which are not to be procured through DGS&D, the controller of stores may procure through weakly Bulletin upto Rs. 3 lakh for each case.
- **Local Purchase of Materials of Small Values:** Controller of stores may pick class small quantity stock items as well not stock items through local purchase; up to a limit of Rs 20,000/ each case.
- **Local Purchase of Items of Stores by DRM'S** CE'C(c), CSTEx(c), CEE,s (c) of Railway, RE, M.T.P. (R)s, up to powers to delegated to them.
- **Opening of Current Accounts against Cash Imprest** by stores officers at major stores depots holding cash imprest for emergent purchases may open and operate 'current account' with Departmental banks or Imprest Nationalised Banks.
- **The supply from** the detail of the procedure employed for accounting for purchases of stores, differ to some extent.
- **Suppliers Challan:** The supplying firm will submitted duplicate challan along with the materials supplied by them. A copy of the challan should also be forwarded to the Purchase officer.
- **Combined Receipt and Issue Note:** On correct receipt of material, the Receiving officer will prepare the receipt and issue note. On the Railways where inspection of stores is not centralized, the form shall be prepared in rise parts, which shall be distributed in between the manager.

Inspection and Receipt of Stores Purchased by the Controller of Stores

- **Inspection:** All materials purchased by the controller of stores, should be inspected by an inspecting officer of the Railway, for materials directly dispatched to Indenter and the Indenter is responsible for its inspection.
- **Inspectorate of DGS & D:** The facilities provided by the DGS & D should also be smaller for Inspection of stores. The facilities provided by the RITES can also be utilized for inspection of store. Government Text House of DGS & D at Calcutta should also be utilized.
- **For Materials Purchased Abroad:** Senior of Railway Adviser, London, RITES, Leyod, JIC. etc should be used for inspection.
- **Rejected Stores:** Rejected stores should be removed to a place set apart for the purpose to avoid any possibility of their mixed up with other stores. In a store depot, the inspecting officer should see that this is done in his presence.
- **Rejection Memo:** Where material is rejected, a rejected form should be made out in chapter code by the receiving staff, an entry also being made on the back of the purchase order the rejection forms should be submitted with the challan or invoice form to the officer incharge for signature. One copy should be forwarded to the controller of stores, and one retained as an office record.

CHAPTER

9

PURCHASE THROUGH DIRECTORATE GENERAL OF SUPPLY AND DISPOSAL

1. **List of items that may be purchased only through the agency of the Directorate General of Supply and Disposal.**

   The items included in the above list; the purchase of them is obligatory through the agency of DGS&D.

2. The above para is exception to following cases:

   (*i*) For the items stores for which the DGS&D has entered into R/c Rg/c, the controller of stores may at his own discretion may make direct purchase up to a limit of Rs. 10,000/- in each case and not exceeding by Rs. 50,000/- in aggregate or up to Rs. 50,000/- in any financial years in each case.

   (*ii*) Instead of other cases, the controller of stores may not use the agency of DGS&D for any purchase up to Rs 1,00,000/- and under in each case.

   (*iii*) In case of emergency the controller of stores may purchase up to Rs. 25,00,000/- in each case.

3. **Rates.** If the rate payable for stores obtained through DGS&D are higher than the rate for similar item obtained by direct purchase, the fact should be brought to the notice of DGS&D indicating supplier and the details.
4. **Inspection.** Controller of stores should indicate the inspecting authority in the contract.
5. **Indents.** Indents on DGS&D should be placed on form prescribed by DGS&D.

   (*i*) *Method of Preparing Indents:* Indent may contain complete description, specification and drawings in absence of which DGS&D may prepare specification/drawings in consultations with the Indenter.

   (*ii*) *Co-ordination of Indents*: DGS&D should co-ordinate with all the Railway and other Government departments to purchase in bulk to achieve most economical rate.

   (*iii*) *Annual Indent*: The annual indent for each class of store should be submitted to DGS&D according to programme issued by DGS&D.

(iv) *Periodical Indent:* Indent for store, which it is not possible for the department. to foreseen their requirement; may be submitted at any time to DGS&D

(v) *Estimated cost of Indent:* Estimated cost should be shown in the indent.

(vi) *Certification Indent:* The indenting officer should ensure that the indents are placed after certification of funds.

6. **Stores for Works:** the procurement of stores for works may be initiated immediately after the works are included in works, machinery and Rolling stock programme.
7. **Types of DGS&D Contract**
8. **Running Contract**
   (i) Rate Contract
   (ii) Fixed Contract
9. **Purchase Order**
10. **Dispatches and Acceptance of Stores**
11. **Receipt Note**
12. **Payments**
    (i) 90%, 95% and 98% payment against dispatch of store
    (ii) 100% payment against bills.
13. **Shortage:** Complaints regarding shortage of or damage of store should be taken up in the first instance with supplier and carrier direct.

    The DGS&D should be addressed in regard to this matter in event of the indentor being unable to obtain satisfaction from the supplier or the carrier.

CHAPTER

10

PURCHASE OF SLEEPERS

Purchase of sleeper is made by the Railway board. General procedure for procurement of sleeper are asfollows:

1. **Kind of Sleeper**
   (i) Wooden Sleeper
   (ii) Metal Sleeper—(a) Cost iron (b) Steel (c) Concrete sleeper.
2. **Demand of Sleeper.** The requirements of sleeper are planned for track renewal work, new construction and doubling approved by Railway Board. The annual requirement finalised in the Chief track engineer conference with Railway Board.

   Keeping in view the actual requirements and funds position and availability of sleeper, in the country, the Railway Board make specific allotments for various types of sleeper to Zonal railway. Purchase of wooden sleeper, steel sleeper, concrete sleeper is inflated by the Board directly on basis of the allotment decided.

   Procurement of Wooden Sleeper. wooden sleeper are arranged by the Railway Board through the conservation of forests of various states.
3. **Sleeper Specification.** Sleeper specification approved by the Railway Board.
4. **Opening of Wagons.** Wagons are opened in the presence of Traffic staff.
5. **Verification by the Traffic Staff.** In case of short receipt the consignee should get the traffic staff to verify and report shortage by Telegram to the sending station.
6. **Telegraphic Report, Discretions Report and Claim Farm:** This should be done a procedure in vogue.

7. **Missing Consignment.** In case of missing consignment, the consignee after a fortnight should remind to the chief operating Manager of the Railway concerned in case of sleeper have not turned up after a month he should send a missing store report to the Chief commercial manager.
8. Missing sleeper on receipt should be acknowledged under a fresh form and parties concerned should be advised. So that the claim on the Traffic department may be withdrawn.
9. **The Bills for part or full consignment** should be passed and sent to Account officer with necessary remarks. The Bills for defective sleepers should not be passed.
10. **Procurement of Steel Sleepers.** They are procured by Railway Board.
11. **Concrete Sleeper** are procured through the concrete sleeper plants. These plants are in private sector also on the railways and Public sector units are also doing this Job.

CHAPTER

11

PURCHASE OF STATIONERY, PRINTING STORES AND PRINTING OF FORM

1. **Purchase Policy:** The Purchase policy for stationery and form, is same as for other items discussed in the previous chapters. In case of purchase through DGS&D the procedure followed by DGS&D should be followed.
2. **Purchase in India:** All primiting and stationery store required to be purchased for the Railway should be purchased on the condition that the delivery is made in India for payment in Rupees.
3. **Tender:** Same procedure as discussed in earlier chapter.
4. **Preference:** Purchase preference should be followed in the same order as described for other items.
5. **Inspections:** All items should be inspected before acceptance and item for which specification tests are prescribed should be required to conform to such specification or satisfy such tests.
6. **Inter-departmental Purchases:** These can be made whenever required.
7. **Power of Purchase:** The Controller of printing and stationery of India exercise full powers.
8. **Power of General Managers:** In case of emergency, the GM has full power to purchase, of at a time three months requirements should be purchased. COS has power up to Rs. 1,00,000/-
9. **Indent for Stationery:** Various departments, stations and officers of the railway should submit annual indent to Controller of stores or Superintendent printing and stationery as per programme decided by COS.
10. **Scale of Supply of Stationery:** The scale for supply of stationery to ordinary offices is prescribed in store code, which should be followed. For Traffic and other special officer, scale of supply may be decided by the General Manager. While preparing indents, the officers should see that the scale is not exceeded and sufficient funds should be provided in the budget for meeting the cost of stationery indent.

11. **Check of Indents:** Indent should be checked with sanctioned scale from scale officer. When the items are not in the sanctioned scale or when the items are included in the indents which are not included in the scale the indent should signed by HOD.
12. **Consolidated Indent:** From the indent received one consolidated indent should be placed with the Controller of printing and stationery for compliance.
13. **Payment for Stationery** obtained through the Controller of printing and stationery as same procedure is followed in case of supply received through the DGS&D.
14. **Stationery Depots:** Stationery depots just like any store depot and same procedure is followed for receipt, issue and custody.
15. **Receipt and Accounted:** The supply should be checked with the entries in annual and emergent indents, and the bill for the cost of the stationery which accompanies the supplier should be accepted and sent to Store account officer for audit and payment.
16. **Issues:** Only those items are issued which have been demanded in the indent. The items, which are not permissible for issue, should not be issued.
17. **Durable Articles:** Durable articles should not be issued on annual indent.
18. **Inspection of Stationery in Officer Stocks Held by Officer:** It Should be checked by Accounts verification staff or special staff deputed by Controller of stores or by the Manager of the railway press. If the stock is in excess than the quantity sanctioned then it should returned to stationery depot and taken on books by credit to stock adjustment account.
19. **Categories of Forms:** There are two catagories of forms:
    (*i*) Standard Forms
    (*ii*) Local Forms
20. **Schedule of Forms:** Each Railway should maintain a complete schedule of standard and local forms and print registers in use on the Railway.
21. **Printing of Forms:** The forms are printed in the Railway Printing press, against the indent placed by the Head of each officer.
22. **Printing in Outside Press:** In case printing in the Railway press is not possible due to overload or absence of necessary machinery, there of printing of forms should be got done by outside processes as per rule in vogue.
23. **Alteration or Modification of Standard Forms:** No alteration or modification should be made without approval of the Railway Board.
24. **Introduction of Local Forms:** No local form may be introduced without the approval of the General manger.
25. **Cost of Forms:** The Manager of printing and stationery should advise the departments each year at the time of preparation of budget of the sum which should be provided for debit for form in their budget.
26. **Accountal of Form:** Only numerical ledgers should be maintained from accounted.
27. **Verification of Balances of Stationery, Forms, and Printed Register:** Departmental stock verification should be carried out as prescribed or other general stores. The accounts stock verification should be done once in three years.

CHAPTER

12

INSTRUCTIONS TO TENDERERS

SECTION (I) INSTRUCTIONS

1. Tenders must be sealed and submitted in special envelopes and addressed to the COS/ CON N. F. Railway. Guwahati-781011/Assam before 14.30 hrs of the day specified, superscribted with the title of the Tender. Tender will be opened on the same day at 14:45 hrs. Tender, which is not submitted on the printed schedule annexed hereto, is liable to be rejected.
2. Tenderers for manufactured items must give the address of their workshop where the items will be manufactured.
3. When offering IMPORTED stores, the Country of origin must be clearly stated.
4. In all Tenders, makers' name, specification and brand of the items offered, must be stated.
5. Any reference made to this office in respect of IRS, ISS, DGIS & RDSO drawings or specifications will be ignored as these are priced publications and are obtainable on payment from:

(*i*) Manager of Publications, Civil Lines, Delhi.	} **IRS, ISS & DGIS**
(*ii*) The Director Research Research Design & Standards Organization, Alambag, Lucknow.	} **RDSO**

6. **Tender Papers.** The intending tenderer is advised to study these tender papers carefully. Any submission of tender shall be deemed to have been done after careful study and examination of the Tender papers with a full understanding of the implications thereof. The specification for the stores shall be deemed to have been accepted unless otherwise specifically commented upon by the tenderer in his Tender. Failure to adhere to anyone or all of these instructions may render their liable to be ignored without any reference.
7. **General.** All documents and entries in the Tender shall be either typewritten or in ink, in English. All prices shall be written both in figures and in words. Tenders with rate/unit overwritten erased or rates not expressed in words are liable to be ignored. If rates expressed in figures and words do not agree, then the higher of the two rates will be ignored.

8. **Clarifications.**
   (*i*) Any clarifications required in regard to this tender may be obtained from the Controller of Store/CON. N.F, Railway, Guwahati-781011, Assam.
   (*ii*) Where stipulated, the firms may see the sample/drawing in the office of the Controller of Store/CON, on working days up to 15:00 Hrs.
9. **Signing of Tenders.**
   (*i*) Any individual/s signing the tender or other documents connected there with should specify whether he is signing
      (*a*) As sole proprietor of the concern or his attorney.
      (*b*) As a partner or partners of the firm.
      (*c*) For the firm per procuration, or
      (*d*) As a director, manager or secretary in case of a Limited company.
   (*ii*) In the case of firm not registered under the Indian Partnership Act, all the partners or the attorney duly authorized by all of them should sign the tender and all the other connected documents.
   (*iii*) The original document empowering the individual or individuals to sign the original Partnership Deed with registration certificate, if any, in case the Tenderer is a firm and Memorandum and Articles of Association in case the Tenderer is a Company, should be furnished to the purchaser for verification, if required.
10. **Tender Forms.** Tenders not submitted in the proper Tender Forms are liable to be rejected, The Tender should be signed by the Tenderer on each page.
11. **Deviation.** Tenderers must note that deviations from the following will not normally be allowed. If however, they are required, the tenderers, must clearly indicate cogent reasons for deviations, indicating the reference of the particular clauses against the following sections and the deviations offered:
   (*i*) Instruction to Tenderers — Section (I)
   (*ii*) General Conditions — Section (II)
   (*iii*) Special Conditions — Section (III)
   (*iv*) Schedule to Tender
12. **Memorandum or Descriptive Matter.** The Tenderer may, if he deems it necessary, submit on his letterhead a short and concise memorandum or descriptive matter which cannot be incorporated in schedule to tender. The tenderer shall keep the length of such memorandum or descriptive matter to the minimum.
13. **Alternative Offers.** Should the tenderer desire to offer suitable stores to an alternative design/ specification, which in his opinion would improve the performance of the stores, reduce initial cost or costs of maintenance but without altering the basic use of the stores. The tenderer shall incorporate the alternative proposal in the tender, for the consideration of the purchaser. He shall clearly indicate in detail, the technical and/or financial advantages which would accrue to the purchaser by the adoption of the alternative proposal.
14. **Prices**
   (*i*) All prices shall be in rupees and paise, in figures and in words and FIRM without escalation. The units of rate shall be in the metric system and as indicated in the Schedule to Tender. Under no circumstances shall the unit of rate be changed or altered by the tenderer.

(ii) The unit price should indicate clearly—

(a) *Current Duties such as Customs, Countervailing, etc.* The Particular item (items) of the Indian Customs Tariff and other publications, on the basis of which the duties have been computed, should be mentioned.

(b) *CIF Value i.e., the Amount on which Duties are Paid.* The total of items (i) and (ii) will indicate the unit price, excluding Sales Tax, if any.

(iii) The total unit prices shall be furnished in the "Schedule to Tender" and shall be F.O.R. port of entry in the case of fully imported stores and F.O.R. nearest goods booking station from the manufacturer's works or destination as required in the case of semi-indigenous or indigenous stores. The prices for fully-imported or semi-indigenous stores shall clearly mention the CIF value of the imported stores, components or raw materials, to indicate the foreign exchange portion. List of imported components has to be furnished in case of semi-indigenous stores.

(iv) For entitlement to get re-imbursement of Sales Tax, the Tenderer MUST quote his State/ Central Sales Tax Registration Number in the Tender. Where this is not done, no claim for Sales Tax will be admitted at any later stage and on any ground, whatsoever.

(v) The prices shall be inclusive of suitable packing to withstand conditions in transit, as per rules laid down in the Goods Tariff, Part-I obtainable from Indian Railway Conference Association, New Delhi, and in accordance with the prescribed specification, if any, to ensure receipt of stores in good condition by the consignee.

(vi) The rate of exchange adopted for working out the prices of imported stores, components or raw materials based on International Monetary Fund ruling at the time of tendering shall be indicated at the bottom of the Schedule to Tender.

15. **Schedule to Tender.** The stores offered shall comply with the specification/s and/or drawing/s indicated in Schedule to Tender.

16. **Delivery.** The Tenderer shall indicate in the Tender, the period in months after the issue of Letter of Acceptance of Tender/import license, when he would commence supply and the monthly rate at which supply would be effected and the period in months from the date of issue of Letter of Acceptance of Tender/import license, when supply would be completed. This delivery should conform to the required delivery wherever so indicated.

17. **Make.** Tenderers are requested to clearly specify at the bottom of the Schedule to Tender the name of the manufacturer's, country of origin and brand, if any, of the stores tendered for.

18. **Earnest Money.**

(i) The Tenderer shall deposit with the F.A. and C.A.O./CON, N.F. Rly. Gauhati-781011, the sum specified in the Schedule of Tender as Earnest Money. The Earnest Money may be deposited on any working day, except on the first working day of the month between 10.30 and 14.30 hrs. The Earnest money may be paid in cash or in any of the following forms:

(a) Deposit receipts at call, pay orders or demand drafts of a Scheduled Bank drawn in the name of the F.A. and C.A.O, / Maligaon.

(b) Guarantee bonds executed by the Scheduled Bank, provided the amount is within the limit approved for the Scheduled Bank by the Reserve Bank of India in the attached form with Schedule to Tender and subject to confirmation in writing by the Reserve Bank of India. (See Annexure 'A' for the form for Guarantee bond.)

Note: 1. Cheques, National Plan Savings Certificates, National Savings Certificates and Government Securities (Stock certificates, bearer bonds, promisory notes and cash certificates) WILL NOT BE ACCEPTED.

2. The guarantee bonds are to be executed on non judicial stamp paper.

3. In the event, Tenderer has deposited the Earnest Money in cash, the number and date of the cash receipt should be furnished in the offer letter in the space provided thereon. Pay orders, demand drafts and guarantee bonds shall be attached to the original copy of the Tender.

(*ii*) *No interest will be paid on the Earnest Money.* It will be refunded in full to the unsuccessful Tenderer/s on application. In the case of the successful Tenderer/s, the deposit may be retained as part payment of the security deposit for due fulfillment of the contract.

(*iii*) In order to facilitate early release of Earnest Money to the unsuccessful tenderers. Tenderers are advised to deposit it in the form of demand drafts.

19. **Income Tax Clearance Certificate.** The tender shall enclose with his tenderer a valid Indian Income-Tax clearance certificate, issued, by the appropriate Income Tax Officer under his seal, which will be returned when done with, without which the tender is liable to be rejected. In the case of new firm, or firms which have no taxable income, a sworn affidavit to that duly countersigned by the Income Tax Officer, shall be furnished. The firms held on the approved list of the Railway and who have already submitted a valid ITCC to the Railway may refer to their Registration Number with the Railway.

20. **Samples.**

(*i*) Where samples are specifically called for along with the tenders, the same should be submitted by the tenderer to the authority specified in the tender simultaneously with the tender with indication given in the tender itself to the effect. Tender received without samples are liable to be rejected without further reference to the tenderer.

(*ii*) Samples shall be supplied "free of cost" freight paid without any obligations on the part of the purchaser as regards their safe transit and custody.

(*iii*) Samples shall be properly labelled and sealed.

(*iv*) If the sample are not destroyed in the course of testing the purchase will advice the unsuccessful tender/s to take the samples back at his/her own cost. In case the samples are not taken back by the tender/s within 15 days of receipt of the intimations, the samples will be considered as unclaimed property and disposed of by the purchase in the manner considered fit by him.

21. **Quota/Essentiality Certificate.** Quota/Essentiality Certificate for restricted categories of steel required for fabrication, if specified in the tender and included in the contract, will be issued to the contractor at his written request for such quantity as may be necessary for fabrication allowing a reasonable wastage in fabrication. The quantity of restricted categories of steel for which a Quota/Essentiality Certificate is required specifying the percentage of manufacturing wastage required shall be indicated in the tender. Quota/Essentiality Certificate will be issued only to genuine manufacturers on replacement basis. For this purpose, the tenderer shall furnish a declaration in the following form in the tender.

"I/We declare that I am/we are the manufacturers of the stores tendered for".

22. **Validity.** The tender shall remain open for acceptance by the purchaser for a minimum period of 90 days from the date of opening of the Tender, during which period, the tenderer shall not withdraw his offer nor amend, impair or derogate therefore, subject to the period being extended further, if required, by mutual agreement from time to time. Any contravention of the above condition by the tenderer will lead to failure of his earnest money.
23. **Tenderer's Address.** Each tenderer shall state in the tender his postal address, fully and clearly. Any communication sent to the tenderer by post at his said address shall be deemed to have reached the tenderer duly and in time, even if the communication does not reach the tenderer at all or in time for whatever reason. Important documents will be sent by Registered Post.
24. **Purchaser not Bound to Accept any Tender.** The purchaser shall not bound to accept the lowest or any tender or to assign any reason for non-acceptance or rejection of a tender. The purchaser reserves the right to cancel or to accept any tender in respect of the whole or any portion of supply specified in the tender papers or to sub-divide the quantum of supply among different tenderers to reduce the quantum of supply or to accept any tender for less than the tendered quantities without assigning any reason, whatsoever.
25. **Tenders Confidential.** The tenderer (whether his tender be accepted or not) shall treat the contents of his tender as private and confidential. He shall also treat the prices quoted by him as strictly confidential till the tenders are opened.
26. **Indian Manufacture.** Tenders for stores of wholly Indian manufacture will be given preference over those for imported stores and those which call for import of components or raw materials only. In any case, the foreign exchange requirements shall be kept down to the bare minimum.
27. **Result of Tender.** The successful tenderer will be advised by letter of the decision on his tender. No tender shall be deemed to have been accepted until and unless such acceptance has been notified in writing to the tenderer by the purchaser.
28. **General Instruction for Submission of Tenders.**
    (*i*) Each tender shall be enclosed in a sealed cover superscribed with Tender No......... due for opening on.........and addressed to the Controller of stores/CON, N.F. Railways, Guwahati-781011.
    (*ii*) The tenders may be deposited in the Tender Box provided for the purpose at the office of the Controller of Stores/ CON, N.F. Railway, Guwahati-781011, or sent through Registered Post. If tenders are deposited in the Tender Box, before doing so the tender envelop should be got registered with the office Supritendent, COS's/CON office, N.F. Railway., Guwahati-781011.
    (*iii*) Each item appearing in the schedule should be considered as a separate and distinct tender in itself.

SECTION (II)-CONDITIONS

- **Condition of Contract**

The supply shall be governed by the Indian Railways Standard Conditions of Contract—A1-63, A2-63, A3-63, as amended from time to time and is applicable on the opening date and as supplemented by the following Special Conditions.

In the event of any of the conditions is Special Conditions, coming in conflict with the IRS conditions of contract, the Special Conditions herein specified shall prevail.

SECTION (III)-SPECIAL CONDITIONS

1. **Deviations from Conditions of Contract**

   All printed conditions of Sale, Contract or Business or any other terms of like nature (in whatever mode or fashion may have been or are described by the Tender) will be considered as withdrawn and inapplicable to the quotation submitted.

2. **Security Deposit**

   (*i*) On receipt of the Letter of Acceptance of Tender from the purchaser, the successful tenderer shall, within a period of 14 days, deposit with the F.A. & C.A. O./CON, N.F. Railways, Gauhati- 7810 11, the sum of 5% of the total value of the Contract, subject to a maximum of Rs. 50,000/- as Security Deposit for due fulfillment of the Contract. The Security Deposit may be made on any working day, except the first working day of the month, between 10:30 and 14:30 hrs. The earnest money already paid by the successful tender may be adjusted towards payment of the Security Deposit, provided the additional amount is paid in anyone of the following forms:

   (*a*) Cash

   (*b*) Government securities at 5% below the market value.

   (*c*) Deposit receipt of any scheduled bank.

   (*d*) Guarantee bonds executed by the State Bank of India or a Scheduled Bank as defined in the Reserve Bank of India Act of 1934, and provided the amount is within the limit approved for the Scheduled Bank, by the Reserve Bank of India (See form of Guarantee Bond for Security Deposit— Annexure 'B'). A written confirmation by the Reserve Bank that the Guarantee Bonds in question are acceptable will be required in this connection.

   Please see form "Guarantee Bonds" for Security Deposit, (Annexure 'A' and 'B').

   (*e*) Demand drafts of the State Bank of India.

   (*f*) A deposit in the Post Office Savings Bank.

   (*g*) National Savings Certificates, (12 year National Defence Certificates, 10 year Defence Deposit Certificates and National Defence Bond).

   Note: Government securities and Post Office Savings Bank Account shall be hypothecated and discharged in Favour of the President of India represented by the F.A.& C.A. O./CON, N.F. Rly., Maligaon and Deposit Receipts, Guarantee Bonds and National Savings Certificate etc., shall be in the name of the F.A. & C.A.O./Con. N.F. Railway, Maligaon, Gauhati-7810 11. The Tenderers, tendering paper securities in any of the forms specified under items (*ii*) to (*vii*) above shall advise the Controller of Stores/ CON, N.F. Railway, Maligaon, Gauhati-781011, in good time regarding refund or renewal of the paper securities in question, as the purchaser will not be responsible for any loss of interest, if timely intimation for refund or renewal of the paper security is not given to the purchaser.

   (*ii*) No interest will be paid on his Security Deposit.

3. **Price**

   (*i*) Prices should be quoted in the schedule to Tender.

   (*ii*) Pries quoted should be FIRM and without escalations.

(*iii*) In exceptional cases, escalation may be allowed on prices due to :

(*a*) Cost of raw materials, and

(*b*) Duties on raw materials, provided the tender gives in his quotation in clear and unambiguous terms the formula applicable. It should be noted that the tenderer is responsible for correctness of details of rates, duties, etc., given in the format and no subsequent alterations on the ground that these details were wrongly furnished, will be allowed.

(*iv*) Tenderers are responsible for correctness of rates in which the Customs Duty countervailing Duty (excise duty), etc., are included in their quotations and that no increase in price will be allowed on ground. These duties originally included in their quotations were wrongly calculated at rates lower than those prevailing at the time of tendering. Adjustment due to statutory variations in the case of variation or in the rate of Custom duties and similar other charges, the actual amount of such duties or charges as on the date of importing supply of the materials, to the re-imbursed which shall have to be supported by documentary evidence of payment of these duties or other charges.

4. **Test Certificate**

In case, tests are prescribed in the specification, it is obligatory of the successful tenderer to furnish the manufacture's test certificate or any other test certificates in the tender along with the supply of stores. In the event of their inability to furnish the test certificate, the cost of the test to be carried out will be to the tenderer's account.

5. **Warranty**

(*i*) Contractor shall warrant that everything to be furnished shall be free from all defects and faults in material. Workmanship and manufacture shall be the highest grade and consistent with the established and generally accepted standards for material of the type ordered and in full conformity with the contract specification, drawings or samples if any, and shall be operable properly.

(*ii*) This warranty shall survive inspection of payment for and acceptance of the goods, but shall expire 24 months after their delivery and ultimate destination in India, or 18 months from the date of placing in service at ultimate destination in India, whichever shall be earlier notified to the Contractor within 4 months of such date. Any approval or acceptance to the purchaser of the stores or of the materials incorporated herein shall not in anyway limits the Contractor's liability.

(*iii*) The contractor's liability in this respect of any complaints, defects and or claims shall be limited to the furnishing and installation of replacement part, free of any charge or the repair of defective parts only to the extent that such replacement or repair of attributable to or arise from faulty workmanship or material or design in the manufacture of the stores, provided defect are brought to the notice of contractor within 4 months of their being first discovered during the guarantee period and 4 months from the date of expiry of warranty period or at the option of the purchaser to the payment of the value, expenditure and damages as hereafter mentioned.

(*iv*) The contractor shall, if required, replace or repair the goods or such portion that thereof as is rejected by the purchaser free of cost at the ultimate destination or at the option of the Purchaser, the contractor shall pay to the purchaser value thereof at the contract price and such other expenditures and damages as may arise by reason of the breach of the condition herein specified.

(*v*) All replacements and repairs that the purchaser shall call upon the contractor to deliver or perform under this warranty, shall be delivered and performed by the contractor within

3 months (promptly and satisfactorily). If the contractor/s desire/s' the replaced parts can be taken over by them/him or their/his representative in India for disposal as they he deem/deems fit within a period of 3 months from the date of replacement of goods/ parts. At the expiry of this period, no claims whatsoever shall lie on the Purchaser.

(*vi*) The warranty herein contained shall not apply to any material which shall have been repaired or altered by the purchaser or on his behalf in any way without the consent of the Contractor so as to effect its strength, performance or reliability or to any defect to any part due to misuse, negligence or accident.

(*vii*) The decision of the General Manager/CON/Controller of stores/CON, N.F. Railway in regard to the contractor's liability and the amount, if any, payable under his warranty shall be final and conclusive.

6. **Inspection.**

   The stores will be subject to inspection by and approval of the purchaser or his nominee during manufacture or before dispatch and on receipt by the consignee as deemed necessary. No unapproved stores shall be dispatched.

7. **Quota/Essentiality Certificate.**

   It is to be noted that the contractor shall be solely responsible for the procurement of controlled categories of steel and all arrangements both financial or otherwise in connection therewith. He shall ensure that there is no delay on his part in submitting an indent against the Quota/ Essentiality Certificate to be issued to the appropriate authority, as the case may be, and in getting his indents planned for production and supply. The contractor shall also be responsible for making prompt financial arrangements and payment for the supply of materials to the producers etc. The fact that purchaser has agreed to provide Quotas/ Essentiality Certificate, does not automatically imply his acceptance for suitable extension of delivery date due to contractor's failure to procure restricted raw materials in time.

8. **Delivery.**

   Unless otherwise agreed, the delivery period will be counted from the date of receipt by the tenderer of the acceptance letter issued by the purchaser.

9. **Rejected Stores.**

   The contractor will be advised by the purchaser or his nominee of the rejection of any stores with instruction to remove the rejected materials within 14 days from date, failing which the railway's responsibilities will cease and after that time they will remain at Contractor's entire risk and if not removed before a further period of 7 days. Ground rent will be charged at the rate of Rs. 1/-per day for one or more articles weighing upto 250 kg and Rs. 2/-per day for one or more articles over 250 kg or demorrage at the goods tariff rate as the case may be or book the material "freight to pay" without any further reference. If in the opinion of the Inspecting Officer, the material is not worth returning, the same will be thrown away or destroyed without affording any credit to the firm.

10. **Higher Price for Earlier Delivery.**

    It should be noted that if a contract is placed on a higher tenderer as a result of his invitation to tender. In preference to the lowest acceptable offer, in consideration of offer for earlier delivery, the contractor will be liable to pay the government, the difference between the contract rate and that of the lowest acceptable tender on the basis of final price F.O.R. destination, including all elements of freight, sale tax, local taxes, duties and other incidentals. In case of failure to complete supplies in terms of such contract within the date delivery specified in the tender, and intercorporated in the contract. This is in addition to and without prejudice to other rights under the terms of contract. Before placing an order on this basis *i.e.*, "Time preference Basis " the express consent of the tenderer will be obtained.

11. In respect of those acceptance of tenders wherein inspection by RITE RDSO has been stipulated or where inspection is at the seller's premises, the seller should notify the inspecting authority availability of materials for inspection at least 20 days before the delivery date with copies to consignee and the buyer. In case where the inspecting authority delays the inspection by more than 10 days from the date of notification, the delivery date in the contract to be deemed to be extended without penalty/L/D by the period in excess of 10 days.
12. For purpose of despatch as provided for in the contract, the seller should arrange to offer his goods for booking by complying with the railway booking regulation on the subject,10 days before the expiry of the delivery date under advise to consignee or buyer. In such a case if booking offered by the Railway is delayed beyond 10 days, delivery date will be deemed to be extended without L/D and penalty to the extent of delay in securing the booking in excess of 10 days, on production of papers showing seller's stamps towards booking of goods and SM's certificate regarding delay in booking.
13. Ex-stock delivery will mean delivery within 20 days from the date of recent order in case where inspection at firm's premises has been stipulated and in other cases it will mean 10 days.
14. Where quotations are called for fabrication charges only *i.e.*, raw materials to be supplied by Railway, the raw materials will be supplied to the successful tenderer after he has paid the value thereof to the Railway. On receipt of intimation of acceptance of Quotation the successful tenderer will have to deposit the amount with the F.A. & C.A.O./ CON of this railway and the amount will be refunded to him on the satisfactory completion of the contract. Fabrication charges quoted by the tenderer will include transport charges of raw materials from the stores depots to the tenderer's place of business and also for the fabricated materials from the place of business of the tenderer to the station of despatch.
15. All articles ordered are subject to inspection, test and approval by an officer of this railway, irrespective of any other inspection indicated in the Purchase Order. Supplies found to be below the standard called for will be rejected and inward freight if paid by the administration will be recovered from any money due to the supplier and controller of Store/CON will be at liberty to cancel the order and re-purchase at the risk and cost of the defaulting supplier.
16. The Railway shall be entitled to appropriate towards the payment due to the Railway by the supplier in respect of any unfulfilled contract whatsoever from any payment due to the supplier or from the security deposit of both lying with this Railway or any other Indian Railway or other Central Govt. or the State Govts. Deposits.
17. Right to increase or decrease the contract quantity controller of Stores/CON. reserves the right to decrease or increase the contract quantity to the extent shown in the schedule.
18. **Imported Stores.**
    - (*i*) ***Remittance to Foreign Supplier:*** The Tenderers should note that the remittance to their foreign suppliers will be permitted only in the national currency of such foreign suppliers.
    - (*ii*) ***Exchange Rate Variation:*** If the tenderers are desirous of quoting any exchange variation clause, the clauses will be as follows:-
        - (*a*) *Rupee-Sterling Variation:* The prices quoted are based on a rate of exchange of Re. 1/-equal to .... and no adjustment will be made, provided the rate of exchange ruling at the time payment is made, does not very beyond the limit of –1%. In the event of a greater variation, prices quoted are subject to adjustment up or down in accordance with the Calcutta Exchange Bank Association T.T. rate of exchange ruling on the date the payment is made by the firm to their Principals. It may,

however, be noted that the exchange variation, if any, will apply only to that portion of the F.O.R. price which is required to be remitted to the firm's Principals in Sterling.

(*b*) *Rupee-Dollar Swiss-Francs:* The prices are based on a rate of exchange of 100 Swiss Fr. to Rs. .... according to the Calcutta Exchange Bank Association T.T. rate approved by the Reserve Bank of India ruling on .... (date of quotation). In the event a variation in the above rate on the date on which payment is made by the firm to their Principals, the price will be subject to adjustment (up or down). It may, however, be noted that exchange variation, if any, will apply only to that portion of F.O.R price which is required to be remitted to the firm's Principals in Dollar/ Swiss Francs.

Note: The term " the date of the payment is made by the firms to their Principals" occurring in the above clause will mean the date on which the payment is affected through a bank.

(*c*) As regards other currencies tenderers are required to quote their rates based on the par value as accepted by the International Monetary Fund prevalent at the time of tendering. The tendered should note that no variation shall be allowed if such variation from the par value of the currency is within the limit of – 1%.

(*d*) Tenderers should furnish the rate of exchange in respect of currencies mentioned at (*b*) and (*c*) prevalent on the date of quotation, as per the standard exchange variation clauses given above.

(*e*) To facilitate scrutiny of claims arising out of the above clause, tenderers are required to indicate clearly in their quotation the C.I.F. components of the F.O.R. prices quoted by them which are subject to exchange variation.

(*iii*) ***Sea-freight, marine insurance, war risk insurance variations:*** Claims for variations in Sea freight, Marine insurance and War risk insurance are not acceptable.

(*iv*) ***Insurance:*** Insurance charges included by the Tenderer in his quotation should cover not only risk in transit while at sea but also risk in transit from warehouse to warehouse in India.

(*v*) ***Import Licence:*** Tenderers should note that the Purchaser does not undertake to grant an Import License for the supply of stores detailed in the tender and that the acceptance of any tender shall not imply such an undertaking on the part of purchaser. A request from the successful tenderer for recommendation of his application for the grant of an Import Licence will, however, be considered.

(*vi*) ***Assistance for Import Licence:*** If assistance for the procurement of Import Licence is promised to the successful tenderer at the time of order by this administration, the successful tender should submit his Import Licence application, addressed to the chief controller of Imports, New Delhi complete in all respects to this office within 10 days from the date of receipt of the acceptance of the tender to enable this administration to forward the same to the competent authorities for arranging issue of Import Licence. The application should be in the prescribed from and accompanied by the Treasury receipt of prescribed amount as per extant rules. By forwarding the sellers' application for Import Licence, the purchaser does not undertake any liability etc., ultimate responsibility to fulfill the contact will be of the seller.

(*vii*) ***Submission of document:*** The documents detailed below should be submitted by the supplier to the Finance Directorate of Railway Board, New Delhi/F.A. & C.A.O./CON, N.F.Rly HQrs. Guwahati-781011 as may be directed by the purchaser.

(*a*) Foreign supplier's Invoice (original or typed certified copy.),

(*b*) Banker's certificate of remittance of the amount by the supplier to his principals abroad indicating clearly the currency of payment.

(c) *Evidence of shipment* : A copy of the bill of lading, pertaining to the shipment of goods included in the invoice, an freight bill or a certificate in absence of freight bill indicating the freight paid on the consignment.

(d) A copy of claim bill submitted to the accounts officer concerned marked 'paid' for the goods supplied.

The amount of sales Tax should be indicated distinctly on the claim bills.

19. Earnest money of Rs. .... /- should be deposited in cash with the F, A& C.A.O./ CON, N.F Railway, Headquarters, Maligaon, P.O. Guwahati-781011, and cash receipt granted by the F.A.& C.A.O./ CON, should be submitted with the quotation, failing which the tender is likely to be ignored.

(i) Firms who have no taxable income and therefore are unable to produce Tax Clearance Certificate will have to submit a duly sworn affidavit to that effect, countersigned by the Income Tax Officer as to its correctness.

(ii) Firms who are registered with D.G.S. & D, New Delhi/other Railways, should quote their registration number and date mentioning the validity date of I.T.C.C. if submitted to D.G.S.& D/other Railways.

(iii) Supply of stores will be subject to inspection by the Director of Inspection / D.G.S.& D.

(iv) Quantities mentioned in the Tender Schedule are subject to increase or decrease by 25%.

(v) It should be noted that if a contract is placed on a higher Tender in preference to the lowest acceptable offer, in consideration of offer earlier delivery, the Contractor will be liable to pay the Government the difference between the contract rate and that of the lowest acceptable tenderer on the basis of final price F.O.R. destination including all elements of freight, Sales tax, local taxes, duties and other incidentals, in case of failure to complete supplies, in terms of such contract and within the date of delivery specified in the tender and incorporated in the contract. This is in addition and without any prejudce to the Railway's other rights in terms of the contract.

(vi) In case of quotations on forward deliveries, subject to assistance for grant of Import Licence, Tenderers will have to submit the following information, duly signed, with the Tender:

Ref: Tender No. ....

Dated .... due on......................................

Our quotation is on forward delivery, subject to assistance or grant of import Licence. The following additional information is furnished to enable you to release necessary Foreign Exchange.

(i) C. I. F. value in Indian currency ....

(ii) Custom duty at ....

(iii) Landing, clearance, profit, etc ....

(iv) Total value of quotation ....

(v) Country of origin ....

In case, the actual C.I.F.I as per Bill of Entry lower than the quoted C.I.F. by more than 5% the price will be based on the actual C.I.F. The Bill of Entry will be sent along with the bills for verification of C.I.F. rate which will be returned by the Accounts Officer of the consignee to us after passing the bill for payment.

Signature of Tender (s)

Controller Stores/CON
N. F. Railway,
(Guwahati-781011, Assam)

ANNEXURE 'A'

Applicable to the Scheduled Bank when securities/ money are to be deposited as to cover against Guarantee etc.

In consideration of President of India having, at our request agreed to accept this .... Bank .... Guarantee in lieu of cash deposit (address) required from Messrs .... for the due fulfillment by them, of the terms and conditions of the Agreement dated .... made between .... and .... for .... (herein after called "the said Agreement") during the period commencing from .... and ending on .... or the extended period, if any We .... Bank do hereby undertake to indemnify and keep indemnified the President of India (herein after called "The Government") to the extent of Rs. .... (...............) against any loss or damage caused to or suffered by the government, by reason of any breach by the said .... of any term or condition of the said agreement and authorise the Government to recover the same from the Reserve Bank of India, from our deposit of cash and / or Securities with the said Bank. The said Reserve Bank of India have at the request of the .... Bank agreed to pay to the Government under the said Agreement and in respect of which we .... Bank hereby give this guarantee for payment. We .... Bank further agree that the guarantee herein contained shall remain in full force and effect upto nine months beyond the contract period and inclusive of the .... date referred to above or the expiry of the extended period, if any, and that it shall continue to be enforceable till all the dues of the Goverment under / or by virtue of said agreement have been fully paid and its claims satisfied or discharged or till .... Ministry of .... certifies that the (Name of the department) terms and conditions of the said agreement have been fully and properly carried out by the said .... and accordingly discharges the Guarantee subject, however, that the Government shall have no right under this bond after the expiry of nine months beyond the contract period. We................Bank lastly undertake not to revoke this Guarantee during its currency except with the previous consent of the Government in writing.

Dated, the .... days

of .... 19 .... for .... Bank

ANNEXURE 'B'

Applicable to the Scheduled Banks when securities/money are to be deposited as to cover against Guarantee etc.

In consideration of the President of India (hereinafter called "Government") having agreed to exempt .... (hereinafter called the said contractor/s) from the demand under terms and conditions of the agreement dated .... of Security deposit/Earnest money of Rs .... (.....................), we .... Bank do hereby undertake to indemnify and keep indemnified the government to the extent of Rs. .... (........................), against any loss or damage caused to or suffered by the Government by reason of any breach by the said contractor/s of any of the terms and conditions contained in the said agreement. We .... Bank further agree that the guarantee herein contained shall remain in full force and effect during the period that would be taken of the performance of the said agreement and that it shall continue to be enforceable till all the dues of the Government under or by virtue of the said agreement have been fully paid its claims satisfied or discharged till the .... (Name of department).

Certified that the terms and conditions of the said agreement have been fully and properly carried out by the contractor/s and accordingly discharges the guarantee, subject however, that the Government shall have no right under this bond after the expiry of nine months beyond the contract period.

Our liability under this guarantee is restricted to Rs .... (........................) and shall not extend 9 (nine) months beyond that contract period. All claims under this guarantee must be presented to .... Bank before the expiry of the above period. We the .... Bank, lastly undertake not to revoke this guarantee during its currency except with the previous consent of the Government in writing.

Date, the .... for .... Bank

NORTHEAST FRONTIER RAILWAY
(Construction)

Sold To ____________________
M/S ____________________
____

To be closed at 14.30 Hrs. &
To be opened at 14.45 hrs. on
....

To
The President of India
Acting Through the Controller of Stores/ CON
N.F. Railway, Maligaon, Guwahati —781011 (Assam)
Schedule of Tender No. ____________________

Sl. No	Description of Material required	Draswing No./ Specification	Unit	Quantity required	Place of Delivery required

To be Completed by the Tenderer

Sl. No	Quantity offered in words	Rate in figures & Words	Place of Delivery offered	Term of Delivery	Delivery Period

Special Instruction to Tenderers

Your attention is drawn to the special conditions enclosed. In case you do not indicate to the contrary, it will be presumed that you agree to abide by all these conditions. The tenderers are requested to quote their rates of F.O.R. destination basis.

I/we——————————carrying on business at——————————do hereby agree to supply at the price quoted and Subject to the Terms & Conditions laid down herein and in the annexed Tender form for which I/ We have entered rates in the schedule.

I/We hereby agree to abide unconditionally by the Indian railway standard condition of contract (Latest)

Signature ____________________
Name ____________________
City ____________________

Special Instruction

1. Quantity may be increased or decreased to the extent of 30% if required.
2. Firm who are not registered for this item with this Rly. other zonal Rly. DGS & D & NSIC must deposit Earnest Money of Rs—————————— with Financial Adviser and Chief Accounts Officer/CON/N. F. Railway, Maligaon, Guwahati—11 and cash Receipt obtained thereof should be affixed on the space provided otherwise offer will not be considered. Firm who are registered with Rly. DGS & D and NSIC must quote their Regd. No——————
3. Successful tender will be required to furnish security Deposit to the extent of 5% value of the contract for the fulfillment of the contract before placement of Purchase Order.
4. The supply is subject to Inspection by RITES/RDSO/DOI (Met) before dispatch.
5. Current and valid Income tax clearance certificate should be furnished along with the tenders.
6. Performance statement should be furnished as per specimen enclosed along with the tender.
7. One Important Note of tender is also enclosed vide Annexure 'A'.
8. Producer's Test Certificate/Government Laboratory Test Certificate/SSI Test certificate should be furnished along with the supply.
9. Tenderer should quote rate for the Rounds to the re-rolled using their own billets.
10. No essentiality certificates will be issued by the Railways for Billets.

To be Completed by the Tenderer

1. Place of delivery offered——————————
2. Terms of delivery——————
3. Whether or not exact to specification as called for (Yes/No)——————
4. ——————Remarks and full particulars of offer if strictly to requirement as called for.
5. Delivery period.

   I/We——————carrying on business at——————do have HEREBY AGREE To supply at the price quoted and subject to the terms and conditions laid down herein and in the annexed tender form for which I/We have entered rates in the schedule.

   I/We Hereby agree to ABIDE UNCONDITIONALY BY THE INDIAN RAILWAY STANDARD CONDITIONS OF CONTRACT (LATEST).

NORTHEAST FRONTIER RAILWAY

Check List

(Enclosure To Tender Documents)

Office of the Controller of Stores (CON) Maligaon: Guwahati—781011.

Against the enclosed tender, kindly ensure certain clarification/confirmations compliances as indicated below, in your offer so that no back references are required. This will help in quicker decision of the tender enquiry.

Failures to comply is liable to result in rejection of the offer.

1. *Tender Form* : The tender from must be returned duly signed and total and unconditional acceptance of the Indian Railways Standard Conditions of Contract (latest) MUST BE CONFIRMED.

2. *Validity* : Please ensure that the validity of the offer is for 90 days from the date of opening as mentioned n the tender.

3. *Earnest Money* : (*i*) Please deposit Earnest Money as required.

   (*ii*) Please indicate the Registration No. of your concern with Rlys. NSIC/ DGS & D and submit photostat copy of your Registration with N.F. Railway or other Railway or NSIC, and/or DGS & D.

4. *Security Deposit*: (*i*) Please confirm that you will deposit 5% value of the contract as security deposit before placement of order if your offer is found acceptable.

   (*ii*) If a Bank Guarantee is furnished. It will need to be certified for adequacy of stamp value by the collector. In terms of the Indian Stamp Act.

5. *Inspection* : Please confirm that you are agreeable to inspection of the stores by RITES/ RDSO/Director of Inspection before dispatch.

   Please indicate manufacture's name and address in case you are not the manufacturer.

6. *Test Certificate* : Please confirm that you will submit producer's/Govt. Laboratories'/SSI Test Certificate along with the supply.

7. *Payment* : (*i*) Please confirm that you are agreeable to 90/95% payment against proof of dispatch under CLEAR Rly. Receipt and Inspection Certificate direct from Financial Adviser and Chief Accounts Officer/Con,N.F. Railway, Maligaon guwahati-781011 or the concerned Accounts Officer. The balance will be payable on receipt and acceptance of the goods by the consignee, and his certificate for the same.

   (*ii*) Payment through Bank will entail many formalities to be observed and you will be required to submit a power of attorney duly hypothecated in favours of the F.A. & C.A.O. (Construction) of this Railway. The power of attorney may need to be approved/ vetted by the Financial Adviser and Chief Accounts Officer/ Con & Law officer of this Railway before its acceptance. You will also have to confirm that the Bankers will not withhold the documents pending payment. Bank charges will have to be borne by you.

   (*iii*) Please confirm that you would be agreeable to receive payment direct from the Financial Adviser and Chief Accounts Officer (Con), N.F. Railway, Maligaon or the concerned Accounts Officer, instead of through Bank, being generally, a quicker procedure.

8. *Conformance* : A performance statement, showing successful past supplies of this item, must be submitted as requested in the tender form, indicating your successful supply of the item tendered.
9. *Income tax* : Please submit your current and VALID Income Tax clearance certificate.
10. *Guarantee Certificate* : Please confirm that you will submit Guarantee certificate in accordance with the conditions of contract for 12 months from the date of receipt of material/18 months from the date of dispatch with condition of free replacement in case any defect is found in the Supply made by you.
11. *Excise Duty* : Please indicate the percentage of excise duty, and other duties or taxes and surcharges applicable/ or included.
12. *Sales Tax* : Please indicate percentage of Sales Tax applicable/included in the price.
13. *Packing and Forwarding Charges,* : Please include the packing and forwarding charges, indicating the station of despatch for dispatching under clear R/R., or indicate the same clearly. "Ex-Works" or "Ex-Godown" offers are liable to be rejected.
14. *Delivery Terms* : (*i*) Please confirm that your offer in on F.O.R. destination basis,

    (*ii*) The purchaser does not accept any liability or responsibility for arranging booking by rail, as explained in Clause 0602 of the IRS Conditions of Contract.

    (*iii*) In view of difficulties often reported in obtaining booking by rail to consignees on N.F. Railway, the contractor may offer at his entire risk, free Road delivery to the consignees subject to re-imbursement of equivalent railway freight by Goods Train, with 100% payment after receipt and acceptance of the stores by the consignee.
15. *Price Variations/Market Fluctuation* : Please quote a firm price in exceptional or unavoidable cases, the basis/ break up of any price variation clause if quoted, should be given indicating clearly the base price and the rate of variation. Offers not on firm price basis are however liable to be rejected.
16. *Tender Form* : Please purchase the tender form and submit the same duly signed.
17. *Raw Material* : Raw material assistance like Essentiality Certificate for steel etc., cannot generally be given. Offers which are conditional on any such assistance or offers seeking such assistance are liable to be rejected.
18. *Delivery* : Delivery date and delivery terms must be firm, unconditional and clear.

Your quotation confirming/ clarifying/ complying the above should reach this office before the date and time specified in the Tender. This is issued without any commitment from the purchaser.

ANNEXURE 'A'

Office of The Controller of Stores/CON,
Maligaon : Guwahati-781011

Important Note

Attached to Tender Enquiry No. ....

1. Supply is subject to inspection by M/s. RAIL INDIA TECHNICAL AND ECONOMICAL SERVICES (P) LTD/Railway Representative/RDSO/DOI (Met).

2. Please quote F.O.R. Destination price.
3. Illustrated least/pamphlet, catalogue etc., showing full details of the offer must accompany quotation.
4. The machine/plant/material spares should guaranteed for one year trouble free service after commissioning of the materials.
5. In case you are not interested to your offer, you must return the tender enquiry with your remarks to that effect. In case tender is not returned by you, this office may not issue tender enquiry to you in future.
6. Drawing enclosed with this tender must be returned along with your offer failing which this office reserves the right to recover the cost of the drawing.
7. In case tenderer stipulate price variation clause the full and complete basis of price variation must be clearly stated and they will also be required to furnish documentary evidence duly supported by their internal auditors who should be a Chartered Accountant, for any such price ———— increase otherwise their offer will be ignored.
8. (*i*) Any firm stipulating for material price escalation clauses will disclose in the quotation the stock of raw materials and finished stores available with them for the items at the time of submission of the tenderers. The following date will be given in the quotation.

Description of raw materials used and or different components in finished Products	Quantity included per/item/unit	Treak up of price under different categories such as price of raw materials excise import duty etc., with rates as rolling on the date of submission of tender	Authority for rate adopted

(*ii*) In the event of the materials price escalation clause being accepted by the Railway Administration the following clause will be included in the Purchase Order/Contract placed. "The materials price escalation clause has been accepted by the Railway Administration as per the following basis".

Description of raw materials used and different components in finished materials	Quantity included per/item/unit	Break up of price under different categories such as price of raw materials excise import etc., with rates as ruling on the date of submission of tender /or any subsequent date before placement of purchase order	Authority adopted

9. The firm will given manufacturer's Test Certificate and the Test Certificate must bear the test identification mark which should be stamped by the manufacturer on the stores to establish genuineness of test. The tenderer must confirm this specifically otherwise their quotation will be ignored.
10. That the tenderer will please note that the direct payment to the firm by F.A. & C.A.O./C.O.N./ N.F. Rly., /Maligaon of bills submitted by them along with relevant Railway. Receipt and inspection Note is not convenient and quicker that the payment through Bank, he must furnish duly executed power of attorney in favour of the Rlys. Banker such as State Bank of India/ Maligaon Branch which should be acceptable by F.A. & C.A.O./and Law Officer of this

Railway authorizing it to receive payment on behalf of the firm and to given receipt their of before any actual payment is made. The firm shall have to bear Bank charges to be incurred for the same.

11. Firms not registered with this railway should submit current Income Tax clearance certificate along with the offer unless exempt under the pilot scheme.
12. Firms who are not registered with this Railway but Registered with other Railway/DGS & D, New Delhi, should quote at their Registration No.
13. Firms not registered with this Railway/other Railway/DGS & D, New Delhi, will have to deposit earnest money of Rs.———————— with Chief Cashier, N.F. Rly/ Maligaon, Guwahati-781011, and the cash receipt should be attached with the tender enquiry.
14. Successful tenderer if not registered with Railway or DGS & D/, New Delhi, will be required to deposit 5% value of the contract as Security Deposit before placement of the contract.
15. Any claims for increase in the price of materials under the profits of materials escalation clause will be subject to acceptance by FA & CAO/CON/N.F. Rly., on the basis of examination certificate of original records of the firm for the proof of payment enchanted rate made by the firm on the quantities of items supplied to the railway, which will be produced by the firm to F.A. & C.A.O., whenever, called for, this will in addition to the certificate issued by the firms auditors, who will be Chartered Accountants.
16. Excise duty should be shown separately if applicable.
17. Sales tax if applicable should be quoted extra.
18. Firm not registered with this Railway should quote the Registration No. of DGS& D, NSIC and other Railway/Railways production unit if they are registered with them. In case they do not have any registration No. it will be presumed, without further reference to them that they are not registered with Railway/ DGS & D/NSIC.
19. The firm will give guarantee of their product along with supply for correctness & specification of the materials and will also indicate the guarantee will held good for one year.
20. If the firm desires advance payment after RITES/Kolkata Inspection dispatch must be made on clear R/R if nothing is mentioned by the firm, it will be presumed that the firm as in for advance payment agrees to the condition of supply on the basis of clear R/R.
21. In case the firm wants advance payment on qualified R/R extenuating circumstances for not submitted clear R/R must be brought out with clear and convincing reasons. In this connection it is mentioned at unqualified R/R can be obtained by the firm it they comply with the conditions of packing required to enable the Railway to issue unqualified R/R.

    Besides, submission of documents such as Inspection Note and clear R/R when advance payment is stipulated the firm will also be require to submit the certificate in body of the bill itself as belows.

    I/We have personally examined and verified and do hereby certify that good in respect of which payment is being claimed have been actually dispatched under R/R No. date and further that these goods are the exact materials indicated in Challan No.———————— dated———— and covered by Inspection Certificate No————————dated ————.
    I/We hold myself/ourselves personally responsible for the correctness of this statement.

    If the firm is not prepared to supply on clear R/R and still desire advance payment then the firm should clearly state so in the tender quotation are liable to be ignored.

22. Firm must quote firm price.
23. In respect of the Stores mentioned in the schedule to the tender, the period for making risk purchase shall be 9 months inspite of 6 months as provided in Clauses 702 (b) of IRS Conditions of the contract.

ANNEXURE 'B'

Special Notes

1. Excise duty will not be paid separately. The tenderer must quote rates inclusive of excise duty at current ruling rates, if any.
2. If the tenderer desires to claim statutory variations in the excise duty within the original delivery period, then the tenderer must indicate in his offer "the rate and quantum of excise duty included" in the quoted rates. If this information is not given, if will be deemed that the tenderer does not desire to claim statutory variation in the excise duty and no claim at a later date may be allowed.
3. The delivery of the stores is required to be completed within 12 months from the date of placement of the purchase order. The tenderer must indicate in his offer the time required by him to commence the delivery of the stores after placement of the purchase order and the assured rate of monthly supplies. The tenderer may take this delivery requirement into consideration while indicating "quantity offered for supply" by him against this tender.
4. The tenderer would be required to produce, if called for by the purchaser, proof of date regarding his ability to supply the stores "at the assured rate of monthly supplies" indicated in his offer.
5. In addition to terms and conditions contained in I. R. S. conditions of contract, the contract, as may be placed against this tender would also be governed by the following special conditions:-
   (*i*) in cases where only a portion of the stores ordered is tendered for inspection at the fag end of the delivery period and also in cases where inspection is not completed in respect of the portion of the stores tendered for inspection during the delivery period, the Purchaser reserves the right to cancel the balance quantity not tendered for inspection within the delivery period fixed in the contract at the risk and expense of the contractor without any further reference to him. If the stores tendered for inspection during or at the fag end of the delivery period are contract in respect of the same at the risk and expense of the contractor. If, however, the stores tendered for inspection are found acceptable the purchaser may grant an extension of the delivery period subject to the following conditions:-
      (*a*) The purchaser has the right to recover from the contractor under the provision of clause "702 (*a*) of I. R. S. conditions of contract liquidated damages on the stores which the contractor has failed to delivery within the period fixed for delivery.
      (*b*) That no increase in price on account of any statutory increase in or fresh imposition of Customs Duty. Excise Duty, Sales Tax or on account of any other tax or duty leviable in respect the stores specified in the contract which take place after the date of the delivered period stipulated in the contract shall be admissible on such of the said stores as are delivered after the date of the delivery stipulated in the contract.
      (*c*) That not with standing any stipulation in the contract for increase in price on any other ground on such increase which takes place after the date of the delivery stipulated in the contract shall be admissible on such of the said stores as are delivered after the expiry of the delivery period stipulated in the contract.

(*d*) But nevertheless, the purchaser shall be entitled to the benefit of any decrease in price on account of reduction in or remission of Customs Duty. Excise Duty. Sales Tax or on account of any other tax or duty or on any other ground as stipulated in the price variation clause which takes place after expiry of the date of delivery stipulated in the contract.

(*ii*) The contractor shall not dispatch the stores till such time as an extension in terms of para (5) (*a*) to (*d*) above is granted by the purchaser and accepted by the contractor. If the stores are dispatched by the contractor before an extension letter as above said is issued by the purchaser and the same are accepted by the consignee the, acceptance of the stores shall be deemed to be subject the condition (*a*) to (*b*) set out in paragraph 5 above.

(*iii*) If the entire quantity is not tendered for dinspection within the delivery period stipulated in the contract and purchase chooses to grant an extension of the delivery period, the same would be subject to conditions (*a*) to (*d*) mentioned in paragraph 5 above.

The tenderer who intend to quote on 'FOR DESTINATION basis, while quoting for such of the goods as attract Excise duty on ad valorem basis will take note of Section 4 (2) of Central Excise and Salt Act, 1944 as amended and indicate the element of transportation and insurance; if any, included in their 'FOR DESTINATION' rate, otherwise the purchaser shall estimate the freight element involved.

THE PRICE TO BE QUOTED BY THE TENDERERS SHOULD TAKE INTO ACCOUNT THE CREDIT AVAILED ON INPUTS UNDER THE MODVAT SCHEME as the tenderer should give a declaration as per the certificate given below:-

Declaration

To,

The President of India,

Through Controller of Stores (Const.)

N.F. Railway, Maligaon

Guwahati—781011

Sub :- Cur Offer against the T/No. ——————————

—————————— due to open on ——————————

for the supply of ——————————

We hereby declare that while quoting the price against above mentioned tender, we have taken into account the entire credit of inputer available under MODVAT scheme introduced as per current order of the Govt.

We further agree to pass on such additional duties as set offs as may become available in future in respect of all the inputs used in manufacture of the final product on the date of supply under the MODVAT scheme by way of reduction of prices and advise the purchaser accordingly.

Signature of Tenderer

Designation——————————

Telephone No.——————————

Date——————————

Performance Statement

Date of Opening————————

S. No.————————

Name and address————————

SI. No.	Purchasing Agency	Order No. & Date	Brief Description	Quantity	Total Value	Delivery Period	Quantity		Rejection if any	Remarks
							Supplied	Balance		
1	2	3	4	5	6	7	8		9	10

The above list included all orders for material, tendered for or similar above Rs. 50,000 from Central Govt. State Govt. and public sector undertaking during the last one year.

OFFICE SEAL

N.F. Railway

Block Copy			**Requisition No.**	**Date**
Requisition for Stores/		**S.1302A**		
Indentor	**Consignee**	**Consignee Code**	**Material Required at**	**Depot**
Description	**Nomenclature Number**		**Quanlity Demanded in Figs.**	**Unit**
			Quanlity Demanded in Words	
			Allocation	

Last Purchase Particulars	Rate	Value	Purpose

1. Quantity in stock with indentor/still to be indented for construction requirement.
2. Total quantity outstanding coverage against other indents.
3. Total Quantity due on outstanding purchase orders.
4. Consumption during the past 3 years ——— ———— ———
5. Details of outstanding indents (this should include the indents for closely similar items)
6. Details of outstanding purchase orders with rates. (this should include the purchase order nos. for closely similar items)

   (attach separate sheet if space insufficient)
7. Likely supplier (if any) (attach separate sheet if space insufficient)
8. Is proprietary article certificate enclosed?
9. Reason for urgent purchase
10. Certificates:
    (*i*) Certified that no/adequate stock of the same or closely similar item is available.
    (*ii*) Funds are available for Rs. ———— during the year————
    (*iii*) Part (s) indented here is /are required for maintenance of assets actually in use under the charge of the indentor.

Indenting Officer *Controlling Officer* *Approving Officer*

For use of stocking depot only:

(*i*) Certified that the item is not stocked in this depot

(*ii*) Certified that the demand cannot be met out of surplus/alternate materials.

(REGISTERED ACK.DUE)

NORTHEAST FRONTIER RAILWAY

(Construction Organisation)
RISK PURCHASE NOTICE

Office of the
Controller of Stores (CON)
Maligaon, Guwahati—781011

No ....
Dated ....

To, ...
....
....

Sub:- P.O. No ....
....

Dear Sir

1. This office Store Order No .... dated .... for delivery by .... was placed according to terms of delivery quoted by you against this office tender No ....
2. It has been reported that the supply against item No .... of the order still remains outstanding in full/to the extent of (Qty.) .... although the date of delivery has expired.
3. Please show cause why the order should not be cancelled and purchase made from elsewhere at your risk and cost. Your reply must reach this office within 10 days from the date of receipt of this letter failing which "RISK PURCHASE" action will be proceeded with without further reference to you and any loss or expenditure that the Administration incurs, because of failure on your part, to report the correct position within the specified period, will have to be borne by you.
4. This is without any prejudice to the rights of the administration to recover liquidated damage for late supply.

Yours faithfully

For Controller of Stores (CON)
N.F. Railway, Maligaon,
Guwahati—781011
For and on behalf of President of India

Copy To:

1. .... (in duplicate). He will please, after a lapse of 15 days, return one copy of this notice with the position re-supply against this order and should thereafter refrain from accepting further supplies without prior approval from this office, If the order has already been complied with one copy of this notice should be returned immediately stating the position.

Enc: 1. Extra copy of this letter
Confidential section
To score off in appropriate titles

For Controller of Stores (CON)
N. F. Railway, Maligaon
Guwahati—781011,

For and on behalf of President of India

V.S. Ghy,- 1- SC/82/5373/11237 dt. 11-11-82/50 Pkts.

Dated for information to lathes :-

1. Indenting Officer
2. Consignee
3. Inspecting Officer (2 copies)
4. P.& A.O. Department of Supply & Technical Development, New Delhi/ Calcutta/ Bombay.

Notes: Copies of the requisitions placed by Direct Demanding Officer are required to be forwarded only to the Inspecting Officer and the P. & A.O. Department of Supply and Technical Development, New Delhi/ Calcutta/Bombay. Copies need not be sent to the Supply Officers who placed this contract.

The identing department is Government or non- Government / Central or State (in the case of Central) } Civil or defence / Commercial or non- Commercial

* The alternative not applicable should be scored out.

Special Instructions

1. On all letters, invoices and bills please quote the number and date of this order, the name of the Indenting Officer, the number and date of indent and the number and date of the contract mentioned on reverse.
2. No direct payment should be made to the supplying firm by the indent or consignee himself for supplies made against the Supply Order.
3. All columns of this form should be carefully typed or filled in ink and should be complete in all respect before issue.

Supplementary Schedule

Item No. of Indent	Item No. of Contract	Descriptions of Goods	No. or Quantity in the same Unit as in the Contract	Unit	Rate per Unit		Total Cost	
					Rs.	P.	Rs.	P.
			Total					

(For use in the Pay & Accounts Office)

CHECKED AND FOUND CORRECT

Noted on page .... of Payment Register,

(Index No ....)

A/cs Clerk Accountant G.O.

SUPPLY ORDER AGAINST DIRECTOR GENERAL OF SUPPLIES AND DISPOSALS RATE OR RUNNING CONTRACT

The Director General of Supplies and Disposals is not authorized to arrange for the purchase of stores for Private Parties(or for Private use of Government Officer)

Office of the

Station

Supply Order No .... dated .... against D.G.S. & D.

Rate / Running .... Contract No .... dated .... (Period of Rate/Running Contract ....)

This order which is intended for the supply of the stores detailed in the schedule below, in accordance with the terms and conditions of the director General of Supplies and Disposals/ Running contract mentioned above and in the manner specified herein, shall operate to create a specific contract between the contractor (with whom the contract referred)

Here enter the name of Govt. concerned to which the requisitioning officer belongs, *e.g.*, President. Governor .... of .... State.

To and the requisitions are placed of the one part and the .... of the other part.

To be filled in when requisitioning different

Designation of Indenting Office

INDENT NO ....

Dated ....

Item No. of Indent	Item No. of Contract	Description of Goods	No. or Quantity in the same Unit as in the Contract	Units	Rate per Unit		Total	
					Rs.	P.	Rs.	P.
		(For supplementary schedule see reverse)	Total					

(Total inclusive price to the nearest rupee/f.o.r./delivered free at in words) Rs.

Date of delivery.

Authority holding Sealed Particulars.

Designation and address or Inspecting Officer.

Designation and address of the Consignee.

Railway Station to which goods are to be consigned.

To be dispatched by train at † Risk Freight of Rate

Designation of the Accounts Officer of the Consignee.

Head of Account to which the cost is debitable.

The necessary

Railway Material Concession Note	is enclosed herewith
Military Credit Note	should be obtained in direct communication with

Certified that a copy of Supply order has been dispatched under endorsement No. (s) .... dated .... in a registered cover to the Pay and Accounts Officer, Department of Supply and Technical Development .... (here fill in the destination) and Director/Deputy director of Inspection .... (here fill in the destination).

Please acknowledge receipt of this letter and arrange supply of above stores.

To Signature...

Sarvashri Designation....................................

FOR ENDORSEMENT AND SPECIAL LINSTRUCTIONS SEE ON REVERSE

The alternatives not applicable should be scored out.

†Passenger or goods train, owner's railway risk, freight paid or to pay or public tariff, railway material or military concession note should be mentioned.

ANNEXURE-D1

NORTHEAST FRONTIER RAILWAY

(Construction Organization)

Office of the
Controller of Stores/Con.
Mailigaon, Guwahati-781011:

To Dated ....

M/s. ....

....

Sub: ....

....

Ref: Your letter no ....

Dear Sir,

1. You have failed to deliver the stores within the contract delivery period and have vide letter under reply asked for extension. In the circumstances stated the date of delivery of stores stipulated in the purchase order is hereby extended from to.................subject to .... levy of liquidated damages for the delay in supplies as per terms and conditions of the contract and subject to the following conditions.

(*i*) No increase in price on account of any statutory increase in or fresh imposition of customs duty excises duty sales tax or on account of any other tax leviable in respect of the stores specified in the said Purchase Order which takes place after the expiry of the ORIGINAL CONTRACT DELIVERY PERIOD shall be admissible on such of the said stores as are delivered after the original contract delivery period, and

(*ii*) Notwithstanding any stipulation in the contract for increase in price on any other ground, no such increase shall be admissible on such of the said stores as are delivered after the expiry of the ORIGINAL CONTRACT DELIVERY PERIOD.

(*iii*) We shall be entitled to the benefit of any decrease in price on account of reduction in or remission of customs duty, excise duty sales tax or on the price variation clause which takes place after the expiry of the above mentioned date (*i.e.*, original contract delivery date).

2. Please intimate immediately your acceptance of the extension on the above conditions. Please note that in the event of your declining to accept the extension on the said conditions the contract shall be cancelled and the outstanding quantity of stores shall be purchased at your risk and cost under the terms of the contract.
3. You are hereby further warned that outstandings at the expiry of the finally extended date will be cancelled at your risk and expense without further reference to you.

Yours faithfully,

Controller of Stores (Con)
N.F.Railway, Maligaon, Guwahati-781011
For & on behalf of the President of India.

Copy to:
(1) FA & CAO/CON/N.F. Railway
Maligaon, Guwahati-781011

Controller of Stores (Con)
N.F.Railway/Maligaon, Guwahati-781011

PROPRIETORY ARTICLE CERTIFICATE

One Equipment/Stores wanted is/are manufactured by M/S

(*i*) No other make is acceptable for the following reasons ....

(*ii*) Approval of the Director/Head of the Depot/Head of the Deptt. or his nominee has been obtained.

(*iii*) The Associated Financial Adviser has concurred in the proposal.

Signature of the Indentor

Designation.................

Date..........................

Note. If more than one Head is to be debited, give details on item sheet

*Strike out whichever is not applicable.

Separate indent should be placed for General Purpose and Works Requirements through the same time.

Indent on the $\frac{\text{Railway Board}}{\text{DGS \& D}}$ by Controller of Stores .... (Railway Code) ....

Item Sheet

Indent No. of the Railway and date ....

<table>
<tr><th>Item No. of Indent</th><th>Detailed Description including Specification and Drawing</th><th>P.L. No.</th><th>Accounting Unit (Words)</th><th>Unit Code</th><th>Quantity in Figures</th><th>Quantity in Words</th></tr>
<tr><td rowspan="3"></td><td rowspan="3"></td><td rowspan="4"></td><td colspan="4">Name and Full Address of Consignee and Quantity:</td></tr>
<tr><td>S. No.</td><td colspan="2">Address</td><td>Quantity</td></tr>
<tr><td rowspan="2"></td><td colspan="2" rowspan="2">Total</td><td></td></tr>
<tr><td colspan="2">Estimated Rate & Unit. Estimated value in Rs.........
Requirements for Period/Demand Ref etc.</td><td></td></tr>
</table>

1. Quarterly installments desired with quantity and date.
2. Dispatch particulars
   (*i*) *by Goods, Passenger train/Parcel Postal and
   (*ii*) *To be booked freight to pay/paid at own Rs. Risk/Rly. Risk
   (*iii*) *To be insured/Not to be insured
   *Strike out whichever is not applicable.

for Estimated Rate, including contract ref. and date, quantity, inclusive or Es-duty, Sales Tax, Name of Supplier etc.

List of Successful suppliers in the last.

Any other relevant information.

....

Signature of Stores Officer

(Name and Designation)

Instructions

1. Separate form item sheets should be used for GENERAL PURPOSE WORKS REQUIREMENTS.
2. Accounting Unit should be the same as in Board's circular Unit for estimated rate should also be the same.
3. List of successful suppliers, particularly for bulk supplies should be invariably furnished.
4. The address of consignees should be complete in all respects for booking of materials.

TC/GHY-1 5000 Sets

Seoi Cards	Card Code	Indent No............			Date	
	Punch On Ailseq 1 Cards	Stock Non. St.	PL. NO.	Category	BDL. No.	COL. 79
	S. No.	Consignee Code	Delivery Date		Quantity (3 Decimals)	

Seq 2 Cards	Unit Code	Demand Regn. Date	Allocation Code	No. Of Consig-Ners	No. of Ite Ms	NO. of De Li Ver Ies	La St S No.	Bn Dl E No.	COL 792

Note: 1. Seqi Card—COL. 25-38. and COL. 44-47 Blank.

2. COL—To IN SEQ2 Card Same as SEQ1 and COL—To Blank.

GOVERNMENT OF INDIA

DGS & D–85(A)

Indent Form

(Top Sheet)

........................Railway

1. Indent placed by:
   (Designation and Full Adress,
   Telegraphic Address & Phone No.
   Telex No. etc.

1. 1. Type of indent (For DGS & D only)
   *Programme/Supplementary/AD-HOC/Works Programme/Express.

2. Indent No. and date:
3. Non. of Items included in the Indent.......Total estimated value Rs..........
4. Designation and address of the Accounts Officer :
5. Head of Account debitable:
6. Expenditure whether Voted or Charged: *Voted/Charged.
7. Name of Inspecting Authority:
8. In case of demand for proprietory stores, has proprietory certificate in a set form been given by the Indentor? *Yes, See reverse/Not Proprietory.
9. In case of purchase of stores involving foreign exchange, has the requisite allotment of foreign exchange been sanctioned by the competent authority? *Yes/No/Not applicable

(i) If yes, the number and date of financial sanction may be quoted:

(ii) Reference of Development Wing for clearance of Stores from Indigenous angle:

10. The name of Technical Officer from whom clarification, if any required, can be obtained:
11. Statistical information for the DGS & D 11.1 *Plan/Non-Plan. 11.2 Sector of Use-Railways 11.3. Required for—*Capital/Maintenance.
12. Copies of A/Ts. to be endorsed to:
13. Funds certificate. (For Railways):

(i) Stores are required for General Purpose. The value of stores will be met as below: Rs..............from Current Grant Rs..............from Advance Grant.

(ii) Stores are required for sanctioned Works and necessary hands to the extent of Rs.....................are available.

....	....
For F.A. & CAO	For Controller of Stores.

14. In case of proprietory stores a proprietory article certificate in the following form should be furnished.

P No. **Code Details of the Fields**

XX	XX	XXXX	X	XXXXX
Purchase Sec	Year	File No.	Source of Supply	Five Digit Sl. No.

Code for Source of Supply		**Tender Type Code**		**Category Code**	
Import	0	Bulleting	1	New	1
COS	1	Sp. Limited	2	Second Hand	2
DGS & D (R/C)	2	Limited	3		
				Repairable	3
DGS & D (RGC)	3				
Fabrication order	4	Open Advt.	4	Emergency	4
Controller of Stationery	5	Single non PAC	5	Con & Sepcial	5
DGS & DAT	6	Global	6	Surplus	6
		PAC	7		
Rly. Board	7				
Production Unit	8				
Other Zonal Railway	9				

Code for mode of Despatch		***Nature of Industry Code***		***Payment Mode Code***	
Direct Delivery	0	Importd purchased India	1	100% on Receipt of the material	1
By ordinary goods train	1	SSI or Cottage Industries excluding Khadi	2		
By Road	2	Public Sector	3	On proof of despatch & inspection	2
Goods QTS	3	Other Rlys	4		
				Proforma Invoice	3
Passenger/Parcel	4	Other Govt. deptt.	5		
By Registered Post Parcel	5	Khadi Industries	6	Advance Payment Along with PO	4
6/Sir	6	Other Industries	7		

N.F.RLY./STORES DEPARTMENT (CONSTRUCTION)/PURCHASE ORDER

CCI Please put the Applicable field Rev. 87

Ordinary Purchase	1	Tender type code	P.O. No. 3-16	Date 17.22	Nature of Ind. 23	Supplier 24-28
Emergency Purchase	2					

Tender No.	Opened on 29-34	Price Variation 1 2 Yes No	Time-pref 36 1 2 Yes No	Risk puech 37 1 2 Yes No	F.E.X CD 38 1 2 Yes No	PO-LST-SR No. 39-40	Perment Mode CODE 41

From To

With reference to your quotation No ... dated ... Please deliver to the Consignee mentioned below, the undermentioned articles free of incidental chares subject to Indian Railways Standard Conditions of Contract latest edition and General Conditions of Contract for the Stores Department of this Railways and to addendum to the same subject applicable to this contract.

Description

Total Quantity in Figures
In words

Rate in Figures 51-58
Rs. [ ]

Buying Unit
Buying 59-60 | UNI NLU 61-62

In words

Excise Duty 63-66 [ ] %

Packing & Forwarding charges 67-69 [ ] %

Sale-Tax-CST/AST/AFT 70-71 [ ] %

Yes | No
Form enclosed
Total Value

PL NO. 42-49 CAT 50

Mode of Despatch
Code 72 [ ]

Inspection Authority
Code 73 [ ]

Delivery term__________
FOR/Free at
To be delivered/despatch to
or to be sent direct to consignees
mentioned below
Bill Passing Officer
Bill Paying Officer
Payment Terms

Controller of Stores/CON

For & on behalf of The President of India

Following condition of attached conditions sheet shall also apply:

PO SR 6-77	Consignee	Consg. CD DP-WD 78-82	Demand No 83-90	Dem Reg. Date	Coverage Code in 91	Quantity in 92-99	Delivery Date 100-105	Allocation 105-113

Tender for Supply of Stores

NORTHEAST FRONTIER RAIWAY (CONSTRUCTION)

Stores Department
(To Be Filled In by the Tenderer)

From

To
The President of India
Through Controller of Stores
(Constn.)
N.F. Railway,
Maligaon, Guwahati - 781 011
To be Closed at 11.30
To be Opened at 11.45

Tender No.
Bulletin No. Dated Item No.

<table>
<tr><td>PL. No. Catagary.</td><td colspan="2">Quotation No</td></tr>
<tr><td rowspan="4">Description

Quantity</td><td colspan="2">Rate at which articles will be supplied including at Charges</td></tr>
<tr><td colspan="2">QUANTITY (in figures)
(in words)</td></tr>
<tr><td>RATE (in figures) Rs.
(in words)</td><td>Rate unit</td></tr>
<tr><td>Excise Duty</td><td>Sales Tax</td></tr>
<tr><td>Specification/Drg, No</td><td>Place required at</td><td>Maker's Name/Brand</td></tr>
<tr><td>Counter offer, if any</td><td></td><td></td></tr>
<tr><td>Inspecting Authority</td><td>Delivery period</td><td></td></tr>
<tr><td>Payment terms</td><td>FOR/Free at</td><td></td></tr>
</table>

I/We engange to supply to the Northeast Frontier Railway (Constn.) with the articles specified above upon the terms of the Indian Railway Standard Conditions of Contract latest edition and upon the terms of the special Conditions printed in the Stores Bulletin and the instructions for the guidane of the contractors issued by the Railway.

This quotation will hold good for 60 days from the opening date or any such time otherwise specified in the tender.

The acceptance of this Tender shall constitute a binding contract between me/us and the President of India acting through the Controller of stores (Construction) Northeast Frontier Railway.

....
Signature of Tenderer

Regist. No. with Rly.................................... Designation...................................
Regist. No. with NSIC................................ Office Seal Telephone No...............................

Regist. No. with DGS & D.......................... Date..

IMPORTANT NOTICE

1. Firms must not quote for groups for which they are not registered.
2. The rate unit must not under any circumstances; be altered.
3. All entries in the tender form should be either typewritten or in ink.
4. Sales Tax where leviable and intended to be claimed form the purchaser, the rate of Sales Tax and the Sales Tax Registration Number should be distinctly shown along with the price in the tender form where this is not done. No. claim for Sales Tax will be admitted at any later stage and on any ground whatsoever.
5. Ambiguity must be avoided in filling tenders.
6. Tender number and due invariably be quoted on the top of envelope and in all correspondence.
7. Whenever samples are called for on tender lists, samples must invariably accompany quotations duly sealed and stamped otherwise offers are liable to be passed over.
8. All articles supplied by successful tenderers shall be to description and quality and in strict accordance with and equal to the approved samples, specification or drawings. Each article manufactured and supplied by successful tenderers must bear their trade mark or identification stamp.
9. Receiving depots will entertain supplies against orders upon 3 p.m. on and working day and up to 1a.m. on Saturdays. In special cases supplies will be accepted upon to the closing of the depot.
10. All rejected articles must be removed by the Vendors at their own charge and cost within 14 days of the rejection notice. The Railway administration will give reasonable care to all rejected materials but will not be responsible for any loss or damage that may occur to it whilst on their premises. If the rejected supply is not removed within the specified time, the railway shall be at liberty to charge ground rent or book the material freight to pay to the firm without any further reference, if in the opinion of the inspection officer, the material is not worth returning the same will be thrown away or will be destroyed.
11. Suppliers bill will not be passed for payment until, the goods have been received, accounted for and accepted by the consignee.
12. Any moneys due hereunder from the supplier to the Railway may be either deducted by the railway from the supplier's bill or may be recovered form the supplier direct.
13. The Controller of Stores reserves the right to publish names and rates of successful tenderers.
14. Where material is asked for to a specification either I.R.S.I.S.D.D.G.S. & D.I.S.S.B.S.S. or as printed in the tenderes must guarantee that supplies offered are upto specification Samples submitted with the tender. Tenders are not tested and the submission of sample or quotation of a brand or make will above the tenderer from the responsibilities arising out of rejection of supplies, which when tested prove to be not upto specification. All supplies made against this tender will be subjected to inspection or test. Cost of test on supplies rejected will be recovered from supplies.
15. The Railway administration reserves the right to accept any offer either in part or whole without assigning any reason whatsoever for the same.
16. The Railway administration reserves the right to cancel, reduce or divide the contract without assigning any reason for such action.

17. The railway administration does not bind itself to accept the lowest offer and any offer or offers may be rejected or not accepted by the railway administration without assigning and reason whatsoever for the same.
18. In the case of special tenders, firms not able to quote must return the tender by due date with the words "No Quotation" written across the face of it.
19. Unregistered forms should pay to the chief Cashier of the Railway earnest money equivalent to 2% of the proposed contract and enclose proof and in the event of purchase Order being placed, should deposit security money as required to due fulfillment of the contract.
20. A Firms should submit current ITCO failing which the tender is liable to be ignored.
21. Unregistered firms should apply for registration with the railway simultaneously.
22. Price preference for prompt earlier delivery is applicable.
23. Price variation linked with raw materials is not generally acceptable.

MINISTER OF RAILWAYS

↓

MINISTER OF STATE FOR RAILWAYS

↓

MEMBER MECHANICAL
(RAILWAY BOARD)

↓

ADDITIONAL MEMBER (RLY. STORES)

↓

EXECUTIVE DIRECTOR RAILWAY STORES (G)

↓			↓
Policy Directives to zonal Railways & Production Units & Co-ordination ↓ General Manager ↓	*Diesel, Elec. Loc, EMU Car Shed Depots Scrap Yard Cutting up Yards for Condemned rolling stock Clothing Factory *Printing Press	*IRON & STEEL CELL Kolkata Particapation in JPC *Planning and Supply of steel to Wagon Builders *Liasion with Steel Plants for Supply of steel to Railways and production Units.	Liaison with other Ministries
Controller of Stores Purchases (HQ) Organisation Inventory Control (HQ) Cell	CENTRALISED PURCHASE ↓	*INVENTORY CONTROL ↓	
*Budgetary Control	*Rolling Stock (Complete units)	*Evolution policy integrated Materils Budget	
*Sales Organizer	*Imported Steel, Wheels, Tyres, Axles,	*Monitoring of inventory Performance and issue of Policy Directives	
*Depot Organizer			
*General Depots	*Processing all purchases of Rlys. and Production Units valued over Rs. 2 Crore in each case.		
*Workshop Depots			

CHAPTER

13

LEGAL ASPECTS ON PURCHASING

13.1 CONCEPT OF COUTRACT

1. In the case of purchase of stores by Government, apart from the need to comply with the departmental instructions issued from time to time, the legal aspects assume importance because of the huge stakes involved and also because of the formalities involved in the conclusion of a contract. These are purchases in which the public are interested and the Government are answerable to the public through the Parliament. The Audit and the Public Accounts Committee scrutinise the dealings from time to time and measures are suggested as to how best the interests of the Government could be protected so that the exchequer does not suffer any loss.
2. Most of us are familiar with the basic concept of contracts. Even to satisfy our daily needs, we enter into so many contracts. The two positive elements which are essential for the formation of a contract are: (*i*) consensus ad idem; and (*ii*) consideration. Consensus ad-idem means that the two contracting parties must be agreed as regards the subject matter of the contract at the same time and in the same sense. To find out whether the two parties are thus agreed, law adopts a test. The test is whether all the terms of the contract can be put in the form of an offer made by one party to the other and which can be accepted by the other saying 'yes'. There can be no contract unless there be a consensus. The existence of this consensus is ascertained by the test of offer and acceptance.
3. The word 'consideration' is understood as some matter accepted or agreed upon as a return or equivalent for the promise. The law presumes that the benefit offered induces the party to make the promise. Under Section 25 of the Indian Contract Act, an agreement made without consideration is void unless it is expressed in writing and registered under the Law for the time being in force for the registration of documents made on account of natural love and affection between the parties standing in a near relation to each other or is a promise to compensate for something done or is a promise to pay a debt barred by limitation.

Characteristics

The characteristics which every offer must possess before it can become a contract on acceptance may be stated as follows:

(*i*) An offer must be one intended to give rise to legal consequences;

(*ii*) It must be one capable of creating legal relations;

(*iii*) The terms must be certain or at least be capable of being made certain; and

(*iv*) Every offer must be communicated.

1. An offer must be distinguished from a quotation or invitation to offer. An offer may be general or specific. It is specific when it is addressed to a definite individual or body or individuals. It is general when it is addressed to an unascertained body of individuals, even though it may be accepted by an ascertained individual.
2. The tendering firm may withdraw its offer at any time before it is accepted even though it might have offered to keep the offer open for a specified period. It is equally open to the tenderer to revise or modify his offer before its acceptance. Such withdrawal, revision or modification must reach the accepting party before the acceptance is put in communication. Where, however, a tenderer agrees to keep his offer open for a specified period for a consideration, such an offer cannot be withdrawn before the expiry of the specified date. This would be so where earnest money is deposited by the tenderer in consideration of his being supplied the tender documents etc. In such a case, there would be subsidiary contract and withdrawal of offer by the tenderer before the specified period would entitle the accepting party to forfeit the earnest money.

Legal Requirements of Contract

The legal requirements of an effectual acceptance may be formulated as follows:

(*i*) It is open to the offerer to prescribe any method of acceptance;

(*ii*) Acceptance must be communicated;

(*iii*) Acceptance must be put in the course of transmission before the offer lapses or is terminated;

(*iv*) Acceptance must be absolute and unconditional;

(*v*) Acceptance must be by the offeree, or by an authorized person on behalf of the office.

1. An acceptance under Indian law may be revoked at any time before the communication of the acceptance is complete as against the acceptor but not afterwards. The communication of an acceptance is complete as against the proposer when it is put into a course of transmission to him so as to be out of the power of the acceptor; as against the acceptor when it comes to the knowledge of the proposer. The communication of a revocation is complete as against the person who makes it when it is put into a course of transmission to the person to whom it is made, so as to be out of the power of the person who makes it; as against the person to whom it is made when comes to his knowledge.
2. What results in a contract is only the acceptance of an offer as made by the offerer. Where acceptance is not absolute and unconditional, the so-called acceptance is only counter offer even though the accepting party may actually use the word "acceptance". In such a case, a contract will stand concluded only when the counter offer is accepted by the offerer.
3. Under law, any person who has attained majority and of sound mind or not debarred by law to which he is subject may enter into contracts. It follows that minors or persons of unsound mind cannot enter into contract nor can any insolvent person do so.
4. *Parties to a contract may be an individual, a partnership, a limited company or a corporation other than a limited company.* There is no difficulty where the contract is with an individual. A partnership is an association of two or more individuals formed for the purpose of doing business jointly under a business name. It is also called a firm. Partner is an agent of the firm for the purposes of the business of the firm – Section 18; So far as third parties are concerned, a partner has the implied authority to bind the firm in a contract coming in the purview of the usual business of the firm. The implied authority of a partner, however, does not extend to entering into arbitration agreement on behalf of the firm. While entering into a contract with a

partnership firm, care should be taken to verify the existence of consent of all the partners to the arbitration agreement. It must be borne in mind that a partnership is not a legal entity by itself apart from the individuals constituting it. In order to bind a firm, the agreement shall be executed in the firm's name or in any other manner expressing or implying an intention to bind the firm-Section 22.

5. *A company is an artificial legal person which has an existence distinct and separate from the members or shareholders comprising the same.* The powers of a company to do business is limited to the purposes set out in the Memorandum of Association of the Company. In the case of a company, the authority of the person seeking to bind the company should be scrutinized, though normally any one of the directors is empowered to represent the company. Likewise in the case of a corporation other than a limited company, it is necessary to verify the capacity of the association to enter into a contract and the authority of the person to represent the association.
6. *A contract can be concluded by sending what is known as an advance letter of acceptance, satisfying the requirement of the law that it is an unqualified acceptance of the terms of the offer.* Where however the parties intend that a contract is to come into existence only on the execution of a formal contract and not merely on the issue of an advance letter of acceptance it is only the formal contract that will bind the parties. Where the intention is that the advance letter of acceptance should conclude the contract it is advisable to state in that letter that this letter of acceptance concludes the contract. While issuing the advance letter of acceptance, care should be taken to scrutinize that the letter does not amount to a counter offer; otherwise, an enforceable contract will not come into existence.
7. Sometimes negotiations have to be undertaken after receipt of tenders. Negotiations after tenders have been opened are severely discouraged. Where competition is restricted ab initio, the negotiations may be more advantageous than calling for tenders. In all cases where firms are called for negotiations after the opening of the tenders, the following clause should be incorporated in the letter calling for negotiations:

   "This invitation to negotiation is without prejudice to the terms and conditions as also the validity of the offer as tendered/agreed to by you."

   Where the validity period of the original offers will expire during the course of the negotiations, steps will have to be taken to get their validity period extended. In other words, offers should not be allowed to lapse in such cases thinking that negotiations are in progress. The specific object/purpose for which the firms are called for negotiations should be clearly indicated in the letters calling them for negotiations, since in the absence of this information; the representatives of the firms will not be in a position to come prepared for discussion. The firms should also be asked to send for negotiations such representatives who are authorised to take decisions on the spot on their behalf. As far as possible all the firms who have quoted against the tender enquiry and whose quotations are technically acceptable should be called for negotiations.

13.2 CONSTITUTIONAL LAWS FOR CONTRACT

1. In the case of a contract which is to bind the Government apart from the ingredients of offer and acceptance, there are certain other formalities. Everyone of you must be familiar with Article 299 of the Constitution. The three main requirements of this article are:
   (i) *The contract must be expressed to be made by the President of India;*
   (ii) *It shall be executed on behalf of the President;*
   (iii) *It shall be executed by such person and in such manner as the President may direct or authorise.*

It is clear from a reading of the Article that there cannot be an oral contract binding the Government; in other words, a contract with Government must be in writing and all terms must be specifically provided therein.

2. *The requirements of Article 299 are mandatory. If any of the requirements are not complied with, the contract is not binding on or enforceable against the Government.* The reason is that such a contract is void and is not even capable of ratification. In AIR 1954 SC 236 the Supreme Court held that though a contract not satisfying the requirements of Article 299 would not bind the Government, a suit would lie against the officer because under Section 230(3) of the Contract Act, 1872 where the principal could not be sued, the agent would be personally bound by the contract and could, therefore, be sued. However, in recent decision (AIR 1971 SC 2210) the Supreme Court has clarified that even the officer will not be personally liable. According to the Supreme Court, if a contract entered into without complying with the conditions laid down in Article 299 is void and there is no contract in the eye of the law, even Section 230(3) of the Contract Act would become inapplicable in such a case.

3. *The Supreme Court has held that a contract in order to bind the Government need not be a formal document.* Even correspondence exchanged in the name of the President of India will bind the Government. The authority for this proposition is the decision of the Supreme Court in Union of India Vs. Ralia Ram (1964 (3) SCR 164). This was a case under Section 175(3) of the Government of India Act, 1935 which is practically in the same terms as Article 299. The Supreme Court expressed themselves as follows:

   "It is true that Section 174(3) uses the expression 'executed' but that does not by itself contemplate execution of a formal contract by the contracting parties. A tender for purchase of goods in pursuance of an invitation issued by or on behalf of the Governor General and acceptance in writing which is expressed to be made in the name of the Governor General and is executed on his behalf by a person authorises in that behalf would conform to the requirements of Section 175(3)."

4. In the case of M/s N.K. Private Ltd., the firm strongly relied on this decision and contended that the letter dated the 15th July, 1968 concluded the contract. The firm succeeded in persuading the High Court to accept this argument. However, when the matter went on appeal to the Supreme Court, the supreme Court decided the case in favour of the Government on the ground that the person duly authorized by the President to accept the offer was the Director (Stores) and so the letter dated the 15th July, 1968 signed by one of the Deputy Directors for Secretary, Railway Board would not bind the Government. The Supreme Court was also satisfied that on the relevant date Secretary, Railway Board was not a Joint Secretary to the Government of India and so any letter issued on his behalf could not conclude any contract binding on the Government.

5. One other point of interest is whether the words "for and on behalf of the President of India" should follow the designation appended below the signature of the officer authorized in this behalf under Article 299 of the Constitution. One of the arguments urged by the Government in M/s N.K. Private Ltd., case was that these words were necessary and in the absence of these words there was no concluded contract. But in Union of India Vs. Ralia Ram, the Supreme Court had already decided that the emission of these words would not be fatal to the authority of acceptance. But as pointed out, Government succeeded before the Supreme Court on the other ground that the acceptance was not by the officer duly authorized by the President of India, namely the Director (Stores). It was true that in the notification of the Ministry of Law issued in exercise of the powers under clause (1) of Article 299 of the Constitution, the Director,

Railway (Stores) was not one of the authorities duly empowered to execute the contract which was before the Supreme Court but then the Supreme Court had earlier held in Brijraj Jaipuria Vs. Union of India (AIR 1962 SC 113) that the authority to execute contracts could be conferred on a person not only by rules expressly framed and by formal notifications issued in this behalf but could also be specifically conferred. Various other arguments advanced on behalf of the firm which were not accepted by the Supreme Court. The judgment of the Supreme Court is reported in AIR 1972 SC 915.

When a contract is arranged on a F.O.R. basis (Free on Rail), the contractor undertakes to deliver goods of the contract description within the time named in the contract into Railway wagons or at the station depending on the practice of the particular railway at his own expense. Under Section 39 of the Sale of Goods Act, 1930, in the absence of a contract to the contrary, delivery by the Contractor of the goods to a carrier or to a wharfinger for safe custody is deemed to be delivery of goods to the Purchaser.

6. *When goods are sold on F.O.B. basis, the duty of the contractor is to deliver the goods on board ship at his own expense for carriage to the Purchaser.* The purchaser is liable for freight and other subsequent charges. These include freight, cost of export duties and import duties and obtaining when necessary, a licence to export. In this type of contract, it is the contractor's duty to give such notice to the purchaser as may enable him to insure the goods in sea transit but it would be more satisfactory to insert a clause in the contract itself instructing the contractor to effect the desired insurance as agent for the purchaser and add the premium to the price. If nothing is said, payment for the goods is due upon delivery of the goods by the contractor to the ship.
7. *When a contract is arranged on F.A.S. basis, the contractor undertakes to deliver the goods alongside the ship at his own expense.* The buyer becomes liable to subsequent charges.

C.I.F. Contracts

C.I.F. contracts are contracts for the sale of goods involving carriage by sea. Under such a contract, the duties which should be performed by the seller are as follows:

1. He ships goods of the contract description quality and quantity at the port of shipment.
2. He procures a contract of affreightment upto the destination mentioned in the contract and obtains a bill of lading;
3. He takes out a policy of insurance;
4. He makes out invoice describing the goods and charging to the purchaser the cost or agreed price, premium on the insurance and the freight.
5. He should tender the bill of lading policy of insurance and the invoice to the purchaser as soon as possible after shipment.

Purchaser's Liabilities

The purchaser's liabilities are as follows:

1. He pays the price on tender of the documents without waiting for receipt of the goods;
2. If the goods arrive, he takes delivery at port of destination in accordance with the bill of lading clauses;
3. He pays al import duties, customs and wharfage charges.

Note: Unlike an FOB contract, in a CIF contract, the contractor has to procure a contract of affreightment.

Classification of Contracts

Contracts can also be classified into:

1. Fixed quantity contracts;
2. Running contracts; and
3. Rate contracts.

   In a fixed quantity contract, the firm is called upon to offer to supply a definite number of quantity by a specified date. In a running contract, the contractor is called upon to supply an approximate quantity of stores at a specified price during a certain period of time. A rate contract is a contract for the supply of stores at specified rates during the period covered by the contract. No fixed quantities are mentioned in the contract and the contractor is bound to accept any order from the purchaser which may be placed upon him at the rates specified by him during the contract period. The purchaser on his part is bound to order from the contractor all stores under the contract which are required to be purchased subject to certain reservations for submitting prices to competition and for dividing the contract between more contractors than one.

4. Extension of delivery period in installment delivery contracts:

   A contract for the sale of goods to be delivered by installments may be:

   (*i*) an entire contract or

   (*ii*) a severable contract.

   The fact that the contract is divisible in performance does not effect the matter. The following stipulation of delivery may be indicated as an example for (*i*) above:

   "Delivery to commence after 45 days from the date of receipt of the order and to be completed within 3 months at the rate of 20,000 units per month right from date of delivery.

   The delivery date in contracts for the type (*ii*) above is generally indicated as follows:

   "Delivery date : 7410 Units by 15.2.08
   8510 Units by 31.3.08

   According to legal advice in the case of a severable contract, each installment constitutes a separate contract though a delivery schedule has been provided. In the case of severable contracts (*i.e.*, contracts providing delivery in installments and not delivery schedule), extensions in delivery period are necessary for each installment separately as according to legal advice if stores are accepted after the expiry of the delivery date of a particular installment without extension in delivery period being given reserving our right to levy liquidated damages, the Govt. will not be legally entitled to claim the liquidated damages. In the case of an entire contract providing delivery schedule, it is not, however, necessary to grant extension in delivery period in the case of delay in intermediate installments and such extensions would be necessary only in case of delay beyond the final date for completion of delivery.

5. *Often a variation in the terms of contract becomes necessary* after conclusion of a contract. But no variation can be made unilaterally. It is also our experience that the suppliers approach for extensions in the delivery dates. An extension letter can operate only if there is an acceptance, absolute and unqualified to all the terms and conditions of extension. Such an acceptance can be evidenced either by correspondence or by contract, that is by making supplies without raising any objection. Mere postal acknowledgment of the letter of extension will not serve the purpose. In view of this, each case may have to be reviewed in order to watch the acknowledgment and the prospect of supplies. Where, however, it is found that the extension letter has neither been acknowledged nor acted upon by the suppliers a notice in the appropriate form

should be issued to the supplier. In the event of failure of the supplier to acknowledge the acceptance of the extension letter by the date mentioned in the notice or his failure to act on the extension letter, the Purchase officer should proceed to cancel the contract for breach.

13.3 POINTS TO DISOLVED A CONTRACT

1. Where it is intended to cancel a contract, it should be done immediately the breach has occurred. In certain cases decision is not, however, taken immediately on expiry of the delivery date or the extended delivery date as the case may be, whether the contract should be cancelled or kept alive. Sometimes correspondence is exchanged with the firm after expiry of the delivery period thereby keeping the contract alive and by such action time ceases to be the essence of the contract. This will create complications as immediate cancellation of the contract will not be possible in that case. The Purchase Sections should not, therefore, enter into correspondence with the firms after the breach of the contract unless it is intended to keep the contract alive. The idea is that they should refrain from entering into correspondence which conveys the intention of keeping the contract alive or has the effect of keeping the contract alive. It is not that every letter written to the firm, after expiry of the delivery period, will have the effect of keeping the contract alive. It is permissible to ask for some information regarding past supplies etc., at the same time making it clear to the party that calling for such information is not intended to keep the contract alive and does not waive the breach and that it is without prejudice to the rights and remedies available to the purchasers under the terms of the contract. The Inspectors should also not enter into correspondence with the firms after expiry of the delivery dates stipulated in the contract. Where as a result of the correspondence exchanged the contract has been kept alive, if time is to be made again the essence of the contract, we are required by law to give a notice to the contractor giving a notice with provision for recovery of liquidated damages for delay in supplies and also with the usual denial clauses included in the standard form of delivery period of extension letter (para 2 of Form No. DGS & D-160) giving a reasonable time for performance and intimating him that time would be the essence of the contract. This notice has to be given by a letter as standardized in consultation with the Ministry of Law, and as indicated in Annexure III of this office order. In such cases where the contract has been kept alive by the conduct of the parties, cancellation would be resorted to only after the expiry of the aforesaid notice period. It should be noted that the date for delivery fixed in such notice cannot be taken as the date of breach of the contract for counting the period of 6 months for the purpose of concluding the risk purchase contract unless it is accepted by the contractor either by correspondence or making supplies. If the contractor does not accept the date either by repudiating it by correspondence or otherwise the date of breach for the purpose of counting the six months period would be the date on which the original delivery period or the mutually agreed extended delivery period, if any has expired.
2. A contract is discharged or the parties are normally freed from the obligation of a contract by due performance of the terms of the contract. A contract may also be discharged; *(a)* by mutual agreement; *(b)* by tender; *(c)* by impossibility; and *(d)* by breach. Where a contract is discharged by mutual consent, *e.g.*, waiver or release, there is no problem. One of the parties entitled to performance or both the parties may waive the performance due from the other; if so, the other party need not perform the contract. In the case of discharge by tender, if one party offers to perform its contract at the stipulated time as per the terms of the contract but the other party wrongfully declines to accept the performance, then the party which has tendered performance is excused from non-performance, impossibility may arise by the destruction of the subject matter of the contract becoming illegal owing to the declaration of war or through

legislation. A contract may also get discharged for impossibility if a condition which forms the foundation of the contract becomes impossible of fulfillment. Section 56 of the Contract Act, 1872 deals with this. This is otherwise known as 'Doctrine or Frustration'. Discharge of contract by breach throws a variety of problems. When there is a breach of contract the breach discharges the innocent party to proceed further with the performance and entitles him to bring an action for damages and to enforce the remedies for such breach as provided in the contract.

3. The three classes of judicial remedies for breach of contract are:
   (*i*) Damages;
   (*ii*) Restitution; and
   (*iii*) Specific performance or injunction.

   Specific performance and injunction are the supplementary and discretionary remedies. Injunction would be granted at the discretion of the Court where damages would not be an adequate remedy. Where damages are an adequate remedy, specific performance will not be granted. We are mostly concerned with contracts where the remedy for a breach is a claim for damages.

4. Chapter VI of the Contract Act, 1872, deals with the consequences of breach of contract. This chapter consists of only three sections of which all of you must be familiar with Sections 73 and 74. Section 73 deals with compensation for loss or damage caused by breach of contract. The principle underlying this section is where a party sustains a loss by reason of a breach of contract; he is, so far as money can do it, to be placed in the same position with respect to damages as if the contract had been performed. According to his section, when a contract has been broken, the party who suffers by such breach is entitled to receive from the party who has broken the contract, compensation for any loss or damage caused to him thereby which naturally arose in the usual course of things from such breach or which the parties knew, when they made the contract, to be likely to result from the breach of it. Such compensation is not to be given for any remote and indirect loss or damage sustained by reason of the breach. In estimating the loss or damage arising from a breach of contract, the means which existed of remedying the inconvenience caused by the non-performance of the contract must be taken into account.

5. Section 73 divides damages into two classes, (*i*) general and (*ii*) special. General damages mean the loss or damage caused by the breach of contract which naturally arose in the usual course of things from such breach. Special damages mean the loss or damage caused to a party by the other party's breach of contract which the parties knew when they made the contract to be likely to result from the breach of it. Cases with which we are mostly concerned are cases of general damages.

6. The measure of general damages is the difference between the contract price and the market price at the time of the breach. If such a rate is not available on the exact date, the court may take into consideration the rate prevalent which is before and just after the date. If the subject matter of the contract is not marketable, the value has to be taken, fixed by the price which actually has to be paid for the best and nearest available substitute. Where there is no such market, damages can be assessed on the basis of tenders opened on or about that date. When the delivery of goods purchased is delayed, the goods are presumed to have been at the time that they should have been delivered; worth to the purchaser what he could then sell them for in the open market. In such a case, the measure of damage will be the resale value of the goods on the date of the breach.

7. Government, however, does not ordinarily purchase goods for resale and often purchases goods which are not available in the open market. The question often arises how the breach of such a contract or delay in the performance of such a contract can be provided for by some

method or measure of compensation. One method is to stipulate for the payment of a lump sum as compensation or a sum calculated per day or per month of delay or breach. This takes us to Section 74 of the Contract Act. According to this Section, when a contract has been broken, if a sum is named in the contract as the amount to be paid in case of such breach or if the contract contains any other stipulation by way of penalty, the party complaining of the breach is entitled, whether or not actual damge or loss is proved to have been caused thereby, to receive from the party which has broken the contract, reasonable compensation not exceeding the amount so named or, as the case may be, penalty stipulated for.

8. The clauses in our contract which have a direct bearing on damages in the event of a breach are the following clauses:
   (i) *Clause stipulating the payment of liquidated damages by the seller for delayed delivery at a rate specified in the contract;*
   (ii) *Clause providing for determination of the contract;*
   (iii) *Clause providing for risk purchase; and*
   (iv) *Security deposit clause providing for forfeiture in the event of failure to perform the contract.*
9. The general conditions of contract provide for recovery of liquidated damages at the rate of 2% per month in respect of delayed supplies. This condition/clause is based on Section 74 of the Contract Act under which a sum can be named in the contract as the amount to be paid in case of breach. It should be noted that liquidated damages accrue only in cases of delay in supplies. Under Section 55 of the Contract Act, 1872, where time is essence of the contract and the promisee accepts performance at any time other than that agreed, the promisee cannot claim compensation for any loss occasioned by the non-performance of the promisee at the time agreed, unless at the time of such acceptance he gives notice to the promisor of his intention to do so. It is because of this provision when we grant extension of time, we take care to specifically provide in our letter, granting extension that an amount equal to the liquidated damages for delay shall be recovered from the seller. Where we fail to give this notice, we cannot claim compensation for delayed deliveries.
10. The scope of Section 74 of the Contract Act, 1872 has been considered by the Ministry of Law on a number of occasions in connection with the right of Government to recover liquidated damages at the rate of 2% per month in respect of delayed supplies. We all are familiar with the opinion of the Solicitor-General of India given in the 1957 year when he gave the following answers:
    (i) Government has no absolute right in all cases of delayed supplies to recover liquidated damages at the rate of 2 per cent per month;
    (ii) Where no loss has been actually caused, compensation could be claimed for inconvenience but there should be some general evidence of the nature of the work contracted for or the goods to be supplied and of the nature of the inconvenience caused and also of the fact that the goods or other supplies could not be made available from any other source;
    (iii) The present provision cannot be treated as a genuine pre-estimate of damages; and
    (iv) There could be no serious objection to the present practice of charging 10% of 2% as token damages.
11. Our right to recover liquidated damages at the rate of 2% per month in respect of delayed supplies has also been recently considered by the Ministry of Law. In the light of the relevant decisions of the Supreme Court, the following principles have been enunciated;
    (i) The expression "contract contains any other stipulation by way of penalty" in Section 74 covers the case of a stipulation to pay money on breach as well as the case of a stipulation

for the failure of money paid under a contract as security for the due performance of the contract.

(*ii*) The expression "whether or not actual damage or loss is proved to have been caused thereby" in Section 74 will not apply to a case where no damage or loss has actually occurred. The expression will apply to cases where some damage or loss has actually occurred but it is impossible for the Court to assess compensation arising from the breach and also where the compensation cannot be calculated in accordance with established rules.

(*iii*) In cases where the Court is unable to assess the compensation, the sum named by the parties if it be regarded as a genuine pre-estimate, may be taken into consideration as a measure of reasonable compensation but not if the sum named is in the nature of penalty.

(*iv*) Where loss is terms of money can be determined the party claiming compensation must prove the loss suffered by him.

12. The Ministry of Law has again reiterated that liquidated damages at the rate of 2% per month, being a general provision applicable to all contractors, cannot be treated as a genuine pre-estimate, and is not, therefore, a measure of reasonable compensation within the meaning of Section 74. The position, therefore, is that before we can recover any compensation, actually loss must occur and in cases where actual loss can be determined, Government claiming loss must prove the loss suffered by it. In cases where it is not possible to prove actual loss, the sum named may be taken into consideration by the court, if it is a genuine pre-estimate of the loss.

13. When the seller fails to have the stores ready for delivery by the time or times agreed upon or when he fails to perform the contract, power is reserved to declare the contract as at an end at the risk and cost of the seller in every way. In such a case, the seller shall be liable for liquidated damages for delayed delivery and for any expenses, losses or damages which the purchaser may be put to incur or sustain by reason of or in connection with the seller's default.

14. Refers to the risk purchase clause, if the contractor fails to deliver the stores or any installment within the period fixed for such delivery or at any time repudiates the contract before the expiry of such period, the government is entitled to cancel the contract and repurchase the stores not delivered at the risk and cost of the defaulting contractor. In the event of such a risk purchase, the defaulting contractor shall be liable for any loss which the government may sustain on that account.

15. In order that the loss at repurchase may be enforced, the following precautions are required to be taken:

(*i*) The stores repurchased should be identical with the stores originally agreed to be purchased and in respect of which there has been a breach;

(*ii*) The repurchase should be made within a reasonable time after the date of the breach.

(*iii*) Risk purchase contract should be on the same terms as the original contract. In other words, apart from the fact that the goods should be of the same specification and liable to inspection by the same authority, the terms of payment, provision regarding liquidated damages, arbitration, etc., should be the same.

(*iv*) Defaulting contractor should also be given an opportunity to quote against the repurchase tender unless it is established that the breach of the original contract was due to his inability to supply goods of the contract description or the repurchase has to be effected on spot delivery in view of the urgency created consequent on the default and it has been established that the defaulter cannot comply with this requirement. The exclusion of the defaulting contractor will not be justified in case the original contract was cancelled on account of his failure to deliver the stores due to rejection in inspection on account of rectifiable defects in the stores tendered.

16. Even though according to legal requirements, the recovery of risk purchase loss could be effected only after materialization of supplies against the risk purchase contract, a demand notice should be served on the defaulting firm as soon as the risk purchase agreement is entered into, asking them to deposit the extra expenditure involved. Since the arbitration/ legal proceedings are protracted, (it may be that in most of the cases by the time we have to produce evidence, supplies against the risk purchase contract might materialize and we would be able to comply with the legal requirements. In cases where the risk purchase contract is not completed, we have to endeavour to produce evidence in regard to the market value of the stores on the date of breach and claim the general damages. The amount recoverable in such cases is the difference between the contract rate and the market rate on the date of breach.
17. The general conditions of contract provide that the contractor may be required to make a security deposit. Defaults in making security deposit is itself a breach of contract which entitles the Government to cancel the contract at the risk and cost of the purchaser. If the security is deposited, it becomes available for recovery of sums payable by the contractor to the purchaser. Sums due for damages may be recovered from the security deposit.
18. Previously we were taking the opinion that the entire security deposit taken for due performance of contract could be forfeited in the event of breach of contract by the contract or irrespective of the fact whether or not Government had sustained any loss on account of such breach. This was based on certain decisions of the High Courts. In Maula Bux Vs. Union of India (AIR 1970 SC 1955) the Supreme Court laid down that the security deposit could not be forfeited when no loss was caused in consequence of such default. In that case the appellant had entered into a contract with the Government of India for the supply of certain goods and had deposited a certain amount of security for the due performance of the contract. It was stipulated in the contract that the amount of security deposit was to stand forfeited in case the appellant neglected to perform his part of the contract. On the appellant committing default in the supply the Goverment rescinded the contract and forfeited the security deposit. The Supreme Court held that forfeiture of earnest money under a contract for sale of property did not fall within Section 74 of the Contract Act if the amount was reasonable because the forfeiture of a reasonable sum paid as the earnest money did not amount to the imposition of a penalty but where under the terms of the contract the party in breach had undertaken to pay a sum of money which he had already paid to the party complaining of a breach of contract, the undertaking was in the nature of a penalty. In AIR 1973 SC 1098, the Supreme Court (Union of India Vs Rampur Distillaries and Chemical Co., Ltd.) have reiterated that a party to the contract is not entitles to forfeit the security deposit on ground of default when no loss is caused to him in consequence of such default.
19. In Union of India Vs. Raman Iron Foundry AIR 1974 SC 1265, the Supreme Court have considered clause 18 of the standard form of contract on the DSG & D side. Under this clause whenever any claim for the payment of a sum of money arises out of or under the contract against the contractor the purchaser shall be entitled to recover such sum by appropriating in whole or in part the security, if any, deposited by the contractor. In the event of the security being insufficient, the balance, and if no security has been taken from the contractor, the entire sum recoverable shall be recovered by appropriating any sum then due or which at any time thereafter may become due to the contractor under the contract or any other contract with the Purchaser, if such sum even be not sufficient to cover the full amount recoverable, the contractor shall on

demand pay to the purchaser the balance remaining due. There is a clause similar to clause 18 in our contracts also. The Supreme Court has held as follows:

"A claim for damages for breach of contract is therefore not a claim for a sum presently due and payable and the purchaser is not entitled in exercise of the right conferred upon it under clause 18, to recover the amount of such claim by appropriating other sums due to the contractor. On this view, it is not necesssary for us to consider the other contention raised on behalf of the respondent, namely, that on a proper construction of clause 18, the purchase is entitled to exercise the right conferred under that clause only where the claim for payment of a sum of money is either admitted by the contractor, or in case of dispute adjudicated upon by a Court or other adjudicatory authority. We must, therefore, hold that the appellant had no right or authority under Cl. 18 to appropriate the amounts of other pending bills of the respondents in or towards satisfaction of its claim for damages against the respondent and the learned Judge was justified in issuing an interim injunction restraining the appellant from doing so."

After this Judgment we have been holding the view that there cannot be any appropriation but that we can only withhold the sums subject to all the consequences that such a with holding may entail in law. The exact implications of the Judgment are still under study and it will be necessary to have this clause suitably modified.

20. A stipulation in a contract of sale with reference to goods may be a condition or a warranty. A condition is a stipulation essential to the main purpose of the contract, the breach of which gives rise to a right to treat the contract as repudiated. A warranty is a stipulation collateral to the main purpose of the contract, the breach of which gives rise to a claim for damages but not to a right to reject the goods and treat the contract as repudiated. It would always be open to a buyer to waive the condition or elect to treat the breach of the condition as a breach of warranty and not as a ground for treating the contract as repudiated.

21. What is known as anticipatory breach, is also referred here that where either party to a contract of sale repudiates the contract before the date of delivery, the other may either treat the contract as subsisting and wait till the date of delivery or he may treat the contract as rescinded and sue for damages for the breach.

Arbitration

Most of our contracts contain an arbitration clause. The parties to an arbitration agreement may agree that any reference there under shall be made to an arbitrator to be appointed by a person designated in the agreement either by name or as the holder for the time being of any office or appointment. Where the contract itself is void, the arbitration clause also would be void. In other words, it would not be open to a contractor to invoke the arbitration clause in such a case. In M/s N.K. Private Ltd., the firm relying on the arbitration clause sent to Govt. a notice appointing their own arbitrator. The Govt. sent a reply challenging the validity of the appointment on the ground that the contract itself was void as not satisfying the requirements of Article 299(1) of the Constitution. The Government ultimately succeeded in the Supreme Court.

1. Where there is a valid arbitration clause, it would not be open to Government to file a suit. If Government ignore, the arbitration clause and resorts to a court of law, it would be open to the party to apply to the court for a stay of the proceedings under Section 34 of the Arbitration Act, 1940.
2. The provisions of Limitation Act shall also apply to arbitrations as they apply to proceedings in court. Even in a case where we are advised that a particular claim is barred by limitation, we would not be in a position to refuse arbitration. In other words, it is the jurisdiction of the

arbitrators to decide the point of limitation also. Where we refuse to accede to a demand for arbitration, it would be open to the aggrieved party to move the court under Section 20 of the Arbitration Act, 1940.

3. Our contracts used to provide for dual arbitration, while on the DGS & D side the arbitration clause provides for sole arbitration. I believe that our clause also has since been amended. An arbitrator is a judge of the parties' own choice. Unless we have full faith in the arbitrator whom we appoint, arbitration as a mode of setting disputes will not be a success.
4. Under the law, arbitrators are not bound to give reasons and so we will have to deal mostly with unreasoned awards. An award shall not be set aside except on one or more of the following grounds, namely:
   (*i*) that the arbitrator or umpire has misconducted himself or the proceedings;
   (*ii*) that an award has been made after issue of an order by the court superseding the arbitration or after arbitration proceedings have become invalid under Section 35; and
   (*iii*) that an award has been improperly procure or is otherwise invalid.

   But normally it would be so difficult to challenge an award which has not given any reasons except on the ground that the award is vitiated by an error of law or mistake apparent on the face of the award or document appended to it. Such errors or mistakes are so rare to find that officers must be more vigilant in the conduct of arbitration cases.
5. Where an arbitration clause provides for the appointment of two arbitrators, one to be nominated by the contractor and the other by the Government, if the contractor appoints an arbitrator and serves a notice of such appointment on the Government, Government should within a period of fifteen days from the receipt of such notice appoint its own arbitrator failing which the arbitrator who has been appointed by the contractor may act as sole arbitrator in the reference and his award shall be binding on both the parties. In the letter of appointment for arbitrator on behalf of the Government, it should invariably be stated that the appointment of arbitrator by the Government is without prejudice to its rights to contend that the matter in dispute does not fall under the arbitration clause or that the claim is barred by limitation or raise other legal objections open to it or to prefer its own counter claims in the arbitration proceedings and also claim proof to the satisfaction of the arbitrators that the appointment of the firm's arbitrator is validly made.
6. Under Article 119 of the Arbitration Act, 1940, the period of limitation is thirty days for the filing in court of an award. This period is to be calculated from the date of service of the notice of the making of the award. Likewise, limitation for setting aside an award or getting an award estimated for reconsideration is thirty days. This is to be calculated from the date of service of the notice of the filing of the award. Where an award is pronounced against the government and the Government is willing to accept the award, the party can be called upon by letter to accept payment of the sum awarded in full and final settlement of all the claims forming the subject matter of the reference. If the party agrees, the payment can be made without making the award a rule of court. A similar procedure may be adopted where an award has been passed in favour of Government. If the party fails to respond, the court will have to be moved within thirty days of the service of the notice of the making of the award.
7. In Chalapan Vs Kerala state Electricity Board AIR 1975 AIR 230, the Supreme Court have hold where the arbitrators fail to make awards within time nothing prevents the umpire to enter upon the reference in lieu of the arbitrators. In view of this decision it becomes necessary that timely action is taken for extension of time whenever an award is not pronounced by the arbitrators within time.

(*i*) In a recent decision (AIR 1973 SC 2479), the Supreme Court has held that an arbitrator can enlarge time for making award if after entering on the arbitration the parties mutually agreed to such enlargement. According to the Supreme Court, it is not the requirement of the law that the power to enlarge time by subsequent agreement must be stipulated in the arbitration agreement. Such a consent must be a post reference consent as is clear from Section 28(2). In essence, where a provision is made in the original agreement that the arbitrator may enlarge the time, such a provision, implies mutual consent for enlargement. But such mutual consent initially expressed in the original agreement does not save the provision from being void.

13.4 STAMP PROVISIONS

1. Under Article 5 of the Stamp Act, 1899, an agreement or memorandum of agreement for or relating to the sale of goods or merchandise not being bought or sold through a broken is exempt from payment of Stamp Act. Where any other document relating to a contract is liable to stamp duty, it shall be open to the Government to take upon itself the liability to pay the stamp in which event by virtue of section 3 of the Stamp Act, no stamp duty shall be chargeable. We must add a clause to that effect in the agreement. Section 3 provides that no stamp duty shall be chargeable in respect of such instrument. That there is a certain amount of confusion in some of the Railway Administrations whether an arbitrator's award should be stamped. It is made clear that an award must be engrossed on a stamp paper the value of which would be determined by the rates of stamp duty in force at the place where the award is signed. Regarding the rates of stamp duty, it would be advisable to consult local revenue authorities.
2. The next question is as regards exemption. As the Government is a party in these arbitration, if the award is in favour of Government and the stamp duty is payable by the Government, then the award would be exempt. As regards the latter point, since Section 29 of the Stamp Act does not provide as to who is to bear the expense of providing the proper stamp in the case of an award, the liability to provide the stamp has to be determined by the arbitrator. It is usual for the arbitrator to call upon the successful party to pay the stamp duty and to include it in the costs which he may award to that party. An arbitrator may, however, make any other direction in this respect. But the award would be exempt from payment of stamp duty under the provision to Section 3 of the Stamp Act only where the Government having been directed by the Arbitrator to pay the stamp duty, the award is in its favour.
3. As to when an award can be said to be in favour of Government is a vexed question. The dispute may have involved simply a claim by the contractor or a claim by the contractor and set off claimed by Government or vice versa or there may be independent claims and counter-claims on either side.
4. Where the Government's claim is the only matter under reference and the Arbitrator awards it in full or part, the award is clearly in favour of Government. It is in material that a part of the claim of Government only has been accepted by the arbitrator. Where the dispute is only in respect of a claim made by the contractor and that claim is dismissed into, the award is again one in favour of Government. Where there are claims and counter-claims by the contractor and the government both or vice versa and the contractor fails fully and government succeeds, whether in part or whole, the award is again one in favour of Government. Similarly, where Government is allowed a set off which wipes out completely the claim of the contractor, when also the award is in favour of the Government. In some cases, even though some relief may have been awarded to Government, the award may also give the contractor relief against the government. In such cases if the Arbitrator directs the government to pay the stamp duty, the

award would not be exempt and Government would have supply the stamp paper. In all other cases, the award would not be exempt and Government would have to supply the stamp paper. In all other cases, the award would not be exempt from stamp duty and if Govt. is directed to provide stamp duty it will have to furnish stamp papers.

5. Wherever as stated above, the award is exempt from stamp duty, the arbitrator must mention in the award that the stamp duty payable in respect of the award shall be paid by the Central Government.
6. There are States which have made provisions for recovery of additional stamp duty on an instrument executed in a different territory or a State. This additional stamp duty will be payable by the party at whose instance the award is filed in court by the arbitrator.

   In a recent judgment, the Delhi High Court has hold that an award is not a instrument executed in favour of the Government. According to this judgment, there may not be any exemption of stamp duty even in the case of an award in favour of the Government. It is understood from the Ministry of Law that this judgment is under appeal.

13.5 SALES TAX

1. Incidence of sales tax paid or payable by the contractor cannot be passed on to the buyer as a matter of course, but only in cases where payment of sales tax in addition to the price of the stores is made a condition of the sale in the tender and the said condition is accepted by the buyer. Sales Tax is payable on the contract price of the finished product and not on the value of the raw materials purchased by the contractor and used in the manufacture except where expressly stipulated.
2. Where the rate of sales tax is increased or new sales tax is imposed after the original delivery day stipulated in the contract, it becomes necessary to consider the terms on which the delivery was accepted in order to decide a claim for payment of sales tax at the increased rate or the new sales tax. Where the delivery date has been extended subject to the condition that no increase in price on account of any statutory increase in the rate of sales tax or fresh imposition of sales tax which takes effect after the expiry of the original delivery period will be admissible and such conditional extension has been expressly accepted or acted upon by the tendering supplier, no increase in the rate of sales tax or newly imposed sales tax should be allowed. Unless a different intention appears from the terms of the contract, in the event of fresh imposition of or increase in the rate sales tax after the making of the contract, the sales tax or the increase in the rate of sales tax has to be allowed on sales, taking place on and after 22nd September, 1963 under the amended Section 64A of the Indian Sale of Goods Act, 1930.
3. No sales tax is legally leviable on works contracts. But it is always a vexed question to decide whether a particular contract is wholly and individually a works contract. If a contract envisages distinct and separate agreements, one for the transfer of materials for money consideration and the other for payment of remuneration for services even though embodied in a single instrument, sales tax is leviable on that part of the agreement which is for the sale of goods.

13.6 CUSTOMS DUTY

1. As a mere statement in the Tender/Contract that the prices are exclusive of customs duty does not entitle a firm to the reimbursement of the duty, it is necessary that it should be definitely stated in the A/T that the duty is payable at a specified rate in addition to the cost of stores instead of mentioning its payment in an indirect manner.

The effect of statutory variation in the ratés of duties of customs, where there is a stipulation in the tender that any variation in the customs duty will be to the purchaser's account, is explained in the law Ministry's note reproduced below:

"Where there is stipulation in the tender to the effect that any variation in the customs duty will be to purchaser's account, the quotation is altered by any alteration in customs duty taking place before acceptance. All variations taking place after the date of tender in such cases have be taken into account and allowed in the acceptance of tender. If it is not allowed and the variation involves increase of price, "there will be no contract between the parties".

Excise Duty

1. As a mere statement in the Tender or contract that the prices are exclusive of Excise duty does not entitles a firm to the reimbursement of the duty, it is necessary that it should be definitely stated in the Acceptance of Tender that the duty is payable at a specified rate in addition to the cost of stores, instead of mentioning its payment in an indirect manner. The effect of statutory variation is also the same as in the case of Customs.

Excise Duty on Raw Materials

""Section 64A of Sale of Goods Act, is attracted on when:

(*i*) There is no different intention apparent from the terms of the contract.

(*ii*) Any duty of customs or excise on goods or any tax on the sale or purchase of goods has been imposed, increased, decreased or remitted in respect of any goods after the making of the contract for the sale or purchase of such goods.

The words, sale or purchase of such goods clearly indicate that the section would be attracted only in cases where the duty is imposed, increased or decreased or remitted in respect of goods sold. These words cannot be interpreted to cover the components or materials which are used in the manufacture or production of goods sold. If any duty is imposed, increased, decreased or remitted in respect of the raw materials used in the manufacture of the stores the seller/purchaser cannot claim the reimbursement or adjustment of the same in terms of Section 64A. Reimbursement of any duty or increase in duty on raw materials used in the manufacture of the ordered stores would depend upon terms and conditions of the contract. If there is a provision in the contract to the effect that any increase in duty on raw materials would be reimbursed to the supplier, then alone it would be possible for him to claim reimbursement of the same from the purchaser. If there is no such provision in the contract, the supplier cannot claim such increase as of right, either under Section 64A or under terms of the contract.

CHAPTER

14

IMPORT PROCEDURE AND CLEARANCE OF IMPORTANT CARGO AT KOLKATA PORT

14.1 IMPORT PROCEDURE

1. **Need for Importation:** Though the policy of the Government of India is to give preference to indigenous stores as against imported stores in order to encourage indigenous industries, due to fast changes in the technologies, the various diesel/electric locomotives and coaches which are presently produced at D.L Works, C.L. Works and I.C.F./RCF respectively are considered techno-economically outdated and therefore recent types are being procured to keep pace with the time. Besides the above stores, some of the spares of existing locos, modern signalling equipments, communication channels, top-hardened rails etc., which cannot be manufactured by the indigenous industries are required to be necessarily imported. Similarly sophisticated medical equipment for life savings purpose, proprietary items of foreign firms from whom, original equipment was procured and any other item which even though developed indigenously, the production is not enough to meet the demands of all the Railways are also imported.
2. **Present Import Policy:** All of us know that from 1991 onwards, Government of India started liberalising industrial regime and the result is that practically all controls on imports have been lifted now-a-days. We can import any item except those stipulated in the negative list. Moreover, the customs duty has been reduced continuously during the last few years and the same has come maximum of 50% and it is expected to come down further in the coming years. Imports into India are also governed by foreign trade (Development and Regulation) Act, 1992 and except for the items, regulated by this policy or any of the law for the time being in force, there is no other restrictions.
   (*i*) The negative list consists of items, the import of which is prohibited/restricted through licensing or otherwise or canalised. This list is available in the Import Policy valid from 01.04.92 to 31.03.97.

3. **Customs Duty:** All the imports into India normally call for levy of import duties and Ministry of Finance issues customs notification for the above purpose. Major changes in the import duty are made on the day of annual budget every year.

   (*i*) To decide quantum of Customs Duty we refer to the Customs Traffic for classification. In the year 1950 a Convention was held at Brussels of Belgium consisting of 35 nations to decide about the common Nomenclature of the merchandise under Import/Export amongst various countries of the World. India is the founder member and nomenclature, as decided there, is known as BTN-Brussels Tariff Nomenclature. This is broadly decided on basis of either material composition or end-use. In 1964 a Tariff Revision Committee was formed by the Govt. of India to overcome the difficulties experienced by different Customs Houses in the Country and placed their recommendations to the Govt. in 1974. Parliament established a Select Committee in July, 75 and the present tariff was passed. It is broadly based on BTN with some modification.

   (*ii*) There are two types of duties at present levied on the imported material *i.e.*, Basic Costoms Duty and Countervailing Duty. Before liberalisation, there were four types of duty *i.e.*, Basic Customs Duty, Auxiliary Duty, Countervailing Duty and Special Duty on Countervailing. Countervailduty is additional duty on goods and normally is equivalent to Excise Duty on like articles if produced or manufactured in India. Basic Customs Duty is as per Section 12 of Custom act.,1962 all goods imported into India are chargeable to duty, for which assessable value is calculated first, which is equal to FON+ Freight (Actual) + Insurance + Landing cost @1% = CIF Value + Landing Cost. If the importer is not in a position to furnish freight and insurance amount, Customs will charge @ 21. 125 % on FOR to arrive at assessable value. Counter- Veiling Duty is calculated on the total amount of assessable value + Basic Duty. For your ready reference, rates of some of Customs Duty are given below:

		Basic Duty	Counter Veiling Duty
1.	Steel Rails	40%	15%
2.	Steel Plates, Sheets etc.	40%	15%
3.	Wheels, Wheel sets, Axle	25%	20%
4.	Bearing- Ball and Roller (All Sizes)	25% + Rs.120/- Per Kg.	15%
5.	Transmission Shaft-Crank, Cam Shaft	25%	15%
6.	Turbocharger Complete	25%	10%
7.	Traction Motor Complete	25%	10%
8.	Valves- All types	25%	15%
9.	Part of Traction Motor	25%	15%
10.	Part of Turbocharger Turbine Bucket and Disc. Assy.	25%	15%
11.	Project Materials (Metro, KREL, Metro)	25%	10%
12.	Computer Software	10%	Nil
13.	Hospital Equipment (Govt. Projects)	Fully Exempted	

4. **Foreign Exchange:** The foreign exchange aspects of the import transactions are governed by Foreign Exchange Regulation Act, 1991, which has recently been liberalised in 1993. The day

to day regulations governing import transactions are done through the Exchange Control Manuals issued by the Reserve Bank of India.

5. The imported items are mostly procured by the Railway Board and balance quantities by the X Zonal railways specially by the production units for the respective production program. As approved by the Railway Board without any monetary limit of estimated foreign exchange expenditure subject to proposal is approved for the essentiality aspect and has been concurred by the Finance.
   (*i*) A resolution was issued by the Govt. of India on the 3rd April, 1992 regarding release of foreign exchange by Government departments and based on the Ministry of Railways issued, vide their letter No. 92/F (FEX) 1/1 dated 01.06.92, the guidelines for payment of foreign exchange under Liberalised Exchange Rate Management Scheme. As per this, Railways will meet all their foreign exchange payment liabilities at market rate. There will be no allocation of foreign exchange from the Ministry of Finance. All the zonal railways will meet their requirements of foreign exchange from the market. There is no need for obtaining Board's approval for floating global tenders for procurement to be financed out of free resources. But import tenders valuing more than 2 crores, the T.C. recommendations duly approved by General Manager is to be submitted to the Board.
   (*ii*) For release of foreign exchange by the Railway Board in case of transactions finance out of various credit import-after clearing the import proposal, the same is sent to the Ministry of Finance's approval to incur expenditure. Allocation is tied up to various long-term foreign credit such as I.D.A. Credit, Yen Credit etc., as available with the Govt. of India.
6. **Type of Import Contract**
   (*i*) *Imported Offers on FOR basis*: In certain cases, the Indian agents directly deal with their foreign Principals and offers are submitted by the Indian agents on their own to supply the materials on FOR basis in which case all transaction including clearance are handled by the agents and they are responsible for the cargo being placed on FOR station of dispatch as agreed upon.
   (*ii*) *Imported offers on FOR/CIF basis* : Contracts on FOR and CIF basis are entered into directly with the foreign suppliers and only agency commission is paid to the Indian agent. Here are clearance of corgo is handled by the Railways but the Indian agent will be responsible for after sale service.
7. **Mode of Payment:** Unlike the internal trade, in import purchases, the supplies have no intimate knowledge of the buyer and therefore they usually insist upon the payment being made either by means of a Letter of Credit arranged with their banker against production of the relevant shipping documents or they deliver shipping documents through their Banker or representative in the importing country against payment by the buyer. L.C. is an order addressed by a banker to his agent or branch in another place instructing the latter to honour cheques or drafts or bills drawn upon by the beneficiary named in the L.C. up to the specified amount and within the stated period of time.
   (*i*) ***Payment against Long-terms Loan:*** Although various types of payment procedures are prescribed under I.D.A. loans, the two commonly used payment terms applicable in Railways are:
      (*a*) *Reimbursement procedure* : The payment is made directly by means of a L.C. This made of payment is a temporary drawing on the foreign exchange reserve of the country. Reimbursement will be obtained subsequently from I.D.A. authorities.

(b) *Direct Payment Procedure :* Suppliers are to send their claim bill supported by Bill of lading and invoices to the F.A. & C.A.O. of the concerned railways who after proper scrutiny of the documents forwards them to the Railway Board under a payment authority showing the amount required to be paid to the foreign suppliers. The Railway Board in turn make necessary arrangements to pay the suppliers from the I.D.A. direct.

8. **Inspection:** The inspection of the imported stores is entrusted to I.S.M./Washington, RA/ BONN, M/s RITES in case of Japan and other countries.

9. **Various Important Documents required for Clearance of the imported Cargo:** The following shipping documents (except item 9.7 & 9.8) will be sent by the Supplier or their agents as soon as shipment is effected.

   (*i*) ***Bill of lading:*** It is signed by the master of the ship and is similar to the Railway Receipt. It shows details like shipping marks on the packages, number of packages, description etc. This is the document based on which the Steamer agent issue delivery order authorising the Port Trust to give delivery of the cargo to the importer. So the original bill of lading is to be surrendered to the steamer agent to obtain the delivery order.

   (*ii*) ***Invoices:*** This is prepared and issued by the supplier showing the cost (FOR or CIF) Contract number quantity, number of packages etc.

   (*iii*) ***Country of Origin Certificate:*** This is also furnished by the suppliers to prove the Origin of the goods. This is required to be produced to the Custom Authorities at the time of clearance.

   (*iv*) ***Fright Note:*** This is furnished by the Shipping Lines indicating the details of ocean freight charges to be paid or payable, where necessary.

   (*v*) ***Packing List:*** This is furnished by the suppliers showing the details of weight. Measurements, number of packages, number of items in each package.

   (*vi*) ***Inspection Certificate:*** This is issued by the government inspector before despatch. This is required for arranging payment and for production to Customs authorities for assessment of duty.

   (*vii*) ***Bill of Entry:*** This is an application signed by the importer and submitted to the Customs authorities for permitting release of goods landed. This bill of entry contains information like FOR value, Ocean Freight, Insurance Charges etc.

   (*viii*) ***Import Manifest:*** This is a document filed by the steamer agent at the landing port with the Collector of Customs and Port Trust, showing complete details of consignment expected by a particular vessel well in advance.

14.2 PROCEDURE FOR CLEARANCE OF IMPORTED RAILWAY MATERIALS AT KOLKATA PORT BY EASTERN RAILWAY

1. The Eastern Railway Shipping Section is acting as a port consignee/clearing agent at the Kolkata Port for clearance of imported goods arriving at the Kolkata Port against contracts placed by different Railway importer, like the Railway Board, and meant for different Zonal Railways and Production Units and also against contracts placed by the Zonal Railways and Production Units, like Eastern Railway, North Eastern Railway, Northest Frontier Railway, Northern Railway, Metropolitan Transport Project, Chittaranjan Locomotive Works, Diesel Locomotive Works, Research, design and Standard Organisation. Clearance of imported

goods is possible only if the Railway Importers mentioned above make available to the Eastern Railway Shipping Section the requisite documents and also render technical assistance for explaining the imported goods to the Kolkata Customs Authorities.

(*i*) Correct and complete documents like Invoice in 4 Copies, Bills of Lading (One Original and three extra copies) Packing, Specification, Inspection/Test Certificates.

(*ii*) The importer should be in a position to explain to the Customs the goods imported as regards their end-use etc., through his technical representatives with the help of documents, such as drawings, catalogues, literature etc., to enable the customs to assess proper Custom Duty and release the imported goods.

2. The type of cargo normally cleared through Kolkata Port/ Airport by Eastern Railway Shipping Section on behalf of different Railways is:

   (*i*) Prime steel section like steel plates, angles, channels, sheet piles etc.

   (*ii*) Steel items like carriage and wagon tyres, axles, wheels and wheel sets etc.

   (*iii*) Case cargoes *viz.*, cargo received in packages or in crates. These are mainly diesel and electric locomotive spares, electronic goods, electrical goods, machinery spares and tools. cable drums, chemicals etc., in kegs and barrels.

3. On receipt of Bill of Lading Invoice and related documents pertaining to a shipment, closing particulars to the concerned Insurance Co. are forwarded for obtaining the Insurance cover as all the imports are covered by open cover contract decided by the Railway Board.

4. Immediately on receipt of the Bills of Lading and Invoices, the Bill of Entry is prepared getting in touch with the concerned steamer Agents with reference to the Bills of Lading and Invoices and submitted the same to Customs with proper categorisation of the imported goods with reference to the Customs Tariff. As soon as the Manifest is filed by the steamer Agents with the Customs and the Rotation of the Vessel is declared, we have to check the manifest, obtain rotation number and line number of the vessel for Calculation of C.I.F. value in the Bill of Entry and submit the same to Customs Noting Section for nothing the B/E in the Manifest and return the office copy of the B/E to us for preparation of Jetty Challan. Immediately the Bill of Entry is received back after noting, it is submitted to the concerned Group of the Customs House for classification and realisation of duty. After finalisation of classification with the help of technical expert and payment of duty, Customs will return duplicate, Triplicate and Exchange Control copies of the Bills of Entry. Duplicate Bill of Entry with all relevant papers is made available for payment of port dues. Triplicate Bill of Entry is sent to CAO (S)/Eastern Railway for recoupment of the amount and for raising simultaneous debit on the Importer. The revolving deposit with Customs should be checked daily at the time of payment of duty to ensure that sufficient balance is always available in the deposit account to ensure payment of duty on any anticipated consignment.

5. **Payment of Ocean Freight:** Arrangement of payment of freight is immediately done after receipt of Freight bills. If there is likely delay in making payment efforts are done to obtain Delivery Order after submitting the undertaking.

6. **Port Charge Payment:** As soon as the duplicate Bill of Entry with all relevant papers are received from the customs along with the delivery orders from the steamer agents, the Port charges are calculated with reference to the bill of lading, shipping specification and duplicate bill of entry and arrange payment of port charges to the Port authorities and also obtain exemption certificate from the entry Tax Authority posted at the Port charge Collection Office. Eastern Railway is having a revolving deposit account with CPT. After making payment receipment is made so that adequate funds already available. Immediately on receipt of one extra copy of Jetty Challan with the Original Bill of Lading, the respective Shipping

Inspector will see the landing condition of the cargo and if the case or cargo damaged, we will immediately apply for Steamer Agent's survey. The time limit for Steamer Agent's survey is 3 days from the date of landing of the cargo. For this purpose necessary prior arrangements should be made *i.e.*, payment of overtime charge towards booking of Customs Officer who is associated with the Survey Co-ordinating with the Steamer Agent's Surveyor, arranging technical personnel from the importer's side and see that the Survey is done within the time allowed. However, all the cases steps are taken to hold Insurance Survey, time limit for which is 60 days from the date of landing of the package/packages. On receipt of complete papers *i.e.*, Bill of Entry out passed by Customs, Jetty Challan, Invoices, Original Bill of Lading, etc., physically clearance the consignment from the Port is taken Rails are normally despatched directly from Kolkata Port to the ultimate consignee loaded in open wagons and with a view to minimise wharf- rent as well as payment of substantial amount by way of sorting and sticking charges to Kolkata Port, the remaining materials are taken to one of the Stored depots of Eastern Railway, mainly Howrah Depot. LCD & NH for transit storage and onward despatch to the ultimate consignee. While clearing the case cargoes from Kolkata Port/Airport if any shortage or/ damage to the package is suspected on Superficial check, arrangement is made immediately for survey of the packages and delivery is taken from the port only after such survey is held and proper remarks obtained from the Surveyor as well as the shed Customs Appraiser on the back of the duplicate copy of the Bill of entry as a token of Customs having witnessed the shortage/damage during survey.

7. **Lodging of Claim:** Materials against various Indents/ Contracts/ Purchase Orders placed by the Railway Board or different Zonal railway's or by the different Production Units are received and cleared at the Docks by the Shipping Section of Eastern Railway. Handling of such imported cargoes are therefore open to short receipt/receipt in damaged condition. Therefore, claim is to be lodged on the various Co-ordination units which are associated with the handling of such cargoes and these associated units are:

   (*i*) Steamer Agent.

   (*ii*) Customs Authority and

   (*iii*) Kolkata Port Trust.

   In addition to the above 3 units there is another unit which is also associated with such cargoes which is the Insurance Unit as all cargoes imported from abroad are insured as per the Railway Board's directive. Therefore, claims are to be lodged on all the above 4 associated units depending on the circumstances and detailed procedure for Lodging such claims for shortlanded/damaged cargoes on all the units.

8. **Air Clearance:** Action on similar lines are taken for clearance of Air Cargo. Constant touch with all the Air lines are to be kept and after collection of documents clearance action is taken, after payment of Customs Duty, Air Freight, Terminal Charges etc.

9. **Method of Settlement of Disputes between one Government Department and another including Public Enterprise:** In course of clearance of cargo at the Kolkata Port this office is to come across various agencies like the Shipping Agents Port Trust, Customs, Insurance Units etc., necessitating claims for short landed/damaged cargo. These claims are attributable to any of the above mentioned agencies. Of late, the Government of India Cabinet Secretariat under cover of Office Memorandum No. 53/3/1/75 - CF dated 19-12-75 addressed to all the Ministries including Railway Ministry circulated under G.M., Eastern Railway's letter No. AW.229/Works/Arbn./Conf. dated 29.10.77 have instructed that litigation between one govt.

Department and another including public sector enterprise should be avoided in settling the dispute by mutual consultation/discussion and arbitration if required. Recourse to litigation should be eliminated. Port Trust, Shipping Corporation of India, Air India, and Insurance Companies fall under the above categories and therefore claims on these agencies should be settled as per the Govt. of India, Cabinet Secretariat's above quoted directive.

14.3 MARINE INSURANCE

1. Marine Insurance is a contract of indemnity with the Insurance Company against any loss or damage to the cargo in the course of marine-adventure either during the duration of the voyage or for a specific period of time after discharging at the port. Total loss or damage to the cargo by fire, sinking and stranding of the vessel, short delivery, non-delivery, theft, pilferage, leakage, breakage, shortage due to leaking/bursting of bags, contamination, damage by extraneous substances etc., can be covered under marine policy depending upon the nature of commodity and as mutually agreed by the Insurer and the Insured.
2. All the Railways cargo imported from abroad are insured and for this purpose Railway Board have taken two open covers with the Oriental Insurance Company Ltd., one for "Free Particular Average 'FPA' risk and other for' "All risk Open cover."
   - (*i*) Under FPA risk cover, risk is covered for loss as per Institute Cargo Clause "C" extended to include the risk of total loss or any package lost over- board or dropped while loading or unloading for effecting recovery towards dropping or Stover- board specific certificate from the Master of the Ship is essential. The risks covered under I.C.C.-"C" are:
     - (*a*) Fire or explosion, stranding, sinking overturning, collision etc., Though war and strike risks are included but radioactive, contamination is not covered. Similarly Gulf countries are not covered against as- coverage. So here the risk is covered for loss when the vessel is stranded, sunk or burnt or any loss or damage which can reasonably be attributed to fire, collision etc.
     - (*b*) In Railways items included under "F.P.A." are - steel items, wheels, tyres, axles rails and other similar items in bulk quantity.
   - (*ii*) All Risk Open Cover insurance covers all types of stores imported by Railway excepting steel and other bulk cargoes *i.e.*, locos, plants and machineries, wheel sets, signalling equipment etc. This policy covers, risk of all sorts *i.e.*, physical loss or damage including risk of theft, pilferage and non-delivery. These are as per Institute Cargo Clause A/Institute Cargo Clause (Air), Institute Replacement Clause/Institute Classification Clause etc., including War and Strike clause but radioactive contamination clause is excluded. In this case also, "Gulf Countries "are excluded against War-Claim.
   - (*iii*) Excluded Risks- Some of these risk are:
     - (*a*) Inherent vice or nature off cargo
     - (*b*) Wilful misconduct of the insured
     - (*c*) Ordinary leakage, ordinary loss in weight or volume or ordinary wear and tear of cargo.
     - (*d*) Insufficient/unsuitable packing.
     - (*e*) Delay
     - (*f*) Insolvency of the owner
     - (*g*) Unworthiness of vessel.

3. **Period Covered by Insurance Policies:** The risk against the above two open covers starts at the place mentioned in the policy for the commencement of the transit, continues during the course of transit and terminates either on delivery at destination or on the expiry of 150 days after discharge at the destination port whichever first occurs. For air consignments it is 90 days. The maximum time limit of 150/90 days is automatic. However, it is better for extension of time limit is obtained before expiry of time limit and subject to payment of additional premium.
4. **Premium Rate:**
   (*i*) For F.P.A.- Steel items, rails, wheels tyres etc. @ 0.10% under deck, 10% more is to be paid if these are loaded on deck. The valuation taken calculation of premium is C & F Value. If contract is on FOB basis then C & F value is assessed by adding 10% extra for the freight.

   (*ii*) For All Risk:

Loco fully assembled	0.19%
Loco Spares, Plants, Machinery etc.	Varies between 0.95% to 1.05%

   (*iii*) In case cargo is delayed beyond 150 /90 days the same will be held covered upto 180/135 days or till such time the cargo is received at the final destination whichever occurs first upon payment of additional premium at a particular rate.

   (*iv*) As per the rule of the Insurance Companies, open policies are not issued with collection of anticipated premium for three months imports. To avoid discontinuity in insurance cover for Railway Imports, Eastern Railway makes an ad - hoc payment equal roughly to three months procurement. Oriental Insurance Co. Ltd. as advance premium. This payment is made on approximate assessment. The Insurance Company will issue premium bills as usual based on the declaration by the Railway Unit. The advance premium fund is to be reviewed so that a minimum of 25% of the quarterly average premium is always maintained with the Insurance Company.
5. **Some Important Points in Connection with the Submission of Insurance Claim**
   (*i*) Payment of advance premium as indicated above.

   (*ii*) Submission of closing particulars- As per the stipulation in the Supply Contract the supplier will have to advise direct the Insurance Company about the shipment of Cargo, duly furnishing all details in prescribed form. It is the duty of the port consignee to ensure that the materials shipped are brought under marine insurance cover immediately on receipt of the documents.

   (*a*) Any unreasonable delay in declaring the shipment shall result in violation of provision of section 64 VB of the insurance act and such declarations are not normally accepted by the Insurance Company.

   (*iii*) The Port Consignee Railway has to substantiate his claims with documentary evidence to prove that the loss or damage has occurred to the insured cargo due to an insured peril. All the relevant documents like bill of lading, bill of entry packing list, insurance survey report, steamer survey report, short landing / short delivery / non-delivery certificate from port and/ or Customs Authorities, copy of the claim lodged on the carriers/ Port Authorities/Custom Authorities who are liable to make good less etc., are to be submitted along with the claim certificate.

(*iv*) Port Consignee Railways are supposed to insist on provisional/on account payment if the claim in prima- facie established. The Insurance Company agreed for on account payment of claims after preliminary survey and pending final settlement of claims.

(*v*) The contract agreement of the Insurance Company stipulates a time table of 15 days, 1 month and 2 months for settlement of claim which are within the purview of divisional, regional and head- office respectively of the Insurance Company after completion of the survey and submission of final documents by the Railway Units.

(*vi*) Continuous efforts need to be made with the Insurance Company to ensue the pending cases. The pending claim cases are supposed to be sent to Railway Board regularly in the prescribed statement.

CHAPTER

15

MATERIAL QUALITY IMPROVEMENT THROUGH STANDARDISATION

15.1 WHAT IS QUALITY?

The dictionary meaning of 'quality' is fitness, merit and excellence. Most people have this meaning in mind when they think of quality. In Materials Management however, quality has an entirely different meaning. Here quality is related to suitability and cost (not price), rather than to intrinsic excellence. The right quality is to be determined by balancing two major considerations:

(*i*) Technical considerations of suitability and

(*ii*) Economic considerations of cost and availability.

The Materials Manager is in an excellent position to contribute to the company's profits that originate in the area of 'quality; because of his knowledge of materials, his knowledge of market trends and his knowledge of reliable sources of supply.

The designing engineering and the production department has a basic responsibility for determining the technical quality of materials to be used in production. The other departments are responsible for determining the quality of materials required by them. The purchasing department is responsible for the second consideration in quality determination *viz.*, the economic consideration of quality. In addition to this, in the progressive companies the Materials Manager is given a major management responsibility *viz.*, the right to challenge the quality requirements of all the requisitions received. The right to challenge means helps to keep all departments alert to their responsibility in determining the right quality.

The Materials Manager contributes to the profitability of the organisation in the area of quality by considerations of materials' availability, selection of right sources of supply, development of new sources of supply, substitutes for existing products as well as substitutes for newly developed products, vendor suggestions, considerations of costs versus prices of materials and above all through standardisation.

Proper specifications and standardisation can materially improve the profitability of the company's operation. The importance of these factors has not been fully exploited by many companies.

Why specifications are so important to a company and why management does not always insist on standardisation are the points worth considering. This is the frame of reference I have in my mind for today's talk.

Purchasing and inventory control are considered as primary materials target areas for cost reduction. More correctly however, the complete materials cycle should be a single target area. Many people start measuring materials costs at the point where requisitions are submitted. In reality however, many materials costs get firmly embedded during the design stage, long before requisitions are submitted to the materials department. The cost investigations should therefore start at the beginning of the cycle *viz.*, at the design engineering phase itself.

Specifications are detailed descriptions of the materials, parts and components used in making the product. In other words specifications are verbal and quantitative descriptions of the product designs. When the specifications are fixed, the final design of the product to be sold is also fixed. Determining the right design of a product and thereby fixing a specification is an important management activity. This task is however, difficult as it involves many variable factors as well as conflicting views of the various departments that must be reconciled before the optimum in design can be achieved .

Preparing specifications for a product involves the following major considerations:

1. Design considerations of the function
2. The sales consideration of consumer acceptance
3. Manufacturing considerations of economical production
4. Procurement considerations of markets, materials availability and prices.

It is quite common that these considerations are conflicting with one another. To resolve such conflicts in the design problem requires highest type of management skills.

Materials Manager's interest in preparation of specifications is frequently not recognised. The design engineers and industrial engineers very often resolve between themselves all the major consideration of specifications mentioned above. This happens despite the fact that the designer and the professional engineer has seldom got adequate experience and information to resolve the procurement considerations. One of the most costly practices of design engineers is the development of stringent specification that do not provide any lattitude or any other basis upon which competition can be developed. Sometimes specifications are written around a specific product, resulting into limited competition. The final authority to resolve the conflict right rests with the department responsible for the product performance - which is usually the design engineering department. There is no reason however, to subordinate manufacturing, procurement and sales consideration unjustifiably to design engineering considerations. From a company view point the right specifications are those that properly blend all these considerations.

As already mentioned above unreasonable tolerances is a common difficulty for an industrial purchaser. It costs more to make materials to close tolerances, it costs more to inspect them and there are more rejections and the costs mount up. It is better to avoid these excess cost by adhering to the most economical method of manufacture while using standard specifications and standard components whenever possible.

15.2 STANDARDISATION

Standardisation is a very broad subject. It encompasses two distinct concepts. The first concept is concerned with materials, their size, shape, colour, physical properties, economical properties, performance characteristics etc. The second concept deals with the managerial aspects of business activities- such as standardising operations, practices, procedures, systems etc. We are considering today only the first concept.

Eli Whitny is known for his role in starting standardisation in United States when he got a contract to supply 10,000/- muskets to the United States Government. Rather than supplying a proportional number of Guns each month after individually making the parts for each Gun as a gunsmith would have done, Whitny designed and made machine tools with which he can mass produce parts which were interchangeable with each other. In other words he has standardised the parts with which he was able to assemble 10,000/- muskets and supply them during the time required.

The three basic systems of production *viz.*, job shop production, line or mass production and process production have their own applications and benefits. Whenever feasible, however, production should progress from a less technologically sophisticated to a more technologically sophisticated system. Even though this concept of advancement is well understood in industry, it is not always realised that production systems are closely related to the problem of standardisation.

Eli Whitny introduced mass production to the United States. But Henri Ford made it practically universal. He once made a statement "The customer can have any colour car as long as it is black". Ford visualised mass production as meaning a standard product produced from an assembly line. More correctly however, mass production implies the production of many diversed product assembled from standardised parts which themselves have been mass produced.

The Materials Manager has considerable interest in standardisation. The existence of standards helps him to achieve the objective of good procurement. The purchasing of specials however, means problems of availability, higher cost, quality and uniformity due to inexperience and lack of adequate field performance data. It also becomes necessary to purchase the specials in larger quantities than are required to meet the exact current needs. The Purchase Manager, therefore, should constantly strive to avoid the procurement of a special and should search for acceptable standards.

15.3 SIMPLIFICATION OR VARIETY REDUCTION

Some people consider simplification as a corollary of standardisation, while people consider it as an integral part of standardisation. Simplification means reducing the number of standard items required to be carried in an inventory. There are many instances where considerable savings have been effected through simplification. In ICF a programme was under-taken for standardisation and variety reduction for steel items as well as for various types of fasteners used. Out of the 1075 different items of steel which were stocked by them they were able to reduce to 264 items. As regards fasteners, out of 1441 different types of items (bolts, nuts, rivets, screws, pins, washers etc.,) they were able to reduce them to 263. This naturally helps in reducing the cost related to materials very considerably.

15.4 STANDARD CLASSIFICATION AND CODIFICATION OF MATERIALS

The discussion on standardisation cannot be complete without discussion of commodity classification and codification of the materials. This is considered as a dry subject. Normally it becomes difficult to get the senior managers interested in it as they consider it as a matter of insufficint importance. The potential of savings involved by using standard codifications systems is seldom realised by these managers.

In many organisations codification system has often been allowed to just grow naturally to meet the immediate internal requirements. Often it is observed that the same component is stocked under different catalogue numbers and description. On C. Railway when the standard codification system was introduced it was observed that one Stores Depot was having about 800 duplicate items out of a total of 10,000/- items stocked.

When we consider two or three organisations belonging to the same industry it will be invariably noticed that each organisation will have separate systems and part nos. for the identical items. A scientific codification system for an industry as a whole can go a long way towards eliminating this duplication thereby achieving both economy and greater efficiency. This becomes more important when a merger of 2 or 3 different companies takes place or when different organizations have to work together to meet a common purpose. It should not be very difficult to go a stop further and visualise an international system of codification even though it is rather difficult to implement it. An attempt in this direction has been made by NATO organisation by developing a NATO codification system for the Defence forces of the different countries under NATO organisation.

Here given below a few requirements and applications of a codification system.

Codification Requirement	**Application**
1. Unique item identification	One name and number applied after positive identification.
2. Division and sub-division of inventories into manageable segments.	Classification which brings together similar items in structured files and records.
3. Knowledge of items relationship in visible format.	Specification of characteristics in various forms of media- in logical uniform sequence.
4. Standard language for internal communication.	Standard terminology, uniform nomenclature and codes.
5. Inventory control	Accurate and reliable date base-elimination of duplication and excessive variety by codification.
6. Improved standardisation	By revealing the true nature of similar items over the total inventory in a form which permits their comparison.
7. Item information in retrievable form	End object of codification collection of data in commodity record and data banks.
8. Database for EDP	Machine sensible code format and uniformity of data facets.
9. Specifications	Description patterns or similar guides for selection and sequencing of item characteristics in uniform format provided by classification structure.
10. External communication	A common language to promote mutual understanding of item information in any communication media.

In our country the time has come for us to give a thought for developing atleast a national standard for classification and codification of items.

Organising a Programme of Standardisation

Very few companies appreciate the importance of introducing a formal standardisation programme. There are many ways in which such a programme can be organised. As there are many departments who are concerned with the subject, a committee effort may be more appropriate. Purchasing is particularly well qualified to perform major role in the standardisation programme. The first task is to see that the standards are written in such a way as to allow as many vendors as possible to fit into the programme. The second task is to inject a very strong dose of value analysis in the written standards.

Purchasing, engineering and other departments can appoint representatives to prepare a priority list of items for standardisation. The items which can offer the highest savings, the items which need most improvement or which would bring greater safety conditions, naturally should get priority. All possible information from company experts, industry sources, vendors etc., is collected and from this data a material standard can be written down.

CHAPTER

16

COMPUTERISATION OF STORES ACCOUNTS AND STORES FUNCTIONS

Computerisation of Stores Accounts and Stores Functions will be implemented in the following phases:

I. Priced ledgers
II. Numerical ledgers—stage I
III. Order progressing
IV. Payment and accountal of bills
V. Numerical ledgers—stage II

PHASE I

16.1 PRICED LEDGER MECHANISATION

Objective : Discontinuance of priced ledgers now being maintained by the Stores Accounts and maintenance of the same on the computer. Production of documents/statements/ reports now being prepared from the priced ledgers manually, or on the computer. Production of special reports and "exception' statements for the stores department which is not now prepared by the Accounts department to enable better management control.

Requirements

1. The first requirement is numeric coding of the following:
   (*a*) Price list numbers in an 8 digit system including one check digit,
   (*b*) Consignee in a 5 digit code
   (*c*) Depots and wards
   (*d*) Unit of accountal
   (*e*) Allocation
   (*f*) Category of stores.

During this phase, "Bin Cards" which are now maintained only in some Depots, should be introduced in all depots for each item. The Bin Card should not be made a duplicate numerical ledger. Instead of posting individual issues and receipts and voucher number, only total issues/ receipts on a day, (quantities) and closing balance, should be posted.

Proper maintenance of "bin cards" is essential, since in a later phase the entire NL card will be discontinued and the depot will rely only on the "bin card", for ascertaining stock on hand etc., as for instance where rationing has to be resorted to due to low physical stocks.

Achievements

At the end of this phase, we will achieve elimination of manual postings of each document in the NL card.

The history sheet, with all the permanent data on the item (description, unit of issue, drawing, specification etc.) details of outstanding estimate sheets/recoupment/orders/A. Ts etc., record of past consumption figures etc., will continue to be maintained. In place of the "movement" card we will only have a balance card indicating physical balance every 10 days. Recoupment, review of outstanding orders etc., will continue to be done by the Stores Depots as before.

PHASE III

16.3 MECHANISATION OF ORDER PROGRESSING

Objective

The object of this phase is to create a "order file" on the computer showing all outstanding orders/ A. Ts/shop work orders to enable progressing of the orders as necessary and also to obtain an assessment of suppliers' performance.

Requirements

A numeric code will have to be given for the following:

(*a*) Suppliers
(*b*) Consignees (part of this has already been achieved in Phase I)
(*c*) Purchase order numbers.

System in Brief

Copies of all purchase orders (including direct delivery orders), shop work orders and ATs will be forwarded to the FDP section. Punched cards will be prepared for each order. The cards will be sorted into Depot, PL no. etc., and then will be read and written on to a magnetic tape in the computer creating an **"order file".**

Amendments/changes in purchase orders etc., will also be forwarded along with new orders to the FDP section for correcting the **"order file".**

In Phase I, all receipt vouchers are already being punched into cards but the order details are not punched. In Phase III, order details will also be punched on the cards.

Before updating the 'stock-on-hand file', the receipt records on the 'transaction file' will be matched with the "order file" thereby closing the orders where they are fully complied with, indicating balance on order where they are partly complied with etc., and an updated 'order file' will be created. As a by-product, a separate tape containing the list of fully complied orders will be produced which will become the supplier's history file.

After the above, the 'order file' will be matched against the latest 'stock-on-hand file' to 'pick out' orders which need to be urged on top priority due to low physical holding, by means of an "exception report".

Reports

It is envisaged that the following reports will be produced in this phase :

1. List of fully complied orders
2. List of over-complied orders
3. List of part-complied orders
4. Statement of orders where delivery is overdue and physical stocks are below minimum,
5. Statement of orders where delivery is not yet due but physical stocks are below minimum,
6. Statement of orders where delivery is overdue by more than 3 months
7. Statement of orders, where physical stocks are in excess of maximum.

   Note : All the above reports will indicate the stocks in absolute quantity and also no. of days the stock will last.

8. Supplier's performance as under:
   - (*a*) List of defaulting firms to be determined by the no. of rejections, extensions etc.
   - (*b*) List of suppliers who have not secured an order for over one year.

Achievements

At the end of this phase we have a system to review every order, but to progress them on a selective basis depending on stock position. We have also a means of evaluating supplier's performance so as to weed out unreliable suppliers and ineffectual suppliers.

Reorder, recoupment functions at this stage continue to be handled mainly in the Stores Depot.

PHASE IV

16.4 PAYMENT AND ACCOUNTAL OF BILLS

Objective

Phase I dealt with mechanisation of priced ledgers in Stores, Accounts office. Phase II and III covered mechanisation of numerical ledgers (stage I) and mechanisation of order progressing. Phase IV deals with the mechanisation of Payment and Accountal of bills in the Stores Accounts office. The brief objectives are:

- (*i*) checking of suppliers' bills in order to pass them for payment
- (*ii*) automatic valuation of all receipts
- (*iii*) better control on outstanding entries in the purchase ledgers.

System in brief

The transactions affecting purchase ledgers are broadly:

(*i*) receipts resulting in credit to the ledger

(*ii*) suppliers' bills resulting in debit to the ledger.

The "order file" created in Phase III will be matched with the receipt order (R.O) in the " transaction file" of Phase I and a tape containing valued receipts will form the credits to the purchase ledger. This will be sorted in order of supplier 's No., purchase order No., PL No., etc.

When the supplier's bill is received, punched cards will be prepared for each bill indicating details such as: Supplier No, Purchase Order No., PL No., Quantity billed for, rate billed, Sales tax, percentage levied, Other taxes if applicable, whether 90% payment or balance payment, total amount etc.

The cards will be read on to a tape and sorted on the suppliers No., purchase order No., and PL No., This tape will form the debits to the purchase ledger.

The tape containing the credits to the purchase ledger will be merged with the tape containing the outstanding Debits and Credits and updated, to produce an outstanding Debits and Credits tape. This tape will then be matched with the debits to purchase ledger to produce two resultant tapes-one containing matched debits and credits and the other containing outstanding Debits and Credits to purchase ledger. These two tapes will then be used to print out the necessary reports.

Reports

The following reports will be printed from the two tapes produced in the system:

1. Purchase ledger
2. Authorisation to pay supplier 's bills
3. List of debits and credits which are outstanding for more than, say, 3 months.

Achievements

At the end of this phase we would have gained:

(*a*) a closer check on suppliers' bills

(*b*) automatic valuation of all receipts

(*c*) a closer control on outstanding entries in the purchase ledger.

PHASE V

16.5 MECHANISATION OF NUMERICAL LEDGER—STAGE II

Objective : In phase I, the transaction portion of the numerical ledger had been eliminated and replaced by transaction statement output by the computer. In phase III the outstanding orders had been transferred to the computer as an "order file". In this phase, the remaining portion of the numerical ledger is to be taken over by the computer and consequently, the computer will take over the onus and functions of stock review and recoupment. At the end of this phase the numerical ledger cards are discontinued.

Requirements

The numerical ledger cards should be reviewed for correctness of data on the history sheet etc., before transferring the information to the computer.

System in brief

During phases I to IV sufficient history information has already been brought on the computer. During this phase, the remaining historical and other data for each item is transferred to the "stock-on-hand" tape in the computer. Such information will include, outstanding recoupments, consumption during the last three years, sanctioned imprest, if any, raw materials required for the item, alternative item which can be used in lieu etc. Once this information is taken over, the numerical ledger cards are to tally discontinued and the depot is left within cards which have been brought up-to-date in Phase III.

At each movement of stock, the stock position is reviewed by the computer taking into account physical stocks, outstanding dues on orders, trend of consumption etc., to indicate action to be taken to reorder, cancel outstanding orders, declare overstocks, surplus etc. The information will be given by means of exception statements, which while indicating the reasons for the report, such as that the item needs reordering, item needs cancellation of outstanding orders etc., while, at the same time, indicating all data for the item, such as past consumption, control parameters (minimum, maximum) details of outstanding orders etc. It will be left to the Stores Officer to take appropriate action on receipt of such reports.

Reports

Reports will be in the form of 'exception statements' calling for action in the following eventualities (in, addition to those already covered in earlier phases).

(*i*) "available stocks" below reorder point-the item needs reorder:

(*ii*) "available stocks" in excess of maximum-review outstanding orders:

(*iii*) actual consumption for current period is in excess of average figures-stock position needs review;

(*iv*) other reports desired by management.

Achievements

At the end of this phase, the full recoupment and stock position review functions of the Stores which has so far been annually done in the Stores Depot is transferred to the computer. Review of stock status is carried out on each item at each movement of stock without fail and exception reports produced for all situations calling for action. Better control information, as laid down by the management, is furnished promptly, enabling better control being exercised on the inventory management. As directed by management, special exercises are carried out on the whole range of stores, analysing enormous date, with ease and speed.

At the end of the above phase, we would have computerised the present manual system of stock recoupment and review, adding on a few control statements and exception reports to ensure 'cent per cent' implementation of the present procedures and systems. This is the starting point for introduction of mathematical and scientific techniques for inventory management. Introduction of most of these concepts would not be feasible in a manual system due to the enormous amount of clerical time that would be required for each calculation and the incidental error proneness. The computer, due to the high speed of computation and enormous capacity for storage of data, can handle these techniques, at high speed and without error. Some of the techniques which could be added in further phases are very briefly mentioned bellow:

(*i*) Forecasting of consumption for advance periods on mathematical/statistical basis

(*ii*) Review of existing parameters *e.g.*, reorder point, danger level etc., based on past consumption and trends.

(*iii*) Determination of "economic order quantity" for each item by evaluating cost of carrying stock vis-a-vis cost of ordering.

(*iv*) Determining 'safety stocks' required for each item on mathematical basis to get a desired service level.

(*v*) Running of simulation exercises for A & B class items to ensure that parameters calculated and fixed are correct and will satisfy the demands arising over the next time periods.

Introduction of each of the above modern techniques will make substantial contribution towards better inventory management.

CHAPTER

17

ROLLING STOCK COMPONENTS

17.1 STEAM LOCOMOTIVES—PARTS AND FITTINGS

1. WP/WG/WL/WT BG locomotives
2. Other IRS steam locos BG
3. Non-IRS locos BG
4. YP/YG/YL/YT meter gauge low
5. Other IRS steam locos MG
6. Non-IRS locos MG
7. All steam locos narrow gauge
8. Rail mounted steam crane BG/MG/NG
9. Rail mounted diesel gauge BG/MG/NG

Policy of Purchase of Steam Locos Parts and Fittings

The items for which there is rate contract are purchased by placing supply order against rate contracts concluded by board items. For where there is no rate contract they purchased directly through limited tender/WSB/Open tender.

17.2 DISEL LOCOS—PARTS AND FITTINGS

1. Diesel electric locomotives BG/MG/NG
2. Diesel electric locomotives vehicle
3. Diesel electrical locomotives Transition
4. Diesel hydraulic locomotives BG/MG/NG
5. Diesel hydraulic locomotives vehicle
6. General motors diesel electric locomotives BG/MG
7. Henchel diesel hydraulic locomotives
8. Henchel diesel hydraulic locomotives
9. Non-Standard diesel locomotives

Policy for Purchase of Diesel Locos Parts and Fittings

For items supplied by DLW; placed with DCW.

Other item are punch through LT/WSB/OP.

17.3 ELECTRICAL LOCOMOTIONS—PARTS AND FITTINGS

1. DC Elec Locos BG(pre war)
2. DC Electric Locos BG (post-war)
3. AC Elec Locos (Japanesedesign)
4. AC Elec Locos
5. AC Elec Locos (CLW)
6. AC/DC Elec Locos BG
7. AC Elec Locos MG

Policy for Purchase of Electric Locos Parts and Fitting

For items which are supplied by CLW-indent is placed with CLW.

Other item are purchase through LT/WSB/OP.

17.4 CARRIAGE, WAGRON, EMU, RAIL CAR PARTS AND FITTINGS

1. ICF coaches BG/MG
2. ICF EMU coaches BG/MG
3. Diesel Rail Car BG/MG
4. BEML Coaches BG/MG
5. Jenop Coaches BG & MG
6. EMU Coaches BG/MG
7. Other Coaching Stock BG/MG
8. Old IRS Design Wagon
9. New IRS design Coaches
10. Other Goods Stock (IRCA & Non IRCA)

Policy for Purchase of (C & W) Items

For items purchased through ICF/RCF indent are placed with ICF/RCF.

For other items are purchased through LT/WSB/OP.

CHAPTER

18

WORK DONE OF PURCHASER IN CON CONSTRUCTIONS OF N-F RAILWAY

18.1 P-I SECTION

- This section deals with procurement of materials of the following major group:
  - (*i*) Permanent way and bridge work.
  - (*ii*) Building materials and sanitary wares.
  - (*iii*) Pipes and pipe fittings.
  - (*iv*) Plant and machinery including complete units.
  - (*v*) Road motors, auto trucks, material handling equipment and spares.
- Procurement of permanent way materials and bridge works.
- Policy of procurement for permanent way materials like Grooved Rubber Pad and Elastomeric Pad are to be procured through RDSO approved firm.
- Procurement of Rail.
- The requirement is submitted by the Engineering Department to the Railway Board. Allotment is made by the Railway Board to the various railways. After receipt of allotment purchase order is placed on M/s. SAIL by the Store Department and material is dispatched by SAIL to the various consignee by a rake load. The movement of rake load is co-ordinated by the Engineering Department with M/s. SAIL and Operating Department.
- Procurement of Grooved Rubber Pad and Elastomeric Pad is made from RDSO approved firms directly by Store Department. Procurement of 6mm thick Grooved Rubber Pad is done by the Railway Board.
- Procurement of Pipe and Pipe Fittings is done by placing supply order against Rate Contract concluded by DGS & D.
- Procurement of Plant and Machinery including complete units.
- Procurement of small track machines is made from firm approved by Railway Board.

- Procurement of Plant and Machinery through open Tender and all concerned including RITES *i.e.*, the Inspecting Authority.
- Issue first reminder, 2nd, reminder, 3rd.reminder final remainder for delay in delivery.
- To ask for receipt note/receipt particulars no loss and no inconvenience certificate from the consignee.
- If the firm failed to supply the material then issue Risk Purchase Tender.
- If the order has been completed in all respect arrange to refund the Security Deposit Money after getting approval of the Competent Authority after getting no claim no due certificate from the firm and after getting no loss certificate from the consignee. In case of dispute or Arbitration case and Court case to hand over the cases to the Finalisation Cell section to further deal the case.

18.2 P-2 SECTION

(*i*) P-2 section deals with the following group of items:
(*ii*) Cement
(*iii*) Petroleum oil lubricants
(*iv*) Fuel other than petroleum products
(*v*) Petrol and diesel

Policy of Purchase

Cement is procured through DGS & D placing Indent on DGS & D. Urgent requirements are purchased directly through SLT or OT. Petrol and diesel for small quantity for three months consumption purchased on local Rate contract with Indian Oil through his various agents in the jurisdiction of N.F. Railway Construction Organisation. Oil and lubricants are purchased from IOC directly on single tender basis.

Duties of the Staff

Following are the duties of the staff:

Office Superitendent Grade-I. To supervise the work of Sr.Clerk and to put up the cases alongwith his remarks to the officer concerned.

Senior clerk. He perform following functions:

(*a*) Drafting of purchase order.
(*b*) Comparing of purchase order and letter after typing.
(*c*) Letters drafting.
(*d*) Maintain purchase order reregister and filed all letters in the case.
(*e*) Noting in PP side for putting up to officers concerned through office Superitendent Grade-I.

18.3 P-3 SECTION

This section deal with the procurement of following item:

(*i*) Major group – Cables, conductors, transmission materials.
(*ii*) Major group – General electrical fittings.

(*iii*) Major group – Electrical measuring instruments, appliances and components.

(*iv*) Major group –Cells of all types, train lighting items of special nature and electrical amenities for passengers.

(*v*) Major group –Electric Sub-station, transmission and distribution equipments.

(*vi*) Major group –Electric machinery and parts.

Policy of Purchase of Electrical Item

1. The item for which there is Rate Contract such as lamps, fluorescent tube, Fan, choke electrical fittings, cable, measuring instrument, switches etc., are purchased by placing supply order against Rate Contract concluded by DGS & D.
2. Item for which there is no Rate Contract and they are procured directly through Limited Tender, WSB, Open Tender etc. The PAC item are prepared through Single tender.

Duties of Office Superitendent Grade-II Incharge

1. He is overall incharge of the section.
2. He supervise the work of the Senior clerk, working under him.
3. He puts up of the paper to the purchase officer concerned after giving his remarks.
4. He prepares monthly statement of demand received and disposed off and closing balance *i.e.*, progress of disposal of demands.
5. He prepares the progress report for disposal of tender *i.e.*, opening balance received during the month and disposed off during the month and balance remained during the month.

Duty list of Senior Clerk

1. He received the demand and registered into the demand register.
2. He checks up specification and drawing etc.
3. He checks up availability of fund and also checks whether this has been countersigned by HOD or vetted by Associated Finance.
4. He asked for drawing or confirmation to the specification from the indentor.
5. He filled up History sheet for procurement of the material.
6. He puts up the proposal through office supdt Gr. I to the concerned officer for approval of enquiry for LT? SLT, WSB, OT.
7. He prepares manuscript copy of the tender.
8. He gets the tender typed.
9. He gets the tender enquiry issued.
10. He prepares the Purchase order and supply order.
11. He compares the typed copy of the purchase order and supply order with the manuscript copy.
12. He gets the purchase order vetted by Finance and deals with the Finance objection.
13. He dispatches the purchase order to the firm, consignee, Accounts and concerned Inspecting Authority.
14. He issues first reminder, second reminder and Final remainder for delay in delivery.
15. He offers receipt note and collects NLC/NIC from the consignee.

16. If the firm failed to supply the material then issue risk purchase notice and issue risk purchase tender.
17. After the order is complete in all respect he put up the proposal for refund of Security Deposit money after obtaining NLC/NIC from the consignee.
18. In case of dispute he hand over the case to the finalisation section for dealing with Arbitration and Court case.

18.4 P-4 SECTION

(*i*) P-4 section deals with Signal and Tele-communication item. These are:
(*ii*) Major Group – Telegraph and telephone equipment.
(*iii*) Major Group –Wireless equipment including electronic components and spares for communication.
(*iv*) Major Group –Mechanical signalling and interlocking equipment not covered by other groups.
(*v*) Major Group –Electrical signalling and interlocking equipment.

Policy of Procurement of Electrical Signalling Item

1. Electrical signalling items are procured from RESO approved firms. The list of approved firms are updated by RDSO from time to time.
2. For tender value more than 3 lakhs, open Tender are issued inviting attention of the RDSO approved firm and below 3 lakhs Limited Tender issued to the RDSO approved firm. PAC item are procured through Single Tender against PAC certificate submitted by the Indentor.
3. Wireless Equipments and Electronic components are procured through firm recommended by Indenting Officer/RDSO approved firm.
4. Signalling item are purchased from NSIC approved firms.
5. Computer are to be purchased from manufacturer only.
6. Before placing for requisition for computer, GM/Con's sanction is required as per latest Railway Board's order.

Duty of the Staff

Following staff working and do their duties in the P-4 section.

1. **Office Superitendent Grade-I.** He is the incharge of the section. He is supervised the work of head clerk and put-up the case along with his remark to the officer concerned.
2. **Head Clerk-I.** Dutues of head Clerk-I are as Fallows:
   (*i*) To receive demand and open case.
   (*ii*) Give case number and enter into the demand register.
   (*iii*) Check specification and drawing etc.
   (*iv*) Check availability of fund etc., and also check whether it has been countersigned by HOD and vetted by the Associated Financers or not.
   (*v*) Ask for drawing confirmation to specification.
   (*vi*) Fill up History sheet.

(*vii*) Put up through office Supdt.Gr.I to the officer concerned for approval of enquiry *i.e.*, Single Tender, Limited Tender, WSB, Open Tender or Indent.

(*viii*) Get the copy typed from the type section.

(*ix*) Issue enquiry WSB, Indent after signature of the Competent Authority.

3. **Head Clerk-II.** Duties of Head Clerk-II are as follows:

(*i*) Prepare manuscript copy of the purchase order.

(*ii*) Compare typed copy with the manuscript copy.

(*iii*) Get the purchase order signed by the Competent Authority.

(*iv*) Send the Purchase order to Accounts for vetting.

(*v*) Deal with the financing budgetting.

(*vi*) Despatch Purchase order to the firm and consignee. and all concerned including RITES *i.e.*, the Inspecting Authority.

(*vii*) Issue first reminder, second reminder, third reminder and final reminder for delay in delivery.

(*viii*) To ask for receipt note/receipt particulars, no loss and no inconvenience certificate from the consignee.

(*ix*) If the firm failed to supply the material then issue Risk Purchase Tender.

(*x*) If the order has been completed in all respect arrange to refund the Security Deposit money after getting approval of the competent.

18.5 P-5 SECTION

The following items are purchased in this section:

1. Major group – Abrasives.
2. Major group –Brushes, brushware, baskets and bamboo products.
3. Major group –Tools, accessories, components and instruments.
4. Major group –Hardware items, fasteners.
5. Major group –Hardware (other than fasteners), wire ropes, chains and allied fittings, oil lamps etc.
6. Major group –Rubber, leather, canvas, plastic, flooring and kindred materials.
7. Major group –Electrodes, cutting and welding accessories, electrical and oxyacetylene.
8. Major group –Paints, varnishes and enamels including painters oil.
9. major group –Crockery, cutlery, napery, kitchen and tableware furniture and other equipments including clocks, watches etc.
10. Major group – Cloth, clothing, and personal equipments, cotton products like cord, twine ropes and Waste cotton etc.
11. Major group – Stationery and photographic goods and equipments and laboratory equipments not covered elsewhere.
12. Major group – Refractories, glass, glass substitutes, asbestods fibre and packing materials.
13. Major group – Ball and roller bearings.
14. Major group – Fire fighting equipment.

Above mentioned items are purchased through Limited Tender, Weekly store Bulletin, Special Limited Tender, Open Tender or by placing Indent to DGS & D or placing supply order on Rate

Duties of Staff

Following are the duties of the staff:

1. **Duties of Office Superitendent Grade-I.** To supervise the work of Head Clerk-I and Head Clerk-II and to put up the cases along with his remarks to the officer concerned.
2. **Duties of Head Clerk-I**

   Head Clerk-I perform fallowing duties:

   (*i*) Purchase order drafting and comparing.
   (*ii*) Letter correspondence through section incharge.
   (*iii*) Tender drafting and comparing.
   (*iv*) In absence of section incharge doing both P-2 and P-5 sections works.
   (*v*) Preparing of stores bulletin and issue of tenders.
   (*vi*) Preparing of position of monthly statement.
3. **Duties of Head Clerk-II**

   Head Clerk-II perform fallowing duteis:

   (*i*) Receive requisitions from CRR section.
   (*ii*) Preparing of purchase note and put up to the competent authority through section Incharge.
   (*iii*) Preparation of draft tender.
   (*iv*) Issue of tender forms.
   (*v*) Issue of purchase order after completion.
   (*vi*) Maintaining guard file.
   (*vii*) Doing the work of P-2 section in absence of staff working in P-2 section.
   (*viii*) Assisting section incharge as and when required.

18.6 P-6 SECTION

P-6 section deals with the procurement of various non-ferrous materials. Following measure group are being dealt in P-6 section:

(*i*) Major Group – Raw materials (ferrous)
(*ii*) Major Group – Non-ferrous metals
(*iii*) Major Group – Timber

- **Steel** is purchased through M/S. Sail. Tisco. IISCO etc. After receipt of the Demand order placed on M/s. SAIL through Iron & Steel Cell/Calcuttta/Railway Board. Regarding small item, procurement made from the stock yard of M/s. SAIL, TISCO, IISCO through the power of COS up to 50 lakhs with advance payment.
- **Timber:** Timber is purchased from Forest department of Assam Govt. and Meghalaya Govt. In case timber is not available from the Forest department, it is purchased by inviting tender from trade.

Duty of the Staff

Following are the duties of the staff:

1. **Office Superitendent Grade-I.** To supervise the work of Head clerk and to put up the cases along with his remarks to the officer concerned.
2. **Head Clerk.** Head clerk do fallowing duties:
   (*i*) To receive demand.
   (*ii*) To register in the demand register.
   (*iii*) To check up with specification.
   (*iv*) To check up availability of fund and countersigned by HOD.
   (*v*) Ask specification.
   (*vi*) To fill up history sheet.
   (*vii*) Put up to officer concerned for approval of mode of purchase.
   (*viii*) Preparing a copy of the tender, indent etc.
   (*ix*) Compare the typed copy with the manuscript.
   (*x*) To issue tender enquiry.

CHAPTER

19

TENDER SECTION

19.1 TENDER SECTION

Following works are done in this section:

(*i*) Opening of limited tender.

(*ii*) Opening of WSB.

(*iii*) Opening of special limited tender

(*iv*) Opening of open tender/advertised tender.

(*v*) Limited tender and WSB are opened every Wednesday and every Friday of the week.

(*vi*) Open tender and special limited tender—they are opened on any working day.

(*vii*) Opening of tenders.

Duty of Office Superitendent Tender Incharge Grade-II

1. To supervise the works of tender section.
2. Opening of LT and WSB.
3. Date stamping and machine numbering of the quotation received at the time of opening.
4. Bunch the offer case-wise.
5. Enter all the tender into the tender register and arrange them in the ascending order in each case.
6. Numbering of the offers in the ascending order and putting up the case to the respective purchase officer and keeping records in the registers in accordance to power of purchase of the respective officer.
7. Referred the firm for clarification etc., as and when required for asking Security Deposit Money and asking of acceptance of IRS conditions of Contract and any other clarification.
8. Check registration of the firm.
9. Preparation of comparative statement in case of OT and SLT and getting it vetted by Associated Finance and enter all the offer received against OT, SLT in the tender opening register.
10. To process for tender committee meeting for open Tender and SLT.
11. To obtain GM's sanction in case it is required.
12. To hand over the case to the purchase section after acceptance of the TCM and keeping record of the tender in the tender register.

Register Maintained

Following registers are maintained in the tender section:

1. Numbering register for LT.
2. Central tender register.
3. Sample register.
4. Register for Dy. COS/CON.
5. Register for SSO/CON.
6. Register for ACOS/CON.
7. Register for OT/SLT.

CHAPTER

20

LOCAL PURCHASE SECTION

20.1 OPENING OF TENDERS

- On the due date and time, tenders are opened. There is an elaborate system for tender opening to ensure that all the tenders submitted by the firms are properly linked in the respective cases and any additions or alterations after opening of the tenders are not possible.
- All advertised tenders and special limited tenders (tenders in which estimated value of purchase is more than Rs 2 lakhs) are opened in public and firms' representatives who want to be present during opening are allowed to be present. Such tenders should be opened by a Gazetted officer from Stores department and at least a Section Officer from Accounts department. All limited tenders are opened by a Chief Clerk/Head Clerk from Stores department and a Senior Clerk from Accounts department. At the time of opening of these tenders, firm's representatives are not allowed to be present.
- After opening they are signed by the tender opening officials on each page and all financial aspects are encircled. All overwritings etc., are also attested. Then the tenderers are sorted tenders case-wise (please note that at this stage, Demand No. is generally referred as Tender No. on some Railways)
- After sorting, tenders are linked in the respective tender cases and then they are transferred to respective purchase officers. However, in all the cases in which lowest tender is valuing more than Rs. 2 lakhs, detailed abstract of all tenders (also known as tabulation statement) is prepared and also got vetted from Accounts department.
- After this, the tender case is passed on to respective purchase officer on the basis of value of lowest tender.

20.2 DECISION OF TENDERS

- The tenders are now to be decided to either accept the suitable offer out of all the tenders received or reject or file them. All the tenders in which acceptable offer is less than or equal to Rs. 2 lakhs can be decided by the respective purchase officer as per the purchase powers delegated to him but, if the acceptable offer is valuing more than Rs. 2 lakhs, then the tenders have to be discussed by a tender committee consisting of 3 officers, one from Stores department one from consuming department and one from Accounts department. From Stores and consuming department officers below the rank of senior scale cannot be the members of a tender committee and Accounts member is generally one grade lower *e.g.*, tenders valuing from Rs. 2 to 5 lakhs are discussed by senior scale officers from Stores and consuming department and an Asst/Junior scale officer from Accounts department. Tender Committee is always a recommending body and its recommendations have to be accepted by a competent accepting officer.

- Some of the points to be kept in mind for deciding tenders are as under:
  - (*i*) The offer should be technically suitable *i.e.*, the material offered by the firm should be exactly as per our specifications given in the tender enquiry. Offers of substandard materials are normally ignored.
  - (*ii*) Out of all technically suitable offers, lowest offer is examined for reasonableness of rates.
  - (*iii*) If the rate of lowest technically suitable offer is considered reasonable, then it is to be seen whether delivery offered by the firm will meet our requirement with respect to delivery period and place of delivery.
  - (*iv*) After satisfying about (*i*), (*ii*) and (*iii*) above, we see that the firm is reliable and has satisfactory record of past performance.
  - (*v*) Finally before accepting the offer, we see that all terms and conditions offered by the firm are acceptable. We normally, place all our purchase orders as per 'Indian Railways Standard (IRS) Conditions of Contract'. As per these condition, we have right to reject the substandard materials, levy liquidated damages for delayed supplies, make risk purchases, etc.

20.3 LOCAL PURCHASE SECTION

Following works are performed in the local purchase section.

1. To receive demand of small value and register in the local purchase register.
2. To obtain order from the purchase officer concerned to make local purchase.
3. To obtain quotation from the local market from the existing firm.
4. To open the quotation in presence of officer.
5. To file the quotation in the ascending order in the case.
6. To put up the case to purchase officer for acceptance.
7. After acceptance of the offer by the officer to collect the material from the supplier after making payment.
8. Making all purchase list and recoupment of the imprest time to time. These are :
   - (*i*) Getting vehicle repaired from the market.
   - (*ii*) Maintenance of CDR and central purchase order register.
   - (*iii*) Machine numbering of the purchase order of the various sections.
   - (*iv*) Payment of telephone bills.
   - (*v*) Maintenance of stationery stock of the office.
   - (*vi*) Preparation of requisition of the office for stationery and other items.
   - (*vii*) Maintenance of imprest.
   - (*viii*) Maintenance of boils and plants register for the office.
   - (*ix*) Repair of typewriter, Ranio machine and xerox machine and other office furniture and equipments.

Duties of Office Superitendent (G)

To supervise the works of Hd.clerk, Sr.clerk and Jr.clerk and put up the cases along with his remarks to the officer concerned.

Duties of Head Clerk

(*i*) Drafting and floating of local purchase tenders.

(*ii*) Drafting of Purchase orders or purchase list after acceptance by concerned officers, chasing of firms for timely supply of materials.

(*iii*) Issue of Purchase orders after comparing the same.

(*iv*) Monthly statement of coverage position of demands and guide the Junior Clerk and Senior Clerk for smooth running of the section.

Duties of Senior Clerk

(*i*) Registration of requisition in CDR and sections register and distribution the same to the section concerned.

(*ii*) Passing of P & T and suppliers bills for payment by F.A. & C.A.O. (CON.)/MLG.

(*iii*) Supply of forms etc., to all sections as and when reuired from Godown and maintenance of records.

(*iv*) Drafting of Tenders & P/orders.

(*v*) Maintenance of Guard file of Purchase orders issued by all sections and sending of Accounts copy of Purchase orders to concerned Accounts Officer.

Duties of Junior Clerk

(*i*) Numbering of Purchase orders.

(*ii*) Entered purchase orders in central Purchase order register and daily statement of purchase orders to controller of Stores/Con and preparing of cases of requisition received by p-6 section.

20.4 LOCAL PURCHASE

- It will be seen from the discussions that for purchasing materials, a set procedure is to be followed and all this adds to costs of purchasing. Therefore, it is not economical at all to purchase items of petty value through centralised purchase office and hence all the field officers have been delegated powers to purchase the materials without following the detailed procedure.
- However, even for local purchases, it is to be seen that canons of Financial propriety are followed and materials are purchased at reasonable prices.

  Powers for local purchases depends upon delegation. Normally, JA grade officers have been delegated these powers upto Rs. 2,500 and senior scale officers and Assistant officers holding independent charge up to Rs. 1,000. However, these powers may vary from time to time and Railway to Railway.

  All Stores officers holding independent charge in the rank of senior scale or above have local purchase powers of Rs. 5,000.

- Some of the important points to be kept in mind by all the officers making local purchase are as under:
  1. There should be a proper system, of entering all the local purchase cases in a register. This register should indicate details of item to be purchased and rate and firm etc., from which purchase has been made.
  2. The purchases should be made at competitive rates after trying number of firms/shops.
  3. Purchases should be made from standard firm *i.e.*, the firm should be either a reputed dealer/authorised stockist/manufacturer or a good shopkeeper. Purchases from persons who do not, own any shop etc., and operate business from their residence and act only as middlemen, should be avoided.
  4. The quotations should be collected only from existing firms. If a firm is doing business in different names from the same premises, only one quotation should be taken from such firms. The practice of collecting more than one quotation from a single shop should not be resorted to.
  5. For collecting quotations per bearer from the local market, officer incharge of local purchase shall nominate the Railway employee by name. The nominated employee shall be required to sign each cover of the quotations subsequently on opening by the officer in charge, each quotation also in token of his having collected personally.
  6. The names of firms from whom quotations are to be obtained are to be suggested by the officer-in-charge of local purchase. The employee, however, may suggest names of new firms coming to his notice, to the purchase officer who could consider including them for subsequent purchases.
  7. If the local purchases are regularly made, a panel of firms should be maintained which should be updated from time to time.
  8. A tender box should also be kept for dropping the tender.
  9. All enquiries should mention time and date by which offers should be received. Any offer received after this should not be considered.
  10. Non-stock items for which standard pattern exists should not be purchased if it can be manufactured by the Railway.
  11. Local purchase of items for which valid rate/running contracts exists, should not be made.
  12. Local purchases from cooperative stores and Khadi Bhandars should be encouraged. Purchase upto Rs. 2,000 from a co-operative stores can be made even on single quotation, while for others single quotation is permissible only up to Rs. 500/.

CHAPTER

21

ESTABLISHMENT SECTION

21.1 WORK DONE FROM ESTABLISHMENT SECTION

In the establishment section the following work are done to deal with the all matter concerning to the **Establishment matter** and **Personnel Department** of COS/CON/Maligaon's office such as maintenance of leave register for casual leave, LAP, LHAP of all staff and officers.

1. Maintenance of currency of work charged post of all non-gazetted and gazetted posts including the currency of OSD/CON, Kolkata office.
2. Dealing with the cases of General Policy matter of Personnel department and maintenance of all policy cases.
3. Transfer and posting of staff from one section to other and booking of staff on duty.
4. Maintenance of register of the staff of class-IV and class-III.
5. The following works are done in the General section.
   (*i*) Maintenance of policy cases like delegation of power.
   (*ii*) Purchase policy.
   (*iii*) Registration of firm.
   (*iv*) Advertisement of open Tender.
   (*v*) Sale of open Tender.
   (*vi*) Taking cash from the firm to whom open Tender documents are sold.
   (*vii*) Depositing cash with the divisional cashier/Construction through MRT.
   (*viii*) Issue of various office order.
   (*ix*) General policy matter.
   (*x*) Issue of petrol oil to the official vehicle of the store organisation.
   (*xi*) Scrap policy and other allied works relating to general policy matters.
   (*a*) *Sale Section*. This section deal with the disposal of scrap and unserviceable released materials arising from gauge conversion projects. This section directly sales the H.T.S. plates which is lying in the premises of M/S. BBJ, Kolkata through open tender and released/unserviceable materials available from gauge conversion project. Survey

Committee meeting is conducted by Store department consisting officers and after certification of survey, the materials handed over to COS/Open Line with the approval of GM/CON for disposal through auction conducted by COS/Open Line from time to time.

(*b*) Released materials such as Rails, Permanent Way fittings and Girder handed over to COS/Open Line and credit realised from F.A. & C.A.O./Open Line.

21.2 DUTY OF THE STAFF WORKING IN ESTABLISHMENT, GENERAL SECTION AND SALE SECTION

There is one Office supritendent Grade-I Incharge of the section, one Office supritendent Grade-II and one Senior clerk in this section.

Duty of the Office Supritendent Grade-I

He is to supervise the work dealt with the section and timely putting up the cases to concerned officer with his remarks.

He is personally supervising the sale/disposal of scrap material and makes out a statement of sale as and when required. Issue of Petrol oil to the official vehicle and supervise the receipt work of various letters and requisitions and any other job assigned by the officers from time to time.

Duty of Office Supritendent Grade-II

Office **Supritendent Grade-II** is doing the following job:

To receive letter and dak coming from firm and outside as well as from different offices including requisition.

He put up the dak pad to the officers concerned and after signatures of the officer he sends the letters to the respective section through a register and requisition sends to the CDR section.

In complete requisition which is pointed out by officers with the remarks sent back to the respective indenting officer for clarification through covering letter for that one policy cases is maintained by office Supritendent Grade-II.

Duty List of Senior Clerk in Establishment Section

He performs the following duties:

(*i*) Enlisted staff name in attendance register every month.
(*ii*) Maintenance of all kind of leave for gazetted or non-gazetted.
(*iii*) Timely putting up of TA and OTA bills to the officer concerned.
(*iv*) Putting up of Sick memo book to office Supritendent/CON.
(*v*) Drafting of letter and noting regarding establishment matter and put up to office supritendent (E) in all establishment matters.
(*vi*) Put up oil position and maintenance of oil coupon book in absence of office supritendent (E).
(*vii*) Putting up staff booking file in Hindi and English.
(*viii*) Preparing of pay order for releasing of security money and service stamps.
(*ix*) Filing all letters regarding establishment in the respective files.
(*x*) Distribution of pay slips of each month amongst the staff.
(*xi*) Putting up tender notices for advertisement to PRO/CON/MLG for publishing in the paper.

(*xii*) Maintenance of disposal and scrap register.

(*xiii*) Chase up credit sale matter to COS/Open Line and F.A. & C.A.O./Open Line during the year.

(*xiv*) Assistance to office superitendent/Sale regarding all scrap matters.

(*xv*) Filing all letters in respective sale files.

(*xvi*) Preparing of open tender booklet under supervision of office superitendent/sale and look after receipt section in absence of office Supdt. Grade II and office Superitendent Grade-I.

These are more that 170 cases are dealt by Establishment/General section.

List of cases are attached here

1. Duty of DSK-II CON Chasing

The following duties are performed by DSK-II/CON Chasing.

(*i*) He receives the chasing letter from the section officer.

(*ii*) He goes to the various firms and government departments for chasing the works assigned to him.

(*iii*) He brings the material urgently required along with him.

(*iv*) He goes for chasing DGS & D, Railway Board/kolkata and various firms and other places in the country.

2. Dispatch Section

Dispatch section is under the control of office superitendent Grade-I, incharge of establishment and general section. He is assisted by one senior clerk.

The following **works** are done in this section:

(*i*) Dispatch of tender, WSB, LT, Indent, OT documents.

(*ii*) Dispatch of letters.

(*iii*) Dispatch of purchase orders.

(*iv*) Dispatch of confidential letters.

The following are the **policies** of dispatch section.

(*i*) Dispatch of tenders valuing below Rs. 25,000/- under certificate of posting.

(*ii*) More than Rs. 25,000 under registered post.

(*iii*) Purchase order of firm's copy should be dispatched through registered post.

(*iv*) *WSB under Certificate of Posting*. Urgent letters are sent through speed post and through FAX after getting approval of the competent authority.

3. Finalization Cell Section

This section is supervised by one head clerk who is assisted by one Senior Clerk. This section deals with court cases and arbitration cases.

Following **duties** are performed by head clerk in this section.

(*i*) Receipt of claim filed by the party.

(*ii*) Preparation of draft reply.

(*iii*) Putting up the draft reply to the officer concerned for approval.

(*iv*) Attending court as and when required.

(*v*) Attending Railway Advocate's house as and when required for clarification and approval of draft reply.

(*vi*) Attend to Law officer (construction) as and when necessary in connection with the court cases and arbitration cases.

(*vii*) To do all the correspondence connected with court cases and Arbitration cases.

Following duties are performed by senior clerk in finalization cell sections:

(*i*) To compare the letter/drafting.

(*ii*) Filing of letter in the file.

(*iii*) Maintenance of all file.

(*iv*) Attending Law officer/Construction in absence of Head clerk.

(*v*) Some time put up the cases to the officer concerned in absence of Head clerk.

4. Type Section

This section consists of one head typist and duties are as follows.

(*i*) To receive manuscript from the purchase section.

(*ii*) To type the tenders such as LT, SLT, OT, Indent, Purchase Orders Official letters, correspondence to the firms as well as field officers.

(*iii*) Maintenance of typewriters.

(*iv*) Reporting the matter of defective type machine to Office Superitendent (G) for repair.

CHAPTER

22

WORK DONE IN THE CONTROLLER SOURCE OF CONSTRUCTION ORGANISATION

22.1 DUTIES OF CONFIDENTIAL ASSISTANT

Duties of confidential assistant are as fallows:

1. To assist and extend necessary liaison as and when required for speeding up the day-to-day work of the HOD.
2. To take out dictation and typing it out and ensure disposal of the same within the quickest possible.
3. To ensure timely initiation of reports on officers and staff of the respective department and its final disposal thereof.
4. To deal with confidential correspondences and disposal of the same at appropriate levels if it is of routine nature and that of policy matters in consultation with superior officers.
5. Help in collection of datas required for finalization of tenders of SAG Level Tender Committee and to type out the TCM as and when required.
6. Assists in all respect for conducting arbitration and drawal of arbitration award, and when HOD is nominated as Arbitrator and take such as may be required for speedy finalization.
7. Keep record of the movement of HOD and accompany if situation so warrant.
8. All other duties being entrusted time to time, as may be called upon to do so.
9. Taking dictation and complete the same duly typed.

22.2 DUTIES OF MOVEMENT INSPECTOR AT KOLKATA

1. Witnessing of disposal/sale of surplus steel materials after fabrication lying with M/s. BBJ and their sub units *i.e.*, M/s. Burn, M/s. Braithwait and Jessop, Kolkata.
2. Co-ordination and chasing M/S. SAIL at the appropriate level for supply of rails, loading into BFRs etc.

3. Co-ordination and chasing of different firms for the details in connection with supply of C.I. sleeper, steel turn out, sleeper, crossing, swithces, turnout grooved rubber pad and other permanent way materials for N.F. Railway/Con unit.
4. Assisting officers for performance of protocol duties and other miscellaneous duties for N.F. Railway (CON), Kolkata as and when required.
5. Assisting official paper works like requisition of materials, important letters, attendance particulars of the office staff etc.
6. Co-ordinating and chasing different railways and firms for placement and movement of wagons and rake for supply of cement, concrete sleeper, wooden sleeper and other permanent way materials.

22.3 DUTIES AND WORKS OF ASSISTANT CONTROLLER OF STORES/CONSTRUCTION

1. Receipt of Demands from various departments of the Construction organisation and distributing the demands to the purchasing sections. Demands not in proper manner/description/ lack of fund, etc., are returned to indentors for necessary clarification/ provision of fund etc.
2. Purchase of materials through L/T and bulletin up to basic value of Rs. 50,000/- in each case. Since next most of the demands are below Rs. 50,000/- the number of cases for purchase is highest in case of ACOS/CON.
3. Matters relating sanction of leave of Class-III and IV staff of the office. To arrange temporary arrangement among sections during leave of other staff.
4. Maintenance of the motor vcehicles of the office, control and approve the movements of the office vehicles and issue of petrol slips, and repairing of the vehicles.
5. Issue/sale of open tender for various to firms and supervise the deposit of the sale proceeds to Div. Cashier from OS/E, and other establishment matters such as transfer and posting of staff etc.
6. Opening of limited tenders by officials of tender section and accounts representative.
7. Purchase of petty value items from local purchase section and from imprest cash.
8. Preparation of monthly imprest bill and submission to Accounts department for recoupment.
9. All matters relating payment of telephone bills of the office.
10. Works relating survey of Engg. materials /houses/zirat etc., and auction thereof.
11. Chasing works for proper delivery of materials in time.
12. To sign the P/Orders of acceptance done by ACOS/CON and SSO/CON.
13. To sign different letters of office relating miscellaneous establishment/administrative matters.
14. To look after the attendance of staff in the office and to do surprise check regarding the attendance and availability of staff in office hours.

22.4 DUTIES OF SENIOR STORES OFFICER/CON

The duties of Senior Stores Officer/CON are funished below:

1. To purchase materials required by the different departments of GM/ CON's organisation within the power of purchases as per sop through Limited tenders and open tenders after thoroughly checked the requisitions.
2. To survey the released materials from various Gauge conversions project and offered by concerned chief Engineers to COS/CON for disposal. He survey the released material along with the nominated members of survey committee. After surveying the materials he prepared the survey sheet and get it signed from other members and Secretary of the Committee than he put the survey sheet in concerned file to GM/CON through proper channel for his approval. After approval of GM/CON he will offers the released materials to COS/Open line for disposed of through auction/tender conducted by Cos/DL. He also chase up the FA and CAD/CON as well as FA and CAD/Open line for credit of the sold materials.
3. He look after the establishment matters relating to class IV and Ii category staff of COS/CON.
4. To reply the audit objection cases.
5. To open the O.T. and special limited tender cases with the accounts representative in front of firm's representative, prepare the T.C.M of his power and put up the same to the authority concern for acceptance.
6. To chase the firms for supplying the materials on whom purchase order and supply orders placed.
7. To sign the P.D. acceptance made by Dy.COS/CON.
8. In addition, important works entrusted by COS/CON and Dy. COS/CON are attended.

22.5 DUTIES OF DEPUTY CONTROLLER OF STORES/CONSTRUCTION

Their duties are under following headings:

1. (*i*) **Procurement of Materials**
   - (*a*) Permanent Way, Tools, Equipment
     cement, Railway Board's item – Steel, rail
     DGS&D items – cement etc.
   - (*b*) Signalling items – cable, equipment, fittings.
   - (*c*) Electrical items – Fittings cables, batteries.

   (*ii*) **Processing Purchase**
   - (*a*) Scrutiny of demands, approval of tender schedules.
   - (*b*) Approval of LT with penal of firms for all items whenever necessary up to value Rs. 3 lakh or below.
   - (*c*) Floating tenders.
   - (*d*) Finalisation of tender cases
     - (*i*) Within direct powers up to Rs. 3 lakh
     - (*ii*) T.C. cases with value more than Rs. 8 lakh to Rs. 50 lakh.
       Issue of P.O.

   (*iii*) Monitoring procurement of material after placement of P.O.
   Chasing with firm over phone, monitoring movement constantly till final receipt of material by consignee at destination.

2. **Disposal of Scrap Surplus Material**
   (*i*) Survey of material
   (*ii*) Offering the material to open line for disposal through auction sale.
   (*iii*) Monitoring realisation of sale credits from open line.
   (*iv*) Finalisation of tender cases for sale through tender and monitoring lifting of sold material.
3. Persuing the legal and arbitration cases to safeguard railway's interest in the matter of disputes in various contracts in liaison with OSD/CON and ALO/CON.
4. Clearance of audit objection cases by supplying appropriately and ensuring implementation of suitable follow up action.
5. General administration of the office of COS/Con and administrative control of the office of OSD/Con/Kolkata.

CHAPTER

23

OFFICE ORDER

23.1 DUTY LIST OF VARIOUS STAFF WORKING IN THE OFFICE OF DYPTY COS/CON/BG

The duty list of various staffs shall be as given under following sections:

Demand Section

The duty list of various demand clerks in the demand section are given below:

1. To receive requisitions and registered them in the Demand Register.
2. To put up proposal to purchase officers, complete with history sheet to decide the mode of purchase after checking up all the particular in the requisitions.
3. To return incomplete requisitions to the indentors asking them to resubmit the requisitions after giving complete details of all the items in the requisitions.
4. To issue limited tender enquiries after getting approval from the competent authority.
5. To issue the tenders against retendered and risk purchase cases promptly.

Work Distribution

The distribution of work of the Demand section as per detailed given below:

1. In this section senior clerk deal with the demands of Engineering and Mechanical department and any other miscellaneous demands of other departments.
2. He will also deal all the demands of Signal and Electrical department.
3. Head Clerk/P, shall supervise the work of demand section and also deal with the major demands of cement and steel.

Purchase Order Section

The following are the works of purchase section:

1. To receive all the accepted tender cases from the tender clerk.
2. To prepare manuscript of the purchase order according to the terms and conditions of the T.C.M/accepted offers.

3. To get all the purchase orders typed by the typist.
4. To get all the purchase orders vetted by the account officer.
5. To arrange despatch of all the purchase orders through despatch section duly completed in all respect.
6. To check the receipt of the acknowledgement from the firm to whom order has been dispatched.

These above mentioned works are performed by purchase order clerk and his work will superwise by head clerk of this section.

Progress Sections

The following are duties of progress section:

1. To chase the firm for dispatching the material according to the terms and conditions of delivery period mentioned in the purchase order.
2. To issue an amendment in respect of extention of D.P. and in respect of change of name of consignee etc.
3. To obtain no loss certificate from the consignee for finally extending D.P.
4. To issue risk purchase notice as per terms and conditions of the order.
5. To hand over the case to the Demand clerk after expiry of the risk purchase notice for issuing tenders accordingly.

Work Distribution

The head clerk concerned will superwise the work progress under their charge. Fallowing are the distribution of work-load of progress section:

1. In this section, Head clerk /Steel will look after the work progress of cement, steel and mechnical department.
2. Head cleark/P will look after the progess of work of A and B catagory purchase order cases of engineering and open tender of electrical department.
3. Head clerk/G will also look after the R/C work of all department.
4. Senior clerk will look after the progress work of 'C' catagory purchase order cases of signal and engineering department, and also look after the progress work of all the limited tender cases of electrical department.

Tender Opening Section

Following are the functions of the tender opening section:

1. To issue tender notice of open tender cases after getting approval of the competent authority.
2. To get the tender schedule prepared and cyclostyled duly approved by the competent authority.
3. To issue open tender documents to the firms after receipt of money from them.
4. To keep complete accountal of the case transaction in respect of sale of tenders.
5. To open limited and open tender according to the opening date.
6. To file all the quotation in the respective tender cases.

7. To prepare a list of tenderers in the open tender register for each open tender case and get it signed by the tender opening officer on the same date.
8. To hand over the tender cases to the confidential tender clerks attached to the officer concerned according to the value of the tender case.

These above mentioned work performed by head clerk, who will look after the duty of tender opening clerk.

Local Purchase Section

Duties of the local purchase section as given below:

1. To receive all the demands for local purchase from the demand clerks.
2. To register all the demands in the Local purchase Register department wise.
3. To issue local purchase bulletin as and when required after, obtaining the order from the competent authority.
4. To obtain quotations per pearer for urgent items dealt with outside the bulletin.
5. To open all the quotations in presence of stores officer and get it initialed and encircled by the officer concerned.
6. To file the quotations in each case according to the ascending order of rates.
7. To prepare history sheet and put up the case to officer concerned for acceptance.
8. To get the material inspected by the I.O. and obtain suitability remarks before delivery of the material to the consignee.
9. To obtain acknowledgement and signature of the consignee in taken of receipt of the material.
10. To arrange payment for the accepted material which has been delivered to the consignee and obtain cash memo from the firm for the same.
11. To prepare purchase list for the item purchased and delivered and get it signed of the officer concerned. Distribute copy of the purchase list to all concerned. One copy of the purchase list should be given to the purchase order clerk for his record.
12. To recoup the cash imprest promptly.

In this section, senior clerk will look after the duties of local purchase clerk.

Confidencial Tender Section

Following are the distribution of work done by confidentcial tender section:

1. Head clerk/G will deal with the tender cases pertaining to the power of Dy.COS/CON till suitable Sr.clerk is posted for the same.
2. Sr. clerk will deal with the cases pertaining to the power of SSO/CON. and also will deal with the tender cases pertaining to the power of ACOS/CON.

Type Section

In this section, typist is the main person who perform all typing work of the office of deupty controller of stores/construction. The work of type section will be supervised by Head cleark/steel.

Receipt and Despatch Section

Senior clerk and Head clerk/G will supervise the work of this section.

Record Section

In this section, seninor clerk, will look after the work done.

Establishment and General Section

In this section Head clerk/Steel will supervise the work done. The distribution of work load of Estt. and General section is given below:

Senior clerk will look after the:

(*a*) Leave of guzzted and non-guzzted staff

(*b*) Transfer, promotion posting etc.

(*c*) Justification for guzzted and non-guzzted staff

(*d*) Parliamentary questions

(*e*) Budget

(*f*) Hindi progress report

(*g*) Fortnightly absentee statement to SPO Con

(*h*) He will maintain all the procedure order and also file pertaining to office order received from COS office

(*i*) The DAR and court cases

(*j*) Casual labour policy, salary Bill

(*k*) Telephone and Typewriter repair bill and other miscellaneous bills

(*l*) Dealing with the cases pertaining to disposal of audit and accounts paras and inspection notes of various officers

(*m*) He will deal with issue of passes and P.T.O.S. and other miscellaneous work ordered by head clerk/steel.

All the casual labour will work according to the work allotted by the O.S. and above duties may be followed with immediate effect.

CHAPTER

24

STEAM LOCOMOTIVES PARTS AND FITTINGS

24.1 PROCEDURE FOLLOWED BY COFMOW FOR PROCUREMENT OF MACHINERY AND PLANT FOR RAILWAY WORKSHOPS AND PRODUCTION UNITS

The COFMOW was established in the year 1979, for procurement of machinery and plant for the Railway workshops and production units under the IDA agreement. Later on, it was procured machinery and plant under BRD loan. Later on, it was continued to purchase machinery and plant under OP and HRD basis.

The following functions are performed by various departments of COFMOW:

1. **Receipt of Indent:** Indents are received from Railway Workshops and production units by the Mechanical branch. After receipt of the indent, the specifications are framed by the mechanical department and key no. is allotted against each indent. While preparing the specification, the manufacturers catalogue are being referred and their specifications are thoroughly studied. After studying the specification of the manufacturers, the COFMOW specifications are framed for the machines to be purchased. Consignees are also being consulted while preparing the specification. Sometimes, RDSO is also involved.
2. After framing the specification, the indent along with the specification is forwarded to the Stores Branch. The specification (part II) of the tender document is printed by the Stores Department. The General conditions of the contract part I is also printed by the Stores Branch. After receipt of the indent, the approval for issue of the tender is obtained from the Controller of Stores. On receipt of the indent in Stores Branch, particulars of the same are noted in the register and then file is put up to the competent authority for floating of OP/Global tender. After approval for issue of the tender by the competent authority, the tender notices are issued to be published in the leading newspapers for wide publicity through advertising agency.

Tender documents are sold to the manufacturers or their authorised agents who approach COS for the same against cash payment/demand draft.

After issue of the tender, if any amendment is required in the specification, as advised by the Mechanical Department, the same is incorporated and amendment to the specification is issued and notice are sent to the manufacturers/agents who have purchased the documents so that they may submit their offer accordingly. For OPB tender, due date is given as 45 days from the date of issue of the notices. For Global tender, due date for opening of the tender is as 60 days from the date of issue of the tender notices.

The tenders received are put into the tender box, which are opened on the due date. After opening the tenders, the offers are read out in the presence of the tenderers. Each page of the tender document is signed by the Stores and Accounts Officers.

All the bids received are filed in a case. The commercial evaluation of each bid is done by the CTC Section, and each offer is commercially evaluated by the Confidential Tender Cell. Brief notes are prepared for all the offers received and marked as L-1-L-2. etc., in ascsending order of the value of the each offer. After commercial evaluation, the case is sent to the Mechanical Department for technical evaluation.

The technical evaluating officer refers the matter to the bidders to give confirmation for clause wise comments against each clause if not furnished earlier and after receiving clause wise comments from the bidder, the technical officer evaluates the offers technically. The technical evaluation duly approved by the CME is forwarded to the COS.

As per the monetary value of the lowest technical acceptable offer, tender is forwarded to the convener of the TC by COS.

Convener of the TC is the Stores member and he fixes the date of the TCM in consultation with technical/financial member of the TC.

The brief note and technical evaluation and commercial evaluations are being perused by the TC and when they agree for a lowest technically suitable offer, the TC recommendations are prepared.

After the recommendation are signed by the convener and technical/financial member, the recommendation are submitted to the competent authority for approval.

The competent authority goes through the recommendation and if it is found in order, the TC recommendations are accepted by the competent authority.

In case, the competent authority does not agree with the recommendation, he gives his observations and referr back to the Tender committee and Tender Committee goes through the observations of the competent authority and submit their recommendations to the competent authority as deemed fit.

After the recommendation are accepted by the competent authority, the tender case is sent to the CTC Section for preparation of the advance acceptance and then sent it to the finance for vetting. The AA is issued duly vetted by the finance to the successful tenderer and they require to submit PGB for 10% of the contract value. After receipt of the PGB, the AT is prepared as per recommendation of the TC and submitted to the finance for vetting the same. After the AT vetted by the finance, the photo copies are taken from each document and AT is prepared and issued to the completion of the contract. In case there is a delay in supply of the machine, the firm is asked to expedite the completion of the machine and put up for inspection by the inspecting authority *i.e.*, RITES. After the machine is inspected by the RITES and inspection certificate is issued, the supplier dispatches the machine as per terms and conditions of the AT.

90% payment is released against inspection certificate and receipt certificate from the consignee for the receipt of the material in good condition. The payment is made by FA and CAO. After receipt of the machine, the same is installed/commissioned by the contractor as per terms and conditions of the contract. After installation/commg. and observing the working of the machine for a period of one month, the PTC is issued by the consignee. After receipt of the PTC, the supplier submit a WGB and claim the 10% payment. On receipt of WGB, the 10% payment of the machine is released by FA and CAO. After receipt of WGB, the PG is released to the supplier. In case, there is an unsatisfactory report from the consignee, the supplier is asked to attend the same and put the machine in working order as early as possible. During the warranty period, any complaint by the consignee is attended by the supplier and after the warranty period is over and there is no complaint against the machine, WG is also released to the supplier.

In case of failure by the supplier to supply the machine within the stipulated DP, the DP is extended reserving railway rights and denial clauses. If the firm fails to supply the machine within a target date the risk purchase notices is issued and AT is cancelled at their risk and cost and risk purchase tender is issued. Firm is required to commission the machine within specified period as mentioned in the tender document, if Procedure followed in the purchase section.

Indent is received from Mechanical department duly key numbered alongwith technical specification in the General section of stores branch. SS(G) put up the indent to the concerned Dy. COSs. after making entry in indent receipt register. After that, the indent is signed to the purchase section concerned.

The indent is entered in the purchase register giving the case no. The proposal is put up to the competent authority for approval to float OP/Global tender. In case of global tender, the finance concurrence is obtained; case is hand over to the SSG who issue tender notices. SS(G) allot the global/OP tender no. For issue of advertised tender, the proposal for issuing tender notice is put up by the SSG and after approval of the competent authority, tender notice is issued to the agency for advertising in the various newspapers.

Tender document are sold by the SS(G). The sealed tender received from the manufacturers of authorized agents, the same are put up the tender box on the date of opening of tender at the specified time. The tender box is opened on the due date and then the tender are opened in the presence of the tenderers. The tenders are opened in the presence of Stores Officer and Accounts Officials. The rate and terms and conditions are read out by the Stores Officer. All the tender document are put in bunch. Each page of tender document is signed by the Stores/Accounts officer at the time of opening of tender. The case handed over to the SS/CTC.

Each offer is commercially evaluated in the CTC. Section in case of single bid system. The briefing note is prepared by the CTC section in the ascending order of the total value of the offer. They are marked as L-1, L-2 etc. The case is sent to financial department for vetting the commercial evaluation. After the commercial evaluation is vetted by the finance, the case is sent to CME through COS for technical evaluation. After tech, evaluation completed, the case is sent to COS by CME. COS marked the case to the concerned Stores officer according to the total value of the lowest technically suitable offer. The Stores Officer in consultation with the other Finance/Mechanical officer fixed the date for holding TC meeting. All the Terms and conditions are discussed in the TCM and the TC minutes are prepared recommending the lowest suitable offer for acceptance.

24.2 FUNCTION OF THE DEPOT SECTION

Depot section deal with for the procurement of items other than the machinery and plant required by the COFMOW office to be purchased through limited. tender. Following procedure is followed in this section. The indents are received from the indentor directly by this section.

The requisitions are entered into requisition register in which the SN and reqn. No., department and description, qty. are mentioned. Then the case is opened. The approval is taken from the competent authority for the purchase of items through the local purchase or ltd. Tender upto the cost of Rs. 2000/- Petty items of small value are purchased through cash imprest upto Rs. 2000/-. For items value of upto Rs. 5,000/- which are available in the Kendriya Bhandar are procured from Kendriya Bhandar. The items which are not available in Kendriya Bhandar, the value of the same is more than Rs. 5,000/- are procured through ltd. tender.

The approval of the competent authority is obtained, for panel of firms to whom limited tenders are issued. After approval is obtained, the limited tenders are issued to the approved firms on panel. For urgent items, per year quotations are obtained. The quotations are dropped in the tender box and opened on the due date. The tenders are opened by ACOS or Section officer of the Accounts or Accounts officer. The offer are signed by the ACOS/Accounts officials who open the tender. The offers are marked as 1/3, 2/3 in ascending order and put up to the competent authority after commercial evaluation. The case is sent to the technical department for examining the technical suitability and certifying reasonables of rates. After suitability is certified by the indentor, the offer is accepted by the competent authority and purchase order is placed. Particulars of the purchase orders are entered into the purchase order register. The supplier after receipt of the purchase order, supply the material to the depot section. On receipt of the consignment the package are opened and material checked and quantity is checked for the correct receipt of the consignment. Then the case is put up to ACOS for inspection. Either ACOS himself accept the material or he may sent to the indentor for technical inspection of the material. After receipt of technical suitability, material is accepted/rejected after inspection report.

For accepted material, RO is allotted and the material is entered in the receipt order register. Bill is verified by ACOS for the correct receipt of material and same is forwarded to FA and CAO for making payment. After allotment of RO and making payment the material is entered into ledger. Particulars of the consignment are entered into ledger. After preparing the issue note, the quantity is sent to the indentor. The items which are purchased through cash purchase, the imprest is recouped by Accounts department.

Insurance Claim

The dispatch particulars are received from the foreign supplier, indicating quantity, amount and total value of the consignment including freight. The premium amount of the consignments are deposited with the oriental insurance co. limited. at the beginning of the every quarter. In case, there is a damage to any package, the same is mentioned in the receipt report by the COS/SH and consignment sent to the ultimate consignee by COS/SH. The damage package are opened in the present of firm's representative, and the insurance survey or and accordingly, the claim is lodged with the insurance company and pursued till its settlement and payment received by the COFMOW.

CHAPTER

25

MATERIAL MANAGEMENT EOQ FORMULA

In Indian Railways, expenditure on staff is 60% of the total expenditure and expenditure on material is 40% of the total expenditure. Expenditure on staff is very difficult to reduce but expenditure on material can be reduced by adopting technique like work study, quality control, value engineering, codification, standardization etc.

For manufacturing firm 80% is the cost of the material and 20% is the labour cost and administration cost. Reduction of cost of material is easier as compared to reduction in cost of staff. We are purchasing material worth of Rs. 6230 crores for every year. If we can reduce material cost by 5%, there shall be saving up to Rs. 311.5 crores. Carrying cost is 25% per year. If we reduce store balances from Rs. 1,000 crores to Rs. 800 crores there will be reduction in store balances by Rs. 200 crores and there will be saving of Rs. 50 crores inventory carrying charges.

25.1 REDUCTION IN CONSUMPTION

This can be achieved by the following means:

1. By avoiding wastage.
2. By avoiding leakage of consumable item.
3. By increasing life of item like train lighting cell.
4. To save money by change in design.
5. By value analysis.
6. By value engineering.

25.2 INVERSE RELATION BETWEEN WORK AND EFFICIENCY

This can be achieved by following ways:

1. Reduce the number of stock item by variety reduction.
2. Purchase 'C' item at a time for two years consumption.

3. Enter into Rate contract for most of the items.
4. Try to reduce non-stock items.
5. By decentralization.

25.3 INVENTORY CONTROL

Cost of inventory. It consists the following:

1. Cost of material.
2. Ordering cost.
3. Inventory carrying cost.
4. Stock out cost.
5. System cost.

Cost of Material. Cost of material is calculated by multiplying unit cost with the total quantity.

Ordering Cost: This is the cost of placing order. For cash purchase, it is Rs. 40/- per purchase. For Limited tender and WSB it is Rs. 400/- per order. For advertised tender it is Rs. 4000/- per order.

Inventory Carrying Cost: Inventory carrying cost consists of cost of capital/interest/opportunity cost which even higher *i.e.*, percentage of money blocked per year interest @ 15%.

storage cost @	5% to 10% per year
obsolescence	2% to 5% per year
loss	1% to 2% per year
Total	20% to 35%

Inventory Carrying cost average is 25% per year over Indian Railways.

Stock Out Cost. If the item is not available Rs.5000/- is going to be lost due to non-availability of item. The stock out cost is Rs. 5,000/- Working out of stock out cost is very difficult.

System Cost. Inventory control means to device a system by which overall cost should be minimum and optimum.

25.4 FORMULA DERIVATION

We can design a formula by which the sum total of the cost of these costs will be minimum. It is cheaper to have sufficient buffer stock and avoid stock out or to have minimum buffer stock and to have out of stock once in five year.

1. **Economic order quantity formula:**

Let S = Annual requirement

Q = Economic order quantity

C_o = Ordering cost

C_u = Unit cost of each item

C_i = Inventory carrying cost

Total cost = Ordering cost (OC) + Carrying cost (CC) + Cost of material ($S_x C_u$).

$$TC = \frac{S}{Q} \times CO + \frac{Q}{2} \times C_u \times C_i + S \times C_u$$

$$\frac{d(TC)}{dQ} = -\frac{S \times CO}{Q^2} + C_u \times \frac{C_i}{2} + 0 = 0$$

$$\because \quad \frac{S \times CO}{Q^2} = \frac{C_u \times C_i}{2}$$

$$CRQ = \sqrt{\frac{2\,CO \times S}{C_u\, C_i}}$$

(*i*) If we divide Q by monthly consumption figure we shall get number of month (M) for which order should by placed on number of month for which quantity should be dispatched at a time.

(*ii*) If we divide S by 12 we get monthly consumption = $\frac{S}{12}$ and by dividing Q by $\frac{S}{12}$ we get number of month (M) for which order should be placed at a time *i.e.*,

$$M = \frac{Q}{S/12} = \frac{12Q}{S} = \frac{12}{S} \times \sqrt{\frac{2\cos}{C_u C_i}}$$

$$= \sqrt{\frac{288 \times CO \times S}{S^2 \times C_u C_i}}$$

$$= \sqrt{\frac{288 \times CO}{S \times C_u \times C_i}} = \sqrt{\frac{288 \times CO}{S^2 \times C_i}}$$

Whereas $S^2 = S \times C_u$ = Value of annual amount of the item.

$$M = \sqrt{\frac{288 \times CO}{S^1 \times C_i}}$$

$$\therefore \quad M^2 = \frac{288 \times CO}{S^1 \times C_i}$$

$$\therefore \quad S^1 = \frac{288 \times CO}{M^2 \times C_i}$$

Assuming C_o = Rs. 400 per order and C_i = 25% and subsitute 1,2, 3, and so on for M. we calculate annual consumption for which order should be placed for one month requirement two month requirement and so on at a time.

$$M = 1 \text{ Month } S^1 = \frac{288 \times 400}{1 \times 0.25} = \text{Rs. } 4{,}60{,}800/-$$

$$M = 2 \text{ Months } S^1 = \frac{286 \times 400}{4 \times 0.25} = \text{Rs. } 1{,}15{,}200/-$$

$$M = 3 \text{ Months } S^1 = \frac{288 \times 400}{9 \times 0.25} = \text{Rs. } 51{,}200/-$$

$$M = 4 \text{ Months } S^1 = \frac{288 \times 400}{16 \times 0.25} = \text{Rs. } 28,800/-$$

$$M = 5 \text{ Months } S^1 = \frac{288 \times 400}{25 \times 0.25} = \text{Rs. } 18,400/-$$

$$M = 6 \text{ Months } S^1 = \frac{288 \times 400}{36 \times 0.25} = \text{Rs. } 12,800/-$$

$$M = 7 \text{ Months } S^1 = \frac{288 \times 400}{49 \times 0.25} = \text{Rs. } 9,420/-$$

$$M = 8 \text{ Months } S^1 = \frac{288 \times 400}{64 \times 0.25} = \text{Rs. } 7,200/-$$

$$M = 9 \text{ Months } S^1 = \frac{288 \times 400}{81 \times 0.25} = \text{Rs. } 5,600/-$$

$$M = 12 \text{ Months } S^1 = \frac{288 \times 400}{144 \times 0.25} = \text{Rs. } 3,200/-$$

$$M = 18 \text{ Months } S^1 = \frac{288 \times 400}{18^2 \times 0.25} = \text{Rs. } 1,420/-$$

$$M = 24 \text{ Months } S^1 = \frac{288 \times 400}{24^2 \times 0.25} = \text{Rs. } 800/-$$

(*iii*) For open tender CO = Rs. 4,000/- per order.

$$M = 1 \text{ Month } S^1 = \frac{288 \times 4000}{1 \times 0.25} = \text{Rs. } 46,08,000/-$$

$$M = 2 \text{ Months } S^1 = \frac{288 \times 4000}{4 \times 0.25} = \text{Rs. } 11,52,000/-$$

$$M = 3 \text{ Months } S^1 = \frac{288 \times 4000}{9 \times 0.25} = \text{Rs. } 5,12,000/-$$

$$M = 4 \text{ Months } S^1 = \frac{288 \times 4000}{25 \times 0.25} = \text{Rs. } 2,88,000/-$$

$$M = 5 \text{ Months } S^1 = \frac{288 \times 4000}{25 \times 0.25} = \text{Rs. } 1,84,000/-$$

$$M = 6 \text{ Months } S^1 = \frac{288 \times 4000}{36 \times 0.25} = \text{Rs. } 1,28,000/-$$

$$M = 7 \text{ Months } S^1 = \frac{288 \times 4000}{49 \times 0.25} = \text{Rs. } 94,200/-$$

$$M = 8 \text{ Months } S^1 = \frac{288 \times 4000}{64 \times 0.25} = \text{Rs. } 72{,}000/-$$

$$M = 9 \text{ Months } S^1 = \frac{288 \times 4000}{81 \times 0.25} = \text{Rs. } 56{,}000/-$$

$$M = 12 \text{ Months } S^1 = \frac{288 \times 4000}{144 \times 0.25} = \text{Rs. } 32{,}000/-$$

$$M = 18 \text{ Months } S^1 = \frac{288 \times 4000}{18^2 \times 0.25} = \text{Rs. } 14{,}200/-$$

$$M = 24 \text{ Months } S^1 = \frac{288 \times 4000}{(24)^2 \times 0.25} = \text{Rs. } 8{,}000/-$$

If the deliveries are phased as per above norms it shall be effective to control store balances and to improve turnover ratio considerably.

25.5 CONTROLLING OF TURNOVER RATIO

By classifying items as A, B, C category.

A Category item are 10% in number and 70% in value.

B Category item are 20% in number and 20% in value.

C Category item are 70% in number and 10% in value.

1. If we phase the delivery of A category item by every 3 month we shall get 4 installments in a year. Therefore, each time the value will be $\frac{70\%}{4} = 18\%$

   Approximately average inventory will be 9%.
2. If we phase delivery of B item by every 6 month we will get 10% of total value in every 6 month and average inventory of B item will be 5%.
3. If we phase delivery of C item every 6 month we will get at a time 5% of total value and average inventory will be 2.5%.
4. From the above, the total value inventory balance will be 9% + 5% + 2.5% = 16.5%.

   By the above method we can achieve turnover ratio 16.5%.

CHAPTER

26

STORES DEPOTS-RECEIPT AND CUSTODY OF STORES

26.1 ORGANISATION OF THE STORES DEPOT

1. **The Depot Officer.** Each stores depot of any importance should be under the supervision of Gazetted Officer of the Stores Department directly subordinate to the Controller of Stores. He is referred to in these rules as the "Depot Officer". He is responsible to the Controller of Stores for the efficient maintenance of stocks of stores, for the prompt service of the territory served by his depot, for the safe custody of the stores in stock, for correct tally of such stock at any time with the balances as shown in the ledgers, for the correct preparation and posting of all initial documents, ledgers, bin cards and subsidiary registers, for the submission of the relevant vouchers and documents to the Accounts Officer on Prescribed dates and for the disposals of surplus and scrap stores.
2. **Wards and Section.** The work of a Stores Depot consists of:
   (*a*) Receipt and inspection of stores.
   (*b*) Storage and issue of materials.
   (*c*) Despatch of materials.
   (*d*) Maintenance of "numerical" ledgers/bin cards.
   (*e*) Recoupment of stocks.
   (*f*) Disposal of surplus stores and scrap materials.
3. **The Receipt Section.** This section which should deal with all the documents relating to the stores and materials coming into the depot should be independent of the ward and other sections of the depot; a Yard Foreman or Supervisor should work under the control of this section to deal with the actual receipt of the materials.
4. **The Despatch Section.** This section which should deal with despatch from the depot of all stores and materials outside the depot should also be an independent unit. Material trains and stores vans will be controlled by this section.

5. **The Ledger Section.** The clerical work of the depot relating to stocks of material is best centralized in a Ledger section where all the stock cards of the depot will be maintained up-to-date. This section should be divided into sub-sections, each sub-section dealing with the numerical accounting and recoupment of stocks of the some classes of stores as are dealt with in the corresponding wards. A separate sub-section should deal with the receipt and registration of the requisitions placed by indentors on the depot, (where, on any railway, the stock cards are maintained by each ward for the classes of stores stocked therein, the procedure for the posting of the stock cards and the recoupment of stocks will be the same in all essentials, the vouchers being passed on to the numerical ledger posters direct instead of to a separate ledger section. The Requisition Register, however, should be maintained in the depot's central office.
6. **Surplus and Scrap Section.** This section should deal with the receipt, classification, stocking and arrangements for sale of all scrap, whether received from the line or otherwise accumulated in the depot. This section should also deal with all the work involved in the disposal of surplus stores on the lines.
7. **Duties of Assistant Depot Officer.** His duties should be specified in each case by the Controller of Stores or by the Depot officer. In the absence of the Depot officer, the Assistant officer will be responsible for all the duties prescribed for the former official.
8. **Duties of Depot Store- keeper.** Depending on the section he is placed incharge of, the Depot Store-keeper shall be responsible for the discharge of the relevant items among the list of duties shown below:
   (*i*) All correspondence by wards with departments will pass through the Depot store-keeper, who will put them up to the Depot officer, if necessary.
   (*ii*) The Depot Store-keeper will deal with all correspondence regarding stock verification reports.
   (*iii*) He will check recoupments, figures of consumption, and maxima and minima shown in the stock cards.
   (*iv*) He will attend to complaints regarding shortages and delay in supplies, and bring all serious complaints to the notice of the Depot officer.
   (*v*) He will see that every convenience is placed at the disposal of the Accounts Stock Verifier for accurate and speedy verification of stocks and that store department witnesses attend and varry out their functions properly.
   (*vi*) He will check the figures of stock and consumption shown by wards on Annual Contract Statements.
   (*vii*) He will make surprise checks of packages by opening them and comparing the contents with the corresponding issue notes, and will initial the record copy of the issue notes so checked.
   (*viii*) He will surprise generally that material is properly handed over to the Despatch section, and that material is properly packed, whether packed by the ward or the Despatch section.
   (*ix*) He will maintain general supervision over the wards, and see that material is properly stocked and looked after and kept in the correct bins and shelves.
   (*x*) He will have under his direct control the registration of requisitions and their distribution towards.

(*xi*) He will allot the duties of the clerical relieving staff of the depot.

(*xii*) He will see that shunting operations are properly carried out in the yard, and that wagons are put in their proper places and to time.

(*xiii*) He will maintain an inward and outward Wagon registers and will examine every loaded wagon to see that the contents are properly loaded, occasionally checking in detail the contents of wagons leaving the Yard.

(*xiv*) He will personally check, with the Wagon registers, the authority for removal of wagons and the weekly statement sent by the Traffic department of the wagons sent to, and received from, the Yard. In the event of any discrepancy, he will immediately report it to the Depot officer, for investigation.

(*xv*) He will pay surprise visits at night to the stores yard, and see that the chowkidari staff are alert and at their posts.

(*xvi*) He will maintain an inventory of all articles of dead stock, viz, plant, machinery, furniture, tools, instruments etc., at each depot in Inventory books maintained separately for each depot.

(*xvii*) He will prepare indents for consumable stores and tools and plant required by the depots, and will put them up to the Depot officer for signature.

9. **Duties of other Subordinate Staff.** The duties of the Depot Store keepers Grade III(in direct charge of materials) and other subordinate staff shall be laid down in manuals of instructions issued for each depot detailing the duties of the staff and laying down subsidiary and local procedure for the running of the depot.
10. **Security Deposit by the Staff in Custody of Stores.** The General Manager, in consultation with the Chief Accounts Officer, should fix scales of security deposits to be made by the staff in custody of stores. A schedule of such staff should be prepared and the custody of stores should in no circumstances be placed under any staff other than those who have furnished such securities. In fixing the scale of securities, the maximum money value of stores to be held by the subordinates concerned should be taken into consideration. This does not preclude the holding of excess stocks for temporary periods, but if it is estimated that such excess will continue for more than six months, steps should be taken to place the stores under the charge of a subordinate of appropriate status.

26.2 RECEIPT SECTION PROCEDURE

1. **The Yard Foreman.** Materials arrive in a stores depot in fully loaded railway wagons, in stores vans, as "smalls" whether through parcel or goods, trains, in lorries and carts or carried by coolies; or from the adjacent workshops in trolleys, Lister Trucks & Co. The receipt of the actual stores themselves should be in the charge of a Yard Foreman or other official who should arrange for the weighment of all wagons, trolleys, trucks, lorries carts, & *c*., both when they are fully loaded, and later on after the stores have been unloaded. He should arrange for the unloading of the material, taking care to see that each consignment or part of a consignment is linked with any forwarding documents which may accompany the material or which may have been handed over to him already by the Receipt section.
2. **The "Receipt Shed".** All materials received in the depot should be generally stacked properly in a "Receipt Shed" and should on no account be mixed up with existing stock of stores in the depot. As an exception to the above, only heavy items of stores and large consignments of ferrous scrap may be unloaded on the spot intended for stocking such materials, provided that

the ward-keeper responsible for the stocking of such items witnesses the unloading and acknowledges the receipt of the correct quantity of material.

3. **The Weighment Register.** The materials received by the Yard Foreman should be entered daily in a register which should show the following particulars:
   (*i*) Date of receipt.
   (*ii*) Wagon or cart or lorry, and c., number.
   (*iii*) Railway receipt number and date.
   (*iv*) Receipt note or any other forwarding document number and date.
   (*v*) Station received from.
   (*vi*) Name and designation of consignor.
   (*vii*) Description of material.
   (*viii*) Gross weight of wagon.
   (*ix*) Tare of wagon (actual).
   (*x*) Tare as stated on the wagon.
   (*xi*) Difference between (*viii*) and (*ix*) and initials of tally clerk.
   (*xii*) Initials of Yard Foreman.
   (*xiii*) Remarks
   (*xiv*) Date put into stock.

   This register will also serve as the Inward Wagon Register.

4. **Materials Received without Documents.** Whenever any material is received without the accompanying documents, the yard Foreman should enter all relevant details in the Wagon Register and immediately report such cases with full details to the Receipts Section and obtain the papers, if they are in that section. If they have not been received from the parties concerned the Receipt Section should enter such cases with full particulars, as far as available, from the Railway receipts in a manuscript register and if the documents are not received within three days from the receipt of the material, a letter should be addressed to the party concerned calling for the documents, copy of such letters being sent to his immediate superiors and district or divisional officer. The cases should be pursued till the documents are received and the stores are properly disposed off or if there is delay of over a month or if material is to be issued urgently or the party sending the material cannot be traced, the stores should be taken into stock by credit to stock Adjustment account.

5. **Receipt Documents and Records.** Stores are received in a depot through the following sources:
   (*i*) (*a*) *Indigenous Purchases.* In case the original receipt and inspection of stores from the firms are centralized in one station, the Inspecting and Receiving officer will issue the Receipt note and forward the relevant foils to the stores depot concerned. In other cases, the Receipt section of the depot receiving the material from the firm will issue the necessary Receipt note. In certain cases as when stores are obtained from the National Instruments (Private) Ltd., or the Controller of Printing and Stationary, the supplies will be supported by the forms of the department making the supply.

   (*b*) *Import.* Such stores will be supported by Advices of Despatch prepared by officer landing the stores.

   (*ii*) *Manufactures from Workshops.* The workshops send the materials under "Material supplied to Stores Form".

(iii) *Returned Stores.* These will be received on Advice Notes of Returned Stores from the several departments of the Railway.

(iv) *Depot Transfers.* These will be received on the special issue notes for such transactions.

(v) Sale / Loan of stores from other railways, & c.

(vi) Materials sent by departments to depot attached to workshops, not for stock, but for transmission to the shops for repair & c.

(vii) Sample received from firms.

(viii) Returnable empties (optionally or otherwise).

6. **Receipt Register.** All the documents covering the several kinds of receipts mentioned above and railway receipts in their connection should be received in the Receipts section. Separate register should be opened to record the particulars of each kind of document and to watch for the receipt of the materials. The registers in should show the following particulars:

(i) Serial number.

(ii) Date of receipt of the vouchers.

(iii) Number and date of voucher.

(iv) Consignor.

(v) Station

(vi) Particulars of material.

(vii) Reference to railway receipt.

(viii) Date of receipt of material.

(ix) Date of sending material of ward for stock.

(x) Alphabetical letter index of ward

(xi) Receipt order number and date (to be assigned by ward-keeper).

(xii) Initials of ward-keeper in acknowledgement of material.

When the material has been properly received, checked and inspected, it should be sent without any delay along with the relevant documents and the Receipt Register to the ward where the material should be stocked. The Depot Store-keeper grade III in charge of materials will sign the register in acknowledgment of the stores, assign the Receipt Order Number at the same time and return to the Receipt section all except the ledger foils of the vouchers after signing them, as required by each kind of form. On receipt of the vouchers from the wards, the Receipt section should retain the foil intended for record in the depot and dispose of other foils as prescribed for each kind of form. At the end of the month, record foils should be sent to the record room of the depot office.

The Receipt registers should be inspected by the Depot officer once a fortnight to see that there is no avoidable delay between the receipt of the material in the depot and its accoutal in the depot ledgers and that materials are not allowed to lie in the receipts shed, indefinitely.

7. **Samples.** Samples received from firms should be properly labelled and, after they have been considered and orders placed, they should be stored for comparison with the supply when received. When the quantity of stores ordered on the sample has been fully supplied, (the lable on the sample should quote the date when the supply is contracted to be completed in full) the samples should be returned to the firms if such is the arrangement, and if not, the same should be taken into stock by credit to the Stock Adjustment Account.

8. **Stores on Loan from other Railways.** When due to delay in receipt of stores on order or for other reasons, materials are obtained on loan from other railways, the receipt of such stores should be accounted for on the usual purchase returns , the forms being prominently marked 'Suspense Receipt' The depot receiving the material should keep a record of the receipt in a manuscript register kept by the depot store keeper grade III in charge of materials concerned to enable him to arrange for the return of the loan as soon as the stores on order for the railway are received. The receipt should be credited in the Accounts Office to the head "Deposit Miscellaneous Accounts". The rate of the last stock in the priced ledgers of the Railway may be adopted for the transaction, and, if there was no stock previously, the Depot Officer should give an approximate rate. No debit will be raised by the lending railway. When the material is returned, ordinary issue notes should be prepared and allocated to debit of "Deposits Miscellaneous Account" Reference to the Original Receipt Note should be quoted on the issue note. The issue note should be priced at the same rate as the original receipt However, inter railway sale should preferably by made instead of loan and final accountal done for sale and receipt of such materials.
9. **Miscellaneous Receipts.** A Stores depot receives occasionally materials which are not included in the categories of stores. For instance, when stores have been sent by a store van, a departmental subordinate occasionally refuses to take delivery of the material, due to its not being in accordance with his requisition. In such cases, the van clerk brings back the material with the issue notes. The Receipt section should maintain a manuscript register for such items and after entering the details of such rejected stores in the same should send the issue notes and the material to the ward concerned to prepare a write back issue note, and put the stores into stock. The Receipt section should watch from the register that the minus issue not is actually prepared and sent to the Accounts office for accountal. But when such incorrectly issued stores have been sent through the usual services of the railway, or when an indentor finds that certain material he had asked for is not required subsequently but has been sent by the depot before he could cancel his requisition he should invariably receive the materials except when sent through a store van and later return them through proper Advice Note of Returned Stores.
10. **Monthly Inspection of Receipts Section by Accounts Stock Verifier.** The Receipt Registers maintained in the Receipt section, the Weighment register and the delivery sheets of van clerks should be inspected once a month by an Accounts Stock Verifier attached to the depot and any cases of inordinate delays in the accountal of material received in the depot, as well as cases in which materials have not been received within a reasonable time after the receipt of the relevant documents should be taken up with parties concerned. Particular attention should be paid to cases in which the materials have been received in advance of documents and all such cases pursued to see that the materials are taken into stock either by credit to the department concerned, or by credit to Stock Adjustment Account.
11. **"Short Receipts" and receipt of "Wrong Stores".** In the case of short receipt of material tendered by the firms direct to the depot, the Receipt Note should be issued only for the correct quantity. In the case of purchased stores which have been received from the firms by a centralised inspection and receipts branch and later distributed by the Stores department.

    Depot transfers should be accepted for the quantities as stated in the issue notes and the shortages taken up with the sending depot and the Traffic Department, if necessary. A manuscript register similar to the one mentioned for discrepancies in receipt of purchases should be maintained by the ward concerned to account for the shortages in stock. If, however, material different to the description in the issue note is received, the stores should be accounted for according to the correct description, and the matter taken up with the sending depot for any adjustment of the price of the same. The material should not be ordinarily returned to the sending depot unless it is not likely to be of use in the receiving depot, or the other depot calls for the return of the same. When the materials are returned, the transaction should be considered a new one and fresh depot transfer documents prepared.

26.3 WARD PROCEDURE—ORGANISATION, RECEIPT AND STORAGE OF STORES

1. **Wards.** The stores and materials stored in stores depots should be distributed among different wards, each ward containing material of one or more classes of stores. The wards may be distinguished by alphabetical letters for facility of reference. Each ward or a group of wards may be placed under the charge of a Depot Store-keeper with one or more lower grade Depot Store-keepers and Depot Store-keepers Grade III incharge of materials to assist him.
2. **Duties of Depot Store-Keeper III.** The lower grade depot store-keeper III incharge of materials will be responsible to the Deport Store-keeper for the safe custody of all the stores and materials in his ward, and for carrying out the work in connection with all items or groups of stores in his section or any other instructions designed for the purpose of ensuring the safety of the stores in the wards as may be issued by the Controller of Stores. Work in the wards should be confined to the physical receipt (from the Receipt section), the Storage and issue of materials. Except for the preparation of issue notes, or other documents for transfer and departmental verification of materials, the wards should, wherever possible, have no other clerical duties and the Depot stores-keeper incharge of materials and his staff should devote their undivided attention to the care of the materials; and their correct numerical receipt and issue.
3. **General Rules for Closing and Opening the Wards.** Depot Stores-keeper Grade III incharge of materials should see before closing their wards that all lockers and strong rooms containing valuable material are properly locked, and that no one is left in the wards. They should personally see the closing and locking up of their wards, after which a naik or chowkidar should go round and examine all locks and windows to see that all are securely fastened.

   The keys of the wards should be locked in a despatch box, the key, of it being tied to the handle and sent to the Time-Office, where the despatch boxes should be collected by the Time -keeper and locked in a safe. The duplicate keys of locks of the wards should be kept in a despatch box and locked in the Depot Officer's safe.

   One master key for all wards and the Depot Store-Keeper's office should be kept in a glass covered case in the Time -keeper's office for emergency use or in case of fire. The key of the glass box should be deposited in the time keeper's safe. The key of the safe should be locked in a glass covered case provided in the Time -keeper's office, This should be done by the Time-keeper or his Assistant, and the key of the glass box containing the key of his safe handed over to the Depot Store-keeper.

   A Key Register should be maintained showing the time the keys are received in the morning and returned at the closing hour. Each Depot Store-keeper grade III incharge of materials or the clerk he details will remove the despatch box personally from the Time Office and initial the Key register. He will return this box to the time-keeper on closing the ward and see the time-keeper signs the register as an acknowledgement.

The time-keeper will open and close the safe, and he or his assistant must remain in his office until all keys are received and locked in safe.

The same procedure should be observed for important keys other than keys of the ward.

Each depot Store-keeper grade III incharge of materials should detail a clerk in turn for a period of one week to receive the keys and open the ward. This clerk should attend early so that material from the Receipt section may be removed early and the ward may be swept and cleaned by the time all the clerks come in.

4. **Custody of Stores and Protection.** It shall be the particular duty of the Depot Store-keeper and his staff to take proper precautions for the protection of stores and materials against deterioration and loss. Valuable stores and fittings, and materials which are of common household use and are, therefore, likely to be liable to pilferage should be kept in locked sheds and bins special attention should be given to the care of inflammable materials, like polyster and cotton fabrics, rubber and plastic goods, charcoal timber, hemp petroleum products etc.
5. **Chowkidari Staff.** Proper security staff should be maintained for watch and ward work of the depot. Usually contingent of Railway Protection Force shall be provided for maintaining watch at the depot gate and for carrying out patrolling etc., as required. In cases, however, where R.P.F. staff is not provided, a proper chowkidari staff should be maintained. Chowkidari staff should as far as possible be recruited from Army and police pensioners, who have been passed as physically fit by the Railway's medical officer. The chowkidari staff should always wear the Railway's uniform when on duty.
6. **Hours of Duty.** The hours of duty should be so arranged that they comply with the Hours of Employment Act and Rules. A roster showing the hours of duty, should be prepared for each depot and kept handy inspection.
7. **Night Shifts and Patrols.** For the night shifts, posts should be arranged round the yard, and the members of the shift should have each in turn a portion of the time allotted to them for going round the posts. These posts should be so arranged that the RPF staff/chowkidars visiting them will see all the principal parts of the Yard. While making their rounds, the RPF staff/chowkidars should examine all locks on doors, gates, godowns, wards &c., and report any suspicious occurrence to the Head Rakshak/watchman on duty. The Depot Store-keeper should instruct the chowkidars wherever provided each day at what times they should commence their rounds the following night, which times should vary from day to day. The Head rakshak/watchman on duty, in both day and night shifts, should make a surprise patrol inspection of the yard, and see that all watchmen are at their posts, awake and alert.
8. **Duties of Chowkidars.** (*i*) RPF staff/chowkidars should not on any account leave their posts until they have been properly relieved. Nor should they smoke or idly converse with anyone whilst on duty.

   (*ii*) They should prevent all unauthorized persons from entering the stores premises and personally satisfy themselves that persons so entering have a bonafide reason for doing so. No outsiders, with the exception of merchants on business or men delivering stores, or railway staff on duty, office peons and conservancy staff, should be allowed in the Yard. In the event of anyone wishing to see any member of the depot staff, the interview should take place in the Time Keeper's office, after a note has been sent to the person concerned.

Merchants and their delivery staff should not be allowed to wander aimlessly about the yard, nor should they be allowed into any ward or where their business does not carry them. They should not be allowed into the General office to see or get into communication with any of the clerical staff, the only exceptions being that they may interview the Sample clerk, with the sole purpose of delivering or taking delivery of their samples, and the Tender clerk, for handing over tender, inspecting tender samples & c, or the Depot officer or his Assistant.

RPF staff/Chowkidars should pay particular attention to all material passing out of the stores depot, whether by carts, lorries gharries, motors & c., or carried by any person and should detain the conveyance or persons, at once informing the Time-keeper, or Gate Sergent, if any, who will examine as much of the material as possible with its accompanying documents, taking care not cause any more delay then is absolutely necessary.

9. **Fire Conservancy.** The RPF staff/chowkidars, wherever provided and the Ward staff should as far as possible be trained in fire drill and imparted thorough knowledge of the fire appliances and what to do in case of a fire. Their efficiency should also be periodically tested by trial fire alarms and mock fire fightings. Sufficient and easily accessible fire protection apparatus and fittings such as chemical fire extinguishers, water and sand buckets, water hydrants, hose pipes and portable water pumps should be provided in the stores depots. Particular attention should be paid to the location of stocks of wooden work, charcoal, hemp, oil, petroleum products, polyster and cotton fabrics, rubber and plastic products & c., with particular precautions against spontaneous combustion of material.
10. **Stacking of Materials.** The location and the method of stacking material should ensure that stocks could be worked off in the order of their priority of receipt in the depot, and admit of full advantage being taken of all mechanical facilities of stacking, removal and transport of material thereby reducing any manual about to be employed in such work.
11. **Unit Pilling.** In order to enable the compact stocking of material and to allow of the existing stock at any time to be ascertained at a glance, a system of stocking the stores so many deep to a row and so many rows to a layer of the stores, or in cases of small items, a system of packing in bags uniform quantities of items in convenient weights of number based on average quantities for one issue should be adopted. In addition, wherever practicable, graduation marks should be painted on bins to show certain previously ascertained quantities which would enable a busy depot store-keeper grade III incharge of materials to know at a glance the approximate stocks in his custody and assist him in taking steps prompt recoupment.
12. **Handling of Materials.** The loading, unloading, stacking and other movements of materials should be made under the supervision of a responsible subordinate in order to ensure that materials are not damaged in the process, and to see that labour staff are not involved in accidents through clumsy handling and disregard of the precautions prescribed to be taken when handling heavy material. Certain percentage of the yard and ward staff should be trained in rendering first aid in case of accidents and suitable number of first aid kits should be provided in the received in a ward, it is necessary to assign a separate series of numbers in the ward to the receipt vouchers. Such numbers shall be called Receipt Order Numbers (R.O.Nos.). This number should be a separate serial for each class of material in a ward and in each class there should be a separate serial for each kind of vouchers shown above. The ward

index letters should be shown as a prefix to the numbers. The series may commence from unit each month or half-yearly or annually as may be fixed by the Controller of Stores. The Stores Accounts Officer should be advised of the serial numbers adopted in the depot and no change should be made in any period for which the serial has been designed.

13. **Forwarding Memo of Vouchers.** Each Depot Store-keeper Grade III incharge of materials should maintain separate books of forwarding memos for each kind of receipt vouchers. The forwarding memo shown below, and should be prepared in quadruplicate. One copy will be retained in the ward. The other three copies along with the receipt vouchers should be sent to the Ledger Section of the depot. The vouchers should be checked with the memo in the section and one copy of the memo duly receipted for the correct receipt of the vouchers should be returned to the ward where it should be filed with the office copy.

Forwarding Memo of Receipt/ Issue Vouchers for.......................(date)..............................

Ward Index letter.......................................Class...

R.O. No.	*Voucher No.*	*Date*	*R.O. No.*	*Voucher No.*	*Date*

After the material has been checked and placed in the bin, the ward-keeper should give the R.O. number on the receipt vouchers (all foils) and enter the same in the forwarding memo at the same time. The foils intended to the sent to the Ledger section should be retained and the other foils returned to the Receipt section for disposal. The R.O. number should be entered by the depot store-keeper grade-III incharge of material in the Receipt Register of the Receipt Section when he signs the same in acknowledgement of the material.

14. **Packing Materials.** Any packing material which has not been separately charged for by the firm and has not to be brought to account under any procedure relating to empties should be promptly taken into stock under suitable headings by credit to the stock Adjustment Account. The stock verification sheet should be used for this purpose and remark relating to the transaction made on the form to distinguish it from proper verification sheet.

15. **Book Transfer Returns.** These Should be prepared in duplicate to transfer stocks from one price list number to another. One copy is retained as office copy in the ward, the other being sent to the Ledger Section as usual. The form shwon below should be used in such cases. These should be treated as receipt vouchers, the transaction under the price list number from where the material is transferred being treated as a minus receipt. The depot store-keeper grade-III incharge of materials, will be responsible to see that there exists the sanction of proper authority for the transfer; the reference to the sanction for such transfer should be shown on the voucher alongwith the brief and clear reasons for the transfer. All such transfer vouchers should be signed by a Gazetted officer.

BOOK TRANSFER FORM

The undermoted transfer of material is made on...

Particulars of P.L. Number transferred from	*Particulars of P.L. Number transferred to*	*Authority for transfer and Remarks*
DP/PL' Catg/ Description Qty. Unit Rate Value WD	*DP/PL' Catg/ Description Qty. Unit Rate Value WD*	Closing Balance

Debit/Credit to Stock Adjustment Account Part..is Rs.................................

Depot store-keeper incharge of material **Depot Store-keeper**

Date.................................. Date...Depot Officer

16. **Departmental Stock Verification Sheets.** These should be prepared in triplicate by the person making the verification and should be signed by a Gazzetted officer of the Stores department. One copy should be retained as the office copy and the other two sent to the Ledger section with a forwarding memo as usual. In cases, where there are no discrepancies in stock, no stock verification sheet need be prepared.

CHAPTER

27

STORES DEPOTS-ISSUE OF STORES

27.1 REQUISITION FOR STORES

All issues should be made on written requisition submitted on the prescribed form by the 6indenting parties, or where any issues are made on the orders of the Depot Officer or the Controller of Stores, such orders should be given in writing.

1. The rule for general use of railways, a combined form of requisition and issue note. Where, for any special reasons, such forms are not founa suitable, separate forms for requisition as shown below may be used.

Form No. Stores 1302

REQUISITION FOR STORES

Requisition on the ....Depot for articles required for the use of.................

Class and P.L. No.	Description of Stores	Unit	Quantity No. Weight	Chargeable to	To be forwarded by, and delivered to	Remarks	Reference to issue note under which which stores are supplied
1	2	3	4	5	6	7	8

Countersigning Authority

....
Signature and designation of Indenting officer

Date..

Station.......................................

Date..

Station.......................................

2. The above form should be prepared in duplicate, one copy being retained as office copy and other forwarded through the district or divisional officer to the stores depot. A stores depot is generally divided into self-contained and distinct wards and such divisions should be intimated to divisional and branch officers, who should prepare requisitions separately for each ward. Unless otherwise stated in any part of this code, requisitions should be made out on the basis of "one item, one form".

27.2 NOMENCLATURE, PRICE LIST NUMBER AND UNIT

1. In preparing requisitions, the nomenclature price list number and unit of the published price list of the railway should be rigidly adhered to, and indenting officers should be careful to fill up correctly the entries in the column "chargeable to", as this information forms the basis of the allocation of the value of the stores supplied. It is not always practicable in the case of items of stores, the units of which have to be expressed in terms of weight measures, for the indenting officer to state his requirements by weight. Requisitions stating numbers required should, therefore, be complied with, but the issue note should record the issue by weight with a note to the following effect;

   "Equivalent of X (number) indented for"

   Indenting officers should not indent for costly articles by numbers when the prescribed unit is by weight.
2. Unless otherwise stated in any portion of this Code, all requisitions should be signed by a gazetted officer of the department requisitioning the stores and this signature shall be taken to mean in addition to the approval to the issue of the stores, that funds to cover the probable cost of the stores are available.
3. Stores should not be requisitioned for unless funds are available to meet the cost. The only permissible exceptions to this rule are when stores are required for:
   (*i*) works urgently necessary to safeguard life or property, or to repair damage to the line caused by flood, accident or other unforeseen contingency in order to restore or to maintain, through communication; or
   (*ii*) work to meet the immediate needs of traffic which are considered by the General Manager or other officers to whom such powers are delegated by him, so urgent that they must be started before the earliest date by which detailed estimates could be prepared and sanction for funds obtained.

27.3 REQUISITION REGISTER

Each depot should maintain a separate Requisition register for each division or district from where requisitions are received, and stores depots adjacent to workshops should in addition keep a separate register for each important shop or group of small shops of the local workshops. These registers should be maintained in the depot office in a sub-section. The date under which the requisition is posted should always be the original date of the requisition. The register should show the following particulars:

1. Receipt serial number
2. Date of requisition
3. Requisition number
4. Indentor
5. Price list number
6. Description of material

7. Quantity
8. Movement of requisition with dates
9. Action taken (issue note reference or details of other action).

The requisition filed on receipt from the indentor, should be registered in the Requisition register and then forwarded to the ward concerned within 24 hours of its receipt in the depot office. When the requisition is fully compiled with, the reference to the issue note should be quoted thereon, and sent to the Requisition register clerks for posting.

27.4 WARD PROCEDURE

1. **Issue of Stores.** The wards should be careful to issue stores expenditiously and exactly as requisitioned for, both as regards specification and quantity. In cases, however, when an article has to be "cut" and the piece left over would not be fit for further issue, the whole piece may be issued though there would thus be small excesses over the quantity requisitioned provided the requisition is for ordinary maintenance and regular repair work and the excess material is likely to be utilized by the department concerned and it has no objection to its issue. The previous consent of the department need not however, be specifically obtained in each case, provided that a general understanding has been arrived at between the department and the stores depot.
2. **Part Supply or No Stock.** In cases, where either only part supply is possible on account of insufficient stock or no stock is available, the ward-keeper should, endeavour to meet the demands of indenting officers from other suitable items in stock. In such cases the indenting officer should be asked to state whether articles of a similar kind will not meet his requirements.
3. **Issue of Second-hand Stores.** Unless it is specified in the requisition that second-hand materials are not required, second-hand materials may be worked off against requisition for new stores without reference to the indentor.

27.5 ISSUE NOTES

1. **The combined Requisition and Issue Notes.** Wherever possible, the requisition and the issue note should be combined into the form of "Requisition and Issue Note" shown below.

REQUISITION AND ISSUE NOTE FORM

Requisition No. 14/M.S/F.............. Placed on.............................Depot.

Date.. By...................................(Indentor)

Price List No.	Class	Part of Drawing	Description	Work Order or Head of Allocation	No.	Quantity Demanded			
						Cwt.	Qr.	Lb.	oz.
1496	Gb.4	...	Steel tool cast round temper C. (1.0 to 1.10) Carbon)]'	60 21	...				

Issued Note		Quantity Issued					Rate	Unit	Value		Closing balance after posting	
No.	Date	No.	Cwt.	qr.	lb.	oz.						
1/964	4-9-05		One	qu	arter	only			Rs.	P.	Entered on stock Card No....	on date......
											Initials of Ledger Poster	

Route	Originator	Approved	Material Received by	Remarks
Sign. Date				Depot Officer / Store-keeper

2. The "Requisition and Issue Note" should be prepared in six foils by the indentor who should not enter any particulars in the lower portion of the form which is reserved for the stores ward making the issue. The block copy should be retained by the indentor as his office copy, the other five copies being forwarded to the Stores depot concerned. These should be received in the Ledger section and after registration passed on to the ward. If the requisition can be fully compiled with at once, the ward-keeper should collect the material and 'lay it out' for later removal by the Despatch section. He should then fill in the lower part of the forms by carbon process; the quantity issued being shown in words as well as in figures.
3. Issue notes form the basis of all charges and it is necessary that they should be neatly and correctly, written out and all details filled in without omission. Particular care should be taken to see that the carbon copies are clear and legible. Wherever the nomenclature has not been correctly given by the indentor (in accordance with the price list) or where a substitute has been issued, the nomenclature and price list number, where necessary, should be written correctly in the issue note portion of the form. The nomenclature, as shown by the indentor, should on no account be overwritten or scored out, so as to make it illegible. If a substitute has been issued, a remark to that effect should be made on the issue note. The copy of the Enquiry note returned by the indentor with his consent should be filled with the depot's office copy of the issue note.
4. **Distribution of the Five Foils of the Requisition and Issue Note.**— As stated, the indentor retains the first foil as his office copy. The other five foils are sent by him to the depot office which passes it on to the ward. After filling in the issue note portion by carbon process on all the five foils the ward-keeper should distribute them as laid down below:
   (*i*) **The second and third foils.** These should be handed over to the Despatch Section along with material. The Despatch Section will pass them on to the stores van clerk, if the material is being sent by the stores van, or send them to the indentor by post along with the Railway Receipt for dispatch of the material. The indentor should retain the second foil and return the third foil through the stores van clerk or by post as an acknowledgement

for the material. This foil should be pasted to the depot's office copy of the issue note (the sixth foil). Any delay in returning this acknowledgement foil of the issue note should be promptly taken up by the Requisition Register Sub-section where the office copy foil (the sixth foil) should be inspected periodically in order to take up such omissions. The Indentor should note on his office copy (the first foil) particulars of the Issue Note No., date quantity actually issued by the depot, & c., and latter forward the second foil to the District or Divisional Officer for check with the fifth foil which will accompany the summary of issues sent by the Stores Accounts Office of the District or Divisional Officer.

(*ii*) **The fourth, fifth and sixth foils.** These should be forwarded by the ward-keeper to the Ledger Section alongwith the forwarding memo of issue notes. The sixth foil should be detached by the Ledger Section and handed over to the Requisition Register clerks for posting the column "action taken" in the Requisition Register and for filling as record later on. The other two foils, (that is, the fourth and fifth) will be sent to the Stores Accounts Office (after the numerical ledgers have been posted) where one copy (the fourth foil) will be used for posting the priced ledgers and later retained as record and the other (the fifth) will be used for preparing a summary of issue along with which it will be sent to the departmental officer for posting there form the debits in his Revenue Abstracts or other book of accounts. This copy will be retained by the departmental officer.

5. It is the duty of the departmental officer to compare the particulars of stores as accepted by the indentor on the second foil of the issue notes with those shown in the firth foil of the issue notes accompanying the summary of issues from the Stores Accounts Office. Any discrepancies in quantities or particulars of the materials should be taken up with the Depot Officer concerned.
6. **Issues to Workshop.** The procedure for issues to adjoining workshops has been laid down in chapter XV. In the case of issues to an "out-station" workshops, *i.e.*, note adacent to the depot, the normal procedure or requisitioning for and issue of stores will apply.
7. **Separate Issue Note Forms.** In circumstances where it is found impracticable to use the combined" Requisition and Issue note" the indentor will make his requisition for stores and the issue note will be prepared in the following form in five copies.

ISSUE NOTE FORM

Depot

No................................... Date..................................

The undermentioned stores are forwarded to.............................through or by.............................. in compliance with requisition No............................Dated...

Class & P.L. No.	Description of Stores	Chargeable	Unit	Quantity No. Weight	Rate	Amount	Remarks

DEPOT OFFICER

Received the above in good order

....

Signature & Designation of Receiving Officer

8. **Issue of Consumable Stores.** Each department should prepare a list of items of stores which are considered as consumable stores for different categories of subordinates and departmental officers should fix a monthly scale of consumption for each item of stores for each subordinate working under them. The lists of items and the scale fixed for each subordinate should be intimated to the respective stores depots from which the subordinates are authorised to draw such stores. The fixing of a monthly scale, however, is no authority for the routine monthly issue (without specific requisition) of the quantities shown therein, irrespective of any balances, the subordinate may posses.
9. **Requisition and Issue Note for Consumable Stores.** The subordinate should submit monthly a requisition in the form shown below (signed by himself) on a specified date for the items of consumable stores sanctioned to him. It will be prepared in six copies. It should also show the balances in hand of each item, and the quantities demanded shall not exceed the sanctioned limit, less the balances exhibited in the requisition. The depot should see that a subordinate does not requisition for consumable stores more than once in a month. Items of stores, the sanctioned quantities of which appear from the average consumption of three or more months to be excessive should be reported to departmental officer concerned.
10. **Authority to Sign Issue Notes.** All issues notes, except those debited to suspense, may be signed by the Depot Stores-keeper (wherever he is the store holder) provided the issues have been made on proper requisitions placed on the Stores Department. All other issue notes including the "write back" issue notes should be signed by gazetted officer of the Stores Department.

27.6 SPECIAL PROCEDURE IN CERTAIN KINDS OF ISSUES.

1. **Stores Issued on Loan.** Issue of stores on loan to other railways, should be witnessed by an accounts representative and the relevant issue notes countersigned by him in token of his having done so. They should then be signed by a gazetted officer of the Stores Department. Ordinary issue note Form should be used and allocated to "Miscellaneous Advances Account". No debit will be raised against the borrowing railway. The loan should be entered up in a manuscript register by the ward keeper/ ASKP concerned to enable him to watch the return of the loaned stores. The borrowing railway should be asked, at the time the stores are loaned, to return them by a stipulated date and this date should be entered on the issue note and in the remarks columns of the numerical ledgers/ bin cards. The Account office should take up any case of delay in return of the loaned articles. The issue note should be priced like other returns; when the articles is received back, a minus issue note should be prepared to write back the original debit to "Miscellaneous Advances", and priced at the same rates as the original transaction.

REQUISITION AND ISSUE NOTE FOR CONSUMABLE STORES

Requisition No...............................

Date...

Depot Officer.............................Depot.

Please supply the undermentioned articles of Class.............................in terms of Schedule of Consumable Stores No.............................dated.............................

					To be filled in by the Depot and Account Office				
					Issue Note No.......... Date..........				
1 P.L. No.	2 Sanctioned quantity	3 Balance in hand	4 Quantity demanded	5 Chargeable to	6 Quantity issue	7 Unit	8 Rate	9 Value	10 Closing balance after posting Numerical Leger

Indentor.......................... Material received

Date................................ Indentor............................

Station............................ Station.......................... Depot Officer

2. **Stores Issued for Purpose of Fabrication, Re-conditioning or Repair.** The following procedure should be observed in dealing with the issues of materials (including cloth to be made up into uniforms) from stores depots to outside firms or other railways for new manufacture or re-conditioning purposes or other minor repairs or re-adjustments and their receipt back into stores depots from the firms, after the necessary work. The weighment or count and loading of all issues or such matters should be made in the presence of an accounts representative who should sign all copies of the issue note. The depot issuing the materials should prepare issue notes and submit them as usual in duplicate to the stores account office where they will be priced and posted in the priced ledgers in the usual manner. The amount of the issue notes should, however, be debited to "Miscellaneous Advances", mentioning the name of the firm to distinguish the transactions, and credited to "Stores".
3. When the material are returned to the depot by the firm, after the necessary work had been done the depot will acknowledge receipt by preparing the usual receipt notes in which the particulars of the issue notes previously issued in connection with the transactions will be entered. The stores accounts office will enter on the copy of the Receipt Note received from the depot, the cost of the materials originally issued. The charges payable to the firm for the work done, as shown in the receipt note by the depot, together with cost of materials issued to the firm will then be debited to "Stores" by credit to "Miscellaneous Advances Account" mentioning the name of the firm.
4. (*i*) **Issue of Stores as Samples for Test.** As stores and materials are subjected before purchase to certain tests and to inspection, cases of tests of materials in stock should ordinarily arise only when any material is proposed to be used for purpose for which it was not intended at the time or its purchase, or when the material is of such a nature that its prolonged stocking is likely to have deteriorated its original qualities or when the item is "returned store" and its qualities have not been previously ascertained. Requisitions for materials for test should be signed by Divisional railway managers or higher authorities. The Controller of stores, however, may have materials tested on his own authority.

(ii) **Quantities of material to be sent for Chemical and Physical Test.** The quantities to be sent for test should ordinarily be in accordance with specification/ procedure for test.

5. (i) The value of the stores sent for test, other which will not be returned should be debited in the Ffirst instance to "Miscellaneous Advances Account" Materials which can be returned intact should be returned to stores after test, and the original issue written back by minus debit to "Miscellaneous Advances Accounts". If such stores are not returned within a reasonable time, the debit to "Miscellaneous Advances Account" should be written back and final debit raised against the department which drew the stores. The cost of stores consumed or damaged in testing will be debited directly to G.3102. If any damages stores are returned in the form of scrap, their scrap value should be taken in reduction of the debit to G. 3102.

(ii) **Allocation of test charges.** Test charges will be debited as under:

(a) *Test Charges on Stores Obtained for Stock Purposes:* If the material obtained for stock purposes is tested and found suitable the test charges should be borne by the railway. If found unsuitable they should be debits to the firm.

(b) *The Charges on Stores Obtained for Trial Purposes.* In the case of samples called for test by the railway, the test charges should be borne by the railway, irrespective of whether the stores are found suitable for note. If on the other hand, samples are sent by firms or test any request from the railway, the test charges should be debited to the firms, irrespective of whether they are found suitable or not.

27.7 DISPOSAL OF VOUCHERS BY WARDS

1. **Submission of voucher to Ledger Section.** The vouchers for the day accompanied by the forwarding memo (S.1256) should be sent to the Ledger section not later than one hour before the closing time of the office. The wards should, therefore, close all receipt and issue of material in suitable time to enable them to send the vouchers punctually to the office.
2. **Cancelled Issue Notes.** If an issue note is cancelled for any reason, it should not be destroyed, but after necessary endorsement of the remark "cancelled" on the several foils and against the entry of particulars of the issue note should be sent to the Ledger Section where they should be separated from the rest and filed separately group by group. The Accounts office should arrange for the inspection of such foils by a clerk daily. Where the Accounts officer is not located in the same station and premises, the cancelled issue notes should be sent by the Depot officer along with other vouchers to the Accounts officer, where, after due check, they should be filled in chronological order.
3. **Monthly Certificate of Vouchers.** At the end of the month, each ward should furnish a manuscript statement showing the commencing number(R.O.Number in case of receipts) and the closing number of the returns for each class, receipts and issues separately and submit the same to the Ledger section with a certificate endorsed thereon that all the vouchers mentioned therein have been correctly submitted on the proper dates to the Ledger section and that no vouchers relating to the dates of the month under reference are detained in the ward. The Certificate should reach the Ledger section on second of the month following the one to which it relates. It should be prepared in four copies, one being retained as office and the other three being sent to the Ledger section which should return one copy (after due check of the statement) as an acceptance of the correctness of the certificate. The other two foils will be dealt with.

27.8 PENDING DEMANDS

1. **Pending Demands in Depots.** Pending demands are requisitions for supplies which have been received by a depot from indentors on the line, but which the depot has failed to satisfy due to the depot stocks of the stores asked for having been exhausted. When a ward is not able to supply a requisition either in part or in full and can offer no acceptable substitutes, the following procedure may be adopted. The ward should attach to the requisition a printed slip carrying the legend 'NO STOCK' or 'Part Supply Made' In the case of the combined "Requisition and Issue Notes", this slip should be attached to the sixth foil which will finally be the record copy of the depot. The requisition should then be sent to the Ledger section. Partly supplied requisitions should be sent along with the relevant issue note foils, and 'No stock' requisitions should be sent by peon book. On receipt in the Ledger section they should be entered in a 'Pending Demand Sheet' maintained in the following from separately for each price list number.

PENDING DEMAND SHEET

PL.No................ Class.............

Requisition No.	Date	Quantity outstanding	Grand Total	Issue Note No.

2. The Pending Demand Sheets and the requisition forms should be retained in the Ledger Section unit a fresh supply of material is received. In cases of part supply on combined " Requisition and Issue Note" Form, the ledger poster should prepare a new set of forms to cover the balance of material not supplied. When the stock of any item is entirely exhausted, the ledger poster should attach a red slip to the ledger card to indicate this fact. When fresh material is received and this is being posted, the ledger poster should remove the red slip. Whenever he does this, he should see whether there is a pending Demanding Sheet for the item, in which case, the usual procedure of transmission of the requisition to the ward should be followed.
3. **Fortnightly Statement of Pending Requisitions.** The Depot Officer should sent to the Controller of Stores once a fortnight (a copy being forwarded to the Chief Mechanical Engineer and the heads of the loco and carriage and wagon workshops) a statement of pending requisitions in the following form. This statement should also shows the outstanding of the current fortnight as well as the previous fortnight and the increase or decrease in the current period under each column. This statement will furnish the Controller of Stores with such information about the working of the Stores depot, as would enable him to take prompt steps to remedy defects in recoupment of stores.
4. **Department Stock Verification.** As an important "back check" on the correct receipt and issue of stores by the wards, it is necessary to have a to department check to see whether the upto date balance of an item in the ledger agrees with the actual physical stock balance: Such departmental verification to be arranged by the depot officer will be in addition to the Stock Verification arranged by the Accounts department.

The department verification need only cover selected item such as items of large annual consumption having regular and frequent issue, items of heavy intrasic value like non-ferrous items, tool steel, etc., and items of a pilferable nature. A list of selective items may be drawn up and approved by the Controller of store. The verification of physical balances should be done by an official other than the ward-keeper-in-charge of the item of stores. The depot officer may postpone the verification if the balances in stock are so heavy that a verification would involve large shifting of stock and the verification could be carried out conveniently at a later date when stocks are at a low level.

The Depot Officer may waive verification in the following circumstances:

(*a*) Where the item has been verified by the Accounts Department within the last three months.

(*b*) Where the Accounts Verification of the particular class of stores is in progress and the item is likely to be verified within the next two months.

(*c*) Where the item has heavy balance the verification of which involves much labour and handling charges.

A list of items the verification of which has been waived under (*c*) above should be prepared by the depot officer and forwarded to the stores Accounts Officer through the Controller of Stores.

5. **Procedure for Verification.** The officer deputed to verify the stock the of item should take down the opening balance in the ledger on the morning of the date of verification and proceed to verify the stock in the ward. He should note down the particulars of weightment, & c., in a field book and obtain thereon the signature of the ward-keeper concerned in evidence of the correctness of the actual balances of stock entered therein.
6. **Stock Verification Sheets.** If the physical balance or stock agrees with the book balance no stock sheets need be prepared. The official making the verification will merely make an entry in the ledger card/bin card to show that the physical balance agree with the book balances. The entry should be initialed by the official making the entry and the clerk-in-charge of the ledger section.
7. If there be an excess of stock or deficiency in stock, the official should prepare a Departmental Stock Verification Sheet and dispose it.
8. The stock sheet should be given a Receipt Order number in the ward before being passed on to the ledger section of the depot. Wherever, possible the explanations for the discrepancies should be given by the ward-keeper before the stock sheet is put up to the officer for signature, the explanation being shown on all the three copies of the stock sheets. The stock sheets should, however, on no account be detained longer than two days after the date of verification.

27.9 DISPATCH SECTION PROCEDURE

1. The work of dispatching stores is an important function in the matter of the issue of stores and is best centralized in a Dispatch section independent of the wards and of ledger section. This section may be divided into sub-section. Certain groups of stores being allotted to each for dispatch. The men in this section should be properly trained in the knowledge of stores in order to avoid mistakes in despatch. The supervisor of the dispatch section should also be in-charge of the store delivery vans and the staff required for working them.
2. **Register of Dispatches.** The Dispatch Section should maintain a Register of Dispatches to record all the issue notes handed over to the section for dispatch of the stores. This register should show the following particulars:
    1. Date
    2. Issue note number and date

3. Consignee
4. Requisition number and date
5. Description of material and price list number
6. Packing particulars
   - Quantity
   - Packing serial number,
   - Packed in box, package, bag or bundle;
   - Net weight;
7. Credit Note No. and date.
8. Railway Receipt No. and date.
9. Gate Pass or Authority to Remove Wagons number and date.
10. Remarks (wagon number, &c.).

This register should also serve as the Outward Wagon Register.

3. **Credit Notes, etc.** The Dispatch Section will prepare the Credit Notes and make all necessary arrangements for the dispatch of the material. The register of dispatch should be inspected by the Depot Officer once a month to see that there are no delays the between the issue of the material by the ward and the actual dispatch from the depot. Local deliveries of stores may be made directly by the ward unless their dispatch involves special packing and carting by lorry or other vehicle, in which case such stores may be trusted to the Dispatch Section. Motor, lorries, wagon, or stores delivery vans should be loaded in the presence of responsible clerks, who should see that there are vouchers for all material loaded in them.
4. **Surprise Checks.** The Depot Officer should make surprise checks on parcels ready for dispatch and check material packed with the accompanying vouchers.
5. **Gate Passes.** No material may be allowed to go outside the gates unless specified on a Gate Pass or Authority for Removal of Wagons. Gate Passes should be prepared in duplicate by the
6. **Check of Materials with Gate Passes.** All material, except material loaded in lorries passing out of stores premises, should be examined and checked with the Gate Pass by the Gate-Keeper, with the Assistance of the Chowkidars. For material loaded in lorries, a percentage only need checked. The Gate-keeper will also be responsible for seeing that all Gate Passes are correctly made out and that for the materials entered thereon, reference to an issue note or indent or some other letter or voucher is quoted. Gate Passes for material loaded in a lorry should show the number of packages in the lorry, and the total number of vouchers.

   The Gate-keeper should collect all Gate Passes and send them the following day, to the signatories for examination and comparison with the record copy, to see that no alteration subsequent to signing them has been made, and the signatories will them counter-initial the passes, if inorder, and return them to the Gate-keeper for record and file.

   If a Gate Pass has been incorrectly prepared or if the gate staff have any doubt as to its genuineness, the Gate-keeper may call for the vouchers or papers in connection there with, and, if still he is not satisfied, he should, report immediately to the Depot Store-keeper investigations.

   The Gate-keeper should occasionally check parcels with voucher at the gate.

   All Gate passes should be scored across in order to prevent their misuse, and them filed by the Gate-keeper in separate files for each section issuing them. The Gate Pass number and date should be quoted against the entries for the material in the register of dispatch maintained by the dispatch section so that issue notes may be readily connected with Gate Pass.

No wagon may be removed from the Yard unless the Traffic Department is in possession of the authority for removal of wagon.

7. **Traffic Statement of Wagon.** The Traffic Department will submit weekly in duplicate statement of all wagon booked from or place in the stores yard showing the wagon number, date of removal from or placing in yard, consignee, net weight, and brief description of contents Both copies will be sent to the Depot Store-keeper.

   On receipt of this statement, the Yard Forman should compare it with his wagon registers and quote the corresponding issue note number and the weight of material shown thereon against the wagons that have gone out of the yard. Similarly, particulars be shown for wagons received, the information should be tabulated on a slip to be pasted to the Traffic Statement. He should them put it up to the Depot Store-keeper who should personally check 10% of the entries with all connected vouchers. If the Yard Forman notices any discrepancy, he should at once bring it to the notice of the Depot Officer. The statement should them be pasted in a skelton file. The Depot Officer should check these statements once a month.

CHAPTER

28

DEPOT LEDGER

28.1 PROCEDURE IN THE LEDGER SECTION

1. The clerical work of the depot in respect of accountal of stocks should preferably be centralized in a Ledger Section where all the stock cards of the depot should be located. The section should be divided into sub-sections corresponding to one or more wards and each sub-section should deal with the same groups of stores as dealt within the corresponding wards. The section should be separate unit under the supervision of a subordinate independent of the ward organization.
2. **The Stock Cards.** The most convenient arrangement is for the Stock Card wherever maintained manually to be in two parts detachable from each other, one part recording the transactions of each item or stores in the depot, called the Numerical Ledger Card, and the other for recording recoupments, called the Recoupment Card. The cards should be maintained in the forms shown below and kept in cabinets of suitable pattern, facilitating posting and filling A separate card for recoupments has two definite advantages. Firstly, entries concerning recoupments being much fewer than those concerning receipts and issues, the card space provided for the former will be used up much more slowly than that provided for the latter. If one card only were provided for each item, it would have to be divided into columns for recoupment, receipts and issues. The space for recoupment being scarcely used up by the time the spaces for receipts and issues has been completely filled in, and extravagant consumption of cards will result. Secondly, wherever only numerical ledgers are abolished in favour of bin cards or mechanization of transaction records, it permits easy transition without effecting the depots' recoupment records.

NUMERICAL LEDGER CARD

Ward.................

Unit.................... Class................. Main Depot......................

Date	Received from or Issued to	Receipt or issue Voucher No.	Quantity		
			Receipt	Issue	Balance
1	2	3	4	5	6

3. **Opening and Closing of Stock Cards.** No card may be opened for the first time for an item, without the Stores Accounts Officer begin advised on the same date to enable him to open a corresponding priced ledger card in his office. Not more then one card should be maintained for an item at a time, unless there is a difference in quality, such as new, second-hand etc., or it is found necessary by reason of different rates of credit to maintain separate records of stock. A manuscript Advice of New Stock Card From should be prepared in triplicate giving the following information, *viz.*, class price list Number, Nomenclature, Category of Stores, (such as Ordinary, Emergency, Special or Surplus) and ward. The copies of the advice should be sent to the Accounts Officer who will return one copy in token of his approval of a new card being opened. When a depot proposes to close, a card, a similar manuscript Advice From prepared in the same detail should be the Stores Account Office. It should state in addition the number and date of the last voucher posted in the numerical ledger/bin card which is to be closed.
4. **Blank Forms.** The Depot Officer should ensure that blank forms of stock cards are kept in proper custody and that issues of such forms for use are made under the orders of the Supervisor of the Ledger Section who should also initial all such issued cards on the right hand top corner. When reconciling the numerical ledger cards with the priced ledgers and when noting the balances of stock verification the Accounts Staff should see that the cards bear the initials of the Clerk-in-charge of the Ledger Section.
5. **Completed Numerical Ledger Cards.** Particular care should be taken to see that all completed cards are carefully stored chronologically, in the order of price list numbers and are easily available for immediate reference, suitable binders or cabinets being used for this purpose. Suitable binders or cabinets may be kept apart for the purpose in which the cards duly arranged by price list numbers should be placed along with a manuscript list of such cards Form which should show:
    1. P.L. No.
    2. Description of stores
    3. period of posting; commencing and closing Voucher No. and date
    4. Opening balance
    5. Closing balance.

28.2 DUTIES OF THE NUMERICAL LEDGER POSTER

1. He should post the receipt and issue vouchers within twenty-four hours of the dates to which they relate, unless any holiday, happens to intervene. He should also keep the "Reeoupment Cards" of the items in his charge duly posted. He is responsible for the timely placing of a

requisitions and purchase orders in connection with the items in his charge except where ledger posting has been mechanized.

2. **Posting of Numerical Ledgers Cards.** There should be no entry in the ledger card ordinarily without a voucher or the transaction. The ledger card should be posted with great care, neatness being a very important factor. No overwriting should be allowed, and in no circumstances should any entry of transaction be scored out. If by a mischance any entry which should have correctly been made in another card had been written in a particular ledger card, the error should be corrected by a write back entry giving reference to the ledger card in which the entry has been since correctly posted. In only such cases can an entry be made without a supporting voucher. All such correction should be made under the initials of the clerks-in-charge of the Ledger Section.

   As stated the wards send the receipt and issue vouchers along with forwarding memo to the Ledger Section. The vouchers should be carefully checked with the forwarding memo, special care being taken to see that continuity of the numbers is maintained. The receipt of the vouchers should be intimated to the wards by returning one copy of the forwarding memo duly receipted. All vouchers received, other than combined "Requisition and Issue Notes" should be passed on to the respective ledger posters for posting the ledgers. Three foils of the combined "Requisition and Issue Notes" will be received in the Ledger Section along with the forwarding memo. The sixth foil should be detached and handed over to Requisition Register Sub-Section for posting the column "Action Taken" in the Register of Requisition and for filling as record later on. Such foils should be filed separately for each division or shop and according to the dates of the requisition in order to facilitate reference in future. The other two foils should be handed over to the ledger posters. In many cases, the vouchers handed over to the ledger section will be in two foils, *viz*, the Accounts Copy and the Bill Copy, but in no case should be foils be separated. The posting in the numerical ledgers should be made from the copy styled "Accounts Copy" and not from the "Bill Copy" After posting each voucher; the closing quantity balance as appearing in the ledger card should be recorded in the voucher in the case provided for the purpose.

3. **Order of Posting of Vouchers.** The purpose of giving the closing balance after each posting in the ledger is to permit of the corrections of the balance being checked by the Accounts Office when the vouchers are posted in the priced ledgers. This cannot be achieved unless the vouchers are posted in both the sets of ledgers in the same order of sequence. The rule should be observed by the depot that receipt vouchers should be posted in a ledger card prior to the posting of the issue vouchers for the day. In posting the receipt vouchers, the following order of posting should be maintained:

   1. Departmental Stock Verification Sheets
   2. Book Transfers
   3. Purchase Vouchers (including Advice of Dispatch) and their adjustment memo
   4. Workshop Manufacture Receipts
   5. Depot Transfer Receipts
   6. Advice Notes of Returned Stores

In posting issues, the following order should be maintained:

   1. Requisition and Issue Notes
   2. Ordinary Issue Notes
   3. Depot Transfers

In posting the vouchers of each of the categories mentioned above (receipts and issue) the posting should be made in the order of the numbers by the ward. In case of receipts. The R.O. numbers should also be posted in addition to the numbers assigned to the receipts vouchers by the suppliers retuning departments, other departs, or the workshop. It would very much facilitate the posting if the vouchers of each category for the day are arranged in the order of price number.

4. **Posting of Accounts Stock Verification Sheet.** These returns which will be prepared by the Accounts Stock Verifiers will be posted in the Depot ledger by the verifiers themselves who should initial all such entries. All such postings will be made before any transaction for sending the copies of their stock sheets to the Account Office Ledger Section for the posting of the period priced ledger.
5. **Disposal of the vouchers after Posting Numerical Ledgers.** After the postings for a date have been made, the vouchers should be checked (if necessary) with the forwarding memo without any re-arrangement in case the voucher have been arranged by price list numbers and the vouchers with both copies of the forwarding memo should be sent to the Stores Accounts Officer who, after checking the vouchers with the memo (without disturbing any arrangement by price list numbers) will return one copy of each forwarding memo to the depot as an acknowledgement for the vouchers.
6. **Monthly Statement of Vouchers.** At the end of month, the clerk-in charge of Ledger Section should countersign the certificate given by the wards in their Monthly Statement of Vouchers and forward both the copies to the Stores Accounts Office. The statement should be carefully checked in that office and if found correct, one copy should be returned to the Ledger Section as and acceptance of the certificate.
7. **Posting of Recoupment Cards Wherever Maintained Manually.** Once yearly, after the Annual Contract Statement has been prepared, the columns in the Recoupment Card headed 'Contract Period' and "Estimated Requirements" should be field in from the figures given in the Annual Contract Statement. The columns "Allotment " and Allotment No." should not, however, be filled in by the Subsidiary Depots as their full estimated requirement will be arranged for by the Controller of Stores and will be available for drawing as required through the Main Depot. The Main Depot for the item is entered on both the Recoupment and Numerical Ledger Cards. In connection with the recoupment of stores the "Maximum" and "Minimum" are important factors. The figures representing maximum and minimum should be entered in the spaces provided for the purpose in both the ledger (if maintained manually) and recoupment part of the Stock Card.

28.3 RECOUPMENT OF STOCK BY SUBSIDIARY DEPOTS FROM MAIN DEPOT

1. When it is found that the balance after posting of an issue in the Numerical Ledger Card is either the "Minimum" or blew it, the stock card poster should immediately insert a colored (blue) signal in the holder at the lower edge of the card. A red signal should be attached if the entire stock is exhausted. Upon completion of the daily posting on the Recoupment and Numerical Ledger Cards the poster should prepare the stock recoupment Requisition wherever prepared manually for all items indicated with a blue or red signal. As the Stock recoupment Requisitions are made out, the blue and red signal should be removed. The posters are responsible for dearing all the blue and red signal by the end of each day.

Recoupment Requisitions so made out should be dispatched to the Main Depot by the first available train or post.

2. **Stock Recoupment Requisitions.** These should be made out in duplicate wherever not mechanized in form shown blew, one copy being retained as office copy and the other being forwarded to the correct Main Depot. On each occasion a recoupment is contemplated, the ledger poster should examine the maximum and minimum figures and adjust them with the approval of the Depot Officer, if he finds that the weekly average consumption points to a definite increase or decrease as the case may be, over the previous six months' period.

STOCK RECOUPMENT REQUISITION FORM

Form Subsidiary Depot to Main Depot...............

Requisition No... Date...............

Class................P.L.No................................ Description..................

Quantity now required ....

*Revised forecast of further requirements for

Current Contract Period............................ ....

Recoupment Clerk's Initials

Pending Demands (Quantity only), if any

Depot.......................Date...................... ....

Depot Officer

*To be filled in only if estimated requirement modification

FOR USE OF MAIN DEPOT ONLY

(a) Date of Depot Transfer Quantity Despatched..

Note ....

Purchase Order No..

*(b) ....Date.......................Quantity Ordered.................................

Requisition on Workshop

*(c) Alteration to contact Allotment

No................Date....................Increased Quantity

Requested...

....

Main Depot Officer

*Fill up where action is taken Date...

3. **Quantity for Recoupment.** The smallest quantity of an item to be recouped will be the "Maximum" and this will be the correct recoupment to make when the stocks on hand are down to the level of the "Maximum" when an issue brings the balance below that of the minimum, the correct quantity to recoup should be arrived at by substracting the balance from the minimum and adding the result to the maximum. In the event of the stock being entirely depleted, the quantity to be requisitioned is obtained by adding the maximum to the minimum quantity. Should a sudden rush of demands deplete the stocks entirely and still leave some requisitions uncompiled with, the correct requipment will be the maximum plus the quantity required to cover the pending requisitions. The following formula, may, therefore, be used with advantage. The quantity to be recouped is equal to (maximum plus minimum plus pending demands) minus (stock plus dues).
4. **Revision of Estimated Requirements for Current Contract Period.** After the annual contract for any class of stores has been in operation for a considerable time, it is inevitable that the quantity at first provided for some items will be required reconsideration due to unexpected fluctuations in consumption. Subsidiary depots may in such circumstances call up material from the Main Depots over and above their estimated requirements, but under normal conditions, the Subsidiary Depots should notify the Main Depots in ample time if they require to alter their original estimate. In order to ascertain the time when such a revision should be affected, a comparison of the quantity shown in the "balance of allotment" column of the Recoupment Card (which shows the amount still available to be drawn for the remaining months of the contract period) should be made with the issues already made over an equal period of the time. To facilitate this comparison the summary of the issues of the past two years is kept tabulated at the top of the Recoupment Card. This investigation which should take place whenever a recoumbent is made, will show whether the quantity required increasing or decreasing and if it appears that an alteration is necessary, the revised figure should be entered in the "estimated reuirements" column of the Recoupment Card and the balance of the allotment increased or decreased accordingly. This revised forecast should be notified to the Main Depot on the Stock Recoupment Requisition being sent forward. When such a recasting of figures is being done, a slip giving the past six months' consumption should be put up along with the Stock Recoupment Requisition for the guidance of the Depot Officer.
5. **"Pending Demands"** if there are any "Pending Demands" *i.e.*, indentors requisitions that cannot be complied with, owing to the stock being exhausted, the quantity of such pending demands should be shown on the Stock Recoupment Requisition. This information should be given in order that the Main Depot which would normally make an issue from its own stock unless an over stock exists, may, if possible, sufficient material to clear such pending demands.
6. **Posting of Requisitions in Recoupment Card (S. 1402-B).** Before the despatch of the Stock Recoupment Requisitions from the Subsidiary Depot, all its particulars should be posted in the Recoupment Card and at the same time the balance of the allotment should be struck and brought down and entered in the column headed "balance of allotment" the total amount of material outstanding on Stock Recoupment Requisitions being shown in column "balance due". The stock Recoupment Requisition should be signed by the Depot Officer.
7. **Arranging Supplies for Subsidiary Depots.** A depot which is the Main Depot for a particular item, deals with all recoupments of the item for Subsidiary Depots, in addition to arranging for its own suppliers of the item. The particulars of recoupment made for Subsidiary Depot are not

entered on the Main Depot' Recoupment Card as the entries on that card only concern transactions for the Main Depot's requirements. Where a Main Depot has over stock, it should make issue out of the stock to a Subsidiary Depot and post the transactions in the "issue' column of the numerical ledger card. Care should be taken, however, not to include these issue in the "summary of issue" shown on the top of the Recoupment Card and for this reason, such a posting should be made in red ink denoting that this is a "Depot Transfer" It is the only the retail issue made direct to Main Depot indentors that are shown in the cages for "summary of issue" on the Recoupment Card and note transfers of stock to other depots. Each depot is responsible for giving its estimate of stock that will be required to meet the retail demands that will be made upon the depot by the various indenting departments, and transfer have, therefore, to be excluded.

8. **Supply from over Stock of Main Depot.** The stock card poster having checked the stock card from the item should forward the Stock Recoupment Requisition to the ward-keeper in charge of the material, should there be an over stock. The ward-keeper should then prepare the Depot Transfer Form and arrange with Despatch Section to dispatch the material by stores van. The Stock Recoupment Requisitions should then be returned to the stock card poster in the Ledger Section with the copies of the Depot Transfer Form. The stock card poster should post the 'issues' column of the numerical Ledger Card in red ink to indicate a Depot Transfer issue. He should also enter on the Stock Recoupment Requisition, the date of the Depot Transfer Issue Note, and the, quantity, dispatched. At the same time, the 'issues' column under the heading 'over-stock', allotment on the back of the Contract Allotment Form or the Estimate Advice Form should be posted under the name of the receiving depot and the new balance of over stock calculated and entered in the adjoining 'balance column'.
9. **Purchase.** In cases where the Main Depot has no stock of an item, and a Subsidiary Depot has shown pending demands on the Stock Recoupment Requisition, the Main Depot should dispatch material sufficient to cover the "pending demand" of the Subsidiary Depot, subject to not lowering the Main Depot's Stock below the "Minimum" in such and other cases when purchase have to be made. Purchase Order should be placed against the existing current contract for quantity sufficient to cover not only the balance required for the Subsidiary Depot but also sufficient to replenish the Main Depot Stock up to the "maximum". These quantities for the two depots should be shown separately on the Purchase Order, to enable the dispatch of the material direct to the respective depots.
10. **Recoupment by Main Depots.** The columns headed "allotment" and "allotment number" in the Recoupment Card should be filled by in by the Main Depot when the detailed allotment for depots is intimated by the Controller of Stores through the Contract Allotment Form which is the Main Depot, foil of the Acceptance of Tender Form, or Estimated of Advice Form, in the case of Directorate General of Supplies an d Disposals Contracts. When the Stock of an item in a Main Depot drops to the "minimum" or when a purchase on behalf of Subsidiary Depot is necessary, the poster concerned should at once prepare a Purchase Order Advice in the form shown below to which he should attach the relative Contract Allotment Form or the Estimate Advice Form and put them up to the supervisor who should check the figures and arrange for the Purchase Order to be made out.

PURCHASE ORDER ADVICE FORM

To	To
Leger Station Supervisor,	Tyist,
Purchase Order Required	Type Purchase
(as per Contract Allotment Form herewith),	Order for*..
Material	
Class and P.L. No..............................	Supervisor
Stock..	Date..
Dues..	*State quantity
Past 6 months consumption.................	________________________
Pendings...	Purchase Order No...........................
"Minimum" stock	Dated ....
Quantity required............................	Quantity ....
Depot..	Typist
Stock Recoupment Requisition (S.1416)	....
No..	Initials of Depots Officer
Poster	Date..
Date..	Remarks...

10. The form which is self explanatory and is generally only used in connection with Quantity Rate Contracts should be made out in duplicate, one copy being retained in the Main depot and the other being sent to the Controller of Stores. Reductions in contract quantities are usually dealt with once yearly at the time when Annual Contract Statements for the new year are submitted by depots, and notification are issued to the supplying firms showing by how much it is intended to reduce the quantity in terms of the contract.
11. If a radical alteration to design is made, or drastic alteration to a programme, which necessitates an abnormal reduction of requirements, the Main Depot should advice the Controller of Stores by means of the Alterations to Contract Allotment Form and in such cases the firms concerned should be notified at once. The chief use of this form, however, is when the Main Depot is certain that the total line allotment for any item is insufficient to meet demands. Care should be taken to notify the Controller of Stores of the required alteration atleast five months before the whole of the material originally allocated is drawn from the firm. On receipt of the Form in the Office of Controller of Stores, the particulars of allotments and quantities drawn by

all depots should be shown on the back of the form from the relative Position Cards and put up to the Controller of Stores to arrange for purchases.

12. If the additional material required can be obtained advantageously by opening the clause of the existing contract, allowing the drawing of a certain per cent over and above the contract quantity a Modification to Purchase Order Form should be prepared and distributed.
13. The Depot Officers In charge of the Main Depots may also be empowered to operate on the percentage clause and in such cases the Main Depot should prepare and send to the Controller of Stores copies of the Modification to Purchase Order Form. This form may be used for the modification of contracts as well as for the modification of purchase orders. These forms should be sent to the Controller of Stores from the main depot of simultaneously with the Purchase Order placed under the percentage clause. If the additional material required exceeds the agreed percentage of the contract quantity, or if it more advantageous to enter into a new contract, tenders should be called for and a fresh contract placed as usual. The additional amount of material ordered should be posted on the Possition Card in the usual manner.
14. **Purchase Orders.** Purchase Orders and Alternation to Contract Allotment Form should be signed by the Depot Officer of the Main Depot, who should also initial the Purchase Order Advice Form at the time the Purchase Order is signed. After dispatched of the Purchase Order its number, and the quantity ordered, should be entered in the relevant columns allotted to the Main Depot on the back of the Contract Allotment Form or on the Estimate of Advice Form and the balance struck showing the current balance available for drawing.
15. **Method of arranging for the Supply of Stock Items not Ordered on Annual Contracts.** The Controller of Stores should prepare a list of the items of each class of stores that it is considered inadivisible to order on annual contracts, separate lists being prepared for items purchased by the Indian Stores Department. A copy of each list should be sent to each depot that stocks of the items appearing in the list. The contract period for each class should be divided into quarterly periods to ensure that the quarterly requirements for each class of stores are dealt with on different dates to avoid congestion of work. Twelve weeks before the end of each quarter the Subsidiary and Main Depots should fill in the following form in duplicate, for the next quarter's requirements.
16. **Stock Requisitions on Workshops.** In the case of items manufactured in railway workshops, the maximum and minimum stocks should be fixed into considerations the length of time required by the workshops to deal with the requisition by Stores Depots upon the Depot's stock on an item dropping to the level of the minimum, a requisition form as on shown below should be prepared in triplicate, the first copy being filed in the Ledger Section, while the second and third copies should be passed respectively to the Receipt Section, of the depot and the workshop's Production Department. For 'C' items with value of annual consumption less than Rs.10,000, the replenishment system of recoupment with annual review may be adopted. A replacement level corresponding to 18 months' consumption may be fixed for each item. The item shall be reviewed at the end of a year, and a stock requisition placed for a quantity by which quantity by which on hand quantity on order minus pending demands, is short of the replenishment level.

STOCK REQUISITION ON WORKSHOP

No....................... Date...................... Depot..

Minimum
Maximum

Class and P. L. No.	Description of store	Quantity on hand on...	Stock Recoupment Outstanding		Pending Demands (Quantity) in the depots	Approx-imate yearly consum-ption	Quantity required	Remaks
			Stock re-quisition Number	Quantity asked for				
1	2	3	4		5	6	7	8

Date.................................. ....

Depot Officer

18. Upon completion of the order, the workshops will prepare a "Material-supplied to stores" Form in five copies and distributed among them. The Receipt Section of the Stores Depot having duly checked the items of stores received, should endorse receipt on all the five foils and return the forth foil to the Production Department whence it should finally be made over to the workshop Accounts Officer. The remaining three copies, duly receipted should be sent to the wards with the material. The war should allot R.O. numbers to them and forward them along with the forwarding memo to the Ledger Section where the quantity received should be posted in the 'receipts' column of the Numerical Ledger Card. One copy should be paired with the relevant Requisition on Workshop and retained in the Ledger Section as record. The other two copies should be forwarded to the Stores Accounts Officer.
19. When the manufactured items are required for a Stores Depot that is not adjacent to the workshops, the following slightly different procedure should be followed. The fifth copy of the material supplied to Stores Form should be retained by the workshops and the other four copies passed to the Despatch Section of the local Stores Depot with the manufactured stores, where, after due check, the forth foil, duly received, should be returned to the Production Department for transmission to the Workshop Accounts Officer. The remaining three copies will accompany the consignment in the stores van with the clerk incharge who, upon delivering the stores to the indenting depot should hand over the three copies and obtain a covering signature upon his delivery sheet. The indenting depot, after due and final check should post the receipt of the item on the numerical ledger card and retain the first foil, passing the second and third foils to its Stores Accounts Officer. This Officer should retain the second foil for his record and send the third foil alongwith the advice of Credit to the Workshop Accounts Officer of the Workshops, that supplied the item. After credit has been booked to the workshop, the Workshop Accounts Officer should send the third foil to the depot that despatched the material, for noting the particulars of acknowledgement in the Register of Despatches before finally returning the form to him.

28.4 MISCELLANEOUS

1. **Disposal of Surplus and Scrap.** The procedure to be followed in the depot.
2. **Miscellaneous Cash Receipts.** The Depot Officer receives small sums of money on account of petty private sales and in payment of dues such as ground rent, loading charges & c. Proper receipts on the prescribed forms should be given to the parties tendering the money, on the same dates as the receipts of cash. These transactions should be promptly accounted for in a Register of Miscellaneous Cash Receipts and the money should be remitted as a rule to the Treasurer or the local Station Master on the same date as that of receipt. In unavoidable circumstances, the money may be remitted on the morning of the following working day. Proper arrangement should be made for the safe custody of the money till it is sent to the Treasurer or Station Master. Necessary monthly statement, as prescribed by the Administration, for such accounts, should be submitted by the Depot Officer on the due dates. All entries in the register and documents in connection with such transactions should be signed by a Gazetted Officer.
3. **Disposal of Stock Verification Sheets.** The duplicate and triplicate copies of the stock sheets prepared in triplicate by carbon process by Stock Verifiers or Inspectors of Stores Accounts, will be made over to the ward-keeper who should record his explanations for the discrepancies found through stock verifications, on the both the copies of the stock sheets and make them over promptly to the Section Inspector of Stores Accounts (or to the Stock Verifier) through the Depot Officer. In cases where satisfactory explanations have not been recorded, rejoinders (Accounts Notes) will be issued by the Stores Accounts Officer. These rejoinders should also be attended to and satisfactorily disposed of as expenditiously as possible.

CHAPTER

29

ISSUE TO AND RECEIPT FROM WORKSHOP ISSUE TO WORKSHOP

29.1 WORKSHOPS STORES DEPOTS

1. A railway workshop ordinarily has a stores depot attached to it under control of an official of the Stores Department to meet the requirement and the workshop in connection with custody, receipt and issue of stores and disposal of all surplus and scrap.
2. All stores whether within individual shops themselves or outside, other than those actually being used in repair or manufacture work, should be in the custody of the Stores Department and from part of its stock.
3. Workshop officials are prohibited from holding stock of stores of any kind.
4. **Sub-wards or Shops Stores.** Each Workshop stores depot is divided into wards in each of which is stocked one or more group of stores. When the wards are not located conveniently within the workshop to serve the requirements of the various shops into which the latter is divided and it is found necessary to maintain stock of stores within certain shops, such shop stores should be under the control of a sub-ward keeper and the materials in his custody should from part and parcel of the main wards. These sub-ward should be recouped daily in accordance with the issues of materials, the purpose of the sub-ward being to serve the requirements of the shops "over the counter" and prevent the latter from running a duplicate stores organization. No separate sets of numerical ledger should be maintained for the sub-wards, such working imprest as may have to be maintained with them being shown in the usual numerical ledgers of the depot as having been earmarked for the use of the respective shops.
5. The sub-wards should carry stocks only of such items as are constantly required by shops which they, serve, for their day-to-day requirements.
6. **Forecast Schedules of Stores Required for Periodic Overhauling of Rolling Stock.** Forecast schedules of all stores, tools, assemblies and component parts required by the workshop for periodical overhauls of rolling stock should be prepared as early as possible in advance of the

actual day which they would be required and these schedules should be furnished to the sub-ward-keeper to enable that latter to keep such materials ready for early issue. These schedules should be submitted over the signature of the Works Manager or a gazetted officer working under him. Such forecasts should not be issued piecemeal, one consolidated forecast should be made out for the rolling stock expected to be overhauled in the month.

9. **Advance Lists of other Materials.** Chargeman or other responsible subordinates of the respective shops should prepare manuscript advance lists, incarbon duplicate, of materials likely to be required by them during the next few days. These lists should be scrutinized and countersigned by the foreman concerned and copies thereof furnished to the sub-ward-keeper whose duty it will be to see that the materials are kept ready for delivery.

10. **Issue Tickets.** All materials required by the shops shall be drawn, only as and when required, the requisitions being made in carbon duplicate on "issue tickets" in the form shown below:-

Workshop Issue Ticket

Serial No. .... Date. ....

Machine No.. Shop. ....

Index No. of Chargemen........................

Sub-ward-keeper, pl. issue....................

PL No.	*Description*	*Quantity & Work Order No.*

Received

....

Signature of Indentor

29.2 WORKSHOP ISSUE NOTE

1. Early every morning, each shop office should arrange the chargeman's copies of the issue tickets of the previous day (which give particulars of the materials received that day) in the order of 'class' and price list number. The issue tickets bearing the same price list number should than be re-arranged, work order by work order, and a pencil abstract made on the back of the last issue tickets for the day of each item of stores issued, of the total quantity of that item for each work order. Combined 'Requisition and issue Notes' in the form shown below, should then be prepared in carbon quintuplicate, all items of one group supplied during the day being entered in one workshop issue Notes.

WORKSHOP ISSUE NOTE

Serial No.................................

No...Shop..Date..

Class.................................

P.L No.	Description	Quantity				W/O	Rate	Unit	Value	Remarks
		Nos.	MTs.	Kgs.	Gms.				Rs. P.	

Received | Signature of Indenting Foreman & Date

Date | Signature of Sub-Ward-Keeper

All the foil of the issue note should be signed by the Foreman and the Sub-Ward-Keeper.

2. These workshop Issue Notes should be checked by the sub-ward-keeper with his copies of the issue tickets. In the case of issue tickets left with the parent ward, a remark should be made to this effect on the Issue Note. The sub-ward-keeper should retain three copies and return the fourth and fifth copies to the indenting foreman.
3. Separate Workshop issue note should (preferably) be prepared in respect or materials obtained from the parent ward as distinct from the sub-word. The sub-ward-keeper (or ward-keeper in the case of an issue from the parent ward) will retain one foil of the workshop issue note as his record and send two copies alongwith necessary forwarding memo to the Ledger Section of the depot for the posting of the numerical ledger. They should later on be passed on to the Stores Accounts Officer who after pricing the issue note and posting his priced ledgers will send one foil, with a Daily Summary of Issues to the Workshop Accounts Officer.
4. The sub-ward-keeper should hand over his record copies of the Workshop issue notes to the main ward-keeper in order to recoup himself. The items for which Issue Tickets had been left with the parent ward will not be recouped.
5. The foreman will daily submit one copy of the issue notes received by him to the Works Manager or a Senior Subordinate specially empowered by the Chief Mechanical Engineer, who should scrutinize the issue notes, as they indicate the nature and the scale of the daily consumption of materials, sigh them in token of having accepted them and forward them to the Workshop Accounts Officer, daily. The other copy will be retained by the foreman as his record. The shop foreman will be responsible for seeing that the workshop issue notes for the day are obtained from the Stores Department and submitted to the Works Manager before noon of the day following.

6. Bound books of printed forms of workshops Issue Note Form which should be machine-numberd should be issued to workshop foreman who will be responsible for their safe custody and accountal, in the same manner as for the Issue Ticket books, a manuscript register being maintined for the purpose.
7. **Issue to workshops from Out-Station Depots.** In cases where the workshops have to requisition for stores from out-station depots, the procedure mentioned should be followed.

29.3 STORES MANUFACTURED FOR STOCK

1. No articles may be manufactured in workshops for stock, purposes, without a requisition on From for such article (s) being placed by the Stores Department.
2. All article so manufactured in workshops should be issued to the stores depot, as expeditiously as possible, after inspection, on the authority of the foreman, conveyed on a from "material supplied to stores by workshops. It should be prepared in quintuplicate and four copies should be sent by the originator duly accompanied by the material as a rule, the fifth being retained as his record. Such materials should not be used up in the shops, by the setting them of against requisition of shops pending in depots.
3. **Issue Rates for Workshops Manufactured Items.** The Issue rates for workshop manufactured items should be fixed according to the price list rate in force for each year as decided vide para 1535.
4. **Re-valuation of Balances in Priced Ledgers for Workshops Manufactured Items.** On the price list rates being revised by the Works Manager and intimated though the Workshops Accounts Officer to the Stores Accounts Office, the balance of stores in stock under such priced ledgers on the date of the coming into force of the revised Priced list rates should be revalued at such rates which will prevail as the issue rates for the item till the price list rate is revised again. The differences arising out of such re-valuation should be debited or credited to Stock Adjustment account, Part II, being collected under a separate heading titled "adjustments on account or revision of rates for workshop manufactured items." The total amounts thus accumulating under this head each half-year should be cleared finally by debit or minus debit to the heads of Accounts abstracts B.2129 or C 2128 or C.2138 or C.2327 in consolation with the Mechanical Department. The general rule against writing up of the value of stores in the priced ledgers does not apply to items of stores manufactured in workshops as the adjustments between actual and approximate costs of workshop manufactured items and on account of re-valuation of stocks on such items in priced ledgers both go the same heads of revenue account.
5. **Workshop Requirement of Manufactured Parts.** All requirements of workshops for Manufactured Parts should be indented be for in the usual manner through requisitions on the sub-ward-keeper or ward-keepers.

29.4 MATERIAL RETURNED BY WORKSHOP

1. **Stores Returned by workshops.** Returned Stores may consist of:
   (*i*) Surplus Stores being balance of new materials that have not been used on a work.
   (*ii*) Stores released from works.

(*iii*) Tools and plant no longer required; and

(*iv*) Scarp.

All such material should be handed over promptly. On the authority of an Advice Note of Returned Stores to the sub-ward-keeper of the shop, whose duty it shall be to see that the material are valued by the Stores Department, despatched to the respective wards and taken into account therein. There is no objection to the sub-ward-keeper avoiding a physical transfer of such of the material asit is possible for him to set off against the issues of the day. He is prohibited from accumulating any stores or scrap that are not required in the shop to which his sub-stores is attached. The Advice Note of Returned Stores should be prepared in five foils, a form such as the one indicated below being used.

2. The materials should be checked with the Advice Notes and arranged for inspection and valuation by the Depot Officer or a gazzeted office on his behalf. Immediately after the stores are valued, the sub-ward-keeper should complete the four foils in this respect, take the stores into stock (either his own or that of the parent ward) and initial the advice Notes and send them to the depot office through the parent ward where they should be assigned R.O. numbers as usual.
3. The four foil, after signature by the Depot Officer or a gazzetted Officer on his behalf, should be disposed of, as follows:
   (*i*) The first retained as record.
   (*ii*) The second foil sent to the returning officer.
   (*iii*) The third and fourth foils sent to the Store Accounts Office after the numerical ledgers have been posted.
4. The Stores Accounts Office after posting the priced ledger should prepare a summary of credits to the shops, for stores returned to the depot each day.
5. The third foil of the Advice Note alongwith a summary of credit will be sent by the Stores Accounts Officer to the workshop Accounts Officer to post the Register of work orders or Allocation Registors for revenue abstracts, the fourth foils of Advice Notes will be filled in the Stores Accounts Office.
6. **Scrutiny of Advice Notes.** The second foils of the Advice Note should be submitted to the Workshop Accounts Office through the Works Manager, who will scrutinize them before counter-signature to see that the credits are afforded at reasonable rates by the Stores Department. This scrutiny may be carried out by a selected subordinate specially empowered to do so by the Chief Mechanical Engineer.
7. The Workshop Accounts Office should arrange the second foils of the Advice Notes by shops and the order of the numbers and dates given by the shops and should pair such foils with the third foils received from the Stores Accounts Office along with the Advice of credits. Any cases of delay in affording credits or discrepancies in quantities etc., should be taken up each fortnight for the Advice Notes of the previous fortnight with the depot Officer.
8. **Advice Notes for Stores Returned to Out-station Depots.** In such cases, the procedure will be followed both by the Workshops and Accounts Offices.

29.5 PROCEDURE IN WORKSHOP ACCOUNTS OFFICE

1. Workshop Issue Notes prepared by the shops would be received daily in the Workshops Accounts Office after scrutiny by the Work Manager or other Officer of the Mechanical Department.
2. The Accounts Office is responsible for seeing that:
   - (*i*) The shop serial number 9 *i.e.*, Requisition Numbers of the issue notes for each shop are continuous and that breaks in such continuity, if any, are satisfactorily explained;
   - (*ii*) The Issue Notes are received strictly according to schedule, *i.e.*, by the evening of the day following the date of issue; and
   - (*iii*) The Issue Notes have been correctly prepared according to the instructions issued for this purpose. The Accounts Office should then pair them with the copies received alongwith the Daily Summaries of Issues and take up any discrepancies with the Stores Department.
3. The forth foil of "Material Supplied to Stores" Forms will be received in the Workshop Accounts Office from the Stores depot through the Production Office. This should be filled by the order of numbers and dates for each shop separately. On receipt of the Advice of Credit duly supported by the second foil of the Form, these foils should be paired with the corresponding fourth foils, and it should be seen that the quantities and rates agree. The calculation of the values as shown on the second foils should be checked in all cases and any errors taken up with the Stores Accounts Office. Any cases of delay in affording credit should also be taken up with the Stores Accounts Office.

29.6 CUSTODY STORES

1. **Explanation of the term "Custody Stores".** These stores chiefly consist of items obtained for the Mechanical Department for the construction of rolling stock/sanctioned under the Capital or Revenue Programme. Directly the stores are received and paid for, the cost is at once debited to the works concerned. Instead of the stores lying in the workshop until they are required, the Stores Department should keep them in safe custody, proper numerical records being maintained by the department.
2. **The Material Schedule.** A Standard Material Schedule is prepared for each type of railway carriage that is constructed; the Schedule shows the part number, description and quantity of every item required per vehicle of the particular design of coach shown on the schedule. Three copies of this schedule (blue prints) are forwarded by the Officer incharge of the carriage and wagon shops to the Depot Officer (of the depot attached to the workshop), who should fill in the columns of the schedule headed "Available" and "To be arranged" One copy should then be retained in the Stores Depot, the second copy returned to the Workshops Progress Office as a notification of the items that are available in stock and the third, forwarded to the Controller of Stores for making arrangements purchase the items required. Tenders for such items will be issued as usual and definite quantities of the item ordered, with deliveries on suitable dates to fit in with the carriage construction programme. In such cases, a copy of the Purchase Order should be sent to the Officer incharge of the workshops to keep him advised of the transaction.

Material Schedule

Class & P.L.	Name of Parts	Mate-rial	Draw-ing No.	Quan-tity per vehicle	Total Quan-tity	Re-marks	Avail-able	To be arran-ged	Purchase order or Requisition on Workshop No. Date	Quan-tity	To be filled by sub ward		
											Rece-ipts	isuue	Bal-ance
1	2	3	4	5	6	7	8	9	10	11	12	13	14

3. **The Receipt and Storage of Custody Stores.** The purchased stores should be delivered direct to a sub-ward in the shop premises which should stock only these "custody stores", the stores being kept in a separate enclosure with definite bin or stacking space allotted to each part or price list number. The Invoice and Receipt Notes or the Receipt and Issue Note printed on paper different in colour to the forms which are used for dealing with stores for stock purposes of the stores depot, should be prepared in four parts only and distributed as follows. Part I will be the block or record copy, Part II should be forwarded to the firm, Part III to the Workshop Accounts Officer of the workshops that requires the stores who should debit the work order for the Works in question with the cost of the stores advised by credit to "Purchases", and Part IV to the Workshop Progress Office as a notification that the stores are available for drawing.
4. The firm should submit their bills supported by Part II of the Receipt Note direct to the Workshop Accounts Officer for payment. Payments should be made as usual.
5. **Numerical Ledger for "Custody Stores".** After the checking of the consignment, the receipts should be posted in the Material schedule and also on a Stock Card which should be maintained in the sub-ward for each item appearing on the Material Schedule.
6. **Issue of "Custody Store".** It has been explained that the workshops progress office is notified by means of the Material Schedule of the stores available in stock and of the stores to be specially purchased for works. The Workshops Progress Office should enter the particulars of receipt of the stores from the above documents on the Progress Office copy of the Material Schedule. As and when required, the stores should be drawn on the authority of Pink Issue Tickets.
7. Workshop Issue Notes printed also on pink paper, should be prepared in quadruplicate every morning by the foreman of the shop concerned for the Issue Tickets. One copy of the form should be retained by the Foreman and three copies sent to the sub-ward-keeper who should check them with his copies of issue tickets sign all the three copies in token of the issue of the stores and return two copies to the Foreman of the shop concerned, retaining the third copy from which he should post the issue on the stock card for "Custody Stores", and on the Stores Depot copy of the Material Schedule. The Foreman should pass on the two copies of the Issue Notes to the Progress Office where one copy will be retained and the other forwarded to the workshop Accounts Officer. The Workshop Accounts Officer should check the Issue Note to see that the stores issued to the Workshops have been duly accounted.
8. Only the stores and quantities shown on the Material Schedule should be issued by the sub-ward-keeper. If any alteration to the Material Schedule are required, particulars should be given on the alteration sheet which should be prepared in duplicate by the Progress Office one copy being retained for record and the other forwarded to the Depot Officer who should alter his copy of the Material Schedule accordingly.
9. **Annual Return of "Custody Stores".** A return of all "Custody Stores" in stock on 31st March each year should be prepared by the Stores Department and furnished to the Workshop Accounts Officer by the 20th April each year.
10. **Verification of "Custody Stores".** These stores should be verified annually by the store verifiers of the accounts Department.
11. **Workshop Patterns.** All patterns including those for stock items manufactured should be in the custody of an official of the workshop who will maintain a proper account for the same.

NUMERICAL LEDGER OF PATTERNS

Class..*Part/Price List No..

Drawing No...................................*Nomenclature...

+Bye No. of Pattern	*Date of Manufacture	Receipt or Issue Voucher No. Date	Requisition for Casting Issue to No. Date	Received from or	Receipt	issued	Balance

* The particular under these heading should be the same as that of the casting for which the pattern is designed.

\+ If there are more than one pattern for a casting, each of them should be assigned a bye-number which should also be indelibly marked on the pattern itself.

‡ This date should invariably be shown on all receipt and issue documents.

The Cost of the patterns including those for stock items manufactured should not be debited to Store Department but should be dealt with in accordance with the foot note. The patterns should be verified alongwith the other items of the tools and plants of the workshop in the normal course.

CHAPTER

30

RETURNED STORES

30.1 PROCEDURE FOR RETURNED STORES

The following procedure for returned stores applies to all departments, other than those workshops to which stores depot and Stores and Workshop Accounts Office are attached. All stores which have been previously issued for the services of the railway and are no longer required on a work should, in the absence of special instructions to the contrary, be returned to the stores depots. If there is more than one stores depot on railway, the Controller of Stores may nominate the depot or depots to which particular classes or stores may be returned and advice the various railway department accordingly. In doing this, he should have in view the depot most suitable for the final disposal of the returned stores, either by reissue to consumers, or by reclamation, or sale by auction, as the case may be.

Advice Notes

The Officer returning stores to stores depots should prepare Advice Notes in Form (S.1539) in six foils by carbon process. Separate Advice Notes should be prepared for each class and for new, secondhand and scrap stores. When the Officer returning the stores is unable to suggest the 'rates' in the Advice Notes, it will be the duty of the divisional or district officer to have this done before passing on the documents to the Depot Officer. In the case of scrap, the classification prescribed in the schedule of rates for different classes of scrap should be strictly observed.

1. **General Criterion for Valuation.** The valuation of material returned from works, particularly of specialised material, is difficult problem. Engineers and other parties returning stores and plant are prone to claim (and provide in their estimates for) as large a credit as possible for them. But the value of such materials to the railway depends largely on the extent to which they can be made use of. Railway Administrative Officers should examine in consultation, if necessary, with the Controller of Stores or whoever may be thought likely to take the material over, the sums provided in estimates as credits for returned material and see that the theoretical value of the material based on its further life is ignored, and the estimate is based instead of the possibilities of the material being used again within a reasonable period after return. If there is no likelyhood of the material of plant being required again within a reasonable period

of return, the credit allowed in the estimate for returned value should be kept within the figure likely to be realized for it as obsolete material or as scrap.

2. **Disposal of the Foils of Advice Notes.** One foil of the Advice Note should be retained by the subordinate returning the stores to the stores depot as his office copy, three foils (the 2nd, 3rd and 4th) should be sent to the depot direct along with the Railway Receipt. Of the remaining two copies, one copy (the 5th) should be sent to the Accounts Officer, Stores, and the other (the 6th) to the Divisions of District Officer through the immediate superior of the subordinate returning in the stores.
3. **Departmental Register of Advice Notes.** The Advice Notes (6th foil) should be carefully examined in the divisional or district office to see that they have been correctly prepared. They should then be listed in a Register of Advice Notes or Returned Stores maintained in the form shown below.

DEPARTMENTAL REGISTER OF ADVICE NOTES FOR RETURNED STORES

Designation of the Officer returning the stores

Advice Note			Materials stated by returning Officer to have been returned		Date of dispatch of the 6th foil of of the Advice Note to the Depot Officer	Material acknowledge by depot to have been received			No. & Date of Advice of Credit received from the Stores Accounts Officer	Remarks
S. No.	No.	Date	Description of materials.	Quantity		Date of acknowledgement and Ro No. and date	Description of materials acknowledged	Quantity acknowledged		
1	2	3	4	5	6	7	8	9	10	11

4. A separate page of this register should be allotted to each returning officer or subordinate as may be found convenient. If the particulars furnished by the subordinates returning the stores regarding nomenclature, rates &c., are found to be incomplete, the Advice Notes (6th foil) should be completed in the divisional or district office in these respects. The Advice Notes (6th foil) should then be forwarded to the depot to which the stores have been returned.
5. The disposal of Advice Notes and the maintenance of the register mentioned above may be entrusted to the Accounts Office, if any, attached to the division or district. The Register of Returned Stores should be inspected frequently to see that there is little avoidable delay on the part of the stores depots in acknowledging he stores. Any cases of omission to acknowledge the stores. And /or to afford credit for the same within one month of the Advice Notes should be taken up with the Depot and Accounts Officers.

6. **Procedure in Stores Depot.** Returned Stores should be dealt with in the store depot in its Receipt Section. The work should, if possible, be divided between two sub-sections, one section dealing with the receipt of the material and the other sub-section being responsible for the accounting for it.
7. **Depot Register of Advice Notes.** As soon as the Railway Receipts and the Advice Notes (the 2nd 3rd and 4th foils) are received in the depot direct from the consignors, the Advice Notes should be entered in a register and serially numbered, the serial number being entered at the same time on the top right hand corner of the Advice Note in red ink or by means of a numbering machine. This register should show the following particulars, *viz.*
   (*i*) Serial Number.
   (*ii*) Date of receipt of Advice Note in Depot.
   (*iii*) Number and date of Advice Note.
   (*iv*) Number and date of Railway Receipts.
   (*v*) Wagon number.
   (*vi*) Designation of subordinate returning stores.
   (*vii*) Particulars of stores returned (*a*) Description (*b*) Quantity
   (*viii*) Date on which stores are received in the depot.
   (*ix*) (*a*) Date on which copies of Advice Notes (6th foil) are returned duly acknowledged to the Divisional/district office (*b*) Receipt order number and date.
   (*x*) Date on which stores are posted in the numerical ledger.
8. On receipt of the stores in the depot, these should be checked with the Advice Notes received direct from the subordinate returning the stores, the date of receipt noted in column (8) of the register and the quantities actually received entered in the prescribed column of the Advice Notes against each item of stores as shown therein. Particular care should be taken to see that the quantities entered in the columns "quantity returned "and "quantity received" agree. In case there are any differences, the depot officer should show the quantity received in the unit adopted by the consignor in addition to that in which the same will be accounted for the depot, so that the returning officer will be able to investigate discrepancies. In such cases brief reason should be stated in the Advice Notes, and the returning officer should be advised of the differences, without delay. On no account should there be any lumping up of entries in the Advice Notes. The depot should then check the classification stores nomenclature, price list number &c., complete all the foils in every respect and inform the divisional or district office of any differences that may come to light.

Inspection and Valuation

The material should then be inspected and valued by the gazetted officer of the stores depot. In the case of store, the depot's stock of which has already been declared as dead surplus, scrap value only should be afforded. Second-hand serviceable stores will be credited at half the price list rate for new stores except in those cases where a different method of valuation has been authorized. If the officer returning the stores does notes accept the valuation by the Depot Officer the matter should be referred to the General Manager whose decision will be final.

1. **Valuation of Second-hand Rails.** Each railway should annually fix a rate for second-hand rails returned to stores ; but in the case of second-hand rails released from existing lines and supplied to new projects (whether financed by the Central Government or not) or to other administrations, their price should be taken as 65% of the market price of new rail.

2. **Valuation of plant and Machinery**

   (*a*) In the case of serviceable plant/and machinery their value should be determined according to the following formula, *viz.*, R-N/L (R-S) where, R is the present day price of new boiler or pump, N is the age of the article, L is the estimated life of the same and S is the scrap value. The scrap value should be pre-determined for each class of plant and machinery. When the article is repaired, the cost of repairs should be added to the book value arrived at using the above formula. If the article is condemned and cut up in the workshops, a work order should be allotted to which should be charged the book value of the article and the cutting up charges. The credit for scrap and any serviceable parts should be booked to the work order. Any outstanding balance should be adjusted against the department which retuned the article.

   (*b*) in case of Machinery and plant, the returning officer should furnish the following information in the advice note.

   (*i*) Source of receipt.

   (*ii*) maker's name.

   (*iii*) Year of purchase.

   (*iv*) Original cost.

   (*v*) Period it has been in use.

   (*vi*) Whether it is good working order for sale or for offer to other railways.

   (*vii*) Reason for return.

   (*viii*) Whether the material is likely to be redrawn in the near future. If not, proposal if any, with regard to its disposal.

3. **Valuation of Boiler Tubes.** In the case of boiler tubes removed from engine boilers and returned to the stores depot from running sheds or workshops, it cannot be determined whether they are serviceable or not unless they are "rumbled". They should not therefore be credited at half value of new stores but at scrap value. When the tubes have been rumbled, the serviceable tubes should be held as second-hand stock at half the value of new stores .The difference between the book value of the "unrumbled" tubes, plus the cost of rumbling and the second-hand value of the tubes when taken into stock after rumbling should be credited to Stock Adjustment Account

4. **Valuation of Repairable Items.** Advice Notes for material which though un-serviceable, could after reconditioning or repairs be rendered serviceable and would thus be useful for another term of life, should be accepted as "Repairable." Credit should be afforded by the Stores Depot for wholly and partly famous articles at $1/3^{rd}$ and non-ferrous articles at half of the current book rate for the new articles. Such articles would generally be stock items of locomotive, carriage and wagon parts and fittings.

   Separate ledger cards under their relevant price list number affixing the correct category code to the price list number of the new article, should be maintained for repairable ones. As soon as it is desired or advantageous to do so, the Stores Depot should get the repairable material made serviceable for issue to consuming department for adding to serviceable stock instead of ordering for new materials.

   The repaired articles should be taken on books at the book rate for repairable ones plus the actual cost of repairs or average cost of repairs, as converient. No distinction should be made between new and repaired articles in the matter of storage, and the issue prices of the e material should be the same.

Note: In case the stock of repairable article exceeds the annual consumption of the new repaire articles investigations should be made and necessary action taken for the disposal of the excess stock

5. The actual cost of repairing or reconditioning such material will rarely be identical with th difference between the new value and rate at which the material has been taken into stoc before repairs.

   The difference should be debited or credited to the appropriate Revenue Head of Account fo overcharges and under-charges manufacture and repairs. A watch should be kept on suc adjustments and wherever it is found that they are very heavy, the rates for repair should b reduced or increased by a suitable percantage to make then accord as near as possible with th actuals as indicated by past transactions.
6. **Non-stock Repairable Items.** In case of non stock items, such materials should not be re claimed or repaired until a requisition is received for the material.
7. **Delay in Receipt of Stores.** In the event of any stores not arriving within 14 days after receip of the Advice Note, the Depot Officer should take up with the traffic department and inform th subordinate returning the stores at the same time. If such stores are not received within 3 days after submission of the report, the Depot Officer should take necessary action accordin to the rules for stores lost in transit.
8. **Stores Received in Advance of Documents.** If any returned stores are received in a depo before arrival of the Advice Note, the fact should at once be reported to the subordinate returr ing the stores, giving details of the stores received, the station of dispatch and the number an date of the Railway Receipt. If the Advice Notes are not received within a week after th submission of the above report, a special report should be made to the divisional or Distric Officer. If the concerned Advice Notes are not received within 14 days after the arrival of th stores, these should be dealt with at "excess found in stock" and accounted for accordingly.
9. **Posting of Numerical Ledgers.** The Depot Officer, after having the necessary enteries made i the numerical ledgers bin cards as well as in the Depot Register of Advice Notes should retai one copy of the Advice Note (2nd foil) as his office record and send the two copies (3rd and 4 foil) duly completed in all respects to the Account s Officer, Stores.
10. **Disposal of Receipt (6th) Foil.** The sixth foil of the Advice Note should also be sent by the Depo Officer duly receipted to the divisional or district officer concerned to be retained as the latter office record after making the entries in columns 7 to 9 of the Departmental Register of Advic Notes (S.1605). He should take up with the depot and returning officers any discrepancies i quantities (vide columns 5 and 9 of the Register) if the reasons given on the Advice Notes ar not satisfactory.
11. **Accounts Register of Advice Notes.** The three copies of the Advice Note ereceived by th Stores Accounts Officer will be dealt with in his office according to the following procedur On receipt in the Stores Accounts Office of the 5th foil direct from the returning officer, th particulars of the Advice Note should be entered in a register containing the following co umns:
    - (*i*) Number and date of Advice Note.
    - (*ii*) Designation and station of subordinate returning stores.
    - (*iii*) Date of Receipt of 5th foil.
    - (*iv*) Date of Receipt of 3rd and 4th foil.
    - (*v*) Receipt order No. and Date.

(*vi*) Date and No. of Advice of credit.

(*vii*) Remarks.

A separate portion of the register should be reserved for each sub-ordinate or division or department with separate pages for each date or month.

12. This register will enable the Stores Accounts Officer to watch the prompt accountal of returned stores by the Depot officer concerned. The Stores Account Officer should inspect this register once a fortnight to see that there is no avoidable delay on the part of the Depot Officer in acknowledging receipt of returned stores and accounting for them. Any delay in accountal should be promptly taken up with the Depot Officer. Any items outstanding for over three month should be extracted in a summary to avoid their being lost sight of and a special report of such items should be made to the controller of Stores.
13. **The Pairing of Advice Notes.** The 3rd and 4th foils received from the depot should be paired with the 5th foil received direct from the returning officer, and the date of their receipt entered in the register.
14. **Pricing of Advice Notes and Posting of Priced Ledger.** The 3rd and 4th foils should then be priced at the valuation fixed by the depot officer. The 4th foil will be used for posting the priced ledger and kept as the record for the Stores Accounts Office.

Advice of Credits

Advice of Credit will be prepared and sent to the Divisional/District Officer. The number and date the Advice of Credit should be noted in the Accounts Register of Advice Notes against the entries of the Advice Notes included in the Advice of Credits. The Advice of Credits with the 3rd foils as supporting vouchers and the corresponding 5th foils should then be sent to the divisional or district officer concerned.

1. **Procedure in the District or Divisional Office:** On receipt of the copies of the Advice Notes along with the Advice of Credit from the Stores Accounts officer in the division or district office, the 5th foil should be transmitted to the subordinate concerned after noting on it the fact of credit having been received. The Advice of Credit supported by the 3rd foil should then be carefully checked with the noted in the Departmental Register of Advice Note. The Divisional or workshop Accounts Officer concerned will be responsible for taking up with the Stores Department any discrepancies in quantities, shown in the copies of the Advice Notes. (When there is no Accounts officer attached to the office of the head of the returning department, this check should be exercised by his own office). Necessary adjustments should then be made by debiting "Transfers Stores" and crediting the head of account concerned. In case where there is no Accounts Officer attached to the office of the department returning the stores, the latter should send the Advices of Credit to the Accounts Officer concerned for necessary adjustment.
2. **Freight on Stores returned to Stores Depots.** In the case of materials returned from revenue maintenance, the freight should be debited to the head "Carriage of Revenue Stores" under the various revenue abstracts of the returning departments. In the case of materials returned from special works, the freight should be debited to the estimate of the work concerned, *i.e.*, Capital Depreciation Reserve Fund or Revenue as the case may be. But if the stores are returned on account of incorrect issue by the Stores Department, the freight should be charged to the head.

CHAPTER

31

EMPTIES

1. **Classes of Empties.** A Railway receives, in course of time a large number of empties or containers of different kinds—packing cases, barrels, and drums. These are of three categories *viz:*
   (*i*) *Non-returnable Empties:* The cost of such empties is included in the cost of their contains and the empties are not returned to supplying firms.
   (*ii*) *Optionally Returnable Empties:* The cost of such empties is charged for by the firm alongwith the cost of the contains, but supplying firms undertake to refund the full cost of the empties, if they returned in good condition within a specified period.
   (*iii*) *Returnable Empties:* These are not charged for by the firms alongwith the cost of the contents, but the agreement is they are not retuned to the firm in good condition within a specified period, the cost of the empties will be payable to the firms.
2. **Serviceable Empties.** These should be held in stock in Group 98 in Class 'S' under a separate section styled 'Empties'. Unserviceable empties should be classified as scrap under the relevant heading, such as metal, and timber.
3. **Non-returnable Empties.** No separate ledgers should be opened for non-returnable empties at the time they are received with the materials as their cost is included in the cost of the materials themselves. When the materials for which the empties are used are issued to the indenting departments, they will be debited with the full cost of the materials including the cost of empties. If, and when, the empties are subsequently returned by the indenting departments of the stores depots, credit should be afforded to the former at scrap rates, and the empties brought on to the numerical and priced ledgers under the proper head for such serviceable empties under Class 'S' Group 98.
4. If by retail issue or owing to other reasons any empties of this category are left in the depot, such empties should be taken into stock at scrap rates under the roper headings by credit to Stock Adjustment Account.
5. In the case of direct supplies, *i.e.*, materials which are not issued form any stores depot, but are supplied direct through the Controller of Stores to the consuming department, the empties

should be returned by the latter to the stores depot form which it usually draws stores and the procedute relating to 'returned stores' should be adopted in this connection.

6. **Empties Returnable to Supplies at Option.** Firms supplying materials charge, in many cases, separately for the empties and undertake to refund full cost of the latter, of they are returned in good condition within a specified period of time. In all such cases the Receipt Note should show the cost of the contents separately from and exclusive of the cost of the empties. The Depot Officer should bring the contents as distinguished from the empties on the numerical ledgers for the contents and the Stores Accounts Officer should also do the same and post only the values of the contents as shown on the Receipt Notes in his corresponding priced ledgers. The particulars of the empties should also be brought on the numerical ledger under a separate head opened for all the purpose in Class 'S' unless it is already in existence and the Stores Accounts Officer will also similarly account for the empties in the priced ledgers.
7. **Issue to Departments.** When such empties are issued to the indenting departments along with the materials contained therein, the issue note should show separate entries for the contents and empties, corresponding entries made in the numerical and priced ledger under the headings for the materials as well as for the empties. The indenting departments should also be informed that, if the empties are returned in good condition within a specified period (which should leave sufficient margin of time for the depot to return the empties to the firm within the time stipulated by it) the cost of the same will be credited to them. This is best done by stamping the relevant issue not by a rubber stamp as follows:

   'If empties are returned in good condition within ....(date) a credit at the rate of ....per receptacle will be afforded to the indenting department'.
8. **Return by Departments.** When the empties are returned by the department concerned, they should be treated in the same way as ' returned stores' and the procedure relating to such stores should be followed. The credit to the returning departments will be afforded by the Stores Accounts Officer at the rate previously intimated to the former when the empties were originally issued, provided they have been returned within the stipulated time and in good condition.
9. If an empty is returned (*a*) after the specified time, or/and (*b*) in a condition unfit for return to the firm, credit should be given at scrap rate only (which should be fixed for each kind of empty in stock). If the empty is not unserviceable, but has been returned after the specified time, a numerical ledger card for such serviceable empties should be opened under the same heading, but separate from the one on which it was originally taken into account on receipt from the firm.
10. If the empty is returned in a totally unserviceable condition, it should be treated as scrap and accounted for as such and not as an 'empty'.
11. **Return to Firms.** When the empties are returned to the firms by the Depot Officer, the transactions will be treated as minus receipts by the Depot Officer and accounted for accordingly in his books. He should issue minus Receipt Notes to the firms and send copies to the Accounts Officer, Stores for necessary recovery, being made from the firms.
12. **Review by Accounts Officer.** The Accounts Officer should maintain a list of the priced ledgers for "Optionally Returnable Empties" and should review them from time to time, and not less than once in three months, to see that the empties are promptly returned to the firms.
13. **Direct Supplies.** When materials in empties returnable at option are supplied direct to consuming departments, the latter should be instructed, through suitable endorsement on the

Receipt Notes for such consignments, to return the empties to the store depot from which the department ordinarily draws stores. Both the depot concerned and the Accounts Officer, Stores should be advised, at the same time of the full particulars of the empties which the department will return. The Advice should be made on the form shown blew.

OPTIONALLY RETURNABLE

ADVICE OF DIRECT SUPPLY OF RETURNABLE EMPTIES

Advice No........................ Date........................

To

The Depot Officer,

The Empties as detailed below have been directly supplies to .... on Receipt Note No. ....Date. ....Purchase Order No. ....Date. ....and would be returned to your depot:

Empties should be promptly returned to the firms and necessary adjustments made.

P.L.No..................Nomenclature of Empties ....Quantity .... Rate..............................Name and address of the firm..

Category of Empties *Optionally Returnable/Returnable empties.................................

Due date of return to the firm...

Date......................

....

Controller of Stores

Copy to the Stores Accounts Officers...

*strike out term not required.

14. **Return by Departments.** The Advice Notes for Returned Stores under which departments return the optionally returnable cmpties (received with the direct supplies) to the stores depot should show full particulars of the Receipt Note, the name and address of the firm, rate and date by which the empties should be returned to the firm, the minus Receipt Note, issued for this purpose, bearing a reference, both to the original Receipt Note and to the Advice Note.

15. **Retuned Empties.** These are note charged for by the firm supplying the materials (contained therein) but there is an agreement that if the empties are not returned in good condition within a specified period , the railway will have to bear their cost, which is generally very heavy. When dealing with commodities carried in such empties, the Depot Officer should bring the contents on his numerical ledger and the Stores Accounts Officer should also do the same so far as the priced ledgers are concerned. The empties will not be brought on the numerical ledgers or the priced ledgers as they are not railway property. The Depot Officer should, however, maintain a manuscript register showing the particulars of the receipt of the emplies and their issue (alongwith-the contents) and their subsequent return by the indenting officer. Separate Pages should be set apart for empties received under each Receipt Note.

16. **Issue to Departments.** The issue notes relating to the original issue of the contents and the receptacles should bear a rubber stamp endorsement to the following effect "if the empties are not returned to this depot in good condition within.........a debit at the rate of ....per empties will be raised against the indenting department.

17. **Return by Departments.** When the empties are returned by the indenting departments within the stipulated period and in good condition, the form shown below should be used for the purpose and not the Advice Note for Returned Stores.

**MEMO OF RETURNED "RETURNABLE EMPTIES"
FOR WHICH NO DEBIT WAS RAISED BY THE DEPOT**

No........................ Date........................

Reference: To Issue Note number and date ....(Through which the contents of the receptacles were received).

The undermentioned empties received from the Depot/Officer................Depot along with the contents through the above issue note, are hereby returned under Free Service Way-bill/Railway Material Consignment Note.

NO........................ Date........................

Description of Empties

Quantity..........................

Station...........................

Dated.............................

Designation of Retuning Party

18. **The form should be prepared in quadruplicate and distributed as follows.** 1st foil: Block copy , to be retained by the Returning Officer 2nd and 3rd foils— should be sent the Depot Officer concerned along with the empties . Both the copies should receipted by the Depot Officer in acknowledgement of the empties and 3rd foil returned to the Returning Officer. 4th foil: Accounts copy, should be sent by the Retuning Officer direct to the Accounts Officer, Stores. These foils should be filed in chronological order in the Accounts officer and checked by the verification staff periodically and not less than once in three months with the register maintained by the depot and any irregularities reported to the Stores Accounts Officer for necessary action.

19. **Returned to the Firms.** The Depot Officer should send the empties on to the firms promptly after making the necessary entries in his register. Proper acknowledgement should be obtained from the firms and filed carefully, reference to the acknowledgement being entered in the register. No entries should be made in the ledger nor should the transactions be treated as 'returned stores'.

20. **Non-return of Empties to Suppliers.** When the empties are returned by the indenting department after the stipulated period and the suppliers cannot be prevailed upon to waive the delay, or when the empties are not received by the depot in good condition, the department or depot should submit Advice Notes of Returned Stores to cover the empties. The empties should be taken at a valuation to be made with reference to the rates given in the scrap Schedule for Scrap empties. The Advice Note should be posted in the priced ledger and credit afforded to the returning department.

21. **Payment to the Firms.** In such cases, the following adjustment should be made to credit the firm to whom the empties belong, and to debit the department concerned with the originally stipulated cost of the empties. A Receipt Note should be prepared for the empties, crediting the

firms concerned, and the several foils thereof distributed in the usual manner. This Receipt Note should quote reference to the original Receipt Note through which the empties along with the contents were received. As issue note should be prepared at the same time debiting the department concerned with the original cost of the empties.

22. The Receipt and Issue Notes should be posted in the priced ledgers as usual. Necessary entries regarding the adjustments and date of submission of the vouchers to the Stores Accounts Officer should be entered in the register under the initials of the Depot Officer or any other responsible subordinate nominated for the purpose.
23. When the payment to the firm is made by the Accounts Officer, Stores intimation of the same should be sent by him to the Depot Officer of noting in the register.
24. Similar adjustments should also be made when department fail to return the empties. Such adjustment should be made within a month of the due date of return of the empties to the Firms.
25. The Depot Officer should inspect once a month the register maintained in forms.
26. **Empties rejected by Firms.** When the empties returned by Depot Officer to the firms are not accepted by them and all negotiations fair to mark them do so even at a reduced price, they should be asked to send the empties to the nearest depot. If such empties belonging to the "Returnable" category adjustment should be carried out in regard to the rejected empties by the depot which sent them to the firm. The same depot should also raise debits at scrap sent by firm. If, however, the empty belonged to the "Optionally Returnable" category, the minus Receipt Note will be withdrawn. The credit to the department afforded at full original value of the empties will be adjusted at scrap value and corresponding debit raised against the depot to which the empty has been returned by the firm.
27. **Direct supplies.** The instructions should be followed to advice the Depot and Accounts Officers of the direct supply of 'returnable' empties.
28. **General.** If due to a department not returning them in time, the number of returnable (optionally or otherwise) empties is less than the quantity due for return and there are suitable empties held at scrap rates that can be substituted for such stock, they may be used to make the quantities, in order to avoid a loss to the administration.
29. In order to avoid loss to the Railway administration from any delay in the return of empties to supplying firms, depot and departments should, whenever possible, decant into or transfer to railway owned empties the contents of empties belonging to firms and release the latter for delivery to the firms. The depot or departments may held as part of their tool and plant a certain number of such empties according to their stock requirements of the contents thereof at any one time.
30. In handing and opening the empties, care should be taken to avoid mutilating or denting or damaging them in any manner. Bungs or other covers should not be lost.
31. Accounts Officers of the departments concerned should scrutinize credits at scrap rates or debits for failure to return the empties (in time or at all) and bring such cases to the notice of the Divisional or District of the subordinate concerned.

CHAPTER

32

IMPREST STORES (OTHER THAN ENGINEERING STORES)

1. **Definition of Imprest Stores.** Materials whether stock items or non-stock items, held in stock at Running Sheds, Train Examining Stations etc, not for specific works but as a standing advance for the purpose of meeting day-to-day requirements in connection with the repair and maintenance and operation of rolling stock shall, including consumable stores such as cotton waste, jute, oil, grease, etc., be treated as imprest stores, so long as they are under the control of the authority in charge of the executive unit, and have not been issued to works. The material required to upkeep of rolling-stock, by divisional electricians and that required for house lighting purposes at various stations by electric chargeman should also be treated as imprest stores.

   Note. Firewood used for lighting up purposes is not an item of imprest.

2. **Object of Imprest System.** The main object of the Imprest System is to control the expenditure on materials used each month in the running repairs of rolling-stock, etc., But this involves inter alia, effective financial and departmental control on the stocks of materials held at out-stations and their issue and recoupment.

3. **Two Systems of Imprests.** These imprest stores may either be "charged-off stores" in which case thir cost would have already been finally debited to Revenue working Expenses, or stores forming part of the stores balances of the Railway, the cost of which be at the debit of capital suspense. The railways on which the cost of all or most of the imprest stores held at running sheds etc., has been charged off to revenue.

4. A railway may follow only one of the two systems of accounting for imprest stores at "out-stations", If both systems exist on a railway, the system in which the cost of imprest is "charged off" should be adopted in the alternative system.

5. **Schedule of Imprest Stores.** Schedule of items of such materials showing the quantities of each item which should be held as an imprest should be prepared separately for each imprest holder.This schedule shall show the following details:

(*i*) Group of Stores.
(*ii*) Price List or Part List Number
(*iii*) Brief description of Stores
(*iv*) Sanctioned Imprest
(*v*) Rate
(*vi*) Value
(*vii*) Revision of quantity from time to time with referefice to authority and a nnual revaluation.

6. Copies of the schedule and any subsequent modifications of it should be supplied to the Divisional Superintendent or the immediate superior of the imprest holders, the Stores Department and Accounts officer, Stores, who should each keep the same up date.
7. **Basis for fixing Quantities.** The Quantity of each item of Imprest Stores which each imprest holder may hold at a time should be generally based on two months average consumption and should be approved by the General Manager of the railway, or any lower authority whom he may authorize.
8. **Requirements of Interchange Stations.** Where interchange stations are required to supply, spares for the repair of home line rolling stock damaged on foreign lines, an allowance for such spares should be included in the imprest stock and they should not be arranged for by special demands on the stores depot. Where the depot cannot supply the demands of all outstations in full, preference should be given to interchange stations.
9. All materials in hand in excess of such fixed imprest on the date of the application of these rules should be returned to the Stores Department through Advice Notes of Returned Stores (1539) and the cost thereof credited to Working Expenses.
10. **Monetary Limits.** The imprest stores fixed for each subordinate should be priced at Price List rates and the cost worked out by the Accounts Officer, Stores and the total value thus ascertained fixed at the approximate limit, in terms of money, of the cost of imprest stores that may be held by each imprest holder. These monetary limits for each impress holder as revised from time to time should be formally approved by the General manager, once every year.
11. **Control of Imprest.** It should be the duty of the Divisional Officer incharge of the imprest holders to see that the imprests are revised from time to time so as to ensure that they are the lowest possible both as regards quantity and value, consistent with actual working requirements. The imprest holder should be held responsible to ask for a reduction or deletion of any item of imprest on the basis of the consumption in his shed or station.
12. The imprests of imprest holders of one division could be increased or decreased under the orders of the Divisional Officer responsible by a corresponding decrease or increase in the sanctioned imprests of other imprest holders in the same division wherever a charge is made in the transportation arrangements involving the transfer of work from one imprest holder to another.
13. **Provision for Special Demands.** In case of special demands arising for such work as reconditioning certain classes of rolling stock, which is not expected to be completed within two months, the Divisonal Officer may authorize a temporary increase in the imprest stock. A copy of this authority, showing the amount of the increase, the reason for it and the probable duration, should be sent to the Accounts Officer, Stores, and to the Controller Stores.

14. **Excess Stores.** The sanctioned allotments present the fixed quantities which should be stocked by the imprest holder. Should any excess arise, it should either be used under the instructions of the controlling authority to recoup other imprests on the Division, or be returned to Stores Depots promptly and the cost thereof credited to Revenue in the usual way. Such recoupment of imprest should be shown as minus issues with relevant allocation by the receiving imprest holder.
15. **Numerical Ledgers.** Each imprest holder should maintain a numerical ledger showing all receipts, issues and balances of imprest material.
16. **Issue of Materials.** All issue should be made on Issue Ticket which should be signed by person duly authorized to approve of the drawing of the material. The issue Tickets will be prepared in a from such as that shown below:

TICKET FOR IMPREST STORES

Serial No. Machine Number

Rubber Stamp of Impress Holder

Store Clerk,

Issue the following			
Class and PL No. (To be filled in by the Stores Clerk	Description of Stores	Allocation	Engine Carriage Wagon No.

....

Signature and date of receiving chagemen

17. A separate Issue Ticket should be made out for each item of stores and should show the head of account to which the cost of material is debitable. The correct part or price list numbers should be entered by the Imprest Ledger Clerk.
18. **Daily Abstract of Issues.** At the end of each day issue Tickets should be arranged by classes price list numbers, and head of allocation. A daily abstract in a from ruled as shown below should then be prepared separately for each class of materials showing the total quantity of each item issued for the day and the quantities debitable to each head of account.

DAILY ABSTRACT OF ISSUES-CHARGED OFF STORES

Date.................

Head of Allocation		B II	B III	C II	C III	
Class and P.L.	Issue Ticket No.	Quantity	Quantity	Quantity	Quantity	Total quantity for the day for each item

19. **Posting of Ledgers.** The ledgers should be posted daily from the abstracts of issue tickets for each day.
20. **Monthly Summary of Issue.** A monthly summary in a from designed as shown below should be posted daily from the daily abstracts and totaled at the end of the month.

MONTHLY SUMMARY OF ISSUES.-"CHARGED OFF" STORES

Class

		P.L.No.		P.L.No.		
Date	Allocation	Allocation	Allocation	Allocation	Allocation	Allocation
	Quantity	Quantity	Quantity	Quantity	Quantity	Quantity
Total quantity for each head under each						
Total Issues						

21. **Returned Stores.** Supplies of Serviceable stores should generally be obtained from the stores depots. But such serviceable materials as may be received from line or reclaimed from scrap and is not used up immediately on work, should be taken on to the imprest Ledger besides which there should be no other account. If the balance is thereby increased to a figure in excess of the fixed miprest, all such excess should be returned to the depot on Advice Notes of Returned Stores.
22. Whenever such stores are taken into imprest stock, the transactions should be shown as minus issues and accounted for accordingly.
23. Scrap material received back from the line should not be taken on to the Imprest Ledger but should be returned to the stores depots under Advice Notes. These Advice Notes should be given a separate serial number for each shed of station and be marked "Imprest".
24. **Transfer.** No transfer to stores between imprest holders should be made except in emergencies. In such exceptional cases, the stores required may be obtained from a neighboring imprest holder, who will however account for them as an issue made by himself to work and will give a suitable remark on all connected documents to show where the material has actually gone.
25. **Closing of Ledgers and Recoupment of Imprests.** The Divisional Officers should fix the dates of accounting period for each imprest holder and intimate the same to the Accounts Officer, Stores.

    Each Imprest holder close his ledgers monthly on the dates fixed for him and check them with the issue and Recoupment Schedule which should be prepared in the form shown below from the Monthly Summary of Issues.

COMBINED ISSUE AND RECOUPMENT SCHEDULE

For period from ....to ....of (Designation of Imprest holders) Station ....

Class.......................

Serial No. of imprest	PL No.	Brief description of stores	Sanctioned imprest	Closing balance	Qty. demanded for Recoupment	Qty. issued by depot	Rate	Unit	Value of Qty.
1	2	3	4	5	6	7	8	9	10

Stores depot balance after	Date of posting and initials of poster		Head of accounts and value			
	(a) Stock	(b) Period	B	II	B	II
			Qty.	Value	Qty.	Value
11	12			13		

The issue and recoupment schedule should be prepared in four copies all of which should be sent to the Stores Depot, which the Controller of Stores may assign as the supply depot for each imprest holder. Items of stores relating to different classes of stores should be prepared on separate sheets. The first six columns should be filled in by the imprest holder and the quantity shown under column 6 should be no more or less than the quantity issued by him to works unless certain receipts from other sources than the depot had been received during the recoupment period of there has been less recoupment on the last occasion. The imprest holder shall ordinarily recoup the full quantity necessary to bring up his balance to the fixed imprest. The Stores Department will carry out a (percentage) check to ensure that the above rule is not infringed and bring to the notice of the Transportation Department any irregularities that may be detected.

Allocation. The imprest holder should split the quantity under column 6 by heads of account debit able and show the same in column 13. The value debitable to each head of account would then be split up accordingly by the Accounts Officer, Stores and shown along side the quantities. If the depot had "less –recouped" any item, the debit should be made by the Accounts Officer in the order of the heads of allocation shown in column 13, the quantity "less recouped" being worked off against the last head of account. In the recoupment schedule for the following month, the imprest holder should take care to show the quantity "less recouped" in the previous month against the corrected head of allocation. The columns for the allocation and values are shown on the sample form but should not be printed, being left to the imprest holder of columinize in manuscript as and when required.

Column 7 will be filled in by the ward of the Depot making the recoupment and column 11 and 12 (a) will be entered by the Depot Ledger Section. The figures of rate, unit and value by each detailed head of account and for the total will be filled in by the Accounts Department.

26. **Authority to Sign Indets.** Indents for recoupment may be made directly by the imprest holders under their signature and the counter signature of District or Divisional Officers for such indents is not necessary.
27. **"New for Old".** In respect of repairable materials, the general principle should be followed that old items of stores should be returned in exchange for each new item demanded. A list of items which should be invariable returned in this way should be issued by Railway Administrations. An illustrated list is printed as Appendix VIII to this Code. Reference to the Advice Note under which such stores have been returned should be quoted on the Recoupment Schedule against the relevant items. If an item on such a list has been lost or cannot be returned for some reason, a statement should be sent detailing the shortage and giving brief explanation why the item could not be produced in exchange.
28. **Depot Procedure.** On receipt of the recoupment schedules in the depot, they should be checked to see that in all cases of failure to submit an old item in exchange for a new one an explanation has been given. The statement should then be sent by the Depot Officer to the Divisional Officer concerned for any action he may consider necessary.
29. **Recoupment of Imprests.** The Depot Officer should enter in the copies of the Recoupment Schedule the quantities of materials actually issued against the quantity demanded. If the former is different from the latter, the balance of the indent is automatically cancelled. The imprest holder may recoup the balance through the next schedule or through a special recoupment schedule as and when necessary.
30. **Review of Scales of Imprests.** Suitable arrangements should exist for the periodical examination, at intervals of not less than six months, of the scales of Imprests with reference to the actual issues for the purpose of seeing of the Imprest can be reduced.
31. **Despatch of Imprest Stores.** The depot will dispatch the material by the usual railway services or stores vans and the supply will be treated as having been issued to imprest holder as soon as stores are made over to the Traffic staff or the subordinate incharge of the stores van
32. **Disposal of the foils of the Recoupment Schedule.** Two copies of the issue and recoupment schedule as completed by the Stores Depot should be sent along with the material. Acknowledgment for the material supply should be obtained on both the copies from the imprest holder. One copy will be held by the depot as receipt, while the other copy will be submitted by the imprest holder to his District or Divisional office for check with the copy received from the Stores Accounts Office.
33. **Accounts Officer Procedure.** The Stores Accounts Office should insert the rates on the schedules, and after valuing the actual quantities issue by the depot separately for each head of account, should post the relevant priced ledgers, and forward one copy to the Divisional or District Officer concerned in support of the Daily Summary of Issues. The other copy will be retained for record in the Stores Accounts Office.
34. **Special Recoupments.** As far as possible, recoupment of imprest should be made at monthly intervals through the issue and recoupment schedules; but in the event of the whole imprest stock of any item being exhautsted, a special recoupment demand may be made if this is considered absolutely necessary.
35. **Ordinary Requisitions.** Ordinary requisitions should not be submitted for items appearing in the imprest schedule and if so submitted, should not be complied with by the Stores Depot.

36. **Requisition for non-imprest Items and Specific Works.** All Stores other than those specified in the imprest schedules which may be required for the purpose of meeting urgent requirement will be obtained on ordinary requisitions countersigned by the controlling officer as and when required, and the cost of these will be charged to the final heads of revenue account. The controlling officer will be held responsible for scrutiny that the articles indented for are really required and that one of the articles available in the imprests could have been used instead.
37. If stores on the imprest schedule are required for specific works, they should be obtained on ordinary requisitions such stores should be issued immediately to the specific work for which they have been obtain and should not be brought on to the quantity accounts maintained by imprest holders for the accountal of imprest stores.
38. **Annual Revaluation and Accountal.** The imprests should be valued at price list rates by the Stores Accounts Officer on the 31st of March each year (the extent to which the increase or decreases in the value of the imprests as compared with sanctioned amounts of the previous year, is due to a variation in the quantities or prices of material should be explained by him, for purpose of incorporation in an annexure to the Annual Statement of Stores Transaction. The Stores Accounts Officer should intimate every departmental head at the same time of the revised money value of the imprest with each of the imprest holders under his control.
39. Wherever there has been an increase in the value, he amount of the increase with brief remarks as to the cause, should be given to enable the departmental officer to examine the imprest sanctions before obtaining the General Manager's formal sanctions.
40. A schedule should be attached to the Annual Statement of Stores Transactions showing the value of these imprests with each imprest holder in each Division.
41. **Verification and Inspection.** Departmental verification of imprest stocks should be carried out annually and a certificate thereof appended to the Annual Statement of Stores Transactions.
42. The Stocks should also be verified by the Accounts Stock verifiers, at least once in two years along with the departmental verification. They should then draw up a report for each imprest holder, which would detail any discrepancy or irregularity found; the imprest holder should furnish on the stock verification sheet itself full explanations for all such irregulations. On the occasion of such verification, opportunity should be taken by the Stock Verifiers to examine whether the schedules are based on actual consumption. Copies of reports of such investigation should be sent to the General Manager and the Divisional Officer concerned. Any revision of imprests necessary on a consideration or therse reports should be made by the General Manager or the Divisional Officer.
43. **Inspections.** Officer and senior subordinates of the Mechanical Engineering Department should see, during their visits to sheds and stations, that the orders regarding the maintenance of imprests are being faithfully followed and that the ledgers, abstracts and summaries are being maintained up to-date in accordance with the rules and that there are no stores kept on hand other than those in the sanctioned imprest.

Form these Daily Abstract, should be posted daily two Monthly Summaries, one by quantities for each item of stores and another by detailed heads of accounts on the lines indicated in the two forms shown below.

MONTHLY QUANTITY SUMMARY

Class ....

	P.L.Nos.				
Date	Quantity	Quantity	Quantity	Quantity	Quantity

MONTHLY ALLOCATION SUMMARY

Date	Head of account		Head of account		Head of account	
	Rs.	Ps.	Rs.	Ps.	Rs.	Ps.

44. **Issue and Recoupment Schedules.** The Recoupment should be made on a Printed Imprest Recoupment Schedule in form, such as that illustrated below in which column 1 to 4 will be printed showing all the items of the imprest sanctioned for each imprest holder. Colums 5 to 12 except 10 will be posted by the imprest holder. The 'rate' in column 5 should be the latest rate at which recoupment was made.

ISSUE AND RECOUPMENT SCHEDULE OF........................

For the period from ....to ....

S.No.	Class	Description of Stores	Unit	Rate	Fixed Imprest	Opening Balance	Receipt from stores & Sources	Issue	Value
1	2	3	4	5	6	7	8	9	10

Closing	Required	Supplied by stores	
		Qty	Value
11	12	13(*a*)	13(*b*)

45. **Recoupments.** The Recoupments Schedules on receipt from the Depot should be posted direct into the ledgers and the total values of the recoupments posted in the register of impress at the end of the month, the issues from stores depots to the imprests should be adjustment though a Journal entry crediting the head "Transfers Stores " and debiting "Capital Imprest Suspense Account".

46. **Increase or decrease in Imprest.** On receipt of intimation from the District or Divisional Officer regarding an increase or decrease in the imprest stock with certain imprest holder the increase should be noted in the respective Imprest Schedule and discrepancies discovered I the Recoupment schedules later on, should be pointed out to the imprest holder.

47. **Stock Verification.** Stock sheets showing the results of verification should be sent to the Accounts Officer, Stores who will deal with them on the lines of the procedure mutatis mutandis for stock sheets relating to stores depots.

48. **Annual Revaluation.** At the close of every financial year, the value of the closing balances shown in the latest Issues and Recoupments Schdule for the month of March should be calculated at the latest price List rates. The total value of stock with each imprest holder should then be entered in the Register of Imprests opened separately for the new year. The total value for each kind of imprest should then be compared with the figures shown in the Registors of Imprests for the last year and the difference adjusted by debit or credit to the Stock Adjustment account after full reasons have been recorded for the discrepancies after careful scrutiny.

49. **Engineering Imprest Stores and Surplus Stores.** The detailed for the maintenance and accountal of Imprest and Surplus Stores with Engineering Subordinates have been laid down in Chapter of the State Railway Code for the Engineering Department. Such stores will be borne at debit of Capital Suspense 'Stores' under the following heads of accounts.

    Engineering Stores..................Imprests...................Permanent-way
    Engineering Stores..................Imprests..................Other than Permanent-way
    Engineering Stores..................Surplus...................Permanent-way
    Engineering Stores..................Surplus...................Other than Permanent-way

    The intitial document and accounts vouchers affecting these heads of accounts will be dealt with by the Accounts Officer of the Engineering Subordinates. Each month, these Accounts Officers will send necessary Transfer Certificates for the amounts of debits and credits to the several heads of accounts to the Stores Accounts Officer who will take them into account and post the Subsidiary Registers for the heads of accounts for purpose of the monthly reconciliation with the General Books.

CHAPTER

33

ENGINEERING PLANT RESERVE COSTUDY, RECEIPT AND ISSUE

1. **Object of a Reserve.** In order to avoid losses from forced sales of serviceable and useful plant left over from special works which is likely to be required for future special works, an "Engineering Plant Reserve "may be created on each railway, with the previous sanction of the Railway Board, who will fix the maximum financial limit of such reserve.
2. **Nature of Plant in Reserve Stock.** The Engineering Reserve would include items of construction plant with the following description:
   - (*i*) Air compressors
   - (*ii*) Air receivers
   - (*iii*) Boilers
   - (*iv*) Boring plant, special, hand and power driven
   - (*v*) Concrete mixing machine
   - (*vi*) Cranes (derrick scotch)
   - (*vii*) Dregers, crab
   - (*viii*) Drilling machines, hand or power driven
   - (*ix*) Drilling machines, pneumatic
   - (*x*) Driving gear
   - (*xi*) Engines, portable, steam
   - (*xii*) Engines, internal combustion
   - (*xiii*) Engines, locomotive, 2 feet gauge
   - (*xiv*) Gantries for girder erection
   - (*xv*) Hammers (pneumatic), rock drilling
   - (*xvi*) Jacks, hydraulic
   - (*xvii*) Jacks, screw
   - (*xviii*) Jolly boats

(*xix*) Lathes (for construction)
(*xx*) Lorries (moter)
(*xxi*) Mortar mills, steam power
(*xxii*) Pumps and pumping plant of all description
(*xxiii*) Pile driving frames
(*xxiv*) Pile hammers, steam
(*xxv*) Screwing machines
(*xxvi*) Steam hoists
(*xxvii*) Stone crushers
(*xxviii*) Winches, crab
(*xxix*) Winches, steam

The list may be added to or any item deleted there from under the orders of the Chief Engineer.

The Stores department should not hold separate stock of these items of the Engineering Plant eserve for use in building new work (not in the ordinary operations of the railway).

3. **Transfer of Plant to Reserve.** On the completion of special works and constructions, all useful plant, for which there is no demand on the open line, should be returned by the divisional or the executing Engineer-incharge to the nearest stores depot accompanied by an Advice Note which should give the following additional information.
   (*i*) Type of plant and maker's name in addition to full description.
   (*ii*) Date when the plant was received.
   (*iii*) Cost of plant originally debited to work.
   (*iv*) Allocation of the work on which the plant was employed and that to which credit for its return value is to be afforded.

   The advice Notes should be prominently marked "Engineering Plant Reserve".

   Note: Where under existing arrangements the Engineering Plant Reserve is concentrated in the Plant Depot under the control of the Engineering Department, the existing arrangements may continue provided the rules in the chapter are followed mutatis mutandis.

   The Engineering Department will, in all cases, be responsible for deciding what material is to be maintained in the "Engineering Plant Reserve".
4. **Custody of Reserve:** The Stores Department will be responsible for all material in the Engineering Plant Reserve and should maintain records of their receipts, issues and balances.
5. **Storage:** When any new material is sent to the Reserve or where an item is retuned from works to the Reserve, the Controller of Stores should decide at which point it is to be stocked. It is desirable that the plant should be stocked at some place close to where it can be overhauled. It is not necessary that all the material should be held in one place, provided that separate records are kept for all such items and the materials themselves are clearly marked and stocked separate so that they do not get mixed up with ordinary stocks.

   For convenience, the material may be held in three localities:
   (*i*) Plant such as winches, dredgers and pumps, which required overhauling in the workshops, may be kept in or close to the shop concerned.
   (*ii*) Plant like portable engines, which have boilers, should be kept in or close to loco shops, where the boilers can be inspected and tested.

(*iii*) Plant like disintegrators, pulsometers, tip wagons which may require replacement of spare parts but not much shop work, may be kept in the stores depots.

6. **Reserve Plant Number.** Each machine or piece of plant of should be given a separate number and marked in some conspicuous place with this number and the letters "E. R." (Engineering Reserve). This number corresponds to the price list number assigned to general stores items and is conveniently referred to as the Reserve Plant number, If there is more than one machine or piece of plant of the same category, a bye number should be given to each such machine as a denominator with the number allotted to the category of plant as numerator. If the machine or plant has been given by the makers an individual number, such a number should be adopted as bye number.

7. **Reserve Plant Register.** The Depot Officer should maintain a register form for recording the receipts, issues and balances of all "Engineering Reserve" items. This register will show the following particulars:

   (*i*) Reserve Plant Number.
   (*ii*) Returning officer.
   (*iii*) Name of work.
   (*iv*) Particulars of advice note under which returned.
   (*v*) Description of plant.
   (*vi*) Cost of plant originally debited to works.
   (*vii*) Estimated scrap value of plant at end of life.
   (*viii*) Book value on receipt into Reserve.
   (*ix*) Total book value.
   (*x*) Particulars to issue notes under which issued from Reserve.
   (*xi*) Name of work to which issued.
   (*xii*) Amount debited on issue.

   No other numerical ledgers need be maintained.

   On receipt of an item of Engineering Plant Reserve, the particulars of the plant should be entered in the register from the Advice Notes.

8. **Valuation of Plant.** The value of the plant sent to the Reserve will be fixed by the Controller of Stores in consultation with the Chief Engineer, after a consideration of the original value of the plant, the time which it has been in use and its condition at the time of return, as also the current purchased price of new plant. In all cases of 'special plant' purchased for work of a kind that is not frequently undertaken, it should be seen that the value at which such plant is taken into the Engineering Plant Reserve is as low as possible consistent with the possible price the plant may fetch in the market. The following formula may be used as a guide in all other cases. The value fixed should be entered in all the copies of the Advice Note and the several foils disposed of as usual.

   Formula:

$$\text{The second hand value of a Plant} = R\frac{N}{L}(R - S)$$

   Where, R is the present day price of a new plant; if this is not readily available, R may be estimated taking the original price as a bases.

N is the age of the plant.

L is the average total life of the plant.

and, S is the scrape value (previously estimated).

9. **Inspection and Repai ; of Reserve Plant.** On return of a plant to the stores depot it should be inspected, dismantled and all necessary repairs carried out so that it is in though working order and ready for the next issue.
10. **Responsibility for Inspection.** The Chief Engineer will be responsible for arranging inspections of all materials taken into the Reserve and for certifying that all such material is complete in all respects, serviceable and fit for immediate issue to another work.
11. **Requisition for Inspection.** On receipt of the material, the Depot Officer should issue a memo, requesting the Chief Engineer to arrange for its inspection and to fix its monthly hire rates in accordance with th . rules. If work, such as boiler insection, is required, the Depot Officer should also requisition the services of the Mechanical Department for the work.
12. **Estimate of Cost of Inspection and Repairs.** Estimates of the cost of inspection and of any necessary repairs should be obtained and sent to the Chief Engineer for acceptance before any such work is put in hand.
13. **Allocation of Cost of Inspection and Repairs.** The cost of inspection and of repairs required before bringing an item of the Plant Reserve to a fully serviceable condition on return from a work should be charged to the work concerned, which should bear in addition the difference between the second-hand value of the artical as it stood when the item was supplied and as it stands at the time of the return of the item. In those cases where it is doubtful whether the plant will be used in the near future, and it is, therefore, considered desirable not to undertake the repair immediately, the cost of such repairs should be estimated and the value fixed for the plant after deducting such estimated cost of repairs. A note to this effect should be given on the Advice Note for plant, and transcribed into the plant Reserve Register and Priced Ledgers for Reserve Plant. Where, however; the arrangement is for the work to be debited on the bases of for the plant to be inclusive of all charges, the expenditure on inspection and repairs and the deterioration in value should be charged to the head A-2210. No suspense head of account should be operated upon for the purpose of recording the expenditure on repairs to such plants.
14. **Certificate of Inspection.** The Depot Officer should obtain a certificate in the following form for all material brought on or returned to the Reserve:

ENGINEERING RESERVE PLANT INSPECTION CERTIFICATE

Reserve Plant No......................

Description of item...................

Spares included.......................

Remarks....................................

(*i*) The material specified above is complete and ready for use.

(*ii*) The above material has been overhauled and inspected on ....the plant is in good order and ready for reissue to works.

The plant has been inspected and the following items of repair are needed. The estimated cost of such of repairs is Rs.....................................

Dated.....................................

....

Chief Engineer

On the certificate being furnished, the Depot officer should place the item in the Reserve and see that debits for hire charges and cost of inspection and repairs are against the work from which the material was received.

15. **Issue.** Issue will be made under instructions from the Chief Engineer who will countersign any requisitions placed on the Depot Officer by the officials in charge of works. Issue notes coverting issues of plant from the reserve should be marked "Engineering Plant Reserve" in bold letters. The Reserve Plant Number of the plant issued should invariably be quoted on the issue notes which should also show the amount to be debited. This should be the same as the value at which the item was taken into the Reserve. The several foils of the issue note should be distributed as usual.
16. **Freight and Handling Charges.** Freight and Handling Charges incurred in returning the plant from 'works' to the stores depot, or vice versa will be borne by the party returning the plant or indenting for it, as the case may be.
17. **Hiring out of Reserve Plant.** As many of the items of plant taken into the Engineering Plant Reserve are likely to be idle for considerable periods, such of those as are not likely to be required for current railway works may be hired out to other Government Departments, or private parties, with the approval of the Chief Engineer, if the plant is to be used in the interests of public service and is to be handled by Departmental labour only and not by contractors, and with the approval of the General Manager in all other cases. Applications for hiring the plant should be in the form shown below.

APPLICATION BY OTHER GOVERNMENT DEPARTMENTS FOR ENGINEERING RESERVE PLANT ON HIRE

To be filled in by prospective loanee or to be filled in by the Railway:

By whom requireded	Particulars of plant required	Quantity required	Purpose for which required	Period for which required	Original cost	Depre-ciated cost	How long used by Rly	Hire recha-rges
1	2	3	4	5	6	7	8	9

Certified that the above plant will be used by departmental labour only and not by contractors.

....

Signature of Loanee

18. **Agreement Form for Hire of Plant.** A suitable agreement should be signed by the Department of hiring the plant and the Chief Engineer incorporating the points deal with the rules. A copy of this agreement should be supplied to the Accounts Officer, Stores, who will watch the recovery of higher, and the return of the plant through the Register of Agreements into which the agreement will be posted by him.
19. **Terms of Delivery.** Delivery shall be in the railway stores yard and the hirer shall remove and return the plant from and to the same point at his own cost.

20. **Freight and Incidental Charges.** Where the plant or material is carried by rail, the carriage charges shall be at public tariff rates.

    The hiring department shall pay, in addition to the hire charges agreed to actual costs plus 12,1/2 per cent supervision charges of all packing, handling, loading, unloading or other direct charges incurred by the railway in despatching or receiving back the plant.

21. **Hire charges.** Hire shall be charged from the date of delivery of the plant in the railway stores yard to the date of its return to the same point (both dates to be included in the period of hire).

    Hire charges for each item of plant will be fixed by the Controller of Stores in consultation with the Chief Engineer.

22. **Liability for Wear and Tear.** The hiring department should satisfy itself when taking over the plant that it is in satisfactory working order. It shall be liable to replace at its own cost wearing parts, such as washers, packing, pump buckets, gauge-glasses & C. which may require replacement during the period of hire. A schedule giving a list of such parts to the particular plant hired out should be attached to the Agreement of Hire of the plant. Spares for such replacements should be obtained only from the railway, which will supply them ex stores depot, at book rates plus the ordinary supervision and freight charges. The materials will be sent from the stores depot to the railway station nearest the point where the plant is stationed, at Public tariff rates, to be paid by the hiring department. The Chief Engineer may at his discretion permit the purchase of the spare wearable parts from outside sources provided he is satisfied that parts correct to specifications only will be used.

23. **Breakage or Loss of Parts.** In the case of breakage or loss of any part or accessory, other than the parts liable to wear out referred to in the schedule attached to the Agreement for Hire of a plant, the cost of replacement shall be shared between the railway and the hiring departments the railway accepting a fraction of the cost represented by the actual life of the part divided by the assumed life, and the hirer a fraction of the cost represented by the difference between actual and assumed life divided by the assumed life. Unless expressly stated before hand in writing , all parts and accessories shall be taken as having the same life as shown for the plant on the railways' books; the assumed life of all machines when not otherwise stated shall be taken as 15 years.

24. **Loss of the Entire Plant.** In the event of the loss of the entire plant, the cost shall be divided on the bases laid down as in breakage or loss of parts.

25. **Statutory Certificates.** While the machine is in the possession of the hirer, he shall be responsible for seeing that any inspection certificate or licence required under any Government Act is obtained in due time. The hirer is also responsible for seeing that all required precautions are observed in using the plant, and is responsible for any accident which may occur from the use of the plant.

26. **Access to Plant at Hirer's Premises.** The railway shall be given reasonable access to the plant and such facilities as may be necessary to satisfy itself that the plant is being so used as to avoid any unnecessary wear or loss or undue risk.

27. **Right of Recall.** The railway shall reserve to itself the right to recall any plant without assigning any reasons by giving one month's notice, or at any time without notice in the event of its being required by the railway for an unforeseen emergency. The general nature of such emergencies should be specified in the Agreement for the hire of the plant. In either case, the railways shall not be liable to pay any compensation to the hirer for the loss that may be caused by the withdrawal of the plant.

28. **Inspection and Repairs on Return of Plant.** On return of the plant, it should be opened out and examined in the railway shops. A statement should be prepared of any repairs or replace-

ments, other than those due to fair wear and tear, which are considered necessary, and the cost of such repairs or replacements should be estimated and shown thereon. A copy of this statement should be sent to the hirer who should be given reasonable opportunity, during working hours of the stores depot, to check the correctness of this statement by the examination of the plant. Such repairs and replacements as are agreed to be necessary, over the about fair wear and tears shall be shared between the parties on the same bases as for breakage or loss of parts.

If the Chief Engineer or other officer empowered by him in this behalf is satisfied that the breakage referred to in paragraph 1931 or excessive wear and tear is not due to the conditions of service to which the plant has been subjected to by the hirer, but is due to previous wear, inherent defect not incidental to the service on which the plant has been used or the like, the Chief Engineer or other officer empowered by him may waive wholly or in part the recovery of cost.

29. **Accountal of Hire Charge.** The Controller of Stores will be responsible for the due recovery of the hire charges and the charges for inspection and repaires, where lived, and for the correct maintenance of the numerical accounts of the several items included in the Engineering Plant Reserve.

    (*i*) The account of the hire charges of the plant should be kept by the Controller of Stores and this should be inspected by the Accounts Department at the time of inspection of his office. The amount of hire should be credited to Earnings.

    (*ii*) The bills for hire charges should be prepared by the Controller of Stores and submitted through the Stores Accounts Officer to the hiring departments. The Stores Accounts Office will arrange for the check and recovery of the hire charges.

30. **Priced Ledgers.** Separate Priced Ledgers should be maintained in the Stores Accounts Office for each plant or piece of plant represented by a Reserve Plant number. The priced ledger should be maintained in the following form:

ENGINEERING PLANT RESERVE PRICED LEDGER

Description of Plant.............................. Serial No..........................

By No. of plant	Original new cost (estim ated)	Estim ated scrap value	Original debit to work	Advice Note or issue note	Received from or issued to	Name of work	Open ing Bal.	Credit allowed Rs.	Debit raised Rs.	Closing balance Rs.
1	2	3	4	5	6	7	8	9	10	11

The priced ledger should be posted in the same manner as other vouchers. The entire "Engineering Plant Reserve" being teated as one class for the purpose of Class Summaries and Ledgers. The receipt and issue vouchers affecting this Reserve should be dealt with on the same lines as the other vouchers for stores transactions. The balance at the end of each month in the Class Ledger should agree with the debit outstanding under the head "Engineering Plant Reserve" in the General Books of the railway and should not exceed the financial limit laid down by the Railway Board.

CHAPTER

34

CARRIAGE OF RAILWAY MATERIALS

Note. The rules apply to the despatch and carriage of Railway materials by Railway Department only.

34.1 PACKING AND LOADING OF MATERIALS

- **Addressing of Smalls and Packages in Less than Wagon Loads.** Every package forming part of a consignment of less than a wagon load should be fully and legibly addressed. Unaddressed packages should not be accepted for booking. All old addresses should be obliterated before packages are tendered for booking.
- Consignments of less than a full wagon load will be accepted for booking and delivered at the goods shed or parcels office only, as the case may be, and not at the premises of the consignor. Such consignments will be subject to the same rules as consignments by the public in respect of loss of damage.
- **Weight Limit by Passenger Train.** Packages exceeding two quintals should not be tendered for despatch by passenger or parcel trains except by special arrangement.

34.2 CONSIGNMENTS IN FULL WAGON LOADS

- **Requisition of Wagons.** A written requisition stating the number and description of wagon or other vehicles required, accompanied by a Railway Material Consignment Note, in support should be sent by the official indenting for the wagon or wagons to the Station Master or Goods Clerk concerned.
- **Wagon Loads booked from and to Department Sidings.** In connection with the booking of full wagon loads under R.M.C. Note and the loading of such consignments in departmental siding. All fully wagon loaded departmental wagons dealt within a department siding, or elsewhere other than a goods shed should be sealed by the department concerned.

- **Loading of Covered Wagons.** Despatching departments should use covered wagons for all materials and stores that can be loaded in such wagons.
- A list of the articles, with a short description and date of lading must be signed by the loader and placed inside each wagon near the door, in order to facilitate check in the event of the contents having to be transhipped on route. The wagons should after loading be scaled and properly locked before being made over to the Traffic Department for dispatch. The R.M.C. Notes covering such consignments should be endorsed 'Sealed & Locked' and this remark should be repeated on the invoices and Railway Receipt. (if any).
- **Liability for Shortage.** If the seals and locks are found intact at destination or transhipment station and a shortage is discovered on unloading a covered wagon loaded in a departmental siding, the sender will be held responsible for the shortage. If on arrival at destination or transhipment point, one or both seals are found deficient but the locks are intact, the Traffic Department along with RPF staff will withness the check of the contents of the wagon, provided it is done before the wagon is placed in a departmental siding, but responsibility for any shortage discovered will rest with the sender. The Traffic Department will accept responsibility for shortage (not depreciation or damage) only when wagons are received with seals and locks damaged and deficient, provided the checking of the contents of such wagons is done by the consignee in the presence of representative of the Traffic Department at a place arranged by the Traffic Department.

  Note. As all Railway materials and stores are generally carried at Owner's Risk the Traffic Department is not responsible for any loss, destruction or deterioration of or damage to these stores except when it can be proved that it is due to any misconduct on the Railway Administration or its servant. Through Railway materials and Stores can, however, be booked at Railway Risk when a rate which is 20 per cent higher than the Owner's Risk rate is chargeable and in such cases the Traffic Department will be as responsible for any loss, destruction or deterioration of or damage to the stores as a Bailee. Vide Section 72 (1) of the Indian Railways Act. 1890.

  The Despatching department will be held responsible for seeing that all loaded wagons are locked before despatch.

34.3 CONSIGNMENTS IN OPEN WAGONS

Only rails, girders, heavy and bulky machinery, signal posts, and material which cannot be loaded in covered wagon are permitted to be loaded in open wagons, and materials so loaded should be secured by lashing chains or wires.

- **Liability of Shortage.** The Despatching Department will be held responsible for shortages found in material and stores loaded in open wagons unless it is proved otherwise by proper investigation.
- **Shortages in Transhipped Wagons.** When loads of wagons are adjusted or transhipped, the Goods Clerk or Station Master will advise the despatching and destination stations of the date of the adjustment or transhipment, the number and description of the contents, and the owning railway of the wagon or wagons into which the materials had been transhipped.
- When shortages are discovered in transhipped wagons, the Traffic Department will make the necessary enquiries and if no articles are found to be left behind, the sender will be held responsible for the shortage.

34.4 LABELING OF WAGONS

Wagons should be properly labelled by the Goods Clerk before they are despatched. The sealing of the vehicles, where necessary.

- **Rebooking of Consignments.** Consignments which the consignee or consignor require to be rebooked or to be delivered short of destination, will be dealt with in every respect as in the case of public goods.

34.5 DELIVERY OF MATERIALS

- **Notice of Arrival.** Destination stations should, as far as possible, serve notice of arrival on consignees for all consignments whether booked as 'smalls' or in wagon loads.
- The consignee's copy of the Invoice (Railway Receipt) should be surrendered at the receiving station before delivery of a consignment will be given. Full signature (not merely initials) should be given at the time of taking delivery. Should the consignee copy of the Invoice not be available at the time of delivery, an unstamped indemnity bond signed by the Official to whom the consignment is booked should be tendered in place of the missing Invoice copy (Railway Receipt) which should be subsequently surrendered on receipt. Delivery should not be given unless either the Railway receipt or an indemnity bond is tendered.
- **Delivery of Wagons in Departmental Sidings.** For full wagon load consignments which have to be delivered in Departmental sidings, the Receipt Foil of the invoice or indemnity bond should be surrendered and signature given in the usual way before placement of the wagons in the siding. This procedure should be strictly followed as its non-observance will lead to considerable trouble and correspondence.
- **Demurrage and Wharfage.** A department failing to effect delivery of a consignment, within the free time allowed will in the case of 'smalls' be liable for wharfage, and in the case of wagon loads for demurrage at the ordinary public rates.

  Wagons detained in Departmental Siding will be subject to the demurrage rules applicable to ordinary public traffic.

34.6 STORES LOST OR DAMAGE IN TRANSIT

In accounting for stores lost or damaged, the following procedure should be observed.

- **Loss or Damage in Stores Despatched by or to Stores Depots Discovered at the Time of Delivery.** Station Masters should submit to the Chief Commercial Manager the usual missing goods report in the form prescribed for the purpose with necessary documents for all shortage found at the time of delivery.

  In such cases, the Receiving Depot will accept the Depot Transfer Issue Note for the actual quantity received and for the difference either lodge a claim with the Commercial Department and pursue or prepare a Counter Debit Transfer Issue Note after taking up the matter with the Sendinng Depot. In the case where a Departmental Officer receives materials from the Stores Depot will pass remarks regarding the actual quantity received on the acknowledgement foil of the issue note but prefer a claim on the Commercial Department or take up the matter with the sender Depot as the case may be. Any enquiry necessary will be conducted by the Traffic and Stores Department as above but the Accounts should raise debits as per the full quantity

Missing stores Report should be submitted in From shown below to the Chief Commercial Superintendent, within one month from the date of booking. Full particulars as to the number and date of the R.M.C. Note should be quoted in the missing stores report. If the materials or stores reported missing come to hand subsequent to the submission of Form the Chief Commercial Superintendent should be immediately advised without fail.

MISSING STORES REPORT

Wording of Foils 1 (Office copy) and III	Wording of Foils II
____________________Office,	____________________Office,
____________________19	____________________19
To	To
____________________	____________________
Report of missing stores	**Arrival advice of missing stores**
Credit Note__________Date__________	with reference to my report of missing stores
From____________________	serial No.____________________
To____________________	dated____________________ I beg to
in Sender____________________	inform you that the stores there in referred to as
Consignee____________________	per memo at fact has/have been correctly received
No. and description of Packages__________	and acknowledged in Received Return No.___
____________________	dated____________________(if a Storekeeper)
	or Consignee's Receipts No.__________
Contents____________________	dated__________(if other than a Storekeeper).
Received on ________at __________hours	
Nature of deficiency or damage__________	Credit Note No. ____________________
____________________	Date____________________
*Consignee's Receipt____________________	From(Station)____________________
Date____________________	To (Station)____________________
*Despatched in Wagon No.__________	Sender____________________
____________________	Consignee____________________
*Received on ____________________	
Advised to____________________	____________________Signature.
____________________Signature.	____________________Designation.
____________________Designation.	

*To be filled in by Consignee for guidance of Divisional Officer.

: To be filled in by the Officer to whom the report is made – On 3rd foil only.

: Only to be filled in if stores are subsequently received – On 1st foil only.

(*i*) The form will be printed, each foil alongside of the other. Foils I and III will be prepared, and the Foil III sent to the Chief Commercial Superintendent on missing a consignment of stores.

(*ii*) If subsequently, the consignment comes to hand. Foil II will be filled in and forwarded to the Chief Commercial Superintendent to enable him to stop any investigations in hand.

- **Time Limit for Claims.** Claims for losses should be submitted by consignees within six months from the date of booking and should be settled by the Chief Claims Officer within a year of the date of booking as a maximum limit of time.
- **Financial Adjustment.** No financial adjustment should be made against the Traffic Department till the claims have been accepted.

  In the case of a stores Depot, adjustment will be made by the preparation and accountal of an issue note for the quantities and values accepted by the Chief Commercial Superintendent of the claims.

  In other cases, the Accounts Officer of the department concerned will make book adjustments through Advice of Transfer Debits duly supported by an accepted copy of claim against the Accounts Officer of the Chief Commerical Superintendent. The responsibility of the Traffic department in all cases of loss or damage will be subject to the relevant rules regarding liability for loss, shortage or damages etc.; laid down elsewhere in this Chapter.

34.7 RAILWAY MATERIAL CONSIGNMENT NOTE

No Railway materials may be conveyed by rail except on the authority either of a Railway Material Consignment Note or an invoice subject to the condition that the stores, materials etc. shall be for the Construction, Revenue or Stock purposes of an Indian Government Railway and be consigned to a recognized official of the railway covered for a letter of authority for their despatch which must be produced at the sending station. The Free Service Way-bill may, however, be used only in forwarding small consignment of railway materials such as official envelopes, wagon covers and ropes etc. as given in the IRCA Goods and Coaching Tarriff.

In order to accelerate the accounting for freight charges and to reduce the clerical labour involved, it is open to railway administrations to provide for the Credit Note being made out in five parts instead of four and of the particulars of rate and of freight being filled in by the station staff. Of the five parts the first part will be the office and the fourth the receipt. The receipt will be treated in precisely the same way as the receipt foil of a invoice granted to the pubic, the responsibility of the Traffic department and of the consignee being the same in each case. The fifth copy which is meant to be made use of as a voucher for the purpose of accounting for freight, will also be handed over to the consignor for despatch to the consignee. Of the two intermediate parts, the part marked 'original' will be the authority under which the consignment is despatched and that marked 'duplicate' the Guard's Way-bill and delivery order. This part takes the place of the parcels Way-bill or Goods Invoice.

- **Head of Account Chargeable:** The official issuing Railway Material Consignment Note should clearly shows all the three foils of the railway materials consignment note the head of the allocation of the charge and designation and address of the Accounts Officer who will account for the same.

  Before the material is received, the consignee should surrender the receipt copy of the invoice together with credit note in the case of freight 'to pay' consignment to the Traffic Staff.

34.8 ACCOUNTAL OF CREDIT NOTES

- **Outward Return by Stations:** Railway materials will not be accounted for by station (in the station books and balance sheet) as to freight. From the abstract, summaries of railway materials and stores will be prepared for local and through traffic in which all particulars as per invoice should be made. The accounts copy of the Railway Material Consignment note sent in by the station in support of their outward returns will be checked in the Traffic Accounts Office. Accounts Office will complete the returns in regards to freight and prepare the necessary summaries.

Separate Outward Returns will be submitted by stations for coaching and goods consignments of railway materials and separate summaries for these will be made in the Traffic Accounts.

- **Check by Traffic Accounts Office.** The copy of the Railway Materials Consignment Note will be carefully examined in the Traffic Accounts Office as to the official designation of the consignor and consignee and the nature of the material carried to ensure, as far as possible, that the consignments are correctly treated as railway materials. Materials of the Telegraph or other Government departments are opt to be erroneously consigned as railway material and it will be seen that when such errors are discovered, a subsidiary return is prepared debiting these departments at the full tariff rates. Telegraph line stores, for use on the railway, are carried free for the Telegraph Department but the freight computed at the railway material rate is debited to the appropriate head of the revenue account. The Outward Returns of the Forwarding Stations in regard to railway materials are checked with the Inward Returns of the Receiving Stations to ensure that all consignments carried have been accounted for, due allowance being made where necessary for the arrival of consignments at the Receiving Stations in a month other than the month of dispatch. In summarising the return, the freight on consignments erroneously carried as railway material will be shown separately from freight on bonafide railway material. The Traffic Accounts Office will prepare transfer certificates and send to the Accounts Officer of the consignee raising the debit for the freight. Traffic Accounts Office should watch through a manuscript register whether the credits to Traffic Earnings are afforded promptly by the Accounts Officers concerned.

34.9 ALLOCATION OF FREIGHT CHARGES

- **Sea Freights, Customs Duty and Port and Handling Charges.** The expenditure on freight incurred by railways is either in the shape of sea freight upto the port of landing, and rail freight from such port to final destination or purely freight by rail from an inland source of supply to destination. This sea freight, the customs duty and the port and handling charges on foreign shores should be charged invariably to the cost of stores.

34.10 INLAND FREIGHT AND INCIDENTAL CHARGES

The inland freight on railway materials from the source of supply or port (together with the loading, unloading and incidental charges such as insurance, port landing, yard and other charges in India, if any) is incurred on consignments.

(*i*) Directly to a 'work' for which these materials are required, or

(*ii*) to Departmental Depots or imprests of stock held by Executive Officer, or for immediate use on maintenance and repairs, or

(*iii*) to a Stores Depot for custody until issue as and when required.

- **Freight on Direct Supplies to Work or Department.** In the case of the first class of consignments referred to in the previous paragraph the freight &c should be charged to the work such work and the case of the second class of consignments referred as mentioned above, the freight &c charges should be debited to the heads of account provided for the purpose in the relevant Revenue Abstract of the department concerned.

- **Freight on Materials sent to Stores Depot.** Materials consigned to Stores Depot (*i.e.*, the third class of consignments may be either:
  - (*i*) stores returned from works, or
  - (*ii*) stores purchased for purposes of stock, or
  - (*iii*) stores transferred from depot to depot.
- **Freight on Returned Stores.** The freight in respect of Returned Stores should be charged either to the 'work' from which the stores have been retuned (when it will be debited to Capital or the Depreciation Fund Account or /and Revenue as the casé may be) or to the Revenue Abstracts of the department concerned as the case may be.
- **Freight on Purchases for Stock.** In respect of stores purchased for stock (this includes manufactured by workshops). The freight shall be allocated as in freight on coal and other fuel and freight on all other items.
- **Freight on Coal and other Fuel.** Freight on coal and other fuel should be debited to the relevant sub-heads in Abstract 'H' of the Revenue Account. In the case of coal issued for other than locomotive purposes, *e.g.*, pumps, capital works, sales issues to other Revenue Abstracts &c a suitable percentage to cover the freight charges, based on the penultimate year's figures of total value of coal received and freight charges paid thereon, should be added to the value of the coal, the recoveries on this account being taken in reduction of expenditure under Abstract 'H'.
- **Freight on All other Items.** Freight on all items of stores for stock purposes should be charged to Abstract K 670 of the Revenue Account titled "Freight from port or source of supply".
- **Freight on Depot Transfers.** Freight incurred on transfer of stores from one depot to another should be charged finally to Revenue Abstract K 70 titled "Freight from port or source of supply".
- **Incidental Charges.** These charges are in respect of insurance, loading and unloading and yard charges and purchase and inspection percentages levied by the Directorate General of Supplies and Disposal or other Government Departments. All such expenditure will, as a general rule, be debited to the head to which freight charges on the stores are debited. As an exception to the General Rule, the charges on account of loading and unloading done by the permanent labour of the stores Department will be charged to Abstract 'A'.

34.11 RAILWAY MATERIAL CONSIGNMENT RATES

When materials or stores intended for the use of a railway are carried by the railway itself, the freight charges are creditable to the earnings of the railway and debitable either to its Working Expenses or to its Capital or Depreciation Fund Accounts. The freight charges are calculated as per the Railway Material Consignment Rates fixed by the Commercial Department separately for smalls and full wagon loads.

No distinction should be made between the railway material rates for revenue stores and that for capital or construction stores.

- **The Railway Materials Rates by other than Goods Train.** The railway material consignment rates for despatch by passenger or "other than goods train" should be at such rates as may be approved by the Railway Board.

CHAPTER

35

SURPLUS STOCKS

35.1 PREVENTION OF STOCKS FROM BECOMING SURPLUS

Important changes in the design of plant and equipment is the introduction of new standards or procedure in place of old and the scrapping of plant for which there are stocks of spares are amongst the factors contributing to accumulations of obsolete or unusable material. The procedure detailed below should be followed in order to keep the Controller of Stores informed of all such events and enable him to minimize such accumulations and consequent loss to the administration.

Surplus due to Change in Design and Standards

Before any new standards introduced, the consuming department should submit to the Controller of Stores an "Advice of Proposed Changes in Design/Standard of Stores/Procedure" in (manuscript) form given below and obtain from him the particulars of the old standard materials in stock.

ADVICE OF CHANGE IN DESIGN OR STANDARD OF STORES OR PROCEDURE

From ....

To The Controller of Stores, ...

No. .... dated ....

The following change is proposed:

Please furnish the following information for the material hitherto used of P.I.. No. .... and suspend further purchase till a decision is arrived at—

Book Balance						
Qty. in stock	Qty. on order	Total	Total Value	Average monthly consumption based on past year's issue	Other consumers	Remarks

....

Head of Department

N.B.—In the case of shop manufactured articles, the stock position of raw material required for the manufacture of the item under reference should also be incorporated,

Part "B"

No.. date ....

From .... To ....

The Controller of Stores,

To use up the stocks, the change should not be made before .... If made at once it will involve a loss of .... in write off/in interest,

....

Controller of Stores

Part "C"

From To

.... The Controller of Stores,

The change will be made when stocks are exhausted

From

An estimate showing justification for the loss involved in scraping old standard material and probable loss to the railway by postponing the introduction of new standards is attached.

....

Head of Department

Seen Approved

Accounts Officer, Stores General Manager

Noted by the Controller of Stores..(Signature) Copy to Depot Officer concerned. Stock may be written off/value may be written down, reference being given to this authority.

....

Controller of Stores

The form is in the three parts as shown above. Three copies of the form should be prepared with portion "A" only filled in and all the copies should be sent to the Controller of Stores who should fill in the required information in the columns provided in part "A" of the form, complete part "B" and return all the copies to the department concerned.

Estimate of Loss

On receipt of the information from the Controller of Stores, estimates should be prepared by the department concerned showing the probable loss to the railway involved in postponing the introduction of the new standard proposed till existing stocks are exhausted and alternatively of the probable loss involved in scrapping the existing stocks. These estimates along with two out of three copies originally sent to the Controller of Stores should be sent to him again. He should check the loss involved in scrapping the existing stock, seeing that other items are not incidentally involved, and also examine whether there are possibilities of reducing the loss by the disposal of the material to other railways.

Where the Controller of Stores accepts the date proposed for the introduction of the new standard, he should intimate this to the department concerned to enable the latter to issue the orders for the proposed changes. The Controller of Stores should at the same time take necessary steps to regulate future purchases of the article concerned, and arrange to obtain the sanction of competent authority for any loss involved in the proposed change. Where the Controller of Stores is unable to agree with the consuming department that the dates of making the proposed changes are in the best interests of the railway as a whole, he should submit his reasons to the General Manager for final decision. Until the consuming department forwards its final orders on a proposed change, new standards in subsstitution for the old should not be stocked by the Stores Department nor should any further purchase of the existing article be made.

Surplus Spares due to Replacements of Rolling Stock, Plant or Machinery

1. When budgets are under preparation involving the replacement of old rolling-stock, plant or machinery, lists of the equipment to be replaced should be submitted to the Stores Department as early as possible. The Stores Department should prepare a statement of the spare parts in stock for the equipment and refer to the consuming departments to ascertain whether these spare parts will become obsolete or can be used on other similar equipment. As soon as the details of spares to be scrapped have been fixed, the Stores Department should prepare a financial statement showing the funds to be provided in the budget for the loss involved in scrapping such material.
2. At the time of actually replacing or scrapping such rolling stock, plant or machinery, & c. a manuscript "Advice to Write off spares" should be prepared in triplicate and sent to the Controller of Stores.

ADVICE TO 'WRITE-OFF' SPARES

Estimates are being prepared for the replacement of the following.

Rolling Stock/Plant/Machinery,

Full description of the article being replaced.	To be filled in by the Stores Department			
	Spare in stock			Value
	P.L. No.	Description	Qty.	Rs. P.

Total value of spares in stock included in the estimate for replacement is Rs. ....

....

Controller of Stores

Estimate sanctic:ıed .... date ....

(Signature of departmental officer),

Depot Officer .... Depot

The plant under this estimate is expected to arrive about .... On receipt of the new plant, the spares detailed above should be (a) transferred to .... / (b) sent to the auction yard and their cost adjusted according to the rules.

....

3. The Controller of Stores should fill in the quantity and value of spares or fittings which are in stock and return all the copies of the departmental officer concerned. The value of such spares should be included in the estimate for replacement and on sanction of the estimate, two copies of the form with particulars of the estimate should be sent again to the Controller of Stores.
4. When orders for new plant have been placed, the Controller of Stores should fill in the probable date of its arrival and send one copy of the form to the depot concerned with instructions for the disposal of the spares and fittings. When the old plant is scrapped and sent to the auction yard, spares and fittings should normally be sent with it; if however the plant is transferred for use elsewhere, the spares and fittings should be kept in stock.
5. In cases where the spares are scrapped along with the plant, the difference between the original book value and the scrap value should be debited to the estimate for the replacement of the rolling-stock, plant or machinery. When the spares are actually sold later on, no further adjustment against the estimate need be made whether the articles fetched over or below the scrap rate.

Cancellation of Orders for Material for Specific Works

1. If, on account of charges in plan or specification, or the dearth of funds, materials obtained for a work, or for which a requisition has been placed will not be required, the indentor should notify the Controller of Stores at once and three copies of which should be forwarded through the divisional or district officer concerned.

ADVICE OF NON-REQUIREMENT OF STORES ORDERED FOR SPECIFIC WORKS

From .... Station ....

No......................Date.......................

To

The Controller of Stores

The materials noted below, ordered on requisition No. .... dated .... will not be required owing to a change in the design having been arranged.

alternatives.

P.L. No.	Description of item	To be filled in by Stores Deptt.	
		Value	Remarks

From To...

No......................Date.......................

The Controller of Stores

(*a*) The order has been cancelled.

(*b*) The material can be used elsewhere, credit will be given at full value.

(*c*) The material is not likely to be used for .... years, credit can only be given at .... percent of full value.

(*d*) The material cannot be used elsewhere and credit can only be given at scrap value, amounting to ....

....

Controller of Stores

Copy of Depot Officer, ... depot, to take the material when returned for auction/for stock at .... value.

....

Controller of Stores

2. If the railway is not actually committed to the purchase, the Controller of Stores should at once take steps to cancel any arrangements made, returning one copy of the form to the indentor through his divisional or district officer stating that the order has been cancelled. If the supply of materials has already been received or the railway is committed to the purchase, the Controller of Stores should return one copy of the form to the indentor through his divisional or district officer stating the rate (whether full or part or scrap) at which the Controller of Stores is prepared to take the material into stock after its original purchase cost has been debited to the department which indented for the stores. The third copy of the form should be sent by the Controller of Stores to the depot which should stock the material.
3. In case the divisional or district officer or head of the department concerned decides in favour of the changes in design & c. proposed by him, notwithstanding the loss involved thereby, he should accept the loss as a debit to the work for which the material was obtained, the sanction of the competent authority being obtained to the additional expenditure involved.

Definition of Surplus Stocks

1. The procedure prescribed for the preparation of Contract Estimates of stores for purchase it should act as a deterrent to any accumulation of stocks beyond the ordinary requirements of the railway. Purely temporary excesses over immediate or estimated requirements are not really surpluses, so long as they can be worked out by issues over a comparatively short period of time. Stores may be considered as really surplus to the requirements of the railway only if they have not been issued for a long time. Even amongst such items there may be some which it is known could be utilized for the purpose of the railway in the near future, and these may with advantage be distinguished from the surplus stores which cannot be so consumed.
2. An essential prerequisite condition to declare any items of stores as "surplus" stock on railways is that such items have not been issued from stock for railway consumption for a period of two years. Such "surplus" stock should be further classified under two heads, *viz.*,
   (*a*) movable surplus and
   (*b*) dead surplus, the definitions of which have been given below are reproduced for facility of reference.
   - **Movable Surplus.** Comprise items of stores which have not been issued for a period of 24 months but which it is anticipated will be utilized in the near future. Such items should be marked in the Price Lists.
   - **Dead Surplus.** Comprise items of stores which have not been issued for the past 24 months and which it is considered are not likely to be utilized on any railway within the next two years. No article, may, however be classified as "dead surplus" unless it has been duly inspected by a Survey Committee. Such items should be marked in the Price Lists.
   - **Emergency Stores not Surplus.** There are items which do not ordinarily wear out, or require renewal and stocks of which are not readily obtainable in India, but which it is essential to maintain to meet occasional emergencies. Amongst such items may be mentioned spare parts and duplicates of electrical machinery to be maintained for emergent

use in case of failure. Such stores are emergency stores and though not issued for period of two years or more, should not be classed as surplus stores.

35.2 SURVEY COMMITTEES

- **Functions of Survey Committees.** A Survey Committee should be formed on each railway for the purpose of inspecting critically the condition of all the stores:
  1. that have deteriorated in value, for any reason.
  2. broken or damaged in transit, or while in stock.
  3. lying in the custody of the Stores Department for a long time and considered by the Controller of Stores has having become unserviceable owing to obsolescence of other causes, and
  4. received as scrap from the line.

  The Committee should determine after such inspection:
  1. what stores held in the depot s should be treated as Dead Surplus Stores or as scrap?
  2. what stores should be classified and rate second-hand?
  3. at what rates and values such stocks should be held in the accounts books? and
  4. how such stores should be disposed of *i.e.*, by sale or by issue to particular uses of particular departments?

  1. (*a*) No stores in stock should be reclassified, and rated second-hand or scrap without the sanction of the General Manager obtained on the recommendations of the Survey Committee. However, Controller of Stores may, on the recommendation of the Survey Committee, reclassify stores in stock and rate them second-hand or scrap upto a limit of Rs. 25000/- per item, this limit being applied with reference to the book value of the item before reclassification. The power delegated to the COS may be redelegated to the Dy. COS & Depot Officers upto a limit of Rs. 10,000/- per item and Rs. 1000/- per item respectively.

     (*b*) Depot Officer may also reclassify stores in stock and rate them, 'Second hand' or 'scrap' without processing the same through Survey Committee upto a limit of Rs. 1,000/- per item. However, before classifying an item costing upto Rs. 1000/- as dead surplus, the Depot Officer should where considered necessary ascertain from the user departments and other depots that the item is not likely to be utilised by them in the next two years.
  2. No sale by auction of any article of whatever category in the depot, and no sale of scrap by private treaty should be made unless the article has been recommended for sale by the Survey Committee.

- **Composition of Survey Committees.** The Committee which should be appointed by the General Manager, will consist of the heads or the Senior Officers of the consuming departments of branches with a Secretary nominated by the General Manager who will be an officer of a department other than the Stores Department.
- **Meetings of Survey Committees.** The Committee should meet not less frequently than once in a half year, at the request of the Controller of Stores or the Depot Officer who should arrange to collect and list the articles to be surveyed.

- **Survey Sheets.** Separate lists of the articles should be made out in quadruplicate, group by group, in the form shown below:

SURVEY COMMITTEE'S REPORT

Item No.	P.L. No.	Description of Stores	Quantity		Book Value			Total	Total	Name of Deptt. Concerned	Reasons of Survey*	Recommendations of S. Committee	Remarks by the Controller of Stores for G.M.'s order
			No.	Weight	Rate	Per	Amount	Scrap Value	Loss Incurred				
1	2	3	4	5	6	7	8	9	10	11	12	13	14

* Here state briefly how stores become obsolete, surplus, & c.

The Committee should, after the most careful investigation, have their recommendations recorded by the Secretary against each of the items on all the copies of the list, both as regards prices and the manner of disposal. The Secretary of the Committee should initial each such recommendation and the members of the Committee including the Secretary, should sign all the copies of the list.

- **General Manager's Sanction.** The Survey Committee's report should be submitted by the Depot Officer to the Controller of Stores. The Controller of Stores will deal with the items falling within the powers and obtain orders of the General Manager for the others.

  The orders of the General Manager/Controller of Stores should be communicated to the Stores Accounts Officer, the Statutory Audit Officers and the Depot Officer and prompt action should be taken to implement them.

- **Revaluation of Undisposed of Items.** Such surplus stores as are not disposed of by sale, transfer of issue within twelve months of the recommendation of the Survey Committee should be classified as scrap and the book value adjusted in accordance with the rules.

35.3 OVER-STOCKS OF "ORDINARY STORES"

The maximum stock that may be held, at any time, of ordinary stores in stock (other than surplus stores and emergency or special stores) should not ordinarily exceed 50 percent of the issues of each item during the year. This limit is applied only to 'ordinary stores'. It should be the objective of every Controller of Stores to see that the stocks on hand of all items of 'ordinary stores' are maintained well within this limit. But inspite of the best of plans, overstocks of 'ordinary stores' develop which have also to be reduced in the best manner possible.

- **Factors Responsible for Overstocks of Ordinary Stores.** Amongst the factors that tend to increase balances may be mentioned:
    1. An unanticipated falls in consumption which it has been impossible to off-set by smaller purchases, owing to contractual obligations on the basis of annual contracts, and
    2. Stores returned by consuming departments in larger quantities than anticipated.

These factors should be particularly taken into account in preparing the Annual Contract Estimates.

35.4 DISPOSAL OF OVER-STOCK AND SURPLUS STOCK OF STORES

- **Surplus Stock Section.** The Stores Department of every railway should be organized to deal effectively with the disposal of surplus stock either by sale or issue, or transfer to other railways. The section of the office dealing with this work corresponds to the sales organization of a commercial concern. It should be in active touch, not only with the stocks of the different items of surplus stores, but also with markets and market prices (if any such exist) for the articles in question.
- **Selection of Items for Sale.** The 'Grouping Forms' prepared, as already explained for the purpose of estimating the items and quantities for which annual contracts should be let contain particulars of all those items of ordinary stores (Stock items) for which there have been no demands for purchase either during the current contract or the new contract periods or both. As the Grouping Forms for such items will be sent to the Surplus stock Section for disposal. The average time lag between the date of the preparation of the estimates of the annual requirements of each class of stock and the end of the new contract periode being about 18 months, the stocks of such stores for which no demands for purchase have been made for one or more contract periods are really in excess of the requirements of the railway, and the surplus Stock section should take all steps necessary to reduce such stocks, if possible, by sale to other railways who may be requiring them, during the new contract period. As the estimates for annual purchases for each item of stores will be made, by all railways, on or about the same date, the time would be opportune for the Section to collect and offer such items for sale to other railways.
- **"Over-stocks" Disposal Register.** A register in the form shown below should be maintained for recording the quantities of over-stocks of "ordinary stores" which it has been considered desirable to sell or dispose of during the next 12 months. This register should be posted from the "Grouping Form" for the items of "ordinary stores" concerned.

"OVER-STOCK" DISPOSAL REGISTER

Group ....

P.L. No.	Description of Stores	Depot Qty.	Depot Qty.	Depot Qty.	t Qty. Sold	Sale order ref.	Buyer	Remarks

- **Register of Non-stock Items.** The Surplus Stock Section should not only try, in this manner, to dispose of the over-stocks of "ordinary stores", but should make use of the same opportunity to dispose of the stocks of "moveable" and "dead surplus" stores, detailed information about which would be available in the Statement of Non-stock items submitted by the depots a register. The items classified as "moveable surplus" will be generally "stock items" for other railways and the best time for offering them for sale is that at which railways make up estimates of their requirements of the class of articles to which the item belongs.
- **Disposal to other Railways and Government Departments.** The Surplus Stock Section should scrutinize every public call for tender, stores, bulletins and Home indents issued by other railways, the Directorate General of Supplies and Disposals or any other Government Department or public body, and in addition examine advertisements in papers, such as the Indian Trade Journal in order to discover suitable opportunities of effecting the sales of surplus stores and over-stocks. When such occasion arises suitable offer may be made for sale.

  The sales will be affected by means of sales orders duly sanctioned by competent authority. The sanction should be communicated by the sanctioning authority direct to the Accounts Officer, copy being furnished to the Audit Officer also.
- **Invitation to Tender for Purchase of Surplus Stores & c.** The disposal of over-stocks and surplus stores may also be made by advertising invitations to submit tenders to the Railway for the purchase of such stores, in the most open manner possible.

CHAPTER

36

SALE OF RAILWAY MATERIALS

Railways purchase and stock stores only in such quantities as their requirements warrant and a need for the sale of such stores should not arise under normal circumstances. Sales of railway materials are therefore generally of obsolete and unserviceable stores and scrap the accumulation of which, it has not been possible to avoid. Occasionally, excess stocks of ordinary stores have to be disposed of. Railway stores should therefore be sold only when it is found that for financial and administrative reasons, it is expedient to sell then keep them in stock. Exceptions to this rule are cases of materials urgently required by other railways or Government departments and of petty sales to quasi railway institutions providing amenities for the railway staff.

Sales may be affected in one the following ways :

1. by public auction;
2. by inviting tenders for purchase or submitting tenders Offering to sell and
3. by direct sale.

No materials which are not overstocks or surplus to requirements or obsolete, unserviceable or scrap should be sold by auction or tender. Subject of the above restriction, the actual method of sale adopted should be appropriate to the circumstances under which the sales are affected and to the nature of the articles sought to be sold. Except when the amount involved in a sale is less than Rs. 100 (or the sale is by direct negotiations), effective publicity should be given to the sale, by advertisement notices in the daily press and in commercial and technical journals and, wherever this is possible, by mailing special notices to likely buyers.

36.1 POWERS OF GENERAL MANAGERS

The powers of the General Manager to sell railway materials and stores is limited only by the canons of financial propriety. He has, however, to obtain the previous sanction of the Railway Board to the sale of the following classes of assets :

1. a portion of the line;
2. any item of authorized rolling stock or
3. any other asset costing more than rupees one lac.

- **Extent Powers may be Delegated.** The General Manager may delegate to officers subordinate to him his powers to sell railway materials and stores.
- **Sale of Stores to other Railways.** Full powers to sell any stores to other Railways at full book rates or higher plus the usual percentage charges, (Supervision charges are not levied on stores sold to other Government Railways).
- **Sale of "Over stocks" of "Ordinary Emergency or Special Stores" by Tender.** Full powers to sell and adjust the difference between book rate and sale value.

36.2 SALE BY DIRECT SALE OF MATERIALS

Full powers to sell at book rate or purchase rate whichever is higher plus the usual percentage charges.

- **Direct Sale of Books, Forms, Stationery, Petty Stores and Clothing for Menial Staff .** Powers to sell at the book rate or purchase rate whichever is higher, plus freight, incidental and supervision charges, to the following:

  Railway Employees' Cooperative Credit Society Railway Institute.

  Government Railway Police Department, Indian Posts and Telegraph Department.

  Railway Battalions, Railway Regiments and other similar bodies.
- **Sale by tender, of scrap and unserviceable, surplus and obsolete stores and adjustment of the difference between the book value and sale value.** Full powers to dispose such material by tender and to adjust the difference between the book value and sale value.
- **Direct sale of Material.** Power to sell at book value or at a loss not exceeding Rs. 200, on each sale. If as a condition of sale, freight is to be borne by the administration, value of such freight should be taken into consideration in computing the loss.

36.3 CENTRALIZED CONTROL OF SALES

The Controller of Stores is responsible for the sale of railway stores irrespective of whether the stores are in his custody or not and no sale may ordinarily be affected without his knowledge and approval. Stores intended for sale should ordinarily be sent to the nearest stores depot or any particular depot the controller of Stores may assign to particular kinds of stores, and sales shall, as a rule, be affected from those stores depots only.

If the freight and loading charges likely to be incurred on transporting unserviceable and scrap materials to the stores depots for disposal, are likely to be heavy and incommensurate with the value the articles may fetch by sale later on, District and Division officers may sell with the prior concurrence of the Controller of Stores, such stores at the spots at which they lie or at any other convenient center.

The Chief Engineer may arrange for the sale of unserviceable wooden sleepers and bridge timbers without prior reference to the Controller of Stores.

The prior concurrence of the Controller of Stores is not necessary to the sale of such items as grass, tress, fish and fruit, which may be arranged by the Chief Engineer.

- **Sale to Employees.** The General manager may, in consultation with his Financial Adviser, frame suitable rules for lath the sale of small quantities of material and stores for the bonafied use of railway employees.

- **Responsibility for Execution of Sales.** When a definite sanction to or a contract for a sale of certain items is communicated to an executive officer by the Controller of Stores or the General Manager, the duty of taking all further action, such as intimation to tenderers, the quantities available for delivery, the recovery of ground rent & c., will devolve on the executive officer in charge of the material to be sold, who will be responsible for seeing that the terms and conditions of sale are observed strictly and for advising the Accounts Offices, Stores, and the Controller of Stores of the satisfactory completion of the transaction.
- **Sale by Public Auction.** The procedure to be followed in the conduct of sales by public auction.
- **Sale by Invitation Tenders.** Inviting tenders for the sale of stores it should be seen that:
    1. The tender notice which is published gives clear particulars of the materials to be sold, approximate quantities thereof and the place and the probable date of sale; and
    2. Tender forms containing the conditions of agreement are available to intending tenders at nominal prices fixed by the Controller of Stores.

36.4 CONDITION OF SALE AGREEMENT

All agreements for sale should provide *inter-alia,* clauses stipulating the following conditions, *viz.,*

1. Tendering firms should deposit with the treasurer of Railway earnest money equal to 10 per cent of the amount offered, without which deposit, the tenders will not be considered.
2. Failure to adhere to any of the conditions prescribed in the tender will disqualify the tenderer.
3. If the purchaser of any materials desires to send it by rail, it will be carried at public tariff rates only.

   Note: When there is any intention to allow the materials offered for sale to be carried by the purchaser by rail at other than tariff rates applicable to the public, the freight concession, which should have been previously sanctioned by the General Manager for the particular sale and item of stores, should be expressend in unambiguous terms and included among the conditions of sale in the tender notices and advertisements. Such concessions when granted should apply only to :—

   (*i*) condemmed railway materials which are in such a condition that they cannot be readily sold for the use for which they were originally made ; and

   (*ii*) the carriage of such stores from place of sale to first destination.

   Such concession can be granted by a railway on its home line only; necessary certificate regarding the category of stores may, however, be granted by the officer issuing the stores to enable the purchaser to obtain similar concessions on foreign railways if the first destination happens to be on a foreign railway.
4. The purchaser should pay to the Treasures of the Railway the agreed amount less the earnest money already deposited within fourteen days of the date of intimation of the acceptance of the tender by the railway.

   Note : Where, for any reason, the exact amount payable cannot be ascertained or when a system of part deliveries has been agreed to on the basis of part payments, a suitable amount should be stipulated as payable by the purchaser as an advance of purchase price, to be adjusted after the exact amount is known. In such cases, the earnest money of the successful tenderer should not be refunded till the conclusion of the contract and deliveries of materials should be controlled so that the outstanding of the purchaser payable to the railway do not at any time exceed the advance.

5. The purchaser should take deliveries of materials purchased within a stipulated period of time.
6. The Railway should reserve to itself the right of withdrawing from sale any material at any stage without assigning reasons.
7. Misdescription or error in quantity should not invalidate a sale. No sale shall be invalidated by reason of any defect or fault in any of the material. A refund will be made to the purchaser when the weight of number delivered is less than the quantity paid for.
8. Except in special circumstances the delivery of the material sold will only be permitted on production of receipt for the payment of the sale value to the Railway. All weighments, counting and loading of material will ordinarily be done by the stores Department and charge for loading should not be paid to the Railway at the rates prescribed for the purpose before the delivery of the materials.
9. The loading will be done in the presence of the purchaser or his representative but, if he does not attend, such loading will be done in his absence and no claim on the ground that wagons were not loaded properly or that weights were subsequently found to be less, will be entertained in any circumstances.
10. Delivery will not be made on the stores premises nor any weighment or counting permitted for re-sale among the purchasers themselves or to others on such premises.
11. The stores will remain Railway Property until all the conditions of sale are fulfilled. The more payment of the purchase money does not constitute the complete purchase and materials will become the property of the purchaser only after the sale has been completed and the stores have been removed from Railway premises or despatched according to the instructions of the purchaser.
12. In the event of its being found impossible to complete delivery after the payment has been made, a refund of the value of the undelivered goods will be made to the purchaser, who will have no claim for further compensation from the railway.
13. Materials not removed within the stipulated time will be subject to storage charges at rates that will be fixed by the Railway.

- **The Stores Tender Ccommittee.** All tenders for stores amounting to Rs. 1 lakh or over should be submitted to a Stores Tender Committee before acceptance. Acceptances of tenders should be promptly intimated simultaneously to the tenderer, the Accounts officer, Stores, and the Executive Officer for the delivery of stores.
- **Weighment and Delivery of Stores sold.** Weighments and deliveries of any stores sold by whatever manner of sale should ordinarily be made in the presence of an Accounts Stock Verifier who should attest the weighment registers and other initial records.
- Where the successful tenderer is another Railway or Government Department, the conditions indicated above in paragraph (1), (3), (4), (8), (10) and (13) may be suitable modified, as earnest money need not be taken from such bodies and payment will be usually made by book adjustment.
- **Sales by Submission of Tenders.** Railways may also submit tenders in response to public invitation for tenders for supplying materials, whether such invitations are issued by railways, other Government Departments or by private bodies. This method of sale is particularly suitable where the railways is pressed to dispose of its ' overstocks' and surplus stores'.

36.5 DIRECT SALES

Direct sales may be either of :

1. stores of which the railway has only normal stock;
2. items of ordinary, emergency or special stores in which the railway is over- stocked; or
3. surplus stores of any class including scrap, sale of which has been recommended by the Survey Committee and approved by the General Manager.

Note : With efficient store- keeping, over- stocks of emergency of special stores should not ordinarily arise.

- **Direct Sale of Stores with Normal Stocks.** The sale of stores which have not been overstocked, is prohibited. Such sales may, however, be made if they are required to meet that emergent needs of other Government Departments, railways or local authorities or by Railway's contractors for use on the railway 's "works" provided that the selling railway's needs are not adversely affected thereby. The above restriction, however, does not apply to stores, of which the stocks are in excess of the railway's normal requirements. The rate at which the stores will be sold in the above cases will be either the book rate or the purchase rate, whichever is higher.
- **Freight and Incidental Charges.** Freight at public rates should be added to the cost of stores fixed. When such freight is not know or cannot be estimated with reasonable accuracy, the freight should be taken to be 5 per cent or such other percentage as may be fixed for the Railway Board. An additional charge of 2 per cent should be made for 'incidental charges'
- **"Departmental Charges".** The total cost *i.e.,* prime cost, freight and incidental charges, of ordinary stores sold directly should then be increased by 12.1/2 per cent to cover the cost off supervision, storage, interest on outlay, & c. except when the sale is to other Government Railways.

  Note : The levy of the departmental charge on the cost of stores issued to Neutral Control Staff may be foregone by railways by mutual consent.
- **Direct Sale of "Overstocks" and Surplus Stores.** The direct sale of such stores of all classes including scrap, may be either:
  1. petty sales to employees and private parties for total value in each case of not more than Rs. 100;or
  2. sales to other departments of the railway, other railways and other Government Departments.

The rates at which surplus stores may be sold should be the book rates (which would have been suitably modified by the Survey committee) or the rates at which similar articles have been sold in recent auction or tender sales, which may be higher. Where similar articles have not been sold at recent auctions but have been withdrawn owing to the reserve prices that had been fixed not having been reached, such prices should be taken to be the prices applicable in the case of these sales, Additional charges for freight, incidental charges and supervision, and it may be added at full or reduced rates or altogether foregone by the authority empowered to sanction the sales. In the case of petty sales, the cost is payable strictly in advance to the railway.

The rate at which "overstocks' may be sold should be the book rate of purchase rate whichever is higher. Freight and incidental charges and departmental charges and should be levied on all such sales as a general rule, departmental charges may however be waived in any particular case with the sanction of the General Manager.

36.6 SANCTION TO SALES

Whenever the Controller of Stores proposes to make a sale which is not within his powers, he should submit to the General Manager a Minute Sheet (in quadruplicate) containing particulars of the proposed sale, making special mention of the book value of the stores, the proposed rate of sale and the total loss (if any) involved in the transaction, with justification for incurring such losses. The General Manager will intimate his approval by endorsing his sanction to the sale on all the four copies which will then be distributed as follows :

1. One copy each direct to the Accounts Officer Stores, and the Statutory Auditor.
2. One copy to the Controller of Stores.
3. One copy to be retained as office copy.
4. One receipt of the sanction, the Controller of Stores should issue a Sale Order to the Depot Officer concerned.

In cases falling within the powers of sale of the Controller of Stores, the Sale Order itself will constitute the sanction.

- **Sale Orders.** Orders for sale of railway stores should be made out in quadruplicate.
- **Delivery Orders.** The following procedure procedure should be followed in all those cases in which the stores sold are either delivered in installments or when the deliveries are effected by an officer who is not an immediate charge of the stores depot.

Delivery Orders should be prepared in quadruplicate, in a form similar to the sale order mutatis mutandis and distributed in the same manner except that the second foils will be detained by issuer till the entire quantity sold has been delivered. The cash receipt for the full amount due on delivery should be attached to the office copy.

On completion of the delivery, the officer issuing the stores will sent to the Controller of Stores a completion report accompanied by the delivery orders (second foils) after filling therein the particulars of the issue notes and the railway receipts, if any, under which the several installments of deliveries have been made.

CHAPTER

37

SCRAP AND AUCTION SALES

37.1 MEANING OF SCRAPS

- **Meaning of Scrap.** There accumulates on every Railway a large quantity of material of different kinds which is no longer useful for the purpose for which it was originally procured. Such material is generally called "Scrap" and should be distinguished from other stores and component parts which can be utilized after repair or renovation. Scrap also consists of empties, turnings, borings, cut odds and ends of metal, sweeping foundry ashes etc, which accumulates in Railway Workshops. Occasionally scrap may consist of second-hand or even new material which the Railway can neither consume itself nor can dispose of other Railways.
- **Schedule.** A detailed schedule of scrap should be maintained by each Railway Administration under group 98 of the State Railway Classification of Stores. In preparing the schedule the use to which the material could be put by the likely purchasers should be kept in view, so that the items may fetch a reasonable price in the auction sales. Scrap of different metals and alloys should be scheduled as far as possible under separate main headings, with suitable subheadings describing the form in which the material is put up for sale.
- **Collection.** Except for those items of scrap which the consuming departments have been authorized to dispose of, the Stores department should arrange for regular collection of all items of scrap from the consuming departments and for its disposal. If the scrap is to be disposed of by public auction, arrangements should be made for its collection at convenient points the purpose of such sales, determined largely by the freight charges to be met, the room available for storage and the proximity to a market for such scrap.

  The Controller of Stores may however decide to dispose of any particular item of scrap at site or at the point of generation of scrap, it is more advantageous to do so.
- **Scrap for Workshop Use.** Scrap suitable for use as raw materials for foundries &c. in railway workshops should invariably be reserved for such use, only the excess over such requirements being sold.
- In the cases of dispatches of scrap from out stations, arrangements should be made to see that double handing is avoided and that the scrap is sent, as far as possible, direct to the stores depot attached to the workshop concerned or to the depot at which scrap sales are conducted as the case may be.

- **Sorting and Storage of Scrap.** When scrap is returned to the stores depot, the Officer or subordinate returning it, should see that it is sorted out according to the correct nomenclature of the Price List before it is actually dispatched. On receipt in the stores depot, the scrap should be further sorted out, if found necessary.
- Suitable arrangement should exist in the stores depot to ensure that the scrap ready for sales is not mixed with other scrap that is being received. For this purpose, there should be kept, if it is possible to do so, two sets of scrap bins or dumps for each kind of scrap, so that the scrap, accumulated in one set of bins or dumps could be set apart at any time for the purpose of auction sale and pending such sale, the other set of bins will be used for accumulating further scrap for the next auction.
- **Auction Sale of Scrap at Stores Depots.** Before by item of stores can be sold as 'scrap' it should be declared as such by Survey Committee appointed by the General Manager of the Railway and the sanction of the competent authority obtained to such sale. The General Manager may relax this rule in this case of known items of scrap of small value which is generally sold to Railway Employees.
- Scrap will be sold generally by auction but if the administration considers that more advantageous prices are likely to be obtained, other ways of disposal may be adopted.
- **Disposal of Waste Paper.** Waste paper may be sold at the place of accumulation and if in any place there is insufficient accumulation to warrant its sale, it may be collected in the Stores depot by the stores delivery van on its journey wherever convenient.

  It is not necessary to keep elaborate ledgers for the waste paper— A numerical account should however be kept. The value realized by the sale of waste papers whether collected in depot or elsewhere should be credited to 'Traffic Earnings'.
- **"Lot" Register for Scrap.** All scrap material accumulated for the purpose of auction sale should be separated into convenient 'lot' of a size that would suit the bidders at auctions. A 'Lot' Register should be maintained showing the following particulars;
  1. 'Lot' Number
  2. P.L. No
  3. Description of material
  4. Approximate quantity
  5. Book rate
  6. Rate in previous action
  7. Sanction reference of Survey Sheet
  8. Rate at which sold
  9. Name of the purchaser
  10. Total value at auction rate
  11. Remarks
- **Survey Sheets for Scrap.** Particulars of each lot should then be entered on the Survey Sheets which are submitted to the Survey Committee. It is one of the important duties of the Survey Committee to inspect each lot and record its recommendations on the survey sheets. The controller of Stores should then obtain the sanction of the competent authority to the sale of such articles by auction, if he finds he is unable to dispose of the same by transfer or sale to other railway, Government Departments &c.

- **Reserve Price.** Reserve prices based on the bids obtained at past auctions and any other information available should be fixed by the Controller of Stores or the Depot Officer for such item of scrap to be sold in order that the item may be withdrawn from the sale, if the bids are found unsatisfactory. Bids lower than the reserve prices may, however, be accepted by the Depot Officer where found expedient provided the Depot Officer doing so records his reasons in writing.

37.2 AUCTION SALES

- **Agency for Auction Sales.** A Railway Administration may either conduct its actions itself or enter into agreement with an auctioneering firm of repute and financial standing to handle the sale of railway materials by auction.
- **Legal Position of Auctioneer.** The position of an auctioneer unto the fall of the hammer is that of an agent for the vendor., that is, the Railway Administration. The auctioneer thereafter become the agent of the highest bidder (the purchaser) as well, and a proper contract must be made to bind both parties *i.e.*, the Purchaser and the Railway Administration. The conditions of sale should therefore be drawn up before the sale. The auctioneer has no authority as the agent of the Railway Administration to warrant the goods, and he cannot add to or alter the particulars of Conditions of Sale by any verbal declaration made in the auction room at the time of the sale.
- **Agreement and Conditions of Sales.** A skeleton form of agreement between railway administration and a firm of auctioneers is to be followed as given in store codes which is revise time to time from railway board. General Conditions of Sales by Auction" which may be adhered to with advantage.
- **Samples for Assay & c.** Small quantities of scrap required by prospective biders for purposes of assay or other tests may be sold to them at schedule rates out of materials prepared into lots for auction.
- **Auction Arrangement at Stores Depot.** No auction should actually be started without the prior permission of the Controller of Stores. The Controller of Stores while according such permission, should examine whether there is going to be any over- lapping of auctions by the same auctioneer, either in respect of deliveries or payment of sale proceeds or both. Such overlapping shall be avoided as far as possible. When, however, this is unavoidable, the Controller of Stores should consider carefully to see that the interests of the Administrator are not jeopardised in any way.

  The Depot officer or any other officer nominated by the Controller of Stores to supervise the auction will be responsible for the conduct of the auction.
- **Presence of an Accounts Representative at Auction Sales.** The Accounts Officer (Stores) should have received timely intimation of the auction. Auction should depute an Inspector of Stores Accounts or a stock Verifier as an Accounts representative to witness the auction sale.

  From the catalogue and the Survey Sheets prepare for the auction, the Stock verifier witnessing the sales should post a manuscript register containing the following particulars:

1. Date of auction
2. LOT Number
3. P. L. Number
4. Description of the material

Material should not be sold at rates per lot but bids should be registered by a number or weight unit so that a complete check on the quantity delivered can be exercised at any time . The Sock Verifier should see the conditions of sale are being observed and that stores are not being sold at obviously low prices. If he thinks that any irregularity is taking place or proper prices are not being obtained, he should bring the matter immediately to the notice of the Officer in Charge of the sale and report the case in writing to the Accounts Officer, Stores.

- **Deliveries of Stocks:** The Depot Officer should arrange for the deliveries being effected according the agreement and terms and conditions of sale and such other specifies or general instructions as may be issued by the Controller of Stores. He should take every possible step to expedite delivery of the auctioned materials.
- **Auctioneer's Delivery Order:** Before material is loaded for delivery, the purchase has to present to the Depot Officer a Delivery Order, made out by the auctioneers authorizing Stores Department to make such delivery. The delivery order should show the following particulars:
  1. Lot number
  2. Description of material
  3. Purchase's name and address
  4. Approximate quantity in the lot
  5. Rate at which sold
  6. Value realized
  7. Reference to the Cash Remittance Note under which the amount shown in column 6 was remitted to the Railway's Cashier or Treasurer.
  8. Chief Cashier or Treasure's Receipt Note and date
  9. Amount of loading charges recovered by the Depot Officer.

Note : 1. Columns 1to 8 will be filled in by the Auctioneers, and column 9 by the Depot Officer.

2. An auctioneer's delivery order is not necessary when the auctioneer does no function as the Agent of the purchaser. The delivery may be made to the purchaser or his agent on the strength of the Cashier's Receipt.

Ground Rent should be charged if the material is not removed within the stipulated time and the Accounts Representatives will be responsible for seeing that where Ground Rent has become due, it is recovered by the Depot Officer before delivery of the Stores. The amount realized as Ground rent should be noted in the Issue Note by the depot and certified by the Stock Verifier. The Depot Officer will be responsible to remit the cash to the Devil, Casher or the local Station Master. In exceptional circumstances and when the Earnest Money paid by the purchasers is sufficient for the purpose, Ground Rent *i.e.*, Storage Charges may be recovered after the delivery of the stores .

- **Weighment and Delivery :** All materials sole shall be weighed or counted before delivery, this being supervised by:
  1. Stock Verifier
  2. Stores Supervisor of rank not less than D.S.K.Gr. III

3. Representative of the purchaser (if he cares to be present)
4. Representative of the Auctioneer (if he cares to be present)

The Stock Verifier should count, measure or weigh each lot or part of a lot after comparison of the description and quantity shown in the sale catalogue to ensure that only such kinds and quantities of materials as have been shown in the catalogue are being issued; he should sign the gate passes and Issue Notes in token of such check. The Stock Verifier should maintain a Field Book which will be his initial record for recording theirin:

(*a*) The lot number
(*b*) Description
(*c*) Rate
(*d*) Cart or wagon number, carrying capacity, and owning railway
(*e*) Gross Weight, actual tare or wagon or cart
(*f*) Net Weight
(*g*) Purchaser's name and address
(*h*) Particular of realization of value
(*i*) Amount of Loading Charges recovered
(*j*) Issue Note number and date
(*k*) Gate-Pass/ Railway Receipt number & date and
(*l*) Amount and particulars of remittance of Ground Rent, if any.

He should sign the issue note after fully satisfying himself that entries made therein agree with those in the field book. The field book should be attested by the Stores Representative making delivery of the goods in token of his having accepted the correctness thereof.

In giving delivery of scrap material, scrap of non-ferrous items should be weighed on beam scales and the weight of each consignment should be recorded in detail by the Stock Verifier in his field book. For giving delivery of ferrous scrap empty wagons need not be weighed and the marked are of the wagons should be taken as the weight of the empty wagons. The loaded wagons should be passed over the weighbridge and the difference between the two weight will give weight of the scrap. In his field book, the Stock Verifier who should be present all the time, record the number, carrying capacity and the owning railway (marked) tare, gross weight and net weight of the wagons used. He should then seal up the wagons with the special seal supplied to him for the purpose. Particulars of the Railway receipt under which loaded wagons are booked will be recorded.

In cases where local delivery is given, the empty and loaded trucks or carts should be weighed and instead of Railway Receipt, particulars of the Gate Pass issued will be recorded. The Issue Note and the Gate Pass should be countersigned by the Stock Verifier.

- **Loading.** The loading of the sold materials should be done under the supervision of the Depot Officer or his Assistant, not below the rank of D.S.K. Gr. III and should be witnessed by the Stock Verifier. The Depot Officer will be responsible for realising loading charges if any, from the purchaser. The Purchaser should not ordinarily be allowed to use his own labour for loading as the Railway's have little control on such labour.

The responsibility of the Railway ends after the consignment has been loaded and made over to the representative of the auctioneers or purchasers and the railway will be no party to any dispute that may arise after the loading has been completed. It is the duty of the auctioneer to arrange for the dispatch of the consignment to the purchaser.

- **Dispatch of Auctioned Material.** In no circumstances should the Railway department be shown on any of the dispatching documents as consignors. The documents should be in the name of the purchaser of his duly authorized agent who should sign them if necessary.
- **Freight Rates:** If the purchaser desires to send any of the stores by rail, they will be carried at public traiff rate only.
- **Stock Verification:** At the conclusion of the delivery of the lot or lots pertaining to the item of scrap, any stock, left over should be verified by the Accounts Department with the book balance and any discrepancies adjusted. Such "left over" stock may be transferred to the bin in which fresh deliveries received since the auction have been stored.
- **Monthly Lists of Deliveries.** The Depot Office should submit to the Controller of Stores and the Accounts Officer (Stores) monthly verified lists of materials in respect of lots delivered in full every month and valuable metals and stores of special sales *e.g.*, rails, girders and c. as delivered, whether in part of in full.
- **Report of Completion of Auction.** On the completion of the delivery of materials sold in each auction, the Accounts Representative should submit a completion report to the Accounts Officer, Stores bringing to particular notice any outstanding features. The Depot Officer will submit similar report independently to the Controller of Stores and Accounts Officer Stores.

  The Completion reports should show the :

  (*a*) Date of Auction Sale.
  (*b*) Lot Nos.
  (*c*) Description of Stores.
  (*d*) Quantity offered in the auction.
  (*e*) Quantity actually delivered.
  (*f*) Rate.
  (*g*) Value.
  (*h*) Loading charges recovered.
  (*i*) Ground rent recovered.
  (*j*) Auctioneer's Commission
  (*k*) Remarks.

- **Sale Accounts by Auctioneers :** The Depot Office should see that the sale accounts are submitted to him by the auctioneers within the prescribed period. He should check the sale accounts, calling for the Treasurer's certificate of payment granted to the auctioneers, for the remittance made by him. If the sale account is found correct and the remittance has been made correctly, the Depot Officer should issue a clearance certificate to the auctioneer in respect of that particular auction and send a copy of the certificate to the Accounts Officer Stores. The Auctioneer' Sale Accounts should be forwarded to the Controller of Stores for transmission to the Accounts Officer.

  Note : There is no objection to the Sale Accounts being submitted by the Auctioneers direct to the Controller of Stores, provided the checks devolving on the Depot Office are exercised in the Office of the Controller of Stores.

- **Bills for Commission Charges :** Except in cases where the auctioneers are permitted to deduct their commission charges from sale proceeds of the auctioned material in terms of their agreement the bill for commission charges should be submitted promptly to the Depot Officer concerned for verification an transmission to the Accounts Officer, Stores, for payment, advising the Controller of Stores at the same time.

- **Auctions by other than the Stores Department:** The preliminary arrangements for the auction of materials held in the Divisions or Districts should be made by the Division or District Officers concerned under advice to the Accounts Officer, Stores, and the Controller of Stores.
- In signifying his approval, the Controller of Stores should advise the Accounts Office, Stores, to arrange for a Stock Verifier being deputed to witness the sale. The auctions may be held either departmentally or with the assistance of the railway auctioneers. The detailed procedure to be followed will be the same, mutatis mutandis as in the case of the auction sales conducted by the Stores Department.
- **Allocation of Financial Responsibility.** The financial responsibility involved in the sale of stores by public auction, tender, or direct sale is in respect both of expenditure and of receipts. In the assessment and collection of amounts due to the railway, the responsibility is with the Executive. The responsibility of the Accounts Organization is confined to seeing that system of collection is suitable and efficient, to verifying by test-check that such a system operates effectively in practice and to examining that the amounts collected are properly brought into account in the railway's books.
- In the matter of expenditure involved, the Accounts Departments id responsible for seeing theat the expenditure is regular and proper and that the system of accounts is such that there can be no loss of railway money, while the administrative and executive officers will be fully responsible for the correctness of the facts in the original documents.

CHAPTER

38

PRICED LEDGERS

1. **Location of Office.** The Stores Accounts Office is a part of the office of the Chief Accounts Officer, located preferably in the closest proximity to, if not along with the office of the Controller of Stores so that the latter is in close touch with his accounts.

   A 'Local' unit of the Stores Accounts Office may, where circumstances require this, be attached to each of the more important stores depots. Such local offices should work in the closest co-operation with the Depot Officer concerned (being in fact his Accounts Office) and deal with all the accounting of the receipts into and issues of stores from the depot to which they are attached, including:

   (*a*) The issue of periodical and monthly summaries to departments (both debits and credits);

   (*b*) The verification of stocks;

   (*c*) The compilation of monthly statements of stores transactions for the depot; and

   (*d*) Monthly reconciliation of priced ledgers with general books.

2. **Functions of the Stores Accounts Office.** The main functions of the Stores Accounts Office are:

   (*a*) To check the initial documents of receipt and issue, and adjust their value in the books of the railway, maintaining the necessary accounts records therefore;

   (*b*) To compile the stores accounts and prepare the periodical returns due to the Controller of Stores, the General Manager, and the Railway Board; and

   (*c*) To verify the stocks of stores in the depots and on the line annually or at such other periods as prescribed for each category and nature of stock.

3. The more important items of work involved in discharging the first of the three functions, *viz.* The initial check and accountal of vouchers, may be grouped as follows:

   (*i*) The maintenance of priced ledgers and effecting reconciliation of the balances in the priced ledgers with the General Books monthly through the means of group ledgers.

   (*ii*) Arranging for the recovery of the cost of stores issued including any incidental and departmental charges, whether in cash or by means of book adjustments (Summaries of Issues).

   (*iii*) Arranging for the discharge of liabilities incurred in connection with the receipt of stores either by cash payment or by means of book adjustments.

(*iv*) Maintenance of Accounts Registers in connection with the above items of work in order to keep a proper record of the assets and the liabilities and to guard against double or overpayments or the omission of recoveries due.

(*v*) Maintenance of liability registers for stock items to record the liabilities entered into as and when the orders are placed on the suppliers/contractors or indents are placed on the procurement agencies and watch the liquidation of such liabilities.

4. **The Stores Accounts Officer.** The Stores Accounts Office will be under the Stores Accounts Officer, a Gazetted Officer, whose duties are two- fold. He is responsible to the Chief Accounts Officer for the efficient working of his branch and in this capacity he exercises a complete and independent audit of all stores transactions and maintain a distinct set of audit registers and books. Subject to the control and general direction of the Chief Accounts Officer, he also acts as adviser to the Controller of Stores (Deputies or Depot Officer in local offices) in all matters of stores accounts and finance and assists that officer with all information in connection with compilation of stores transactions, including book rates, consumption of stores, balances etc.
5. The maintenance of priced ledgers of stores involves different groups of operations.

Group A : (*i*) The receipt and check of vouchers and forwarding the same to Data Centre.

(*ii*) Periodical listing of the transactions and forwarding the same to Date Centre.

(*iii*) Opening and closing of priced ledgers as advised by the Depot Office, after due check.

(*iv*) Checking of punched data, as per data processing procedures.

(*v*) Accurate and timely maintenance of priced ledgers through EDP Centre.

Group B : (*i*) Scrutiny of all unmatched vouchers, vouchers causing irregular balance items and other rejected vouchers and their clearance.

(*ii*) Scrutiny of printed ledgers for abnormal and unreasonable results and their elimination.

Group C : (*i*) The revision of rates.

(*ii*) The review of the priced ledgers.

The operations should be carefully planned and allocated, in such a manner that the work will not only be up to date, but also the accuracy thereof is also ensured.

All vouchers affecting stores transactions, (except those relating to adjustments of monetary values only, such as the correction of mistakes in such values, etc.) will be received from the stores depot. Every such voucher will represent a physical receipt or issue of a quantity of stock as shown on the document. The exceptions will be cases in which a quantity, short received or erroneously received instead of the correct material and returned since, is permitted to be shown as in stock pending the settlement of the dispute regarding such shortages; and cases of correction of price list numbers discovered after the vouchers have been despatched etc.

6. **Time Table for Submission of Voucher by Depots.** The vouchers should be made over by the Depot to the Stores Accounts Office, daily. The vouchers for a date, say the first of a month, should be completely delivered to the Stores Accounts Office, without fail, wherever no holiday intervenes, on the morning of the third, within the hour of the opening of the office. The vouchers would be accompanied by the Forwarding Memo, where the Stores Depot and the Stores Accounts Office are not in the same station, the time allowed may be modified to suit local conditions taking care to see that there is no avoidable delay in the regular submission of

the vouchers to the Accounts Office. The Accounts Office shall after checking the vouchers, bundle them in batches (according to the voucher code and date) periodically as per programme laid down by the Data Centre and deliver them on these dates.

7. **Check of Vouchers.** On receipt in the Accounts Office, the vouchers should be checked with the Forwarding Memo to see;
   (*a*) that all the vouchers entered therein have been received; and
   (*b*) that the serial numbers assigned to the vouchers are correctly continued from the previous day and have been assigned without any break.
8. **Cancelled or Missing Vouchers.** If any vouchers are missing, or if any have been shown as cancelled, a search should be made for the missing vouchers and if they cannot be obtained at once, a note should be kept in a register and the matter pursued until settled satisfactorily. In the case of cancelled vouchers, the foil of such vouchers should be inspected. In checking the vouchers with the Forwarding the arrangement of the vouchers as received from the depot should not be disturbed, even if this involves some inconvenience.
9. **Scrutiny of the Vouchers.** The vouchers should then be examined to see that:
   (*a*) They have been prepared on the proper forms and with proper voucher code;
   (*b*) They are signed and / or countersigned by proper authority or authorities as required by the rules;
   (*c*) The correct number of foils have been received;
   (*d*) They are legibly written;
   (*e*) All data required to be punched are duly entered in the relevant places;
   (*f*) In the case of receipt notes where the ordering unit is different from the accounting unit, both the units are legibly shown. The extra charges such as ST, Surcharge, Excise Duty, Customs Duty, etc. are indicated precisely and not in general terms;
10. **Rounding off Paise.** In calculating the value of each item of stores in connection with the Receipts or Issues, the value should be taken nearest to the paise.

    In the case of purchases through the centralised agencies, the calculation of values of the item in the receipt note should be reckoned in terms of whole rupees, amounts below being dropped, and 50 paise and above reckoned as one Rupee. If more than one it is entered in a Receipt Note, the rounding off should be done on the total of the items and not on individual items. This is necessary in order that the amount posted in the purchase accounts registers and the priced ledgers agree with the bill forwarded by the Pay & Accounts Officer of the DGS&D Wing, who rounds off paise to the nearest rupee.
11. **Receipt Notes.** In the case of Railways with decentralized inspection. Part III of Form S. 719 will be received from the depot after it has been taken into account. The value of the supplies should be calculated at the rates shown on the voucher, It should then be handed over to the ledger clerk for posting the priced ledgers, after which it should be posted in the Purchase Account Register.

    In the case of railways with centralized inspection of supplies and centralized stores accounting, Part IV of Form S.726 will be received from the depot, after it has been taken into account. The value of the supplies as shown on the voucher should be checked. The voucher should then be handed over for posting the priced ledgers.

    Note : Under an organization of decentralized Stores Accounts Officer, part V of the Receipt Note should be paired with Part IV received with the Daily Summary of Credits of Purchasers Account, the quantities being checked and a remark made on Part V to that effect. The value shown on Part V should be checked with the amount shown in the periodical summary and the date of accountal of the voucher in the priced ledgers should be noted on the latter at the same time.

12. **Receipt Orders for imported items.** Receipt Order for imported items should not only contain the rates for the item but also the rates of packing charges, insurance, freight, customs duty, countervailing duty, etc. The receipt value should then be calculated taking into account all the above factors. The voucher should then be passed on for posting the priced ledgers.
13. **Workshop Manufactures.** The values for these items are calculated by the computer at the pre - determined rates advised by the workshops periodically. Whenever new items are undertaken for manufacture and the pre-determined rates are not available, the estimated rate should be obtained and indicated on the vouchers before they are passed on to the computer centre.
14. **Depot Transfer Receipts (3rd foil).** Periodical summaries of Issues (showing also the rates of issue) against the depots to which materials have been sent will be prepared by the stores accounts section. The same will be handed over to the concerned staff dealing with the Receiving Depot. In case of local Stores Accounts Office attached to each depot, the summary should be sent to the Stores Accounts Officer of the receiving Depot. The rates and values required for pricing the 3rd foil, should be taken from the above summary. The voucher should then passed on to the EDP Centre for posting the priced ledgers and preparation of unified class ledgers.
15. **Advice Notes of Returned Stores.** The pre-determined credit rates will be adopted for valuing returns.
16. **Book Transfers and Departmental and Accounts Stock Verification Sheets (Single Foils).** These vouchers should be priced at book rates by the computer while posting the priced ledgers. All issue vouchers will be received in the accounts office of which one copy is forwarded to the computer centre. The issue should be priced at book average rates except the Sale Issue Notes which will be priced according to the terms of sale.
17. **Adjustments of Loss or Gain on Sales.** The irregular balances in the priced ledgers arising out of the differences in value between the book rates and the tender, auctioner private sale rates should be adjusted on the same day by debit or credit to stock adjustment account, stock adjustment vouchers (one copy only) should be prepared by the computer at the time of posting priced ledgers and posted in the ledgers. Periodical summary of such items should be prepared by computer centre for such transactions separately. On receipt of such summary from the computer centre, the Accounts officer should see whether proper sanctions exist for any losses on sales.
18. **Time Table for Pricing and Valuation of Vouchers.** The Pricing and calculation of values of vouchers should be finished on the same day the returns are received from the depot.
19. Priced Ledgers should be maintained by the Group of Stores. As the ledgers are printed on continuous stationery, the Priced Ledgers printed should indicate the last date of transaction to facilitate back reference. They should be maintained in form shown below or such other convenient form as may be prescribed by FA&CAO. The ledgers are printed periodically in the order of depot, ward, price list number and category.

PRICED LEDGER FOR THE MONTH OF 2009

Depot	Ward	U.L. No.	Unit	Catg.	Description of item	Last date of Accounts Stock Verification	Last Purchase Rate

Date	Posting Printing	Receipt Order or Issue Note No.	Rece-ived from or issued to	Alloca-tion	Quantity			Value			Average Book Rate	Purchase Rate	Last date of Posting
					Rec-eipt	Issue	Bal-ance	Rec-eipt	Issue	Bal-ance			
			Opening Balance										
			Total										

THEN NEXT ITEM AND SO ON

20. **Exhibition of Maxima and Minima on the Priced Ledgers.** It is not obligatory to show the maxima and minima stocks on the priced ledgers. During verification of stocks, the Accounts Stock Verifiers should review the existing stock with reference to the maxima and minima annual requirements and also with reference, if necessary, to the statistics of monthly and annual consumption relating to the item. They should report to the Stores Accounts Officer and the Depot Officer cases in which the maxima or minima appear to be excessive in the light of actual average consumption.

    Note : The information regarding maxima, minima, annual requirements, etc., may be called for by the verifier from the computer centre for the above purpose.

21. **Rules for Upkeep.** The priced ledgers printed and given by the computer centre will be bound and kept monthwise and ward and groupwise.

    A list of priced ledgers opened for the month and closed should be furnished by the Computer Centre and these lists should be filed along with the priced ledgers for the month. A copy of the above list should be sent to the Depot Officer for his information and record.

22. **Opening of Priced Ledgers.** Whenever the depot opens for the first time a ledger for an item of stores, a manuscript advice (ARD for Master file) in duplicate will be sent to the computer centre through Accounts office the same day giving the following particulars, *viz.* unified group, price list number, category and quality of stores, nomenclature and unit and other

particulars as are required for the master file. On receipt of the Advice, the computer center will open the new priced ledger after exercising the necessary validity checks.

3. **Index of Priced Ledger Cards.** The EDP Centre should furnish the accounts office with an up-to-date list of all priced ledgers at least once a year. The list should indicate all the relevant particulars such as depot, ward, price list number, quality, unit of accountal, last date of issue, last date of verification, quantity balance, value balance, book average rate, etc.

4. No change should be made by the depot staff in any of the particulars of the cards opened by the computer centre and accepted by the accounts office without the concurrence of the Accounts Officer. Some important examples of the cases to which this restriction applies are:
   (*i*) Changes in the nomenclature or unified list number as appearing in the existing ledgers.
   (*ii*) Changes of the unit of accountal, such as an alteration from weight to number, number to cubical contents, etc. In such cases, in addition to obtaining the previous concurrence of the accounts officer and computer centre, the actual stock should be verified by accounts stock verifiers in the existing unit and in the proposed unit and any discrepancy discovered under the existing unit should be adjusted before the account in terms of the new unit is posted in the ledgers.
   (*iii*) The splitting up of an existing item of nomenclature or heading into further items or headings.
   (*iv*) The grouping of existing items of nomenclature or headings into a single item or heading. In this and the former cases, such splitting or grouping should be done in the presence of an accounts stock verifier.

5. **Closing of Priced Ledgers.** When a depot proposes to close a card, it will send the Accounts Office necessary advices (ARD for Master file) giving full particulars as in the case of the opening of cards. The advice will also state the number and date of the last voucher to be posted which will enable the accounts office to see that all the vouchers forwarded by the depot upto the time of closing have also been posted in the priced ledger. Before the ledgers are closed it should be seen that there are no irregular balances and there are no outstanding purchase orders against that item. The same should then be forwarded to the computer centre for the closure of the item. The computer centre will ensure that all the closure advices received are given effect to after suitable checks.

6. Items deleted from the computer files and should be listed simultaneously by the computer centre and a copy of the above list should be sent to the depot officer for his information and record.

7. **Re-opening of Cards.** The same procedure as laid down for the opening of cards should be followed in this connection.

   The priced ledgers are the basis of all stores accounting and the utmost care should be taken to avoid errors therein. The following instructions are therefore laid down for the guidance of ledger posters with a view to minimize all chances of errors in ledger posing:
   (*i*) *Up- keep of Priced Ledgers:* The Priced Ledgers should be maintained neatly and safely as receive from the EDP Centre periodically and in proper order of depot and ward.
   (*ii*) *Posting of Vouchers:* Before sending the vouchers for posing for the day, it should be seen by the Accounts Office that the vouchers in hand relate to correct depot, group and correct month.

(iii) During the course of posting, the poster should take care to see :

(a) that the nomenclature add price list number of each item of stores as shown in the return corresponds with the nomenclature and price list number of the same item of stores in the priced ledgers. An item in a return should be sent for punching only when the above particulars agree.

(b) that the number and date of the voucher and the figures of quantities and value are distinctly written in the vouchers without flourish and within the lines/cages allotted to the respective figures.

(c) that no voucher received or any item thereof has been omitted to be punched or posted in the priced ledgers or has been posted twice by the Computer Centre. For this purpose, the punch operator should write the letter 'P' against each item in a voucher after it has been punched and 'V' after it has been verified. A detailed list checking should be made comparing with has totals already arrived at.

(iv) The Computer Centre should punch all the vouchers received by them on the date of their receipt. Should a ledger punching and posting work fall into arrears for any reason *e.g.*, rush of vouchers on a particular day, Computer room/Punch room is expected to work overtime to pull up his arrears. In cases of sudden illness, or other absences beyond one's control, the supervisor of the section should make arrangements, to get the work done with the approval of the competent authority, and a note should be kept of the vouchers for the correct punching and verification of which responsibility will rest on the person to whom the work is allotted.

(v) During the course of posting the vouchers, the Computer Centre should print a statement in Form or such other form as may be prescribed by FA&CAO, giving particulars of Unified list Number, Price List Number wherever it is found that:

(a) The receipt rate varies from the book rate by 10 per cent or more;

(b) Credit balances have appeared either in quantity or value;

(c) Quantities exist without value of values without quantities;

(d) The unit in vouchers varies from the P.L. Unit.

(vi) **Adjustment Receipt Notes :** Sometimes the controller of stores sends adjustment receipt notes to set right mistakes committed in the original Receipt Notes. In such cases, the Adjustment Receipt Notes should bear reference to the original Receipt Note Number, R.O. Number and date and the original rate and value of the item.

(vii) **Other Adjustments such as write-back, under or overcharge statements, etc :** In all such cases, the accounts office should verify the posting of the original transaction and should give a cross reference manually against the posting Adjustment Voucher.

(viii) **Posting of Stock Verification Sheets :**

(a) While posting stock sheets, both departmental and accounts, the computer centre should see the date of verification and carefully compare the opening balance shown on the stock sheet with the balance shown on the priced ledger for the same date and should then proceed to post the stock sheet.

(b) *Discrepancies between Opening Balance and Book Balance as per Priced Ledgers:* If there is any discrepancy in the ground balance on the date of verification, the difference between the ground balance and the book balance should be posted in the priced ledgers bringing the priced ledger balance in accord with the actual ground balance. These differences should be valued at the book average rate prevailing on that date.

(c) When the discrepancy is subsequently traced any further adjustment on account of the resultant deficiency or excess should be adjusted through a supplemental stock verification sheet prepared in the Accounts Office for the purpose. This stock verification sheet should be assigned the same number as the original one with the word 'Supplemental' added thereto.

(i) **Certification of verification :** At the end of verification of the stock of each unified group, the Computer Centre, on a request from the Accounts Officer, should print a list of items, if any, which have not been verified during the programme period, with a view to have such omissions in verifications rectified. This should be ensured by providing for the date of verification in Computer files.

(ii) **Discrepancies between Opening Balance of Numerical and Priced Ledgers:** If there is any discrepancy in the depot and accounts opening balances as on the date of verification the matter should be investigated at once by reference to the numerical ledger card (if available in the situation) and the discrepancy rectified before the results of verification are posted in the priced ledgers.

(iii) If the Numerical Ledger is most immediately available, the priced ledger balance should be inserted in the column provided for the purpose, in the Stock Verification Sheet, and the difference between the balance and the actual balance by count should be priced, value and posted in the priced ledgers thus bringing the priced ledger balance in accord with the actual ground balance. At the same time the discrepancy between the depot ledger and the accounts ledger should be noted down in the register, to be maintained for reconciliation of depot ledgers with priced ledgers. The depot ledger card should be either called for at once or the matter left over till the next reconciliation is due, depending on whether the amount of differences is above Rs. 50 or Rs. 50 and below; when the discrepancy is traced and set right, any further adjustment on account of the resultant deficiency or excess should be adjusted through a supplemental Stock Verification Sheet prepared in the Account Office fort he purpose. This stock Verification Sheet should be assigned the same as the original one with the word "Supplemental" added thereto.

(ix) **Certificate of Verification.** At the end of the verification of the stocks of each class of stores, a ledger poster should go through his ledgers and put up list of items, if any, which have not been verified, with a view to have such omissions rectified.

(a) **Disposal of Completed Ledger Sheets :** The ledger poster should particularly see that completed sheets are transferred to suitable binders or cabinets as soon as new continuation sheets have been opened in their place. All such, binders or cabinets should be suitably labelled and all completed sheets should be put in them in the order of their depots, class and price list numbers and along with the previous sheets for the same item.

28. **Vouchers posted as Minus Receipts.** The following return will be posted in the ledgers as minus receipts:

(i) *Depot Transfer Issue Notes :* These will be posted as minus receipts in the issuing depot and as plus receipts in the receiving depot and accounted for accordingly in all subsequent stages of the accounts.

(ii) *Book Transfers* : The posting in the card, stocks from which has been transferred will be shown as minus receipt and accounted for similarly in all other stages of accounts.

(iii) *Deficiencies in stocks and all other transactions to debit of 'Stock Adjustment Account'*: Will be posted as minus receipts and accounted for accordingly. The Stock Adjustment Account itself will however exhibit the debits and credits separately.

29. **Vouchers Originating in the Accounts Office.** In addition to the vouchers which will be initiated by the depot, will be prepared in the Stores Accounts Office and posted in the priced ledgers only.

30. **Under and Overcharge Returns.** When an issue made on an issue note or a receipt through an advice note has been debited or credited at wrong rates or values, an undercharge or overcharge return in form should be prepared adjusting the error and the return should be posted in the priced ledgers and accounted for by inclusion in the debit or credit summaries of the department concerned.

FORM A & B AS IN THE STORES CODE

31. **A Under and Overcharges advised by the Supplying Departments or Firms.** Such undercharges upto Rs. 200/- in each case may be adjusted direct to Stock Adjustment Account without routing through the Priced Ledgers and where such undercharges or overcharges exceed Rs. 200/- in each case, the same should be accounted for in the Priced Ledgers like ordinary 'receipt' to be merged automatically in the average rates for subsequent issues or adjusted in due course against the Stock Adjustment Account if there is no stock in hand or stock so little that undercharges or overcharges would affect the average rate by 10 per cent or more as compared with the current market rate. Undercharges and overcharges in respect of stores for special works or stores used directly on works excepting those chargeable to Workshop Manufacture Suspense in Production Units should however be adjusted direct against the works concerned.

32. **Stock Adjustment Vouchers.** There are vouchers for money values only in connection with debits or credits to Part II and III of Stock Adjustment Account by contra adjustment against the head 'Stores' with supporting entries in the priced ledgers. The entries in the priced ledgers will be made as receipts and minus receipts. The form shown below should be used for the purpose.

STOCK ADJUSTMENT VOUCHER

Against part..of Stock Adjustment Account.

Depot...

Date..

ALLOCATION :

Group	P.L. No.	Surplus		Deficit		Remarks
		Rs.	P.	Rs.	P.	
	Total					

Stores Accounts Officer

33. **Adjustment for Rupee one or less.** Such adjustment on account of under of overcharges or against the Stock Adjustment Account should not however be made for petty sums not exceeding one rupee. In such cases, a remark should be made on the priced ledger manually against the posting of the item in question to show that the error has been noticed.

34. **Disposal of Vouchers after Posting Priced Ledgers.** After the posting of each day has been completed by the Computer Section, the Computer Section will forward all the vouchers to Priced Ledger Section for onward transmission of the same to the departments/Suspense Accounts Section along with their respective summaries.
35. With the object of assisting the Controller of Stores in maintaining the Price Lists up to date and at the same time of removing from the priced ledgers large differences between the book average rates and the rates published in the Prices Lists, a clerk should be assigned the duty of examining at least once a week the special print outs given by the Computer Centre and of taking action on the proposals relating to rate revision contained in the register. He should consult the relevant priced ledgers and submit 'proposal for revision of price list rates' in form showing the following particulars.
    1. Class
    2. P.L. No.
    3. Description of Stores.
    4. Unit.
    5. Book rate.
    6. Price List rate.
    7. Quantity in stock.
    8. Current Market Rate.
        (*a*) Purchase Order number and date.
        (*b*) Receipt Note number and date.
        (*c*) Rate.
    9. Suggested new rate.
    10. Controller of Stores Orders.

    In order to avoid duplication of work the rate revision clerks of each depot should prepare the statement only for the items for which the depot is the 'main depot'. Where it is not found necessary to have individual clerks for individual depots, it should be ensured that this phase of work is completely covered on a programmed basis.

    The list should then be forwarded to the Controller of Stores who should decide whether and when the rate should be revised, and what such revised rate shall be. The Controller of Stores may also originate revision of rates as in cases of stores obtained on contracts.
36. The correction slips to the Price Lists will be issued by the Controller of Stores.
37. **Revaluation of Balances.** The value of balances in the ledgers will also be corrected at the revised rate by preparing a stock adjustment voucher for all such corrections, subject to the rule that there should be no writing up to the values over the actual cost paid for purchased stores in stock.
38. **Irregular Balances.** With the object of removing from the priced ledgers all irregular balances, ledgers should be continuously over-hauled by ledger reviewers. This work should be arranged so as to complete a review of all the ledgers once every six months. The reviewers are expected to notice all lapses and to so conduct the review works as to ensure that all irregularities are brought to notice .Among the more important irregularities are :
    (*a*) Credit balances in quantity or value.
    (*b*) Value without quantity.
    (*c*) Quantity without value.
    (*d*) Price list rate varying from the book rate by 10 per cent or more.

(*e*) Adjustment carried out without the preparation of vouchers signed by a Gazetted Officer.

(*f*) Items which are overdue for stock verification.

(*g*) Incomplete headings.

(*h*) Stocks not having been issued for more than two years (excluding emergency stores).

(*i*) Stocks heavy as compared with normal issues.

To facilitate review, the Computer Centre should furnish a statement of such irregularities periodically. The Computer Centre should also at the same time ensure that suitable machinery has been provided for in the system to arrest the irregularities (a) to(e) entering the Computer files.

39. **Scrutiny by Section Officer and Stores Accounts Officer.** The Section Officer should serutinise the irregularities pointed out by the Computer Centre at least once in six months. He should submit a report to the Accounts Officer indicating the results off scrutiny. The work of the reviewer should come under the scrutiny of the Accounts Officer at least once in a year.

40. **Review of Registers.** All irregularities noticed by the reviewers or the Section Officer should be noted down in special registers and put up for the information of the Accounts Officer on the Ist of each month. The irregularities noticed by gazetted officer will be recorded in a separate register. All necessary action to set right the irregularities should be taken very promptly.

41. **Importance of Review Works.** The review of ledgers as a daily item of work is of the greatest importance, and when it falls into arrears, differences needing adjustments swell into abnormal figures and considerable time it lost by the clerks in tracing reasons and causes for these differences. The review work should therefore be conducted systematically and properly, a proper programme being dawn up for the work monthly.

42. **Review Procedure.** The Computer center should prepare a statement for all the items of stores scheduled to be taken for review during the month, giving the total value of the quantity on hand, multiplied by the current book rate, the actual book value and the difference between the actual book value and the calculated value. If the difference is less then Rs.200/- a general scrutiny may be made and the difference adjusted. Differences higher than this limit should be investigated and necessary stock adjustment vouchers prepared with full explanations for the differences recorded thereon before submission to the gazetted officer.

43. The reviewers and the staff preparing adjustments are responsible for the correctness of all adjustments specially those affecting the suspense heads of account. For example the stock adjustment account cases in which the facts are not clear and approximate adjustments are proposed to be made should be carefully investigated personally by the Section Officer uncharge of the section and authorized by a gazetted officer.

The Section Officers incharge of the section are personally responsible to see that all adjustments are based on facts, and that no adjustment is based on inadequate evidence. Where a write-off occurs, the sanction of competent authority should be obtained. The existence of a credit balance in the Stock Adjustment Account, is no authority for adjustment without sanction. Any adjustments based on speculative or incomplete data require the previous sanction of the Controller of Railway Accounts.

All cases where the Stock Adjustment Account is affected to the extent of Rs. 500 or over should be examined by the Accounts officer. All adjustments of Rs. 5,000 or over should be reviewed by the Deputy Chief Accounts Officer and these of Rs. 10,000 or above by the Financial Adviser and Chief Accounts Officer.

44. **Other duties or Reviewers.** In addition to the independent review conducted by him in accordance with the foregoing instructions, a reviewer should also conduct the investigation of the items listed by Computer Centre at the time of posting the priced ledgers. He will be responsible for clearing these items.

CHAPTER

39

CHECK AND PAYMENT OF STORES BILLS

The liabilities incurred in connection with 'receipts' of stores are discharged either:

1. by direct payment; or
2. by means of book adjustments.

39.1 DIRECT PAYMENTS

Bills in respect of which direct payments are made, are in respect of :

1. Purchases arranged by the Controller of Stores;
2. 'Local purchases' of petty stores, arranged through the Directorate General of Supplies and Disposals, in cases in which the Directorate General of Supplies and Disposals has authorized direct payment to the suppliers;
3. Supplies of tumbler;
4. Supplies of coal, coke and oil fuel;
5. Sewing and tailoring charges;
6. Customs duty on 'imported stores';
7. Loading and unloading charges due to contractors;
8. Portdues, wharfage, etc.

   These are in respect of bills submitted for payment in terms of contracts placed by the Railways.

- **Book Adjustments:** These are in respect of:
  1. Railway inter-departmental transactions as in the case of stores returned to the stores depots and manufactured stores supplied by railway workshops to stores depots.
  2. Payments due to other Government departments where the exchange account facility is available ;
  3. Payments due to other railways.
- **Payment for Direct Purchases by the Controller of Stores:** In all cases of direct payments, the

procedure for the internal check of bills for stores supplied should generally include:

1. a check of the purchase order on firms,
2. a check of the Receipt notes which notify the actual receipt of the stores ordered for,
3. the maintenance of Purchase Account Registers to enable a record being kept of the liabilities incurred on account of stores purchased from each supplier that have not been discharged by payments, pending the detailed check of bills.

- **Check of Purchase Orders:** A copy of the purchase order will be received by the Accounts Officer, Stores, direct from the Controller of Stores. On receipt of this, he should see:
  1. that there is continuity in the number of Purchase Orders (missing numbers should be reported to the Controller of Stores for necessary action);
  2. that items of stores, purchase orders of which are beyond the powers of purchase by the Controller of Stores have been sanctioned by the competent authority;
  3. that the Purchase order do not infringe the purchase policy rules.
  4. that the Purchase orders do not contain any items of stores which should be purchased through the Directorate General of Supplies and Disposal; and other nominated agencies except in emergencies;
  5. that there is no great variation in the rate adopted from time to time for the purchase of the same kind of material;
  6. that the rates and other particulars are in accordance with the agreement with the contractor in case where a contract for the supply of material is in force;
  7. that there are no erasures, overwritten figures or unattested correction in the purchase orders; and
  8. that the purchase orders have been signed by a gazetted officer of the stores department, authorized to do so.
- **Uncomplied with Purchase Orders:** The Purchase orders should then be kept arranged serially group by group or in any other order as may be decide upon by the FA & CAO.
- **Check of Receipt Notes Part III:** The next document to reach the Accounts officer is usually the Receipt notes in cases where payments are not to be made on proof of dispatch.
  (*i*) The number and date of Receipt note should be entered on the connected Purchase order. The Receipt order no. and date for stocked items should also be indicated on the Purchase Order, for facilitating review of Suspense Register at later date.
  (*ii*) The rates and quantities on the Receipts note should be compared with the rates and quantities shown on the Purchase order and the Receipt note should be enfaced 'checked with purchase order' over the initials of the clerk responsible for the check. In case of part supplies, a note of the quantities supplied should be made on the purchase orders.
  (*iii*) The 'value' should be calculated and entered into the 'amounts' column of the receipt note. In calculating the value of each item of item of stores, the total value should be rounded off to the nearest paise.
  (*iv*) It should be seen that there are no overwritten figures, erasures or unattested correction on the receipt note, and that the number of the receipt notes are in consecutive order.
- **Periodical Summary of Credits to Credits to Purchase Account:** Where the stores accounting of a railway has been decentralized it is necessary to provided for the individual stores Accounts offices to be advised of the day-to-day credits to the Purchase account

maintained at the headquarters office in respect of materials pertaining to depots served by such offices. In such cases, therefore, after the above checks have been applied, the receipt notes received each day from the stores depots or any authorized inspecting and receiving agency should be sorted by the depots to which the stores are consigned, and listed separately for each depot in the form similar to the periodical summary of issues showing the number and the date of the Receipt Note and the value. These summaries will be called "Periodical Summaries of Credits to Purchase Accounts" and sent periodical to the local atores account office concerned. The total of these summaries for a month should agree with the total credits for the same month in the Purchase account register for stores for stock.

- **Maintenance of Purchase Account Register:** Generally 'Purchases' are made first and 'Payments' follow. In order to record each transaction as it takes place, Purchase Account Register should be maintained head of accountwise by the Stores Accounts Office in the form shown below:

..............Railway

PURCHASE ACCOUNTS

FOR...

Name of Contractor and Address ....

Sl. No.	AB No. or TC No. and Date	Debit Voucher No. Order No and date	AT No & date	Receipt Note No & date	Receipt Order No. & date	Inspection Note No. & date	RR No. & date
1	2	3	4	5	6	7	8

Quantity	Rate	Opening Balance		Month..................................				AND SO ON
		Due to Vendors	Due to Vendors	Supplies	Payments	Balance		
						Due to vendors	Due to vendors	
	Rs. P.	Rs. P.	Rs. P.					
9	10	11	12	13	14	15	16	17

Purchase Account registers should have separate pages reserved for transaction of each firm or contractor and should be provided with sufficient columns to record details continuously for three years in case of suppliers whose contracts run for more than one year at a time or who are known to have frequent and regular dealings with the Stores department. Where space permits, the same page may be used for more than one A.T. or order, enough space being left between two A. Ts or orders for the number of payments likely to be made on each A.T. or order. In respect of suppliers whose contracts are not expected to run beyond a year, and whose dealings with Railways are infrequent a smaller six of register may be used which provides columns for only twelve months (*i.e.,* one financial year). The Purchase accounts registers should be chronologically numbered for a financial year, and should be capable of being identified by the year and serial number of the register. After checks the Receipt notes, Receipt order number, Railway receipt No. and date, Quantity, Rate and value of supply should be entered in the Purchase account register as a credit to the account of the supplier. Reference to the register no. and the page number of the Purchase account register should be quoted on each receipt Note at the same time. When the bills for stores supplied is received from the supplier, it should, before being passed for payment, be checked against the credit in the Register, and if the amount billed for this found to agree with the credit, the same should be entered as a debit against the entry of credit. Differences if any, should be immediately investigated and rectified. No bill should be passed for debit to 'Purchases' unless the corresponding credit already appears in the Register except in case of advance payments to firms authorized to receive such advance payments.

Note : For hundred per cent supplies, Purchase Account Registers may, if considered, convenient, be maintained depot wise in the serial order of the Receipt Note without allotting a separate page for each supplier. All the particulars prescribed in form should be posted in this form for each entry. If the items are not likely to get cleared within the same year, the register may be designed to accommodate 2 years transaction to save tune in carrying over of Balances.

- **Abstract of Purchase Account Registers:** At the end of each month abstract should be made in the following form by bringing together the transaction-debits, credits and balances of each contractor.

ABSTRACT OF PURCHASE REGISTERR FOR THE ....YEAR

ALLOCATION

Name of Vendors	Balance from last month		Month			Month		
	Due to Vendor	Due by vendor	Credits	Debits	Balance	Credits	Debits	Balance.

- The vertical total of the figures for the month will represent the debits, credits and balance for the month, of the Purchase account. Subject to the exception is a debit balance should not be permitted in the Purchase account register. If a debit balance arises from any other cause it should be investigated and removed at once.
- **Debit Balances in Purchase Account Register :** It occasionally happens that bills for stores supplied are receive, supported by the railway receipt, in advance of intimation of the actual arrival of the stores, and that payment has to be made before the stores have been acknowledged as received in the stores departments. Such cases of payment prior to the actual debit to stores should be permitted only in the case of well known firms of commercial standing; but

when they do occur, the payment made is usually 100/98/95/90 per cent of the value of stores desppatched and should be debited to purchases account even though there is no credit and a debit balance will consequently ensue. When such bills are passed, the postings shall be made in a separate purchase Account.Register reserved for the purpose and immediate steps should be taken to clear the debits in the Purchase account, by debits to 'Stores' on acknowledgements of the Stores by Depot officers, in the Purchases account registers the amount will be posted separately as a debit balance against the account of the supplier concerned.

- **Review of Purchase Account Registers :** It is imperative that the postings of credits in the Purchase account registers should be correctly made and that they should be upto date, as arrears or incorrect postings will cause delay in passing bills for payment. The register should be inspected once a week by the Section officer and once a month by the Stores accounts officer.
- **Bills of Supplies :** Bills for the supply of stores should be prepared by the suppliers according to format given below, and sent direct to the Accounts officer, stores, of the railway for payments.

BILL FOR STORES PURCHASED

The ....Dr.
To...for stores supplied by him on Purchase Order of
No.................................dt...

<table>
<tr><th rowspan="2">Authority for purchase</th><th rowspan="2">Description of stores</th><th rowspan="2">No. or Qty.</th><th colspan="2">Rate</th><th colspan="2">Price</th><th colspan="2">Amount</th></tr>
<tr><th>Rs.</th><th>P.</th><th>Rs.</th><th>P.</th><th>Rs.</th><th>P.</th></tr>
<tr><td></td><td></td><td></td><td></td><td></td><td></td><td></td><td></td><td></td></tr>
<tr><td></td><td></td><td>*Total</td><td></td><td></td><td></td><td></td><td></td><td></td></tr>
</table>

* (In words) Rupees..

Dispatch Details Place and date	RR No..................dt.,............Inspection Certificate..............dt..............

Signature of Supplier

- Bills may not be submitted in duplicate by suppliers. The bills should be supported by Part-II of the Receipt note granted by the depot receiving the supply. Bills that are not supported by the Receipt note should be returned unpaid to the party presenting the bill. An exception is made in the case of 95 per cent bills. Duplicate copies of Part II of the Receipt note should not in any circumstances be issued to the suppliers by the depots. All application of this nature should be addressed to the Chief accounts officer who will take any necessary action in the matter.
- **Check of Supplier's Bills:**
  1. On receipt of the bill it should be stamped with the date and stamp of the office and examined to see:
     (*a*) that the bill is prepared in standard form and if not prepared in that form, that all the necessary particulars required by the form are given, and

(*b*) that is marked 'original' and is free from erasures and unattested corrections and bears the signature and address of the vendor.

2. The bill should then be registered and numbered in a Register of bills and passed on immediately to the rate verification clerk, who should verify the correctness of the rates and quantities charged in the bill with those given in the copy of the Purchase order received direct from the Controller of stores. The certificate of the correctness of rate and quantities should be signed by the Section office, in charge of the section who should also see that the particulars of bills are note on the purchase order to keep a watch over the quantities supplied against an order from time to time. When the order is completed and payment made in full. The purchase order should be stamped 'COMPLETED'.
3. The bill should then be passed on to the clerk responsible for checking the totals and calculations, who should also see:
   (*a*) that the rates, quantities and nomenclature in the bill agree with those given in the Receipt note Part II. The latter being compared with Part III of the Receipt note received direct in the Accounts office.

   (*b*) that the rates are given both in words and figures;

   (*c*) that the Receipt note Part II is signed by the officer authorized to do so and his signature agrees with the specimen signature kept in the Accounts office;

   (*d*) that the purchase is made by the authority competent to do so and in accordance with the rules in force;

   (*e*) the any extra charges claimed by the contractor such as freight and insurance, etc. are accepted by the Stores department and are in accordance with the terms of the agreement; and

   (*f*) that all recoveries due from the contractor are made.
4. The Purchase account register clerks should then verify the amount tying at the credit of the contractor in his ledger. The amount for which the credit is verified should be written on the bill by the purchase ledger clerk under his initials. He should quote the accounts, bill number and the amount passed in his Purchase Register against the entry of credit received through receipt order. Part III and also post the value of the bill as debit in the Purchase account register. It should be ensured that the allocations given in the Bill by the Bill passing section agree with the allocation of the Purchase account in which the credit is outstanding. One this is done, the Register No...............Folio No...............of the Purchase account register should be noted as a proof of posting the item, no bill should be passed unless an credit exists in the Purchase account register. (The Controller of stores should furnish to the Account office a list of the suppliers who are entitled to the concession.
5. In case no credit has been revived through Receipt order. Part III, the bill should be kept pending till the receipt of such credit and inquiries made of the depot regarding the delay in the submission of the Receipt note.

- **Defacement of Part II of the Receipt Note:** After each bill has been audited the head of the sub-section will see that the acknowledgement of receipt of the stores, *i.e.*, Part II of the Receipt Note is punched and enfaced with the following stamp:

  Stores supplies under this receipt have been passed for payment under bill No.............. dated..............................in the Accounts for............................for Rs....................

The number and date will be the number and date assigned to the bill in the 'Register of bill received'. The stamp should be affixed at the part where the acknowledgement of the receipt of the stores by the departments is given.

- **Audit Enfacement:** The audit enfacement of the bills should then be filled up after which the bills should be submitted to the Section officer. The Section officer will be responsible for examining each bill to see that there is evidence that all prescribed checks have been applied and that the audit enfacements are correct. In addition there is evidence thereto, he should himself check completely atleast three bills each day. A notebook should be maintained by the Section officer in which particulars of bills checked by him and the result of the check should be recorded for the inspection of Stores accounts officer. The bills should then be sent up for the Stores accounts officer approval and signature, or approved by the Section officer himself as the case may be, depending upon the financial limits prescribed (by the Board) from time to time.
- **Risk Purchases:** Certain contracts for the supply of stores provide for the purchase of stores at the risk and cost of a contractor in the event of his failure to comply with the terms of the contract during the stipulated period. When under such a provision in a contract, and article is purchased at a higher rate than the one shown in the contract, the Receipt note Part III should be valued at the contract rate and the Purchase register posted accordingly. On receipt of a bill, the amount at the contract rate should be debited to "purchase" and the balance to miscellaneous advances (Revenue), as recoverable from the contractor who failed to supply the article at the rate contracted for. The latter head should be cleared as soon as the recovery is effected. In exceptional cases, when recovery from the defaulting contractor has been effected before payment at the higher rate has been made, the recovery should be credited to deposits and the amount paid in excess of the original contract rate debited to it.

  Note : In the case of production units where suspense head "Misc. Advance (Revenue)" is not operated, the suspense head "Mise. Advance (Capital)" may be operated for the purpose.
- **Abstract of Bills:** As they are completed, the bills should be included in and abstract of audited bills and sent (duly signed by the Stores accounts officer) with cheques for the total amount of the abstract to the cashier for payment. Before the bills are sent to the cashier, reference to the number of the abstract in which they have been included should be entered in the 'Register of bills received'.
- **Prompt Payment of Bills:** No bill should ordinarily take more than four days to be disposed of in the Accounts Office unless there are defects in it which render it inadmissible in audit or call for further reference.
- **Paid Bills:** The bills should be returned by the cashier after payment for record in the Accounts office. The date of the receipt of the paid bills should be entered in the Register of bills and the signature of the record clerk obtained against each entry in the register. The paid bills should then be post-audited on the laid down in the Indian Railway Account Code.
- **Watch over Supplies Against Contracts:** The particulars of supplies received in the depots should be posted in the Contract register from the Receipt note (Part III). At the end of each month, balances should be struck so that the position of each contract may be ascertained.
- **Payments for Direct Purchases from Abroad:** When stores are purchased direct from abroad either through contracts placed by Railway Board or by Zonal Railway./ Production Units, the following procedure should be adopted for making payments for the supplies:

1. The FA & CAO of the Zonal railway or the Production unit indicated in the contract as the paying authority should open Letter of Credit (L.C.) with any of the nationalized Banks.
2. On the strength of the telex advice containing Contract No. and date, description of item (s), rate, quantity dispatched value paid received from the banker abroad, any nationalized bank may be authorized to debit the Railways' account with the Reserve Bank of India without a reference at that stage to the Railway.
3. On receipt of the copy of the telex advice or receipt of a copy of the advice from the Bank whichever is earlier, the Accounts officer who is authorized to make payments under the contract should examine the primafacie correctness of the debit and this should be specifically accepted under his signatures. If this primafacie examination reveals any incorrectness, the matter should be immediately taken up with the bank for resolving the issue.
4. On receipt of the actual shipping documents, if as a result of and internal check there are defects rendering the payments made unacceptable, the bank should on receipt of an intimation from the Railway be required to credit the account of the Railway with the Reserve Bank of India with the actual amount originally debited. This will ensure that the difference between buying and selling rates of foreign exchange is not operated to Railway's disadvantage.
5. The exchange rate applicable on the date the foreign supplier negotiated the documents with their bankers should be taken as the applicable exchange rate for working out the liability of the Railway Administration.
6. Banks may charge interest for the period between the date of negotiating the documents and the actual payment by the Railway administration to ensure that there is no avoidable delay in the bank presenting the documents to the Railway administration, a per-determined time limit for the above period may be agreed upon with the bank. No interest charges should be paid by the Railway administration to the banks for delays beyond this limit. Free time, if any, allowed by the bank for such commercial transactions should be fully availed of an all efforts made to complete the transaction within that period in order to avoid/minimize payment of interest.
7. In addition, banks will claim commission charges for opening L.C. commitment charges, cable charges, etc, which should be checked.
8. In case where foreign exchange payment is covered under foreign loans/ credits/ grants the procedure prescribed in the foreign exchange release/ licensing conditions should be followed.
   (*i*) Sharpening documents usually prescribed are:
      (*a*) Foreign Supplier's invoice
      (*b*) Bill of lading
      (*c*) Packing list
      (*d*) Certificate of country of origin
      (*e*) Marine insurance policy
      (*f*) Any other documents are prescribed in the respective contract

(Authority: Railway Board's letter No 78/RS(G/779/38,dt.14-9-78 and No. 83/F(s)I/PW5/1dt.24-3-83).

- **Register of Bills passed Provisionally:** Items passed provisionally for payment should be entered in the Register of objectionable items, and in all such cases the audit enfacement on the bill should be according to the following form:

  Passed for Rs. ———————for payment as per particulars given below :

  Abstract No———————————date———————Finally—————————Rs————

  ————————Provisionally under orders of FA&CAO/General Manager/ Railway Board.

  Total———————————

  The final disposal of the objections should be recorded in the Register.

Bills other than Purchaser Paid for in Cash

(*i*) **Customs Duty Bills :**

(*a*) The rates charged should be checked with the Indian Customs Tariff.

(*b*) The amount on which duty is charged should be checked with the invoices.

(*c*) Customs duty should be included in the cost of stores on which it is levied and the amounts thereof should therefore be extracted in a statement to enable posting to be made in the ledgers.

(*d*) The correctness of the rate of exchange adopted for conversion should be checked.

(*e*) The insurance charges included to arrive at the CIF value should be checked.

(*f*) It should be ensured that the classification of material has been made correctly and discrepancies, if any, pursued.

All the Customs duty bills should be checked cent per cent in the Accounts office. A manuscript register should be maintained in the Accounts Office to record all the Customs duty bills checked and admitted.

Refund of Customs Duty : All the claims for the refund of Customs Duty arising out of the following be made within proper time and credited to the cost of imported stores (to which it pertained) when refund materializes.

(*a*) Wrong rates adopted

(*b*) Wrong classification of material

(*c*) Refunds on consignments list or short landed, etc.

(*ii*) **Clearing Contractor's Bills:**

(*i*) In the case of imported stores, the quantities should be checked with the account of tonnage and freight. In the case of materials returned by departments, etc. the quantities or weight shown should be checked with the respective vouchers.

(*ii*) The payment to Contractor may be classified into two categories namely :

(*a*) charges for services rendered by him.

(*b*) charges arising out of the import, such as wharfage, demurrage, shed opening charges, infringement charges, etc.

The payments for the services rendered should be checked to ensure that they are in accordance with the conditions of the contract agreement.

It should be seen that rates of wharfage etc. are as per the current scales of rate published by the port trust authorities.

(*iii*) **Check of demurrage charges:** Demurrage charges normally become payable due to one of the following reasons :

(*a*) Non receipt of shipping documents.

(*b*) Short-supply, non-supply or delayed supply of wagons.

(*c*) Customs formalities, etc.

(*d*) Failure to clear in time.

In the Accounts office, the payment of demurrage charges should be carefully checked with reference to the contract conditions before admitting liability. Claims/ Bills for payment of demurrage charges should clearly show the liability of the Railway and the reasons therefore.

In cases whether the charges have to be recovered from the clearing agents or the suppliers, separate registers should be maintained by the Accounts office and the recoveries are watched. Where the demurrage charges have been contested or appealed against, the recoveries should be pursued.

Claims for Short Landing:

Claims for the items short landed should be preferred by the Controller of stores in consultation with the Stores accounts officer, consignments. Necessary bills should be prepared by the Stores accounts officer on the basis of Advice received from Controller of stores. A manuscript register should be maintained by the Accounts office to watch the settlement of these claims. This register should be reviewed monthly by the Stores Accounts Officer.

- **Port Trust Bills:** Rates should be checked with reference to the schedules of rates of the port trust concerned.

39.2 BILL PAID THROUGH BOOK ADJUSTMJENTS

The debits are raised through :

(*i*) Transfer certificates in the case of other railways.

(*ii*) Exchange accounts, if the supplies or service are by government departments, other than railways.

- **Debits by Foreign Railways:** Foreign railway transfer certificates should be subject to the same checks as for bills, before they are accepted and journalized.
- **Exchange Accounts:** The bulk of the expenditure debited through exchange account is for the purchases arranged through the Directorate General of Supplies and Disposals or for supplies of stationery and printing stores by the Controller of Printing and Stationery, India.
- **Purchase through the Directorate General of Supplies and Disposals.** Purchases other than stationery effected through the Directorate General of Supplies and Disposals are dealt with for accounting purposes in the same manner as those made by the Controller of stores, with this difference, that the bills are not paid by the Railway but by the pay and Accounts officer Directorate General of Supplies and Disposals and debits are raised by the latter against the Accounts officer of the Indenting officer concerned through exchange accounts. The duplicate copies of the bills will be received in support of the debit. On receipt of such debits, the bills should be posted in the Purchase ledgers as debits to the firm. The transactions should then be journalized by crediting 'Reserve Bank Suspense' by debit to 'purchases' These debits will be in adjustment of the items previously credited to the Purchases account by debits to 'Stores' on receipt, of the Receipt Note (Part III) from the Controller of stores. A separate set of Purchase register should be maintained for purchases made through the Directorate General of Supplies and Disposals and the outstanding items to this set of registers should be analyzed at the end of each month and agreed with the General Books.

- **Percentage Charges:** The Directorate General of Supplies and Disposals levies departmental charges for the following services rendered at rates laid down from time to time.
  - (*i*) Stores purchased through the agency of the Directorate General of Supplies and Disposals:
    - (*a*) Purchase.
    - (*b*) Inspection.

    Including all sampling and testing before the contract is concluded and also where necessary, sampling and testing during the currency of the contract.
  - (*ii*) **Stores purchased director by controller of stores :** The charges for analysis and test of chemicals and other stores and for inspection and testing of purchases not made through the Directorate General of Supplies and Disposals carried out at the Government Test House, the Metallurgical Inspectorate or any other organization under the Inspection Branch of the Directorate General of Supplies and Disposals and for advisory and miscellaneous work will be in accordance with the 'Schedule of charges' for testing and inspection work done by the Directorate General of Supplies and Disposals for the Army Department, Commercial department and undertaking of the Central Government, all departments under the Provincial Governments, State and Company managed Railways, Indian States and Quasi -public bodies, (Copies of the schedule are obtainable from the Manager of Publications, Central Publication Branch, Delhi).

  The Officer-in-charge of the inspection or testing organization will, as soon as the work is completed prepare a voucher showing the value of work done and forward it in triplicate to the railway concerned, which will countersign and return two copies to such officers and train one copy for record. At the end of the month, the officer-in-charge of the inspection or testing agency will send the accepted vouchers to the Pay and Accounts Officer Directorate General of Supplies and Disposals for adjustment.
- **Supplies of Stationery, etc. by the Controller of Printing and Stationery:** The debits for such supplies will be raised through the Exchange accounts and should be dealt with on the same lines as the debits for purchase through the Directorate General of Supplies and Disposals.
- **Printing and binding work done by the Controller of Printing and Stationery:** Debits for any such work will be raised on basis of statements prepared for 4, 6, 8, 9, 10 and 12 months, *i.e.*, in the exchange accounts for July, September, November, December, January, March and March final, so that the control over expenditure and the framing of revised and budget statements, etc. will not be affected in any way. They should be dealt with on the lines, *mutates mutants*, as the debits for supply of stationery, etc
- In accounting for the purchases of stores, from abroad the books of account in India have to show the progress of the transaction, *i.e.*,
  - (*a*) payment for the purchases;
  - (*b*) the actual receipt of the stores by the indenter in India.

The normal procedure for the accountal of these phases of the transactions is as follows:

(*a*) The payments debited to the suspense head of account 'Purchases Imported by credit to the head of account "Transfer Railway- Secretary, Railway Board, Accounts" in the case off book adjustment or "Reserve Bank Suspense" where direct cast payments are made including Letter of Credit.

(*b*) On the actual receipt of the stores by the indenter in India, the suspense head of account 'Purchases Imported' is credited by debit to the suspense head of account 'Capital Stores' or other final heads of account under Capital or revenue depending on whether the materials are taken into stock in stores depots or are sent on directly for use on works.

Control Over Expenditure Against Purchase Grant

- **Expenditure Register.**— A manuscript register should be maintained for the purpose of watching expenditure on stores purchased in India as against the allotment. The allotments should be noted from the distribution of the sanctioned amount under the various heads appearing in the Funds register. The expenditure should be noted as regards cash payments through abstracts of audited bills and as regards expenditure for a month should be verified with the debits to 'Purchases' in the General Books.

Accountal of Earnest Moneys and Security Deposits for Tender and Contracts

- Tenderers and contractors for making supplies of stores have under conditions of tender or Contract to deposit earnest moneys or security deposits for the due discharge of the obligations under taken by them. The securities may be either in cash or paper securities. Such moneys are held by the Railway till the obligations are faithfully, satisfactorily and completely discharged, when the sums are refunded to the parties concerned. The rules for the accountal of such secutities are prescribed in the State Railway Account Code.

CHAPTER

40

TRANSFER TRANSACTIONS, STORES JOURNAL AND FINAL ACCOUNTS

- **Heads of Accounts:** The following heads of Accounts under "Capital" and 'Revenue' are generally operated upon in the accounts books of the Stores accounts office which is mainly concerned with the accountal of transactions connected with 'Stores'.

  Capital:

  (*i*) Major Head Construction of State Railways—(Commercial) and Construction of State Railways—(Strategic)

  (*ii*) Minor Head Stores suspense and Miscellaneous advances

  Sub-heads :

  1. Purchases Imported
  2. Purchases Indigenous—Purchase by Railways including Railway Board.
  3. Purchases through Centralized Agencies such as DGS & D, etc.
  4. Sales other than Fuel
  5. Sales (Fuel)
  6. Stores
  7. Store-in-transit
  8. Stock adjustment account
  9. Stock adjustment account—Other items

- For facility of reference and reconciliation with the connected subsidiary registers and accounts, the Head 'Stores' is divided into the following sub-heads and detailed heads and sub-detailed heads.

Sub-head	Detailed Head
(*a*) Imported purchases	(*i*) Direct purchase by Railways including Railway Board.
	(*ii*) Purchase through other agencies.
(*b*) Indigenous purchases by Railways including Railway Board	(*i*) Imported stores purchases in India.
	(*ii*) Purchases from cottage and small scale Industries.

	(*iii*) Purchases from public sector undertakings.
	(*iv*) Purchases from other Railways.
	(*v*) Purchases from other Government departments.
	(*vi*) Khadi purchases.
	(*vii*) Local purchases made out of imprest.
	(*viii*) Others.
(*c*) Purchases through centralized agencies such as DGS & D etc.	(*i*) Imported stores purchased in India.
	(*ii*) Purchases from cottage and small scale industries.
	(*iii*) Purchases from public sector undertakings.
	(*iv*) Khadi purchases.
	(*v*) Purchases—fuel (Diesel).
	(*iv*) Purchases—Fuel (Coal).
	(*vii*) Others.
(*d*) Sales other than fuel	(*i*) Sales to Railway employees.
	(*ii*) Sales to outside parties.
	(*iii*) Sales to other railways.
	(*iv*) Sales to other Government departments.
	(*v*) Export sales.
	(*vi*) Sales to public undertakings.
(*e*) Sales (Fuel)	(*i*) Sales to Railway employees.
	(*ii*) Sales to outside parties.
	(*iii*) Sales to other Railways.
	(*iv*) Sales to other Government departments.
	(*v*) Export sales.
	(*vi*) sales to public undertakings.
(*f*) Stores	(*i*) Stores in stock in depots.
	(*ii*) stores in stock—Fuel (Coal).
	(*iii*) Stores in stock—Fuel (Diesel).
	(*iv*) Engineering imprest stores (Permanent way).
	(*v*) Engineering imprest stores (other than permanent way).
	(*vi*) Surplus engineering stores (Permanent way).
	(*vii*) Surplus Engineering stores (other than permanent way).
	(*viii*) Surplus engineering stores awaiting sales.
	(*ix*) Petty repair shop.
(*g*) Stores-in-Transit	(*i*) Stores-in-Transit- Purchases other than fuel.
	(*ii*) Stores-in-Transit-Depot Transfer other than fuel.
	(*iii*) Stores-in-Transit- Fuel.
(*h*) Stock adjustment account	(*i*) Difference between the ledger balances and ground balances discovered by the Stock verifier.
	(*ii*) Difference between the ledger balances and ground balances discovered during departmental stock verification.

(*iii*) Differences arising out of revaluation of stocks due to market fluctuation of Purchased stores.

(*iv*) Differences arising out of revaluation of stocks due to market fluctuation of shop manufactured stores.

(*v*) Differences in book value and value realized in sales.

(*vi*) Loss in classification of new stores as second hand/ scrap.

(*vii*) Other losses *i.e.*, breakage, leakage or losses on Transfer.

(*viii*) Rounding off.

(*ix*) Loss due to enemy action.

(*j*) Stock adjustment account—Other items

(*i*) Miscellaneous items (adjusted through Depot Stock Sheet, Book Transfer, etc.)

(*ii*) Value brought on books through Depot stock sheets pending receipt of vouchers.

- **Revenue**

  The following are the heads of accounts under Revenue:

  Working Expenses :

  (*i*) Revenue abstracts.

  (*ii*) Miscellaneous advances.

  (*iii*) Deposits—Miscellaneous.

  (*iv*) Transfers—Divisional.

  (*v*) Transfers—Railways.

- Transactions of receipts or payments in cash are accounted for in the following manner. In the case of moneys due to the railway, bills or other demands for payment are presented by the Railway to the parties concerned, and the money is paid into station booking offices, or to the Treasurer of the Railway, In such cases of receipts of cash, the foils of Miscellaneous Cash Remittance Notes or other cash receipts given by the treasurer show the particulars of service or stores paid for and the allocation; all such cash transactions should be posted (in Part II) of the Journal, by credit to ' Sales', etc., and debit to 'transfers Revenue'. The journal, is posted from the journal slips, the account registers for the heads of accounts credited being posted directly in detail from the receipts for cash. In the case of payments by the Railway of cash for supplies or services, the Abstracts of bills show the details of allocation for such payments. The Journals is posted directly from these abstracts, the supporting accounts registers being posted directly from bills and the vouchers in support thereof.

  Note : In case off Railways, other than Open Line Railways, where the Capital Heads are alone operated, the Head 'Transfers Revenue' will not be operated.

- Adjustments on account of transactions between the Stores department and other departments of the same railway are generally carried out internally in the Accounts office, while those with other Railways are carried out through (Transfer Certificates). Adjustments with other Government Departments are carried out through either the 'Exchange accounts' or 'Cash payment'.

- **Transfer Certificates :** Transactions not involving the actual receipt or payment of cash relating to other divisions and branches (if the transfer certificate' procedure is adopted for internal adjustments) or other railways will be passed on to the party concerned through transfer certificates, which for facility of reference are called 'Local Transfer Certificates' or 'Advices of transfer debits or credits' in the case of transfers relating to the divisions or branches of the home railway, and 'Foreign Transfer Certificates' in the case of those relating to other railways.
- **Local Transfer Certificates :** The adjustments in connection with the local transfer certificates will be carried out by employing a system of minus adjustments, *i.e.*, the division or branch originating the transaction debits or credits to the head 'Transfers- Divisional' which is accepted by the responding party by a minus debit or minus credit against the above head. The main idea underlying the above system is that the transactions (under the H) under the head 'Transfer-Divisional' for the whole line for a particular month should be nil, unless, of course, there remains certain local transfer certificates unadjusted, at the end of the month. In the case of foreign transfer certificates the creditor foreign railways always raises a debit against the debtor railway, which is accepted by the latter by contra credit against the transfer head.
- Local transfer certificates will be issued from and received in the Stores Accounts office direct, while foreign transfer certificates will be dealt with exclusively in the Book Section of the Headquarters Accounts office. The various processes relating to these are described.
  (i) *Signing of transfer certificates:* Transfer certificates may be signed by the Section officer of a section, provided they are supported by bills or vouchers signed by a Gazetted officer; in other cases they should be signed by a Gazetted officer. Similarly, the acceptance of the transfer certificates received from the various offices should be signed by a Gazetted officer unless supported by a bill or voucher duly accepted by a Gazetted officer, in which case the acceptance of this transfer certificate can be signed by the Section officer.

  (ii) *Date up to which transfer certificates may be issued:* All transfer certificates should be issued up to a date not later than the 12th of the following month, as the Transfer Certificate received in the office against whom it is issued after the 13th will be responded to in the next month's accounts, thus increasing the outstandings at the end of the month under the head 'Transfers-Divisional'.

  (iii) *Acceptance of transfer certificate in full:* All transfer certificates should be accepted in full; but if the entire amount of any transfer certificate does not relate to the office against which it is issued, it should be returned unaccepted under the signature of a Gazetted officer.

  (iv) *Transfer certificates registers:* To watch the proper disposal of the transfer certificates issued and received, two manuscript registers should be maintained one each for outward and inward transfer certificates, in the following forms, separate pages being allotted for each division, branch or section concerned.

Form No. S.2913-A

OUTWARD TRANSFER CERTIFICATE REGISTER

No. and date	Sub-section and name of clerk	Amount of T.C.		Date of receipt		Initials of clerk concerned	Journal slip No. through which adjusted
		Dr.	Cr.	Accepted	Un-accepted		

INWARD TRANSFER CERTIFICATE REGISTER

Date of receipt	Transfer certificate No. and date	Amount of T.C.		Sub-section	Initials clerk concerned	Details of return		Journal slip No. through which adjusted
		Dr.	Cr.			Accepted	Unaccepted	

(*v*) *Schedule of transfer certificates :* After the issue of all transfer certificates for the months for which the last date is the 12th of the following month, a consolidated schedule showing the transfer certificate No. and amount, separately for debit and credit, for all transfer certificates issued against each section, division and branch should be prepared and issued. These schedules are of importance in the reconciliation of the head 'Transfers- Divisional, Branches or Section' and should be very carefully prepared. The Transfer certificates from other offices should be carefully scrutinized, before being retuned.

These schedules should be returned to the issuing office by about the 18th of the following month to which they relate, and in case of non - receipt of accepted schedules, telegraphic reminders should be issued so that the transactions relating to a month may be duly accounted for in the same month's accounts.(relating to a month may be duly accounted for in the same month's accounts.)

(vi) *Adjustment with foreign railways:* In case it is desired to issue a transfer certificate against a foreign railway, the relevant voucher or, in the case of cash payment or recovery, a bill (quoting reference to the authority) along with the necessary certificate should be sent to the Book Section with a memo showing the allocation against the amount to be adjusted in the Stores Accounts office. The Book section, on receipt of the acceptance by the railway concerned will issue a memo, intimating the fact, when necessary adjustment may be carried out. Similarly, the Book Section will send with a memo, any foreign railway transfer certificates received by it for acceptance and the latter should be adjusted in the Stores Accounts Office after necessary verification.

The memo received from the Book section should be registered in the inward transfer certificate register and their proper disposal watched by the Journal keeper in the same manner as in the case of inward transfer certificates.

- **Adjustment with Government Departments other than Foreign Railways :** All exchange accounts with Civil, Military and Postal and Telegraph departments, where exchange accounts facility is a available, will be controlled by the Book section. The items pertaining to the various branches will be intimated to or by it through a memo sent along with the necessary vouchers. These memos should also be registered in the transfer certificates register and adjusted after due verification.

  In case it is proposed to originate an entry under the above head, the Journal slip should be prepared on the authority of a bill accepted by the officer against whom the item is adjustable.
- **Summaries of Transfer Adjustments :** Summaries of all transfer adjustments with other railways, and accounting offices of the Civil, Military and Postal authorities should be prepared and sent along with the consolidated Journal entry to the Book section. Reference should be quoted to the memo of the Book Section through which the intimations for adjustment were received, and necessary vouchers sent in support of adjustments originated by the Stores Accounts office.
- This record should be kept in a form as shown below, to bring together the whole of the debits and credits under the suspense heads mentioned above.

THE STORES JOURNAL

Date of receipt	Vouchers and date	Particulars	Heads of account debitable/ creditable	Heads of account debitable/ creditable	Reference to Journal slip

- The journal will be maintained in two parts with separate folios each month for each part, part I will collect all the transactions connected with the receipt of stores. Part II will relate to the issue of stores. The following will be the nature of the Journal entries affecting each head of account in the Journal.

- **Purchases Imported :** The debit to the head will be through Advice of payments (received from the High Commission of India by credit to Transfers Railways- Secretary Railway Board) or the debit scrolls issued by Reserve Bank of India in cash. This account will be credited through a Receipt advice by contra debit to 'Stores in Stock'. If the consignee Railway happens to be a foreign Railway, the debit to the head will be through a Foreign Transfer certificate.
- **Purchases:** The credit to this head of account will be through a monthly Journal entry prepared from the grand total of the group summary for purchases. The debit to head 'Purchase' will be through the Abstracts of Audited Bills by credit to 'Cash' and through Transfer vouchers and Exchange accounts, by credit to other railways and departments on account of adjustments made on their bills.
- **Miscellaneous Advances:** This head will be debited with the value of stores issued on suspense account by credit to 'Stores' and will be credited when the stores are returned by debit to 'Stores and will be credited when the stores are retuned by debit to 'Stores' or to the final heads of account.
- **Sales:** In the case of cash sales, auction sales or sales by tender where the value of material sold by the Railway is received in advance of actual issue of stores, the credit to this account will appear earlier then the debit. The credit will be by debit to 'Cash'. In other cases, *i.e.*, direct or tender sales to other Railways or Government departments the debit will appear first by credit to 'Stores' for the value of stores at the sale rates. The credit will be received through Transfer certificates or Exchange accounts by debit to the 'Transfer Railways'.
- **'Stores':** The transactions affecting this head are in respect of the value of stores received or issued from a stores depot. The debits to this head are by credit to the following heads.
  - (*i*) The 'Transfers- Workshops' on account of manufactured articles supplied to stores depots and also the value of stores returned to depots.
  - (*ii*) To 'Transfers- Divisional' on account of stores returned by departments to depots.
  - (*iii*) To Imprest accounts (all categories) Engineering plant account and surplus stores account on account of Stores retuned to the Stores depots.
  - (*iv*) To the Depot transfer account.
  - (*v*) To the Stock adjustment account.

  Note : All items that can be identified abinitio chargeable to Works for which separate Works Registers exist, should not pass through 'Stores in Stock' or any other Stores Suspense head and should be debited/credited to final heads of account.
- The credit to the head 'Stores' will be by debits to Transfers Workshop, Transfer Divisional, the Depot Transfer Accounts, Store-in-Transit account and Imprest Account (All Categories).
- **The Stock Adjustment Account:** The debits and credits to this head of account will be chiefly by contra adjustment to 'Stores' (Capital 7160) except in the case of the adjustment against the Revenue Abstracts, in clearance of the half- yearly balances under this head of account.

The other heads of accounts are self- explanatory such as:

- **Journal Entry Slips:** Journal slips debiting or crediting the various sub-heads of accounts noted above will be generally prepared at the end of the month from the several suspense registers. Miscellaneous debits and credits not emanating from any of the suspense registers will be prepared from the original vouchers themselves. Separate journal slips should be prepared for Capital and Revenue and signed by a Gazetted officer. They should then be numbered (separate series being allotted each month to Capital and Revenue), and posted in the journal, Capital and Revenue Journal slips should be separately filed, month by month
- **Consolidated Journal Slip:** The Journal keeper should satisfy himself, particularly with reference to the entries regarding Transfers—Railway and Divisional, that all the transactions of the month have been brought to account. The journal should then be totalled and consolidated journal entries (one for Capital and the other for Revenue) should be prepared. In preparing the journal entry, transactions carried directly into the General Books, *e.g.* cash payments (or receipts) for stores should be disregarded- Special care should be taken to see that:
  - (*i*) the amounts shown as debit and credit against 'Transfers State Railway Revenue' in the Capital account agree with those shown as credit and debit against 'Transfers State Railway Capital' in the Revenue account;
  - (*ii*) the total amounts of debit and credit under 'Transfers, Divisional or Branches or Sections' agree with the amounts as accepted by the sections and branches concerned through the monthly schedules; and
  - (*iii*) The amount shown as minus debit and credit against "Transfer Stores", *i.e.*, responding entries for transfers originated by the divisions, branches, Sections agree with those accepted through their schedules.
- The consolidated journal entry will show only the totals of the debits and credits to each head of account maintained in the Stores Journals.
- The journal entries should be signed by the Stores accounts officer and forwarded to the Book Section for incorporation in the accounts of the Railway.
- **Subsidiary Register for Capital Account:** The transactions relating to the Capital heads of account for the 'month' and from the commencement of operations' should be shown in the schedule of capital expenditure accompanying the monthly Capital account. Current of the Railway submitted to the Railway Board.
- As the heads of account operated upon in the Stores Accounts Office are mainly suspense heads of account detailed headwise, it is necessary that the balances under each detailed head are reconciled and proved with the General Books. For this purpose, a subsidiary register should be maintained by the Book Section for these detailed heads of account, in which should be shown opening balances, debits and credits during the month, and the closing balances in the following form. Separate pages should be opened in the register for each head of account appearing in the Journal and a summary of each head of account prepared at the end. The correctness of balances in this monthly summary should be certified by the Book Section. Any discrepancy found as a result of its reconciliation with the Book section, if any, put up to the gazetted officer within 10 days of the close of the accounts for the month.

When stores accounting has been decentralised, there arises the need for such an office submitting a monthly statement of Stores Transactions to the General office in the form shown below. The form is self-explanatory.

FORM OF SUBSIDIARY REGISTER

Sub-Head..

Detailed Head..

Month	Opening Balance	Debits	Credits	Closing Balance

The opening and closing balances should agree with the balances appearing in the Depot Group Ledger for the month.

- The account should be accompanied by such schedules as may be prescribed by the Chief accounts offices. The accounts of the various account offices should be consolidated in the Head office in the form shown below. The further procedure of accountal will be on the same lines as laid down in the previous sections.

Abstract of Stores Transactions for the month of.. 19 ....

Dr. **Cr.**

	II Receipts during the month							IV Other transaction				V Issues during the month			VI	VII	VIII	IX		
Name of Depot or Stores Accounts (Branch) Office	Opening Balance	Depot Transfers (a)	Returned Stores (b)	Purchases in India (c)	English Purchases	Manufactured in shops	Stock Adjustment Account	Suspense	Book Transfers	Sales	Total Debit of each Depot	Transfers to Depots (a)	Issue to Departments other than shops (b)	Issue to Workshops (c)	Sales	Stock Adjustment Account	Other Transactions	Closing Balance	Total Credit of each Depot	Remarks
TOTAL																				

- **Annual Accounts:** The following annual accounts should be submitted by the Stores Accounts Office to the Book Section on the prescribed dates :

  (*a*) Capital and revenue accounts.

  (*b*) Finance accounts.

  (*c*) Appropriation accounts.

  Detailed instructions regarding the preparation of each of the above accounts appear in the Accounts Department Code. Material in connection with the preparation of (*a*) and (*b*) above is generally obtained from records maintained in the Stores Accounts Branch itself, Whereas the explanations for variations between the original grant and the final grant and between the latter and the actual expenditure under the various sub-heads of the Appropriation Accounts, will be framed in consultation with the executive, if necessary. These should then be incorporated in the accounts submitted to the Book Section. For this purpose statements showing the figures of the original grant as compared with the final grant and the latter with the actual expenditure, should be sent to the Controller of Stores or other executive officer concerned, sufficiently in advance to admit of the accounts being sent to the Book section in time.

- **Exhibition of Losses in the Accounts :** Losses of stores will be exhibited in the Accounts under the following heads:

  (*i*) Physical losses;

  (*ii*) Losses due to variation in prices;

  (*iii*) Losses due to obsolescence and deterioration.

  The physical losses of stores will be generally speaking, the shortages of stores discovered during verification of stocks. But all the deficiencies of stock are not to be considered, ipso facto, physical losses. The losses are generally attributed by the depots to the following reasons.

  (*a*) Retail issues.

  (*b*) Leakage, etc.

  (*c*) Turn of scale.

  Losses arising out of retail issues, or leakages are not strictly speaking, physical losses though the former may partly be a physical loss and as most of the losses will be due to (*a*) and (*b*) ,the entire amount may be taken as physical loss. Clause(*c*) is, however, compensatory and losses attributed to this cause only should not be classes as 'Physical losses'. Losses under (*ii*) will be those shown under relevant detailed head of the Stock Adjustment Account Losses under (*iii*) for which the Stores department is responsible will be shown under relevant detailed head of the Stock Adjustment Account and those for which other departments are concerned will be debited to them and will be accounted directly by the Accounts officers concerned to the Book Section of the General Branch, where they will be consolidated. While scrutinizing the explanations given on stock sheets, Inspectors of Stores Accounts or Stock verifiers should keep note of all physical losses of stores and submit an annual statement to the Stores Accounts Officer by the 30th April each year.

CHAPTER

41

THE ANNUAL STATEMENT OF STORES TRANSACTIONS

1 A statement of the actual balances of stores in hand at the end of each financial year should be prepared by each Railway administration in Form given below and should reach the Railway Board along with its accompaniments by the Ist November of the year following.

STATEMENT OF STORES TRANSACTION FOR THE YEAR ENDED 31st MARCH,.........

Form No S.3001

		Ordinary Stores									Surplus Stores					
	Particulars				Receipts during year						Balance on 31st March			Balance on 31st March		
1	2	3a	3b	3c	3d	3e	3f	3g	3h	3i	4a	4b	4c	4d	4e	4f
	Total															

STATEMENT OF STORES TRANSACTIONS

Emergency Stores		Stores obtained for Special Works				Total All Store	
Balance on 31st March (opening)	Balance on 31st March closing	Balance on 31st March	Receipts during the year	Issues during the year	Balance on 31st March	Balance on 31st March (opening)	Balance on 31st March closing
5a	5b	6a	6b	6c	6d	7a	7b

50% of issues — Balance on 31st March 19 — From Purchases — From materials returned From works

Total — Issues during the year — Balance on 31st March 19.........

Variations from previous balance — Variations from normal maximum

3(g) minus 3(b)			3(g) minus 3(a)		
Movable surplus	Dead surplus	Total	Movable surplus	Dead surplus	Total

Add Amount under adjustment :

(a) Stock Adjustment Account.

(b) Stores-in-transit.

(c) Engineering Plant Reserve

(d) Imprest—Other than Engineering.

Engineering—Permanent-way.

Engineering—Others.

(e) Surplus—Engineering—Permanent-way.

Engineering—Others.

Balances as per General

2. The statement should show the money value of the stores in hand in thousands of rupees under each major group of stores, and the figures should be sub-divided and arranged as to distinguish the ordinary stores, from other categories of stores *viz.*

(a) Stores obtained for special works. *i.e.*, specially obtained for important works of additions or renewals.

(b) EMERGENCY STORES which comprise items which do not ordinarily wear out or require renewal but of which it is essential to maintain stock to meet emergency demand. Due to breakage or unanticipated deterioration and which are not readily available in India.

(c) SURPLUS STORES the figures for which should be sub-divided into two classes viz.

(i) Movable or live surplus *i.e.*, items of stores which have not been issued for a period of 24 months but which it is anticipated, may be utilized in the near future; and

(ii) DEAD SURPLUS which comprise items of stores, which have not been issued for the past 24 months and which, it is considered are not likely to be utilized on any railway within the next two years.

Annexure 'A'

Questions	Replies
(a) Does the balances shown agree with the General Books of the Railway and with the details of the priced ledgers, or what are the items of differences and how are they explained?	

(*b*) Have the quantities in the priced ledgers have been proved or corrected by stock taking during the year, or, if this has not been completly done, what has been the extent of comparison made of stock taking and of correction of books as a result thereof ?

(*c*) Has due allowance been made for depreciation, obsolete pattern, etc. or if not, why has this not been done.

(*d*) Are all the rates at which stores issued are priced being revised regularly to accord with market rates as laid down in paragraph 210-S?

Annexure 'B'

REVIEW OF BALANCES OF THE MATERIAL-AT-SITE ACCOUNTS FOR THE YEAR ENDING 31ST MARCH..................................

Division	Completed works		Works in progress		Works not yet started		Works not to be done		Total	
	No. of works	Amount	No. of works	Amount	No. of works	Amount	No. of works	Amount	No. of works	Amount

Annexure 'C'

STATEMENT OF BALANCES OF "CHARGED OFF" IMPRESTS ON 31ST MARCH..................................

Categories of Imprest Holders

Division	Running sheds		Train examining stations		Electricians			
	Total money limit by General Manager	Balance on 31st March	Total money limit by General Manager	Balance on 31st March	Total money limit by General Manager	Balance on 31st March	And So On	Total balance on 31st March
Total								

3. It should be seen that when the anticipations of movable surplus stores being used do not materialise, the relevant items are transferred to dead surplus. Before classifying any stores as dead surplus, it should be ass certained as far as fasible that the material is not likely to be in demand by other Railways. The value of dead surplus stock should be suitably written down if necessary to scrap values, after survey by Survey Committee.

4. **50 per cent of Issues** (See Statement of Store Transcations): The comparison of actual balances of 'Ordinary Stores with 50 per cent of issues' is with a view to assess the endeavours of the Railway Admistrations to reduce and restrict the actual balance to the limit.
5. **Returned Stores** (See Statement of Store Transcations): The materials returned from works lead to the accumulation, ultimately, of surplus and unserviceable stores on railways. The receipts under 'Ordinary Stores' should show separately:
   (*a*) receipt by purchases; and
   (*b*) receipts of materials returned from works, to enable an idea to be obtained on the proportion of materials returned from works to new stores purchased in the market or manufactured in the market or manufactured in railway workshops.
6. **Balance of Materials-at-Site:** A review of the balances of the material-at-site account for the year should be prepared in the form shown as Annexure B to Form S. 3001 and attached to the statement. This analyses stores balances under this head by each Division and by the following sub-heads:
   (*i*) Completed works.
   (*ii*) Works in progress.
   (*iii*) Works not yet started.
   (*iv*) Works not be done.
7. **Balances of Charged-off Imprests:** A statement of balance of 'Charged-off imprests comparing the balance at the end of the year with each category of imprest holder in each division with the total of the money limits fixed by the General Manager should be submitted as Annexure C on all railways where such system is in force.
8. **Certificate of Balances by Chief Accounts Officer:** A certificate of the balances should be furnished by the Chief Accounts Officer over his signature in the form to answers to the questionnaire which is an annexure to the Annual Statement.
9. **Note Accompanying the Statement:** The statement should be accompanied by a note which should show:-
   (*a*) The balance of stores for the last ten years, in order to show the fluctuations;
   (*b*) The increase or decrease under each individual head of stores in paragraph 201 in the year under review and the reasons for the same; and
   (*c*) The details of the verifications of stores carried out during the year.
10. **Preparation of the Statement:** The statement should be prepared by the Controller of Stores, the assistance of the Accounts Officer being taken for the preparation of the Financial Statements. The Chief Accounts Officer is personally responsible for the accuracy of the certificate. The Controller of Stores should also prepare the note to accompany the statement. The draft statement should be submitted to the General Manager who is responsible for reviewing it carefully before submitting it finally to the Railway Board over his own signature.

CHAPTER

42

THE STORES BUDGET

1. The stores budget for the 'ensuing year' and revised estimate for the current year should be prepared in the following form by the controller of stores with the assistance of the stores Accounts Officer and submitted to the Railway Board by the 23rd December each year, accompanied by Annexures 'A' 'B' and 'C' the forms shown below being used for the purpose.
2. The following instructions should be followed carefully in the preparation of the stores budget except for "Fuel oils. The budget for these items should be prepared by the respective controlling officers and furnished to the Controller of stores for incorporation in the stores budget.
3. The figures to be shown as the opening balance for the ensuing year will be an estimated figure made up of:
   - (*a*) The estimated book value of stores expected to be in stock at the end of the current year;
   - (*b*) The estimated net result of outstanding balance under the Stores suspense heads of Purchases-imported, indigenous, sales, etc., and
   - (*c*) The amount expected to be outstanding in the stock Adjustment Account after the accounts for the year are closed.
4. **Issues to 'Works' :** The expenditure on stores purchased for specific 'works' that can be indentified as initio as such, should be debited directly to the 'Works' concerned and not passed through the general stores suspense head. The figures on this accounts should not, therefore, be included.

   Estimates for stores required for 'Works' which cannot be identified as stated above should be called for from the Divisional Officers/Heads of Departments by the Controller of Stores and incorporated against the relevant items.
5. Modifications are sometimes made by the concerned Heads of Departments in the budget, estimate submitted to them by the various divisions owing to changes in the programme of works. The effect on the Stores Budget of these modifications should be intimated to the Controller of Stores as soon as they are carried out in the Works programmes finally submitted to the Railway Board.

DEMAND NUMBER:16- STORES TRANSACTIONS

(Figures in thousands of Rupees)

DEBITS	Actuals for the past year	Original Budget for the current year	Revised Estimate for the current year	Budget Estimate for the ensuing year	CREDITS	Actuals for the past year	Original Budget for the current year	Revised Estimate for the current year	Budget Estimate for the ensuing year
1	2	3	4	5	6	7	8	9	10
BALANCE AT COMMENCEMENT OF THE YEAR					**ISSUES DURING THE YEAR**				
(*a*) Stores in stock (other than those in Grain Shops)					(I) To Works Capital				
(*b*) Outstanding Stores Suspense balance.					(IV) To Capital Manufacture Suspense				
(*c*) Outstanding on Stock Adjustment Account.					(V) To Miscellaneous Advances (Capital)				
(*d*) Stocks in Grain Shops					(VI) Sales and Transfers				
(*e*) Coal					TOTAL				
(*f*) Coke					(VIII) Deduct for Issues within the Demand				
(*g*) Fuel Oil					(vide item vi (-) per contra)				
Total					**Total Credit During the Year**				
RECIPTS DURING THE YEAR					**ANTICIPATED BALANCE AT THE CLOSE OF THE YEAR**				
I. Purchase:									
1. Stores for Works Construction Depots					(*a*) Stores in Stock (other then those in Grain Shops).				
2. Stores for Production of New Rolling Stock					(*b*) Outstanding Stores Suspense Balance.				
3. Stores for Issues to Coach and Wagon Builders					(*c*) Outstanding in Stock Adjustment Account.				
4. Stores for General Purposes					(*d*) Stocks in Grain Shops.				
5. Grain Shops and Catering Supplies					(*e*) Coal				
6. Coal					(*f*) Coke				
7. Coke					(*g*) Fuel Oil				
8. **Fuel Oil**					**Total**				
Total Purchase					**Grand Total**				

II. Receipt from Manufacture into Stores:	GRAND TOTAL
III. Materials Returned from Works	Net Debit or Credit during the year
(*i*) Workshop Material	Budget allotment required
(*ii*) Other Materials	
IV. Other Debits	
(*i*) Receipts after Fabrication into Stores	
(*ii*) Other Debits such as Stock Adj. A/c., sales, etc.	
V. Total Debits for Purchases and Receipts	
VI. Deduct for issues from Stores Suspense to Service/Books within the demand vide item I, IV & V per vide	
(*i*) Manufacture Operations:	
(*ii*) Misc. Advance Capital	
(*iii*) Works Capital	
TOTAL DEBITS DURING THE YEAR	
GRAND TOTAL	

NOTES:

1. A brief narrative explanation should be furnished for:
   (*a*) Variations between the debits during the year expected to be adjusted under Stores Suspense at the revised Estimate stage and those anticipated for adjustment at the original budget.
   (*b*) Difference between the anticipated debits expected to be adjusted under Stores Suspense during the ensuing year and those provided for in the Revised Estimate of the current year.
2. Separate explanations for variations/difference in respect of credits under Stores Suspense should also be given.
3. The figures of actuals to be shown against the different heads in the above statement should be worked out from the Capital Account Current for March and the supporting departmental summaries of Receipts and Issues. The opening and closing balances should agree with the net figures of actuals of the respective year reported to the Secretary (Accounts).
4. The figures for Suspense should represent the value of inventory to be held in stock with reference to the norms of inventory prescribed.

* *Details of Adjustment through Stock Adjustment Accounts, if any, should be given by Abstracts of Revenue Accounts.*

DEMAND NO. 16- ASSETS-ACQUISITION, CONSTRUCTION AND REPLACEMENT

Break-up of the amount for Purchase of Stores for Works and General purposes excluding Coal, and Fuel Oil and Grain Shops supplied by various Agencies of Purchases.

(Figures in thousands of Rupees)

Particulars	Actuals for last year	Revised Estimate for current year	Budget Estimate for ensuing year
1	2	3	4
I. Through Ministry of Supply (D. G. S. & D.)			
II. Through Railway Board			
III. Inter-Railway Purchases/Sales/Transfers			
1. Through D. L. W.			
2. Through C. L. W.			
3. Through I. C. F.			
4. Through D. C. W.			
5. Through other Railways:			
(*a*) Imports:			
(*b*) Others:			
IV. Direct Purchases by the Administrations:			
1. Imports			
2. (*a*) Steel			
(*b*) Other items			
TOTAL			

6. **Issue to Capital Manufacture Suspense:** These estimates should be initially prepared by the department entrusted with the manufacture and repair operations in consultation with the respective Accounts Officers and furnished to the stores Department for incorporation in the stores Budget. The value of materials budgeted for under this head should represent the value of materials likely to be drawn by the workshops during the year for the different types of products to be manufactured as per the approved production programme in respect of Production Units. The value of materials is assessed adopting the latest book average rates available at the time of preparation of the budget.
7. **Issues to Miscellaneous Advances Capital:** These represent issues of stores for fabrication etc.
8. **Issues to Revenue:** These are general purpose stores issued for use on works of the nature of maintenance, repairs and operation for which no detailed estimates are prepared by the consuming departments. In these cases, the average consumption of the last three years would, after allowing for special items of expenditure, if any, peculiar to each year form fairly accurate guide. Such estimates should be prepared by the Controller of Stores and checked against similar estimates for funds for 'stores from stock' obtained from departments, divisions for the ensuing year with reference to the funds provided by them for "stores in the different Revenue Abstracts. Large variations between the figures communicated to the controller of stores through the departmental estimates and those arrived at on the basis of previous three year's consumption, should be brought to the notice of the principal officers concerned by the controller of stores in order to decide the figure to be finally adopted for the budget.

9. **Sales and Transfers:** While Railways exchange spares and other items, production Unit supply spares to the Railways which is also included in this item. Controller of stores should base his estimate for this item on the value of indents submitted by the zonal Railways and to the extent accepted for supply during the year.
10. **Closing Balance-Stores in Stock:** The "Ideal" balance would be 40 per cent of the average issue of ordinary stores for one year plus the cost of emergency stores. As it will not always be possible to dispose of all scrap as and when received and avoid accumulation of surplus stores in spite of the most efficient store keeping, the value of such scrap and surplus stock should be taken into account in estimating the balance of stores in stock, at end of the year.
11. **Closing Balance Outstanding Stores Suspense Balances:** This is an item corresponding to similar head under opening balance at the commencement of the year and the amount under this head should be as low as possible.
12. (*a*) *Stores for Works and Construction Depots—Item I (1):* The value of stores to be purchased and paid for during the year, for ultimate issue to works which cannot be identified ab-initio as stated in 3104-S and as such passing through stores Suspense should only be included under this head.

    (*b*) *Stores for Production of new Rolling Stock—Item I (2):* The value of stores to be purchased and paid for and passing through Stores Suspense for ultimate issue to the shop for production of new Rolling Stock against Rolling stock budget order should be included under this head. (This will apply cnly to be Production Units and be Railways who are executing Rolling Stock Budget orders for manufacture of certain new Rolling stock).

    (*c*) *Stores for Issue to Coach and Wagon Builders—Item I (3):* The value of stores to be purchased and paid for and passing through Stores Suspense for ultimate issue to Coach and Wagon Builders (in Private and Public Sector) for the purpose of building new Rolling stock should be included under this head. (Steel, bought out components, etc., which are procured and kept under stores suspense for ultimate issue to these builders should only be included).
13. **Stores for General Purpose—Item I (4):** The value of general purpose stores to be purchased and paid for and passing though Stores Suspense for ultimate issue for maintenance, repairs and operation should be included under this head. This should be the last item to be budgeted for in this estimate. When all the other items had been filled in on the Debit and Credit sides, the two sides should be totalled separately. The excess of the total of the entries on the credit side over those on the debit side will represent the amount required for the purchase of Stores for General Purposes.
14. In the estimating the value of stores to be purchased, the following factors should be taken consideration

    (*a*) Estimated throw forward from previous year, (*i.e.*, value of stores, indents for which were certified against previous years grants but which have not been paid before the close of the previous year).

    (*b*) Indents of the current year.

    (*c*) less estimated throw-forward to next year (*i.e.*, value of stores, indents of which have been certified against current year which are not likely to be paid before the close of the year).
15. In order to enable the Ministry of Railways to know the supply position, etc., against contracts placed on their behalf by the Director General, Supplies and Disposals, and to estimate the expenditure involved for budget purpose, fortnightly/weekly reports will be submitted to the Ministry of Railways by these agencies during January/March giving the following particulars.

(*a*) Railway Indenter.
(*b*) Indent Number.
(*c*) Contract Number and date, if placed.
(*d*) Value of the Contract.
(*e*) Value of the Stores supplied during the period under report.
(*f*) Date of shipments.
(*g*) Remarks regarding outstanding.

16. **Receipts from Manufactures into Stores (Item II):** They should agree with the credit in the Manufacture Suspense Budget against "IV-Issues to Capital-Stores Suspense". The amount to be provided should therefore, be settled by agreement between the stores Department and the various manufacturing departments.
17. **Material returned from Works (Item III):** This will be a consolidated figure of the estimates submitted by Departments.
18. **Other Debits (Item IV):** When owing to the operation of the stock Adjustment Account the head 'Stores' has to be debited, such an Item of debit is an item of " Receipt" which is not covered by any of the Item I to III, IV "other charges" is, therefore, provided for this purpose. In the original budget estimate no amount ordinarily be shown under this head. This will also include the value of fabricated items which are kept in stock for issue. The provision for this item should be based on the value of fabricated materials likely to be received during the year based on the estimates furnished by the departments.
19. Reduction in debits on account of issues made to "works and services" debitable to the same head as "Stores" (item VI). The value of stores to be issued to such "Works" Manufacture Operations' and 'Miscellaneous Advances Capital' from stores Suspense will be indicated as a reduction in debits. The same amount will also be shown as deduction under 'credits', against Item XIII.

    The estimates for 'Works' should be obtained from the Divisional/District Officers, those for 'manufacture Operations' and "Miscellaneous Advances-Capital" would be the same as shown against Items IV and V under "Credits".
20. The "Net Debit or Credit" during the year would be the difference between the 'Total Debits and Credits' during the year. This would be the amount by which the closing balance is decreased (or increased) from the opening balance during a year.
21. **Budget Allotment Required:** This would be the total of the Debits during the year.
22. **General:** A brief narrative explanation of the difference between the opening and closing balances should be given. Special features in the estimates should be brought out clearly and a full explanation thereof furnished indicating the amount involved in respect of each item in the debit and credit side.
23. Particular Watch should be kept over the actual booking of debits and credits on account of stores transactions. As soon as the grant for stores is known a complete statement of the expected debits and credits to stores under the various heads should be prepared working up to the net grant.
24. The progress of debits and credits under each head should be watched by the stores Accounts Officer through monthly statement having particulars of debits and credits as in paragraph 3101 against each of which should be shown the figures under the following four heads.

1. Budget allotment (Budget year).
2. Actuals at end of last month.
3. Approximates for current month.
4. Total expenditure to end of the month.

25. A copy of the monthly statement, referred to in the preceding paragraph should be furnished to the Controller of Stores to enable him to watch the progress with a view to regulate purchases and issues or to revise the budget estimates. The attention of the General Manager should be drawn to the progress of debits and credits if it shows the necessity for the curtailment of the programme of purchases. Debits and Credits may be subdivided by more important items of stores, if the railway Administration so require, in order to regulate Purchases.

CHAPTER

43

STOCK VERIFICATION OF STORES DEPOTS BY THE ACCOUNTS DEPARTMENT

1 **Object of the Stock Verification:** The object of verification by the Accounts Department of Stores in the custody of the Depot and other Departmental Officers and Subordinate is to ensure that the materials accord with the description and specification shown in the balances appearing in the books and that excess or deficiencies.

2. **Frequency of Verification:** The Stores, whether in a Stores Depot or with a department should be verified by Stock Verifiers of the Accounts Department. The programme of inspection should be so arranged that all materials are verified as shown below:

1. Materials-at-side-works	Ordinarily verified once a year.(i)
2. Stores with Impress holders	Once in two years.
3. All tools and plant	Once in 3 years.
4. All materials in a Depot as under:	
(*i*) A items—all items having an annual usage value of Rs. 1.25 lakes or more.	Once in 6 months
(*ii*) B items—all items having an annual usage value of Rs. 20000/- and above but below Rs. 1.25 lakhs.	Once in a year
(*iii*) C items—all items having an annual usage value below Rs. 20000/-	Once in two years
(*iv*) D items—all items that had no issue for 12 months and over.	Once in a year
(*v*) Miscellaneous items—Stores under the custody of inspectors entrusted with tools, instruments, etc.	Once in 3 years
(*vi*) Verification of in-proces—inventory in all workshops and Production Units especially in respect of costly and pilferable items as per Board's letter No. 77/RS (TC)/165/28 of 9–01–1978.	Once in 3 years
(*vii*) Machinery and plant	Once in 3 years

The Chief Accounts Officer may, however extend the period between verifications or curtail the items to be verified where he and the General Manager agree that:

(*i*) the reduction in check will not impair efficiency;

(*ii*) the reduction check will provide sufficient safeguards against loss; and

(*iii*) a too rigid application of the rule is not condusive to economy.

3. **Supervision and Control:** The verification should be carried out by Stock Verifiers under the general supervision of the stores Accounts Officer and under the direction of the authorized Inspector of Stores Accounts, assisted where it is feasible and expedient, by the Inspectors of Stores Accounts.

4. **Duties of the Senior Inspector of Stores Accounts:** The authorised Inspector of Stores Account is generally responsible to the Stores Accounts Officer for the proper conduct of all business relating to the verification of stores. He should prepare in duplicate provisional programme of work for each financial year before the commencement of the year and submit it to the Chief Accounts officer for approval. The Chief Accounts Officer will retain one copy and return the other copy duly approved to the Stores Account officer where it should be filed carefully for purposes of comparison with the progress made during the year. The authorized Inspector should distribute the work among the Stock Verifier working under him in such a way as to complete the verification of stores and tools and plant in due time. He should make surprise visits to see that the staff are actually employed on the duties on which they have been deputed. He should also himself lest check the work done wherever he considers it necessary and furnish a report of the results to the Stores Accounts Officer. To ensure the element of surprise which is the essential factor contributing towards the success of such visits, previous intimation of the visit should be given only to the Stores Accounts Officer. Detailed information of his movements should however, be given in the weekly journal of the authorized Inspector. He should submit daily or and weekly reports to the Accounts Officer of the progress made by each Stock Verifier. The Stores Accounts Officer should periodically check the work of the Inspector of Stores Accounts and Stock Verifiers.

   Verification Registers: The authorized Inspector of Stores Accounts should maintain manuscript registers separately for each category of verification to record following information separately for 'depot verification' and for 'line verification.'

   (*i*) Serial number.

   (*ii*) Name of depot and group or division or subordinate.

   (*iii*) Actual number of working days taken in previous verifications

   (*vi*) Name of Stock Verifier on two previous verifications

   (*v*) Date when verification is due in the year as per programme

   (*vi*) Date when started.

   (*vii*) Date of completion.

   (*viii*) Time taken (actual working days)

   (*ix*) Name of Stock Verifier.

   (*x*) Date due for next verification

   (*xi*) Initials of authorized Inpector of Stores Accounts.

5. The authorized Inspector will maintain the Register of Stock Sheet, the Register of Field Books and be incharge of the blank and completed field books.

6. **Duties of Stock Verifiers:** Their duties are :
   (*i*) The routine verification of stocks comprising :
      (*a*) Stores in the custody of the stores department.
      (*b*) Imprest or surplus suspense material in custody of subordinates on the line.
      (*c*) Materials-at-site of works
      (*d*) 'Charged-off' material in workshops, Sheds and other charged-off materials elsewhere generally as far as they are susceptible of check.
      (*e*) Fuel with the loco department.
      (*f*) Timber in the carriage and wagon shops.
      (*g*) Engineering reserve plant.
      (*h*) Type in the printing press.
      (*i*) Tools and plant in the custody of subordinates and offices of all departments of the railway.
      (*j*) Consumable stores.
      (*k*) Material under acceptance in stores depot.
      (*l*) Verification of in-process inventory in all workshops including production units.
      (*m*) Verification of machinery and plant.
   (*ii*) Surprise verification of stocks.
   (*iii*) Inspection of the receipts and inspection section of the depots.
   (*iv*) The witnessing of auction sales.
   (*v*) The witnessing of deliveries of stores sold.

   The Chief Accounts Officer may, however, it is found feasible and expedient, arrange for two or more Stock Verifiers to work under the supervision of an Inspector of Stores Account in which case, the respective duties of the inspectors of Stores Accounts and the Stock Verifiers should be clearly laid down. The Inspectors of Stores of Stores Accounts may in such cases be entrusted with part of the duties allotted to the authorized Inspector.

7. **Authority Cards**: Authority cards being the following inscription should be issued to the verification staff in order to enable them to establish their identity with the Depot or Departmental Officers and Subordinates:

   "This is to certify that Mr. X is an Inspector of Stores Accounts or Stock Verifier of the........................Railway and is authorized to have access to all Books and Records relating to stores at Stores Depots or with Departments."

   PHOTOGRAPH
   Signature of Party
   STORES ACCOUNTS OFFICERS

   A manuscript should be maintained to record the implements and tools and plant issued to Stock Verifiers. I:. this register all articles issued to a Stock Verifier will be noted against his name.

   These will be compared with the annual tools and plant returns submitted by Stock Verifiers every year and all discrepancies looked into.

8. **Field Books:** Field Books for depot verification, engineering and other verifications and blank registers for witnessing deliveries of materials sold by auction or tender or for other similar

purposes, should be issued to Stock Verifiers as and when required by them. Ail field books issued for a category of verification should be allotted before issue of a progressive serial number and commencing from unity each financial year.

9. **Register of Field Books:** A manuscript register should be maintained by the authorized Inspector to record the issue of the field books. The register should show the following particulars.
   (*i*) Serial number
   (*ii*) Number of pages in the field book
   (*iii*) Date of issue
   (*iv*) Name of stock verifier.
   (*v*) Name of depot or department verified
   (*vi*) Acknowledgement of stock verifier.
   (*vii*) Date of receipt back in office.
10. **Completed Field Books:** After the completion of the field books or the verification for which they are issued, all field books should be returned to the office for record, the date of their return being recorded in the register in the column provided for the purpose as soon as they are received back. At the close of the financial year this register should be overhauled to see that no field books are lying with Stock Verifiers which should have been returned to the office. Calls for outstanding field books should be issued, the authorized Inspector being responsible to see that this is regularly done.
11. **Immediate Investigation of Large Discrepancies:** Any large discrepancies found as a result stock verification between the ledger or the records and the actual count balance should be investigated without delay and a detailed report submitted thereon to the Account Officer. For this purpose, difference over 2per cent in quantity over the total transaction since the date of last verification of items or Rs.5000/- in value whichever is higher should be generally investigated by the Verifier and effort made to find out the cause thereof this should not be construed to mean that explanations for variations below these limits will be accepted as a matter of course. Unless in any case, the Administrator or Accounts Officer consider it necessary to call additional, information stock holders should furnish full and detailed explanation in respect of differences over 2 per cent in quantity over the total transactions on each account since the last date of verification of these items or Rs.5000/- in value whichever is more.
12. **Erroneous Classification, Unauthorised Stock and Surplus Stores:** Any wrong classification of the Group of Stores, or unauthorized stocks of stores held by any Officer or subordinate, any items of stores which is surplus to requirements or for which there has been no demand for over a year (provided that such items have not already been reported as such by Depot or District Officer) should be noted and included in narrative report of verification to be submitted by the Verifier.
13. **Arrangements for Custody and Protection of Stores:** The Verifiers should particularly examine and report if proper arrangements exist for the safe custody and proper storage of material against unnecessary from the weather or loss from any other cause. With this object, they should examine the existing arrangements to see:
   (*i*) that the godown floors are pucca or cemented' and in case of subordinates on line where such godowns have not been provided, that no stores are stacked on the ground and that unserviceable sleepers and rails have been used as under packing in case of heavy materials which cannot be stacked in racks or bins;

(*ii*) that racks or other suitable arrangements are provided for storing hand tools and petty and consumable stores;

(*iii*) that items of common domestic use are always kept under lock and key, soap matches, towels, dusters, etc. are instances of this nature;

(*iv*) that in case of material stacked outside the godowns such as sleepers, rails, crossings, etc, enclosures have been provided or chowkidars appointed to watch the same;

(*v*) that proper arrangements exist for locking the godowns and keeping the keys in safe custody;

(*vi*) that proper arrangements exist for locking the godowns and that adequate arrangements exist for fire protections, *i.e.*, fire extinguishers are kept handy and easily accessible spots and that fire buckets area always full of water and/or sand where inflammable articles are stocked. Adequate fire engines are available at call for attending emergencies;

(*vii*) that inflammable stores are near stocked near combustible items, *i.e.*, waste cotton, sleepers or other wooden fittings are not stocked near petrol or oil;

(*viii*) that statutory regulation for strong explosives and such dangerous substances are observed; and

(*ix*) that in order to avoid deterioration of stock, issues are not made from fresh receipt as a matter of course but that articles first received are issued first and to ensure this fresh receipts are not dumped on existing stocks but are so arranged that their turn for issue will come only when the existing stock are exhausted.

14. **Survey of Depots and Yards for Unaccounted for Stores:** In order to ensure that any stocks not on the books are not overlooked, a survey of large depots and yards should be made to see that all materials lying about stocked or unstocked is properly accounted for in the books. If there is any material in stock for which no ledgers exists, it should be examined how the material in question came into stock and steps taken to promptly account for such material in the books of the depots or departments.

15. **Examination of Arrangements for Recoupment and Issue:** The procedure in force in the Stores Depot and Departments regarding the receipt, issue and accounted of stores should be examined with a view to as certain if the orders in force from time to time with regard to these matters are strictly observed.

The Controller of Stores, as a custodian and distributing agent of stores, supplies stores to the entire Railway Administration in accordance with its needs. The Stock Verifiers while overhauling the account of subordinates and of other officers on the line should, therefore, see that stores are not obtained through any other agency or in cases of emergent demands, where the articles can be manufactured in local workshops expeditiously and without additional cost (*e.g.*, squares wooden, boards, inch; or wooden patterns for adding sleepers on renewals). It should be seen that articles locally manufactured are invariably taken on the subordinate accounts.

17. In the case of the following articles, which are supplied in large quantities under contracts approved by competent authority, orders for supply will be placed directly by the departmental officer concerned:

(*i*) Pay Clerks and their Inspector

(*ii*) Sub-Assistant Surgeons on traveling duty

(*iii*) Water Inspector

(iv) Platform Inspector
(v) Refreshment Room Inspector
(vi) Block Inspector
(vii) Publicity Inspector
(viii) Engine Drivers
(ix) Any other subordinate declared by the FA. & CAO.

16. **Dead Stock, Tools and Plant of Low Value:** When verifying articles other than ordinary stores, viz. articles of dead stock, tools, plant and machinery, stock verifiers may use their discretion to omit from certification articles of low value such as notice boards, name board, ticket-nippers, carriage keys, station seals, etc. and concentrate their attention on the check of more important items. Stock Verifiers should show in such cases at the end of their stock sheet the articles that have been omitted from verification.

17. **Small Tools and Hand Tools with Certain Staff:** The verification of small tools and hand tools in minor workshops, running sheds, pump houses and with permanent way Inspector, inspector of works, signal and interlocking inspectors, sanitary inspector and other inspectors need not be carried out by the Stock Verifiers. The Stock Verifier should at the time of verification of other types of stocks with such staff investigate the system in force for the supply and custody of these tools and see that reasonable care is being exercised making issues and ensuring that workmen to whom they are issued return them to stores custody when no lager required.

18. **Petty Consumable Stores:** Petty stores and consumable stores except kerosene oil) as stated in prescribed schedules in the custody of subordinates of the Traffic Department need not be verified by Stock Verifiers, as these stores are supplied in accordance with fixed scales and in very small quantities.

19. **Dunnage:** Charged off sleepers, cast iron pots, etc. used in stores depots or with subordinates line to stock material on need not be verified by Stock Verifiers as it is not always practicable to remove these from under the material stacked thereon and as their detailed verification is too costly in time and money to be commensurate with the value of material. It should however been seen that only material otherwise unserviceable is used for such purposes.

    Though it is not ordinarily the duty of a Stock Verifier to verify the articles mentioned, he should use his discretion to make up full and complete verification, if he spects an irregularity in any case.

20. **Selection of Items for Verification:** On being posted to a Depot, the Stock Verifier should consult the programme of work as to the duties he is required to perform in the Depot. After having given one day's prior notice, in writing, to the Ward Keeper of the group that is to be taken up for verification, he should select the items of the group, he desires to verify each day.

21. **Entering the Field Book:** The stock verifier should then enter in his field book the name of the depot, its section, date of commencement of the verification, group, Nomenclature and P. L. Numbers of the items he proposes to verify on the following day. Book balance should on no account be entered in the field book until after the stocks have been actually verified.

    After the necessary particulars have been entered on the field book and he has satisfied himself that the stores are properly cared for and grouped, the Stock Verifier will being to verify each particular item of stock on detail. He should never accept book balances as correct, but should verify all stores in stock unless special orders to the contrary have been taken from the Stores Accounts Officer.

22. **Descriptional Nomenclature, etc. of Articles:** It must be seen that the articles verified agree with the description under which they stand on the ledgers and that the nomenclature, classification of the group and units for stock are in accordance with the published Price List. If any doubt as to the correctness of the classification of group specially in the case of loco or carriage and wagon fittings, the specification or drawing of the same should be obtained for comparison. If any doubt still exists in the mind of the verifier regarding identification or unified group of an articles of stock (such as engine fittings, tools plant or machinery or component parts thereof) the assistance of the Mechanical Department Officials may be sought.

23. **General Instructions Regarding Depot Verification:**

    (*i*) **Presence of depot stores-keeper essential.-** Stores should be certified in the presence of the Depot Store Keeper or some one deputed on his behalf.

    (*ii*) **Correction of scales, etc.-** Scales should be carefully adjusted at least once during each day before weightment of any article.

    (*iii*) **Personal count and by stock verifier.-** The Stock Verifier should personally count weigh or measure all items of stores he proposes to verify with the assistance of stores coolies where necessary. All details of verification *i.e.*, count, weight or measurement should be recorded in the field book and it should be seen that no stock of the items under verification is lying in any other part of the godown or obscure corner. The Stock Verifier will not only be responsible for certifying what is shown to him but will also be responsible for seeing that nothing is left unverified.

    (*vi*) **Material under issue or receipt.-** The Stock Verification being the first voucher to be posted for that date, the ground balance after verification should be shown as at commencement of the day. Therefore, Stock Verifiers should examine material under issue and receipt. If such vouchers happen to be there, the ground balance should be struck as at the beginning of the day, taking into account the vouchers under issue or receipt. If any articles are found lying without any covering voucher, they should be invariably brought into books. Except under exceptional circumstances, which should be recorded in the field book.

24. **Weighments and Measurements:** The instructions given above should be kept in view when weighing or measuring stock.

25. **Units of Weight:** The Unit for verification should be the same as that of unit of accountal and the quantity shown in stock sheets should be rounded off to the nearest number of decimals as that of Priced Ledger.

26. **Weighment Vs Count:** A Stock Verifier should not waste time in counting large quantities of small articles when a fair result can be obtained in a shorter time by weight and measurement. In such cases 5 per cent or 100 of the articles, whichever is less, should be counted and weighed, and the weight of the whole stock then taken and reduced to count by weight of the sample count. When weighment is made, the maximum quantities which a can weigh should be weighed each time.

27. **Measurement Vs Weighment:** Measurement or average weighment to arrive at the total approximate weight of stocks of an article should be resorted to only if there are heavy balances in hand. To arrive at average weighment, at least 2 per cent in the case of steel and 10 per cent in the case of other material of stores, should be weighed, such stock should then be measured by length, area or cubic contents. The measurements of the entire stock should then be taken and then reduced to weight by the data furnished by the sample quantity measured

and weighed. If the weight thus arrived at is approximately the same as the depot book balance, the latter should be accepted as correct, if however, a heavy difference is disclosed thereby, all figures for measurements and weighments should be carefully rechecked and an additional 2 per cent or 10 per cent (as the case may be) weighed and measured. Appendix III to this Code gives tables of weights and measurements for certain common items of stores.

The method adopted in ascertaining the average and actual weighments or measurements taken in each case should be carefully recorded in the field book.

28. **Valuable Articles:** In the case of valuable articles, such as tin ingots etc. the whole stock should always be weighed, regardless of what the balance may be.

29. **Verification of Heavy Articles:** The weight of heavy stores, such as large steel plates, channels, rolled steel beams, etc. which cannot be easily handled or weighed, should be arrived at by very carefully taking the measurements of such articles, calculating the cross-section and then using appropriate formulae or conversion rate which should be prescribed for the purpose by each Railway Administration. Where no such formula have been prescribed, the conversion factors given in Appendix-III may be used.

30. **Verification of Fluids:** The stock of different kinds of fluids are maintained either:

    (*i*) Litres or

    (*ii*) Kilograms.

    The containers of such fluids are generally:

    (*a*) Portable cylindrical drums;

    (*b*) Tins;

    (*c*) Stationary cylinders, and

    (*d*) Vats which admit of proper measurements to find their cubical contents.

    (*a*) The following formulae should be used to ascertain the cubical contents of the containers.

    (*i*) *Formula for Cylinders:* Area of the base x length or height of the cylinders. The base being always circular, the formula of II R2 is always to be applied to work out the area of the base. II = 22/7, R=Radius

    (*ii*) Formula for tins, vats, etc. which are generally rectangular in shape: Cubical contents = Length × Breadth × Height.

    (*b*) ***Verification of Fluids Accounted for in Litres:*** In case of verification of fluids which are stocked in units of litres, the cubical contents *i.e.*, the part upto which the container is filled with the fluid should be calculated in cubic decimeters to find out the contents in litres, taking one cubic decimeter equal to one litre.

    Note: Unopened receptacles with original sealings, etc. intact may be taken as containing the quantity of the fluid stated on the receipt takes.

    (*c*) ***Verification of Fluids Accounted for in Kilograms:*** In the case of verification of fluids which are stocked in units of kilograms the following procedure should be followed. The cubical contents of the containers should be calculated (in cubit decimeters) and reduced in the first instance to the weight of distilled water at the rate of one kilogram per cubic decimeter and then resultant weight should be multiplied by the specific gravity of the fluid in order to arrive at its weight.

    Note: Unopened receptacles with original sealing, etc. intact may be taken as containing the quantity of the fluid stated on the receptacles.

(*d*) Goods supplied by well known firms of commercial standing may be accepted as per quantity marked thereon, on cases where it may not be either advisable or convenient to open the packages or cases to make a cent per cent check.

31. **Verification of Belting in Machine Rolled Coils Leaving no Space in between the Laps:** The diameter of the hole in the middle (in centimetres) plus the outside diameter (in centimetres) multiplied by the number of laps in the coil and the resultant multiplied by 0.01571 will give the length of the belting in meters.

32. **Unpacked Goods:** In case of imported articles and indigenously manufactured goods packed by the well known firms of commercial standing may be accepted as per weight or number marked thereon or the advice of dispatch, in case, where they are intact and it may not be advisable or convenient to open the packages to make a cent per cent check.

33. **Items of Stores Issued in Weight against Requisitions in Numbers:** In the case of articles which are indented for in numbers but, the prescribed unit for which being weights or vice versa, issues are made by weight, Stock Verifiers should, with a view to preventing or detecting fraudulent practices of over charges in weight, test check, at the time of verification of such items, the weights shown on issue notes as equivalent to the number issued. A report of the result of this test check should be entered in the field book submitted to the Stores Accounts Officer.

34. **Incomplete Count of Weightment:** It is not possible to finish the count or weightment of an item during the May, the stock of such counted or weighted portion of the material should be kept quite apart from the undealt with balance in the godown.

35. **Rearrangement of Stock:** All material taken out of racks, etc. by the Stock Verifier should be put back into the rack properly arranged, and he is responsible to see that this is done.

    Permanent Way Stores: The main items of stocks in permanent way depots are the rails of different types. The distinguishing features of various types are reproduced in Appendix XII to this Code. Other items of stocks are rail fastenings, sleepers and sleeper fittings, crossings and points with their fittings. The materials commonly used with sleepers, the different kinds of crossings and descriptions of crossings and switches are to be found in Appendix XII. In permanent way depot and other verifications, Stock verifier will comes across small fastenings as cotters, etc. Which are stocked either in bins or gunny bags and to facilitate check, the contents of each bin or bag will be painted on it. For all practical purposes, it is enough if the Stock Verifier test checks a percentage (at least 5%) of such full bins or bags and if found correct, he may accept the figures in others as correct ; otherwise the entire stock will have to be checked in detail. He should, however, make sure that all the bags, bins, etc. really contain the correct material.

36. **Acceptance by Ward-keeper of Results of Verification:** The stock found by count or measurement or weighment should then be noted in the field book. Initials of the representative of the stores department in whose presence the stock is verified should be obtained in the field book against the item in question as a taken of his acceptance, on behalf of stores department, or the correctness of the entries made therein. He should also furnish a certificate to the effect that all stocks of the particular item have been accounted and shown to the stock verifier.

47. (*i*) ***Certificate by Ward-keeper:*** After the verification of each group of stores has been completed, the Stock Verifier should obtain a certificate from the Ward Keeper concerned and the subordinate incharge of the Depot that all stores pertaining to that group have been truly and correctly presented for verification and duly verified. This certificate should be submitted to the authorized Inspector for record with the completion repot.

(*ii*) ***Section Officer's Certificates:*** The Ward Keeper's certificate should be countersigned by the Section Officer of Stores Accounts Office to the effect that the stores as per all priced ledger cards of that group maintained in the Account Office have been verified. Omissions of any items should be explained by the stock verifier concerned. This certificate should then be submitted to the authorized Inspector alongwith the completion Report. For the purposes of this certification of the Completion Report, the Section Officer should prepare a list of all items not verified for that group if any from the priced ledgers.

38. **Completion Report of Verification:** At the conclusion of the verification of a group of stores, the Stock Verifier should submit a completion Report in manuscript showing the following details:

Current year Last* year

(1) Depot
(2) Class
(3) Prevailing unit
(4) Date verification commenced
(5) Date verification completed
(6) Total number of working days
(7) No. of days as estimated in programme
(8) No. of days taken last year*
(9) Brief remarks in explanation of any excess of Col. 6 over 7 and or 8*
(10) Total number of items
(11) No. of items with no discrepancies
(12) No. of items with excess
(13) No. of items with shortages
(14) General remarks as to efficiency of stores keeping.

Note: To be filled in by authorized Inspector: wherever particular features of a verification indicate a more detailed report a narrative report of any special features should be submitted alongwith the Completion Report. The Completion Report should be completed and scrutinized by the authorized Inspector and submitted to the Stores Account Officer.

39. **Posting of Verification Results in Ledgers:** After the actual stock figures of an item of stores have been ascertained and accepted by the Ward Keeper, the physical stock verified by the Stock Verifier should be shown in his field book, as well as in the stock sheet prepared by him. The differences, if any between the physical stock and the priced ledger will be brought to account by Stores Accounts Officer at the time of posting the priced ledger. He should prepare stock sheet as follows:

(*i*) If there is no difference, the remark 'Stock verified correct' will be printed on the stock sheet prepared.

(*ii*) If the difference be an excess *i.e.*, the actual stock figures are greater than book balance the difference will be struck and posted as receipt in the ledgers duly giving the date of posting. The difference arrived at should be shown, together with the physical balance and the actual book balance in the stock verification sheets.

(*iii*) The same procedure will be adopted while recording shortages, except that figures will be taken as minus receipt and shown as 'Shortage in Stock' in the printed stock sheets.

40. **Opening of New Stock Cards:** If it is considered necessary to open a new ledger for an item for which none exists, the Stock Verifier should immediately inform in writing the subordinate incharge of the Stores Ledger Section of the fact, who should carefully verify that no ledger is already in use for the item and send an advice for opening a new ledger.
41. **Reclassification:** If materials that are being verified are borne on the ledger as new or second hand but are found to be actually otherwise, the entire quantity should be shown on the stock sheets, as described in the ledgers with suitable remarks as to the condition of the stores. In no case should the Stock Verifier either himself transfer or ask the Depot staff to transfer any material to scrap; the Stores Accounts Officer will do needful.
42. **Stock Verification Sheets:** The stock Verifier should prepare in triplicate (by carbon process) Stock sheets in from (S. 1260) for all items of stores. The verification of which has been complete that day. The stock sheets should be prepared from the date in the field book.The stock so prepared will contain only the ground balance. A Stock Verification Report has to be prepared at the time of posting the priced ledger, in from S.1260, showing the book balance, the ground balance as per the stock sheet and the excess shortage, If any.
43. **Numbering of Stock Sheets:** Stock sheets for Stores Depot Verification should be serially numbered for each unified group of stores and in the case of other verifications for each account, separate series being also used for new, second-hand and surplus stores. (If two more Verifiers are employed in verifying the same unified group of stores at the same time, each of them should have his own series of numbers).

    The numbering will consist of a composite barrel consisting of two position Depots, two positions of Ward, two position of Group and five positions of Series Number.
44. **Instruction for Preparation of Stock Sheets and Stock Verification Report:** The following general instructions regarding preparation of stock sheets and stock verification reports should be carefully observed:
    - (*i*) Stock sheets/ Stock Verification Reports for different categories and qualities of stores should be clearly so marked.
    - (*ii*) Entries should be made on one side only.
    - (*iii*) A space of one or two lines should be left between two entries on a stock sheet/Stock Verification Report.
    - (*iv*) Entries should be made in Stock Sheets/Stock Verification Reports for every articles found in stock.
    - (*v*) The Stock Sheets should be so prepared that all quantities shown in the book are clearly traceable into the stock sheets. This will be done by giving cross reference in every case to the field book number, and its page and item numbers.
    - (*vi*) The columns for 'Priced Ledger Balances' and 'rate' and 'Value' will be filled up at the time of posting of Priced Ledger by the Accounts Office.
    - (*vii*) Brief remarks, such as 'Average weighment', Measurement, 'book balance accepted' should be given in the 'remarks' column of the Stock Sheets against all items that have not been verified in detail.
    - (*viii*) Each stock sheet should be signed by the Stock Verifier and by the subordinate incharge of the stores verified.
45. **Adjustment or Supplementary Stock Sheets:** Stock Verifiers may in some cases come across a stock of items on a date subsequent to their verification of that particular item. Quantities thus found should be entered on a separate page of the field book. References on the two pages

of the field book dealing with the items should be recorded. In such cases, the item should be verified afresh.

46. **Register of Stock Sheets:** As a check on the disposal of stock sheets, the authorized Inspector should maintain a manuscript register containing the following columns:

1. Register serial number.
2. No. and date of stock sheet.
3. Group of stores.
4. Name of verifier.
5. Date of submission of original copy to the Computer Center.
6. Date of submission of duplicate and triplicate copies to the Depot Officer.
7. Date of submission of duplicate and triplicate copies of stock sheet (printed by computer Center) to the Depot Officer.
8. Date of return of duplicate copy by the Depot Officer.
9. Date of final disposal.
10. Remarks.

47. **Scrutiny of Explanations of Discrepancies:** The Stock sheets on return to the Stores Accounts Office, after explanation by the Depot Officers, should be carefully scrutinized by the authorized Inspector to see that every discrepancy has been explained. Further explanation should be called for in regard to remarks that are unsatisfactory. Accounts Notes will be issued in such cases.

48. **Important Points for Scrutiny:** While scrutnising the stock sheets, the authorized Inspector should see :

(*i*) that explanations recorded against discrepancies represents facts;

(*ii*) that they are clear, intelligible and definite;

(*iii*) that independent explanations are furnished against individual discrepancies and that excesses under some items are not adjusted against shortages in dissimilar items. In case of analogous items (where sizes only differ) such adjustments may be passed upto 2% of the transaction since the date of last verification, but any bigger differences must be taken up;

(*iv*) that in case of items accounted for in number large differences do not arise; - that where shortages found as a result of stock verification are attributed to the neglect of the subordinate holding charge of stores, the cost of the missing articles is invariably recovered from the parties at fault. The amount so recovered should be noted in a manuscript register of recoveries maintained in the following form:

(*a*) Date

(*b*) Name of division.

(*c*) Name of person debited.

(*d*) Amount recovered.

(*e*) Authority.

(*f*) Initials of stock verification clerk.

(*v*) At the close of the financial year, the amounts should be totaled up and incorporated in the statement showing the activities of the Stock Verification Section prepared for the purposes of the annual statement of Stores Transactions; and (*vi*) that in case of discrepancies arising as a result of improper classification/grouping, the shortages under one item are not set off compensating improper classification/grouping and excess posted under items.

57. **Admissible Percentages of Shrinkage and Dryage:** The following are the percentages of admissible moisture in weight in various commodities:

1. Chalk, white — Not more than 2-1/2% moisture
2. Pumice
3. Asbestos packing
4. Coir, loose — Not more than 5%
5. Coir, yarn
6. Cotton, raw
7. Cotton, spun
8. Cotton, waste
9. Gum country
10. Jute, country
11. Jute, gasketing
12. Log line
13. Ropes
14. String, scotly — Not more than 5%
15. Wool, worsted
16. Band catgut
17. Brooms, Goa
18. Cane, split
19. Hides and leather goods
20. Moonj, raw — Not more than 10%
21. Moonj, raw
22. Soap

Additional items may be added with approval of the General manager.

The salient features of each case of discrepancy should be pointed out in the form of noted to the Stores Accounts Officer for orders regarding final disposal.

50. **Accounts Notes:** All discrepant items for which satisfactory explanations have not been offered by the executive should be incorporated in an accounts note care should be taken to group all items of similar nature where identical information is required.

51. **Register of Accounts Notes of Stock Verification Section:** To control the issue of accounts notes and watch their final disposal, a manuscript register of accounts notes should be maintained with separate part for the various divisions, departments and depots. All accounts notes issued to the various offices and departments should be recorded in this register under the respective heads and progressive serial numbers allotted to them. The date of final disposal of each accounts note should be noted in this register.

52. **Register of Important Irregularities detected by Stock Verification staff:** To facilitate the preparation of the memorandum of results of internal check required to be submitted to the Railway Board, a register of irregularities detected as a result of the internal check will be

maintained in the Accounts Section. As soon as the investigation of a case is completed by the Verifiers, who will make the necessary entry in the register of important irregularities, in consultation with the authorized Inspector of Stores Accounts, if necessary. The orders of the Stores Accounts Officers should be obtained before entering any case in the register.

It is important that the full facts of the case should be accepted by executive before the irregularity is intimated to the Accounts Section for noting in the register of irregularities.

53. **Half-yearly Report to General Manager:** A general review of stock verification work should be submitted to the General Manager when the aggregate effect of the adjustments is reported to him half-yearly for purpose of adjustment of the balance lying in the Stock Adjustment Accounts.

54. **Depot Stock Sheets:** Depot Stock sheets prepared by the Stores Depots to adjust differences found in stock during their periodical departmental checks should be passed on to the Verification Section by the Ledger Section after the posting of the priced ledger, for the scrutiny of the remarks offered by the depots in explanation of the differences. Their scrutiny and disposal will be on the same lines of Accounts Verification Sheets.

The authorized Inspector should review quarterly the departmental verification carried out by the Depot Officer.